RED, WHITE, AND GOLD:

CANADA AT THE
WORLD JUNIOR
CHAMPIONSHIPS
1974-1999

RED, WHITE, AND GOLD: CANADA AT THE WORLD JUNIOR CHAMPIONSHIPS 1974-1999

ANDREW PODNIEKS

ECW PRESS

CANADIAN CATALOGUING IN PUBLICATION DATA

Podnieks, Andrew

Red, White, and Gold: Canada at the
world junior championships 1974–1999

ISBN 1-55022-382-8

1. World Junior Hockey Championship. 2. Hockey – Tournaments – Canada.
3. Hockey – Records – Canada. 1. Title.

GV847.7.P62 1998   796.962 62 079   C98-933033-8

Imaging by ECW Type & Art, Oakville, Ontario.
Printed and bound by Printcrafters, Winnipeg, Manitoba.

Distributed by General Distribution Services,
325 Humber College Blvd., Etobicoke, Ontario M9W 7C3.
(416) 213-1919, (800) 387-0172 (Canada), FAX (416) 213-1917.

Distributed in the United States by LPC Group,
1436 West Randolph Street, Chicago, Illinois, U.S.A. 60607.

Published by ECW PRESS,
2120 Queen Street East, Suite 200
Toronto, Ontario M4E 1E2.

CONTENTS

Team Canada Guide and Record Book for the World Junior Championships

INTRODUCTION

The World Junior Championships began in 1974 as an almost insignificant, six-team invitational tournament. The games were played in the Communist Soviet Union before sparse crowds. Participating nations were Canada, the Soviets, Finland, Sweden, Czechoslovakia, and the United States. In 1999 in Winnipeg, the tournament will feature ten teams in a highly structured event that will host some 300,000 fans. Today, the WJC is the premier junior tournament in the world, and one of the most significant and exciting hockey events of the year.

In 1976, after three years of invitational play, it was clear the World Juniors was ready for a more formal and sophisticated presentation, thanks largely to the the growing popularity of international competition fuelled by the 1972 Summit Series. By 1977, the IIHF had relented and Canada was allowed to use pros at the World Championships, and so a gap existed where young players (particularly in Canada) had little opportunity to gain international experience. Not coincidentally, the first year of professional involvement at the senior level was also the first year of the official World Junior Championships.

The early years of the WJC were salient to the formation of the Canadian hockey program that exists today. This program has been successful not just here but in every important hockey-playing nation in the world. But in the early years, Canada sent a junior club team to the World Juniors. Not surprisingly, the teams were not very successful. The CAHA realized that a national junior program, like the one Father Bauer proposed for the senior teams in the sixties, was essential to ensure international success.

After finishing a respectable second in 1976 with his Sherbrooke Beavers, coach Ghislain Delage suggested that a winter camp and scouting unit were required. Today, Canada's junior program does not begin with the World Juniors; it ends there. Canada has an under-18 team and an under-17 team, and these teams hold and participate in many regional and world championships. The program helps players develop, and gives early bloomers or late bloomers equal opportunity to participate internationally in their teens. The World Juniors is the culmination of these tournaments, the Stanley Cup for junior hockey.

The success of the WJC is evident. Almost every Canadian world junior player has gone on to play in the NHL, and every elite Canadian of the last twenty years began here. Gretzky, Gartner, Ciccarelli, Lindros, Kariya, Allison, Gilmour, Fleury, Lemieux, Hawerchuk, Nieuwendyk, Patrick, Peca, and dozens of others all played at the WJC. So, too, did the emerging stars of today: Ed Jovanovski, Jarome Iginla, Martin Lapointe, Vincent Lecavalier,

Manny Malhotra, Chris Phillips, and Joe Thornton, to name a small selection.

Because of NHL expansion, the fall of Communism, and increased European scouting, Canadian fans are seeing the development of the finest players from around the world mature at the World Juniors. Ten years ago, the Canadians at the WJC would go on to play in the NHL, but the best from Russia and Czechoslovakia would disappear for another year. Today, the best players from most teams are drafted and play in the NHL. As the quality of the tournament has increased, Canada's domination of the World Juniors has become unparalleled. Before last year's worst-ever eighth-place finish, Canada won five consecutive gold medals.

Perhaps the most enduring quality of the World Juniors is that it is not an isolated two-week event. It is a wonderful piece of a larger puzzle. Many players who do not make the Canadian team have gone on to spectacular NHL careers, and sometimes a star performer at the WJC does not go on to remarkable pro success. For some it is the beginining, for others the apotheosis. Most of all, it is a tournament of emotion, desire, and naturally created experience. The coaches and officials, too, are proud to represent our country. Some go on to coach or ref in the NHL; others remain at the junior level. For Canadian Hockey, it is a tournament to be proud of, a measuring stick for the ambitious programs that help make Canada the hockey capital of the world.

1974 WORLD JUNIOR CHAMPIONSHIPS SOVIET UNION, DECEMBER 27, 1973-- JANUARY 6, 1974

TEAM CANADA
(Peterborough Petes)

Mike Kasmetis, goal
Frank Salive, goal

Doug Halward, defence
Paul McIntosh, defence
Brad Pirie, defence
Ed Pizunski, defence
Greg Redquist, defence
Pete Scamurra, defence
Jim Turkiewicz, defence

Jake Ayotte, forward
Tony Cassolato, forward
Gord Duncan, forward
Paul Evans, forward
Bill Evo, forward
Tom Gastle, forward
Doug Jarvis, forward (captain)
Stan Jonathan, forward
Red Laurence, forward
Ed Smith, forward
Bob Wasson, forward

Mike Fryia, forward (did not play)

COACH ROGER NEILSON

The Petes were coached by the most innovative man of his era, Roger Neilson, who became known as "Captain Video" when he joined the Leafs a few years later. Neilson was in his eighth year with Peterborough, and was devoting himself full-time to coaching in the OHA. Before that, he divided his time between the Petes and a local high school, where he taught phys ed. In Canada's game against Finland, Neilson pulled his goalie with fully two minutes to go, and though the strategy did not eke out a tie, it is almost certainly the first time the Finns had encountered this new Canadian twist to desperation hockey.

At home, Neilson was famous for pushing the rules-book envelope. Once, he put a defenceman in goal for an opponent's penalty shot so that the player could come out and try to check the skater. Another time, with his team two men short in the dying minutes of a game, he put an extra man on the ice because a too-many-men penalty would not affect the number of men on the ice. He pulled his goalie late in a game and instructed him to place his stick across the goal line before skating out; after all, there was nothing in the rule book that said this couldn't be done. He was forever challenging conventional wisdom and, by so doing, felt he kept hockey a topic of conversation and interest.

PETERBOROUGH PETES REPRESENT CANADA

The CAHA elected the Toronto Marlboros as the team that should represent Canada at the first unofficial World Junior Championships in Leningrad. The previous spring the Marlies had won the Memorial Cup in a record-setting, dominant manner. They were clearly the best team in the country. However, the Marlies opted to remain at home and participate in another prestigious international tournament at the Gardens, which featured Farjestad, a club team from Sweden, the Czechs, the Soviets, and a number of other OHA teams.

The Marlies might have demurred because of the effects of the World Hockey Association, which over the summer stripped the team of its powerful nucleus by signing underage juniors (something the NHL could not yet do). In the summer of 1973, the Toronto Toros signed eighteen-year-old sensation Wayne Dillon, as well as the Howe brothers, Marty and Mark. Gone was the core of the Memorial Cup team. Oshawa coach and future World Junior coach Gus Bodnar admitted as much. "If the Marlies had those players, the rest of us could stay home," he said. So the Petes, runners-up in the OHA, were chosen as the second best team in the Dominion.

INTERNATIONAL EXPANSION

The significance of the Summit Series in 1972 to the development and welfare of international competition cannot be overstated. One year after Paul Henderson's remarkable goal, the very landscape of hockey in the NHL, in Canada, and in IIHF circles was changing dramatically and unconditionally. The Marlies were part of an international tournament. The Leafs had just signed, for the first time in NHL history, two Europeans, Borje Salming and Inge Hammarstrom. In Detroit, Thommie Bergman was joined at the Red Wings training camp by three other Swedes, Ulf Sterner, Leif Holmqvist, and Tord Lundstrom. Soon, Anders Hedberg and Ulf Nilsson would be playing in the WHA with Bobby Hull and the Winnipeg Jets.

Referee Rudy Bata, who had been part of the Summit Series, was in Toronto, studying with Canadian referees and linesmen to learn how to incorporate the one-ref–two-linesmen system into the European game, a change made patently necessary through his Canada-Russia experiences. As he confessed: "If we [Europeans] are to play against [Canada's] pros, our officiating must improve, and the way to do that is to have two linesmen and one referee, who is the boss. For the referee, it becomes easy when he can forget about offsides. But for the linesmen, it can be a problem, something the Czechs and Russians must learn. Seeing offsides and icing is one thing, but being in proper position and knowing which man goes to which part of the ice and what lines to be on, that is another thing." In Europe, the days of two referees competing with each other and doing triple duty — calling penalties, offsides, and goals — was coming to an end.

THE UNOFFICIAL JUNIORS

Because this was a tournament held by invitation only, it is not considered the first World Junior Championships. While Canada's third place finish and horrible 9–0 loss to the Soviets might seem wretched to contemplate, the Petes were the only club team in Leningrad. All other entries were the best juniors in the country, thus placing Canada — Peterborough — at a distinct disadvantage. This would be remedied a few years later.

PRE-TOURNAMENT PREPARATION

On December 4, 1973, the Petes travelled to Minneapolis for the first of a home-and-home exhibition series against the United States junior team, comprised of players from the Midwest Junior Hockey League (the St. Paul Vulcans, Minnesota Junior Stars, St. Cloud Junior Blues, and Fargo-Moorhead Sugar Kings). In the game at the Met Centre, the Americans won 2–1 in overtime in a hard-hitting game played under international rules. A couple of days later, the Finnish junior team began an eight-game tour of Canada, playing the country's top major junior teams in preparation for the world juniors. This was surely a testament to the respect with which they held Canada's system — they travelled halfway around the world to play here before heading for the World Juniors in Leningrad.

Six of the Petes joined the London Knights in a game against the touring Moscow Selects. Goalie Mike Kasmetis played along with Doug Jarvis, Stan Jonathan, Tony Cassolato, Paul McIntosh, and Jim Turkiewicz. The Selects lost 9–3 against the mature and experienced Russian team. In the return match against the U.S. juniors, the Petes won 6–4 at the Memorial Centre in Peterborough, beating a team coached by Murray Williamson, a native Winnipegger. Interestingly, the Petes were scouted for much of December by three Soviet officials who were preparing their entry for the World Juniors at the end of the month.

FRIENDSHIPS AND MEMORIES

While the games were all played in Leningrad, the Petes had to travel to Moscow to catch their plane home. On the train ride, they were joined by a number of Soviet juniors who wanted to know everything about Canadian life and how players made it to the NHL. To prepare for the competition, the Soviets had formed a thirty-five-strong training camp for a month and played numerous exhibitions. "I'm certain that if an all-star team of Canadian junior players could be prepared under similar conditions it would beat the Russian team consistently," said Neilson, prophesying the future of the Canadian junior system.

TOURNAMENT FORMAT

This was the first of the annual, simple round-robin format tournaments. Every team played every other team once, two points for a win, one for a tie. Games did not go into overtime, and a tie in the standings was broken by head-to-head results. Canada finished third to Finland's second because of a 4–3 Petes' loss during the tournament. The two-referee system normally used in Europe was replaced by the Canadian system of one referee and two linesmen, with mixed results: "The linesmen were brutal," said Neilson. "They were new to the job and watched the game instead of the lines."

FINAL STANDINGS

	GP	W	L	T	GF	GA	P	GAA	SO
Soviet Union	5	5	0	0	36	12	10	2.40	1
Finland	5	3	2	0	21	23	6	4.60	0
CANADA	5	3	2	0	17	23	6	4.60	0
Sweden	5	2	3	0	32	21	4	4.20	0
United States	5	1	4	0	10	32	2	6.40	0
Czechoslovakia	5	1	4	0	19	24	2	4.80	0

RESULTS

(all games played at Leningrad)

December 27	Czechoslovakia 6	Sweden 4
	Soviet Union 6	Finland 2
December 28	Canada 5	United States 4
	Sweden 9	Finland 4
December 29	Soviet Union 7	Czechoslovakia 5
December 30	Finland 4	Canada 3
	Sweden 11	United States 1
January 1	Canada 4	Czechoslovakia 2
	Soviet Union 5	Sweden 4
	Finland 5	United States 1
January 3	Canada 5	Sweden 4
	Finland 6	Czechoslovakia 4
January 4	Soviet Union 9	United States 1
January 5	United States 3	Czechoslovakia 2
January 6	Soviet Union 9	Canada 0

1975 WORLD JUNIOR CHAMPIONSHIPS CANADA, DECEMBER 26, 1974-- JANUARY 5, 1975

(some games played in the United States)

TEAM CANADA (WCHL All-Stars)

Larry Hendrick, goal (Calgary Centennials)
Doug Soetaert, goal (Edmonton Oil Kings)
Ed Staniowski, goal (Regina Pats)

Blair Davidson, defence (Flin Flon Bombers)
Rick Hodgson, defence (Calgary Centennials)
Rick Lapointe, defence (Victoria Cougars)
Bryan Maxwell, defence (Medicine Hat Tigers)
Kevin McCarthy, defence (Winnipeg Clubs)
Robin Sadler, defence (Edmonton Oil Kings)

Danny Arndt, forward (Saskatoon Blades)
Rick Blight, forward (Brandon Wheat Kings)
Mel Bridgman, forward (Victoria Cougars)
Mark Davidson, forward (Flin Flon Bombers)
Rob Flockhart, forward (Kamloops Chiefs)
Kelly Greenbank, forward (Winnipeg Clubs)
Ralph Klassen, forward (Saskatoon Blades)
Dale McMullin, forward (Brandon Wheat Kings)
Jim Minor, forward (Regina Pats)
Barry Smith, forward (New Westminster Bruins)
Brian Sutter, forward (Lethbridge Broncos)
Bryan Trottier, forward (Lethbridge Broncos)

COACH JACKIE McLEOD

Saskatoon Blades coach McLeod was chosen as national coach largely because of his international experience. After a brief NHL career with the New York Rangers (1949–55), McLeod led Canada's Trail Smoke Eaters to a gold medal at the 1961 World Championships, the last gold Canada was to win until 1994. He led the tournament in scoring and was selected to the All-Star team at right wing. The following year, he played for the Galt Terriers at the Worlds and was again named to the tournament All-Star team. In 1966, McLeod was appointed head coach of this same national team he had played for. He coached the Canadian entry at both the 1967 World Championships and the 1968 Olympic Winter Games in Grenoble, France during his five-year tenure with the National Team, and in 1970 took over as head coach and general manager of the Blades.

TOURNAMENT FORMAT

The six teams were placed in one division and played a round-robin series (five games) to determine final placings. Each team got two points for a win, and tie games did not go into overtime. A tie in the standings would be broken first by head-to-head results and then by superior goal differential. Each country would also provide one referee who would not work a game in which his country participated, and all the linesmen were Manitobans.

FINAL STANDINGS

	GP	W	L	T	GF	GA	P	GAA	SO
Soviet Union	5	5	0	0	22	8	10	1.60	0
CANADA	5	4	1	0	27	10	8	2.00	1
Sweden	5	2	2	1	18	24	5	4.80	0
Czechoslovakia	5	1	2	2	9	11	4	2.20	1
Finland	5	1	3	1	10	14	3	2.80	0
United States	5	0	5	0	9	28	0	5.60	0

RESULTS

December 26	Winnipeg	Canada 9	United States 3
	Brandon	Soviet Union 4	Finland 1
December 28	Winnipeg	Canada 10	Sweden 2
	Brandon	Czechoslovakia 1	Finland 1
December 29	Winnipeg	Soviet Union 5	Czechoslovakia 1

December 30	Winnipeg	Canada 2	Finland 1
	Fargo, ND	Sweden 7	United States 3
December 31	Minneapolis	Soviet Union 3	United States 1
January 1	Winnipeg	Canada 3	Czechoslovakia 0
	Winnipeg	Sweden 5	Finland 3
January 3	Minneapolis	Czechoslovakia 5	United States 0
	Winnipeg	Soviet Union 6	Sweden 2
January 5	Winnipeg	Soviet Union 4	Canada 3
	Brandon	Czechoslovakia 2	Sweden 2
	Minneapolis	Finland 4	United States 2

1976 WORLD JUNIOR CHAMPIONSHIPS FINLAND, DECEMBER 26, 1975-- JANUARY 1, 1976

TEAM CANADA
(Sherbrooke Beavers)

Benoit Perreault, goal
Richard Sevigny, goal

Mario Claude, defence
Robert Desormeaux, defence
Ken Johnstone, defence
Floyd Lahache, defence
Normand Lefebvre, defence
Brendan Lowe, defence
Regis Vallieres, defence

Alain Belanger, forward
Joe Carlevale, forward
Ron Carter, forward
Daniel Chicoine, forward
Jere Gillis, forward
Mark Green, forward
Denis Halle, forward
Bernard Harbec, forward
Fern Leblanc, forward (captain)
Peter Marsh, forward
Robert Simpson, forward

COACH GHISLAIN DELAGE

The apprenticeship from local coach to national representative was a slow, methodical one for Delage. He began coaching in the sixties in Montreal's old Metropolitan Junior league, first with Rosemount and then with the St. Jerome Alouettes. When the Metropolitan league amalgamated with the Quebec Major Junior Hockey League, Delage found himself in one of the most important developmental systems in the world. He joined the Sorel Black Hawks in 1970, and two years later he took the head coaching job with the Sherbrooke Beavers, where he remained for eight years.

Under an agreement with the Canadian junior leagues, it was Quebec's turn to send a team to the 1976 World Juniors. The OHL had sent Peterborough in 1974 and the Western league had assembled an all-star group for 1975. The QMJHL was unwilling to form a similar all-star team, so the Beavers, who had been Quebec Junior League champions in 1975, banded together and decided to go.

THE SENDOFF

Sherbrooke's last game before leaving for Finland was a 10–0 hammering of the Quebec Remparts in front of 4,100 wildly cheering fans at the Sport Palace. The organist played "We Wish You a Merry Christmas," and the Beavers' Fan Club presented the team with a cheque for $3,000. The Drolets, of Sherwood-Drolet hockey stick fame, gave an additional $2,000 and sticks, and a like sum was given by the QMJHL and the Quebec government. O'Keefe Sports gave the players luggage and duffel bags, and the team was on its way.

IN FINLAND

The Beavers played an exhibition game on December 23, beating Palloseura of Forssa in Finland 7–0 before playing the Finn juniors three nights later to open the tournament.

TOURNAMENT FORMAT

A simple round-robin system was used, and ties in the standings were broken by head-to-head results. Canada finished ahead of the Czechs because of an earlier 5–4 victory, and the Finns were placed above the Swedes because of a 7–2 win.

FINAL STANDINGS

	GP	W	L	T	GF	GA	P	GAA	SO
Soviet Union	4	4	0	0	19	10	8	2.50	0
CANADA	4	2	2	0	12	27	4	6.75	0
Czechoslovakia	4	2	2	0	12	10	4	2.50	1
Finland	4	1	3	0	12	14	2	3.50	0
Sweden	4	1	3	0	23	17	2	4.25	0

RESULTS

December 26	Canada 4	Finland 1
	Soviet Union 3	Czechoslovakia 2
December 27	Soviet Union 5	Sweden 2
December 28	Sweden 17	Canada 1
	Czechoslovakia 2	Finland 0
December 29	Canada 5	Czechoslovakia 4
	Soviet Union 6	Finland 4
December 31	Finland 7	Sweden 2
January 1	Soviet Union 5	Canada 2
	Czechoslovakia 4	Sweden 2

1977 WORLD JUNIOR CHAMPIONSHIPS CZECHOSLOVAKIA, DECEMBER 22, 1976-- JANUARY 2, 1977

FINAL PLACINGS

GOLD MEDAL	Soviet Union
SILVER MEDAL	**CANADA**
BRONZE MEDAL	Czechoslovakia
Fourth Place	Finland
Fifth Place	Sweden
Sixth Place	West Germany
Seventh Place	United States
Eighth Place	Poland*

relegated to "B" pool for 1978

ALL-STAR TEAM

GOAL	Alexander Tyznych (Soviet Union)
DEFENCE	Risto Siltanen (Finland)
	Lubos Oslizlo (Czechoslovakia)
FORWARD	Dale McCourt (Canada)
	Bengt-Ake Gustafsson (Sweden)
	Igor Romasin (Soviet Union)

DIRECTORATE AWARDS

BEST GOALIE	Jan Hrabak (Czechoslovakia)
BEST DEFENCEMAN	Viacheslav Fetisov (Soviet Union)
BEST FORWARD	Dale McCourt (Canada)

COACH BERT TEMPLETON

Bert Templeton, in his third year as coach of the St. Catharines Fincups, had a reputation. He was a brawler, more interested in the finer arts of boxing than of skating, shooting, and passing. In one pre-season game, on September 10, 1976, the Fincups and London Knights were involved in a series of vicious fights. The game was suspended, and 554 penalty minutes were assessed. Templeton received a two-game suspended sentence from league commissioner Tubby Schmaltz, even though Templeton was in the press box and Fincups chief scout Bud Mountain was behind the bench. Because he signed the game sheets, Templeton was technically responsible for his team's involvement.

The Scotland-born Templeton had to scramble to go to the tournament. He found out at the last minute he was not eligible for a Canadian passport, and a quick trip to the British embassy in Ottawa and assurances from the Czechoslovakian embassy were needed before he could travel abroad.

ST. CATHARINES FINCUPS — MEMORIAL CUP CHAMPIONS

Although the team was amateur champion of Canada by the time training camp opened for the 1976–77 season, the Fincups were not guaranteed the opportunity to represent Canada at the first official World Junior Championships. That honour would be bestowed upon the team that had the most points in the OHA after ten games of the regular season. This stipulation was a necessary evil of the junior hockey system. In the OHA, a player can only play for four years before he has to leave, sometimes for the NHL, sometimes for OHA Senior A, sometimes for the working world. Turnover from year to year is quite high, and a team that wins the Memorial Cup one spring could be a much inferior team in the fall. For instance, the Sudbury Wolves had the most points in the OHA the previous year, but then lost Rod Schutt, Randy Carlyle, Dave Farrish, Randy Pierce, and Alex McKendry. Kingston, too, lost seven players to graduation. The Fincups, whose roster hadn't changed significantly, looked to be the favourites.

JUNIORS AND THE UNDERAGE CONTRACT

When the World Hockey Association (WHA) entered the hockey wars in 1972, one of its mandates was to lure unlurable NHL players to the new league. These included free agents whose contracts had expired in the NHL but who, according to the NHL, belonged to the team and couldn't move at will to another professional league. In court, it was proved that at the

Captain Dale McCourt, seen here with his junior team
the St. Catharines Fincups, led all players in scoring with
18 points at the first official World Junior Championships.

end of a contract a player could indeed move freely to the WHA without compensation.

Another controversy erupted over eighteen- and nineteen-year-olds. The NHL considered them underage players. When a youngster joined the Canadian junior hockey system (OHL, QMJHL, or WHL), he signed a contract thought to be binding until he graduated from the league at age twenty, when he became eligible for the NHL's amateur draft. The WHA was prepared to draft younger players and challenge the Canadian junior system in court. John Anderson and Marlie linemate John Tonelli stopped playing junior hockey when they turned eighteen, fearing that to continue would explicitly endorse the OHL contract policy. Both resumed their junior careers, Anderson representing Canada at the World Juniors and Tonelli in the NHL. Such was not the case for Mike Gartner. Following his participation in the 1978 WJC, he went directly from junior to the WHA.

THE FIRST TEN GAMES — A RACE

The Fincups won their first game of the 1976–77 OHA season 9–3 over the Windsor Spitfires and followed with a 4–3 win over the London Knights. They lost only once in their first ten, and clinched the trip to Czechoslovakia with a 9–1 slaughter of the Spitfires. Team owners took the players and staff out for a night on the town after the win to celebrate. The standings looked as follows:

Emms Division

	GP	W	L	T	GF	GA	P
St. Catharines	9	8	1	0	60	25	16
London	10	7	3	0	47	28	14
Kitchener	11	5	5	1	52	61	11
Toronto	9	5	4	0	44	36	10
Windsor	10	1	7	2	34	65	4
Niagara Falls	9	0	8	1	23	50	1

Leyden Division

	GP	W	L	T	GF	GA	P
Kingston	10	7	2	1	46	33	15
Sudbury	11	6	4	1	69	47	13
Ottawa	9	5	3	1	42	31	11
Peterbourough	9	5	3	1	35	26	11
Sault Ste. Marie	10	5	5	0	30	46	10
Oshawa	9	0	9	0	22	56	0

THE UNIFORMS

The thrill of clinching the overseas trip could not possibly match the feeling the players had December 13 when they put on their Canada jerseys for the first time. "That's when I really felt proud," admitted Wille Huber, one of the few anomalies in Canada's international hockey history. He was born in Germany, but his family moved to Canada when he was just a few months old.

Although the team going over was primarily the Fincups, there were nine additions. Defencemen Brad Marsh and Rob Ramage came from the London Knights. Defencemen Craig Hartsburg was from the Soo. The Marlies' Trevor Johansen went. Forward John Anderson of the Marlies also went, as well as Sudbury's Dave Hunter and teammate Ron Duguay. Danny Shearer made the trip with the team, but he had a deep bruise to his collarbone that prevented him from playing. Thirty players were selected because Templeton wanted to get as many young Canadians into the games as possible, and because he wanted players to be in top shape.

Templeton's plan backfired, however. When the thirty players arrived in Czechoslovakia via Vienna and Zvolen on December 19, he was told he had to name twenty skaters and three goalies, and only they could play in the tournament. Tough decisions had to be made quickly. The coach immediately ruled out Rob Street, who was over the twenty-year age limit, and Mike Boyd, who was nursing a bad cut to a foot. He cut the Soo's Hartsburg and five of his own Fincups — Brian Ostrowski, Dave Simpson, Brian Anderson, Jay Johnston, and Jody Gage.

One change from training camp to the junior team was in goal. Mark Locken left the Fincups on November 23 after appearing in ten of the team's first twenty-five games. Al Jensen got the majority of the work. Not pleased with his ice time, Jensen went back to high school, and Bob Daly became Jensen's backup.

WHAT THEY TOOK

Trainers Andy Alway and Bill Dynes packed six huge trunks with supplies for the trip, including: 480 sticks and 36 goalie sticks; 100 rolls of tape; 150 rolls of medical tape; players' equipment, for which the players would be responsible in Czechoslovakia; 100 towels; 2 cases of soap, as well as toilet paper and shampoo; and a skate sharpener.

WHAT THEY BROUGHT BACK

In 1977, Czechoslovakia was Communism at its most fervent. Basic supplies were hard to come by, night life was a Western term and a forbidden fruit, and luxuries and amenities that have long been part of Canadian living were nowhere to be seen in depraved Banska Bystrica. As a result, there was a fair bit of post-tournament bartering among players. Mark Plantery got a fur hat made from white rabbit in exchange for a pair of jeans and a Canadian jacket. The trade was consummated with a Russian. Steve Hazlett, Joe Contini, and Dave Draper were also wearing new headgear when the team touched down at Pearson, and Ric Seiling exchanged jackets with a Finn. Once back in St. Kitts, mayor Roy Adams presented the entire contingent with St. Catharines Centennial paperweights, and hundreds of enthusiatic fans provided a supportive backdrop to the civic reception.

AND AFTER . . . A LITTLE SHINNY

It seemed like a good idea at the time. Before leaving Czechoslovakia, the team had agreed to play an exhibition game in Vienna against a top-flight all-star team from Austria. The game would cause a sensation in the city, the Fincups were told. After a nightmarish journey from Banska Bystrica to

Vienna, the team found three hundred fans in the four-thousand-seat Danube Park Hall. The opposition looked so inadequate coach Templeton loaned the Austrians six players, turning the game into a Canadian scrimmage augmented by a few locals. The Austrians won the game 8–7, and the Fincups arrived in St. Kitts the next day.

TOURNAMENT FORMAT

The eight nations were placed in one division and played a single round-robin schedule. Tie games were not decided by overtime, and the first three finishers won gold, silver, and bronze. A tie in the standings would be broken by the head-to-head result in the round robin.

THE OPPOSITION

CZECHOSLOVAKIA

Rene Andrejs, Vladimir Caldr, Frantisek Cerny, Jiri Cerveny, Jan Hrabak, Jiri Hrdina, Jaroslav Hubl, Peter Ihnacak, Jordan Karagavrilidis, Jaroslav Klacl, Jindrich Kokrment, Jaroslav Korbela, Jiri Lala, Josef Lukac, Lubos Oslizlo, Jiri Otoupalik, Pavel Skalicky, Ladislav Svozil, Vladimir Urban, Alexander Vostry

FINLAND

Matti Forss, Jukka Hirsimaki, Raimo Hirvonen, Jarmo Huhtala, Hannu Ihala, Kari Jarvinen, Arto Javanainen, Juha Jyrkkio, Jouko Kamarainen, Hannu Kamppuri, Erkki Laine, Jukka Laukkanen, Ari Makinen, Harry Nikander, Jukka Peitsoma, Reijo Ruotsalainen, Risto Siltanen, Rauli Sohlman, Tomi Taimio, Pertti Vaelma

POLAND

Kazimierz Bednarski, Adam Bernat, Franciszek Bryniarski, Bogdan Dziubinski, Jerzy Gotalski, Henryk Gruth, Leszek Jachna, Andrzej Jarosz, Andrzej Malysiak, Leszek Minge, Witold Pulka, Boleslaw Remlein, Tadeusz Rylko, Dariusz Sikora, Miroslaw Sikora, Andrzej Swiatek, Ludwik Synowiec, Zbigniew Tomaszkiewicz, Stefan Wadas, Slawomir Zawadzki

SOVIET UNION

Ivan Avdeyev, Viacheslav Fetisov, Alexei Frolikov, Irek Gimayev, Valeri Jevstifeyev, Igor Kapustin, Alexander Kubanov, Konstantin Makarocov, Sergei Makarov, Sergei Mylnikov, Nikolai Narimanov, Vasili Payusov, Igor Romasin, Vladimir Shvetzov, Mikhail Slipcenko, Mikhail Sostak, Sergei Starikov, Mikhail Tolochko, Alexander Tyznych, Vladimir Zubkov

SWEDEN

Torbjorn Andersson, Rolf Berglund, Leif Carlsson, Bo Ericson, Kent Eriksson, Robin Eriksson, Bengt-Ake Gustafsson, Dan Hermansson, Karl Lilja, Per Lindberg, Eje Lindstrom, Harald Luckner, Roger Mikko, Mats Naslund, Lars Nyberg, Tore Okvist, Bjorn Olsson, Hans Sarkijarvi, Conny Silfverberg, Reino Sundberg

UNITED STATES

Bob Bergloff, Carl Bloomberg, Jeff Brownschidle, Bobby Crawford, Richie Dunn, Dave Gandini, Keith Hanson, Terry Houck, Mike MacDougall, Charlie Malloy, Kevin McCloskey, Paul Miller, Doug Olson, Mike Parker, Jim Penningroth, Mickey Rego, Barry Ryan, Roy Sommers, Don Wadell, Dave Wilkins

WEST GERMANY

Hans B. Muhlhausen, Helmut Barensoi, Peter Eimannsberger, Bernd Engelbrecht, Andy Groger, Horst Heckelsmuller, Herbert Heinrich, Jorg Hiemer, Ernst Hofner, Matthias Hoppe, Josef Klaus, Harald Krull, Armin Lauer, Verner Lupzig, Dieter Medicus, Holger Meitinger, Albton Paulus, Peter Schiller, Manfred Schuster, Gerhard Truntschka

FINAL STANDINGS

	GP	W	L	T	GF	GA	P	GAA	SO	PIM
Soviet Union	7	7	0	0	51	19	14	2.71	1	78
CANADA	7	5	1	1	50	20	11	2.86	1	189
Czechoslovakia	7	4	2	1	32	17	9	2.43	1	59
Finland	7	4	3	0	35	29	8	4.14	0	104
Sweden	7	3	4	0	28	30	6	4.29	1	115
West Germany	7	2	5	0	18	33	4	4.71	0	152
United States	7	1	5	1	25	45	3	6.43	0	96
Poland	7	0	6	1	12	58	1	8.29	0	88

RESULTS

December 22	Banska Bystrica	Finland 6	United States 3
December 23	Banska Bystrica	Canada 14	Poland 0
	Zvolen	Sweden 5	Finland 4
	Banska Bystrica	Soviet Union 4	Czechoslovakia 0
	Zvolen	West Germany 4	United States 3

December 25	Zvolen	Canada 4	Czechoslovakia 4
	Banska Bystrica	Finland 4	West Germany 1
	Zvolen	Soviet Union 10	Poland 1
	Banska Bystrica	United States 8	Sweden 5
December 26	Zvolen	Canada 6	Finland 4
	Banska Bystrica	Czechoslovakia 8	West Germany 2
	Zvolen	Soviet Union 4	Sweden 2
	Banska Bystrica	United States 2	Poland 2
December 28	Banska Bystrica	Canada 5	Sweden 3
	Banska Bystrica	Soviet Union 2	West Germany 1
	Zvolen	Finland 8	Poland 2
	Zvolen	Czechoslovakia 5	United States 2
December 29	Banska Bystrica	Canada 9	West Germany 1
	Zvolen	Sweden 6	Poland 5
December 30	Zvolen	Finland 3	Czechoslovakia 2
	Banska Bystrica	Soviet Union 15	United States 5
January 1	Zvolen	Canada 8	United States 2
	Banska Bystrica	Czechoslovakia 9	Poland 0
	Zvolen	Sweden 5	West Germany 0
	Banska Bystrica	Soviet Union 10	Finland 6
January 2	Zvolen	Soviet Union 6	Canada 4
	Zvolen	West Germany 9	Poland 2
	Banska Bystrica	Czechoslovakia 4	Sweden 2

TEAM CANADA GAME SUMMARIES

December 23   Canada 14   Poland 0

(all times for this game approximated to minutes in official records)

First Period

1. Canada, Anderson (unassisted) .... 6:00(pp)
2. Canada, Hazlett (Contini) .... 13:00(pp)
3. Canada, Huber (Foster) .... 15:00(pp)

   PENALTIES: Foster (Can) 3:00, Dziubinski (Pol) 5:00, Contini (Can) 6:00, McCourt (Can — misconduct) & Forbes (Can — minor, misconduct) 8:00, Bernat (Pol) 12:00, Bernat (Pol) 14:00

Second Period

4. Canada, Anderson (McCourt) .... 2:00(pp)
5. Canada, Hunter (Shaw) 4:00

27

6. Canada, McCourt (Anderson) 5:00
7. Canada, Hunter (unassisted) 14:00
8. Canada, McCourt (Marsh) .... 16:00 (sh)

PENALTIES: Malysiak (Pol) 1:00, Contini (Can) 6:00, Shaw (Can — major, misconduct) 14:00, Forbes (Can) 18:00

Third Period

9. Canada, McCourt (unassisted) 5:00
10. Canada, Hunter (Duguay) .... 8:00(sh)
11. Canada, Secord (McCourt) 10:00
12. Canada, Shaw (Marsh) 15:00
13. Canada, Contini (Huber) 17:00
14. Canada, Shaw (Forbes) 20:00

PENALTIES: Seiling (Can) 7:00, Rylko (Pol) 13:00

Shots on Goal:

Canada	18	8	17	43
Poland	8	14	4	26

In Goal:

Canada — Jensen
Poland — Wadas

December 25   Canada 4   Czechoslovakia 4

First Period

1. Czechoslovakia, Skalicky (Vostry) .... 10:45(pp)
2. Canada, McCourt (unassisted) 13:42

PENALTIES: Shaw (Can) 1:35, Duguay (Can) 3:40, Urban (Cze) 5:53, Shaw (Can) 8:56, Urban (Cze) 18:26

Second Period

3. Czechoslovakia, Otoupalik (Korbela)... 15:09(pp)
4. Canada, McCourt (unassisted) .... 17:26(sh)
5. Czechoslovakia, Karagavrilidis (Oslizlo) .... 18:18(pp)

PENALTIES: Secord (Can) 1:16, Johansen (Can) 4:46, Cerny (Cze) 7:13, Huber (Can — major) 14:30, Duguay (Can) 16:25

Third Period

6. Czechoslovakia, Korbela (Hubl) 5:55
7. Canada, Contini (unassisted) 7:22
8. Canada, McCourt (unassisted) .... 19:41 (ea)

PENALTIES: Contini (Can) 11:26, Skalicky (Cze) 15:52

Missed penalty shot: Josef Lukac (Cze) stopped by Al Jensen (Can)

Shots on Goal:

Canada	9	14	9	32
Czechoslovakia	10	17	11	38

In Goal:

Canada — Jensen
Czechoslovakia — Cerveny

December 26   Canada 6   Finland 4

First Period

1. Canada, Duguay (Secord).. 3:51
2. Finland, Jarvinen (Kamarainen).. 4:45
3. Canada, Foster (Plantery) 15:14

    PENALTIES: Johansen (Can) 8:29, Forbes (Can) 15:50

Second Period

4. Canada, Contini (Seiling).. 3:47
5. Canada, Marsh (Foster) 6:51
6. Finland, Forss (Ruotsalainen)... 10:36(pp)
7. Finland, Siltanen (Jyrkkio) .... 17:28(pp)

    PENALTIES: Forbes (Can) & Javanainen (Fin) 6:33, Contini (Can — minor, misconduct) 9:09, McCourt (Can) 9:36, Laine (Fin) 12:55, Hazlett (Can) 14:20, Duguay (Can — major) 16:53

Third Period

8. Canada, Anderson (McCourt) 11:48
9. Finland, Forss (unassisted) 16:57
10. Canada, McCourt (Anderson)... 19:53(en)

    PENALTIES: none

Shots on Goal:

Canada	6	6	7	19
Finland	11	12	7	30

In Goal:

Canada — Jensen
Finland — Kamppuri

December 28   Canada 5   Sweden 3

First Period

1. Sweden, Gustafsson (Hermansson)... 8:09(pp)
2. Canada, Anderson (Contini) .... 12:39(pp)

    PENALTIES: Secord (Can) & Hermansson (Swe) 5:07, Plantery (Can) 6:50, Sarkijarvi (Swe) 12:05, Forbes (Can) 13:40

Second Period

3. Sweden, Luckner (Olsson) 6:57
4. Sweden, Eriksson (Mikko) 7:45

5. Canada, McCourt (Anderson) 11:45
6. Canada, Anderson (McCourt, Secord) 12:02

> PENALTIES: Luckner (Swe) 3:39, Gustafsson (Swe) & Anderson (Can) 4:10, Eriksson (Swe) 8:32, Secord (Can) 16:14, Marsh (Can) 17:01

Third Period

7. Canada, Hunter (Foster) 2:40
8. Canada, Foster (Duguay, Huber) 17:29

> PENALTIES: Secord (Can) 3:59, Duguay (Can) 10:21, McCourt (Can) & Naslund (Swe) 19:02, Contini (Can — double major) & Hermansson (Swe — minor, major, misconduct) 19:43

Shots on Goal:

Canada	13	14	9	**36**
Sweden	14	13	12	**39**

In Goal:

> Canada — Jensen
> Sweden — Lindberg

December 29   *Canada 9*   *West Germany 1*

First Period

1. Canada, Duguay (Keating) 5:37
2. West Germany, Hofner (Meitinger) .... 13:37(pp)
3. Canada, Contini (Anderson) .... 15:09(pp)

> PENALTIES: Contini (Can) 9:50, Forbes (Can) 12:05, Truntschka (WGer) 14:15, Lupzig (WGer) 17:48, Seiling (Can) 18:43

Second Period

4. Canada, Seiling (Marsh) 12:59
5. Canada, Anderson (Ramage) 18:08

> PENALTIES: Seiling (Can) & Medicus (WGer) 19:26

Third Period

6. Canada, Hazlett (Contini) 0:22
7. Canada, McCourt (Anderson) 4:24
8. Canada, Shaw (Houle) 5:27
9. Canada, Hazlett (Contini) 5:52
10. Canada, Hunter (Duguay) 18:17

> PENALTIES: Ramage (Can) 6:33, Huber (Can) 7:59, Medicus (WGer) 10:39, Anderson (Can) 10:44, Groger (WGer) 14:19, Schiller (WGer — major) & Duguay (Can — major) 18:36, Foster (Can) & Heinrich (WGer) & Schuster (WGer — misconduct) 19:02

Shots on Goal:

Canada	26	28	26	**80**
West Germany	11	9	13	**33**

In Goal:

Canada — Jensen
West Germany — Engelbrecht

January 1   *Canada 8*   *United States 2*

First Period

1. Canada, McCourt (Johansen) 1:07
2. Canada, Seiling (McCourt)... 5:53
3. United States, Gandini (Hanson) .... 11:50(pp)
4. United States, Penningroth (Wilkins) 16:29
5. Canada, Hazlett (Seiling) 16:41

  PENALTIES: Marsh (Can) 10:49, Huber (Can) 18:43

Second Period

6. Canada, Anderson (Johansen, McCourt) 1:03
7. Canada, Anderson (Ramage) .... 4:16(pp)

  PENALTIES: Huber (Can) 2:13, Parker (U.S.) 2:59, Hazlett (Can) 7:55, Contini
  (Can) & Rego (U.S.) 12:31, Contini (Can) 14:37

Third Period

8. Canada, Hazlett (Seiling, Contini).. 11:11
9. Canada, Hunter (Duguay, Foster)... 11:50
10. Canada, Anderson (McCourt, Keating) 14:15

  PENALTIES: Hunter (Can) 17:08

Shots on Goal:

Canada	12	15	14	**41**
United States	16	4	8	**28**

In Goal:

Canada — Jensen
United States — Bloomberg/Parker (Parker [4 goals] replaced Bloomberg
[4 goals] at 2:13 of 2nd)

January 2   *Soviet Union 6*   *Canada 4*

First Period

1. Soviet Union, Frolikov (Sostak).. 5:12
2. Soviet Union, Zubkov (Romasin).. 5:38
3. Soviet Union, Jevstifeyev (Fetisov).. 9:58(pp)
4. Soviet Union, Sostak (Frolikov)... 13:40
5. Soviet Union, Romasin (Makarov) 14:33
6. Soviet Union, Gimayev (Romasin) .... 16:55(pp)

  PENALTIES: Marsh (Can) 8:32, Johansen (Can) & Gimayev (Sov) 11:52, Johansen
  (Can) 15:01, Marsh (Can — minor, misconduct) 19:41

Second Period

No Scoring

> PENALTIES: Seiling (Can) 8:05, Payusov (Sov) 13:15, Hunter (Can) 18:38

Third Period

7. Canada, Secord (Johansen)... 2:37
8. Canada, Anderson (McCourt) 3:05
9. Canada, Hazlett (Contini) 12:33
10. Canada, Seiling (Hazlett) 15:59

> PENALTIES: Zubkov (Sov) & Secord (Can) 4:21, Contini (Can) 7:08, Kubanov (Sov) 13:10, Romasin (Sov) 13:31, Contini (Can) & Frolikov (Sov) 18:04, Johansen (Can — high-sticking major) 19:44

Shots on Goal:

Canada	10	12	8	**30**
Soviet Union	19	10	15	**44**

In Goal:

Canada — Jensen
Soviet Union — Tyznych

TEAM CANADA FINAL STATISTICS
1977 WORLD JUNIOR CHAMPIONSHIPS
(St. Catharines Fincups)

			GP	G	A	P	PIM
10	F	Dale McCourt(C)	7	10	8	18	14
24	F	John Anderson	7	10	5	15	4
14	F	Joe Contini(A)	7	4	6	10	38
17	F	Steve Hazlett	7	6	1	7	4
11	F	Dave Hunter	7	6	0	6	4
23	F	Ric Seiling	7	3	3	6	8
25	F	Ron Duguay	7	2	4	6	16
29	F	Dwight Foster	7	2	4	6	4
15	F	Geoff Shaw	7	3	1	4	19
20	F	Al Secord	7	2	2	4	10
28	D	Brad Marsh	7	1	3	4	18
7	D	Willie Huber(A)	7	1	2	3	11
5	D	Trevor Johansen	7	0	3	3	13
27	D	Rob Ramage	7	0	2	2	2
21	F	Mike Keating	7	0	2	2	0
6	D	Mike Forbes	7	0	1	1	22
2	D	Mark Plantery	7	0	1	1	2
19	F	Dennis Houle	7	0	1	1	0
1	G	Al Jensen	7	0	0	0	0

In Goal

	GP	W-L-T	MINS	GA	SO	AVG
Al Jensen	7	5–1–1	420	20	1	2.86
Bob Daly	did not play					

Coach   Bert Templeton

CANADIAN OFFICIALS AT THE 1977 WORLD JUNIOR CHAMPIONSHIPS

Blair Graham (referee)   5 games

TEAM CANADA ROSTER SUMMARY

Team Canada players	19
Drafted Into NHL	17 (all but Plantery, Shaw)
Played in NHL	17 (all but Houle, Shaw)

PLAYER REPRESENTATION BY LEAGUE

OHA   19

PLAYER REPRESENTATION BY AGE

19-year-olds	10 (Anderson, Contini, Duguay, Forbes, Foster, Hazlett, Johansen, Keating, McCourt, Seiling)
18-year-olds	7 (Houle, Huber, Hunter, Jensen, Marsh, Secord, Shaw)
17-year-olds	2 (Plantery, Ramage)

PLAYERS' CAREER PROFILES

John Anderson	Toronto Marlboros (OHA)
	Selected 11th overall by Toronto at 1977 Draft
	Played in the NHL 1977–89
Joe Contini	St. Catharines Fincups (OHA)
	Selected 126th overall by Rockies at 1977 Draft
	Played in the NHL 1977–81
Ron Duguay	Sudbury Wolves (OHA)
	Selected 13th overall by Rangers at 1977 Draft
	Played in the NHL 1977–89
Mike Forbes	St. Catharines Fincups (OHA)
	Selected 52nd overall by Boston at 1977 Draft
	Played in the NHL 1977–82

Dwight Foster   Kitchener Rangers (OHA)
Selected 16th overall by Boston at 1977 Draft
Played in the NHL 1977–87

Steve Hazlett   St. Catharines Fincups (OHA)
Selected 76th overall by Vancouver at 1977 Draft
Played in the NHL 1979–80

Dennis Houle   St. Catharines Fincups (OHA)
Selected 123rd overall by St. Louis at 1978 Draft
Did not play in the NHL

Willie Huber   St. Catharines Fincups (OHA)
Selected 9th overall by Detroit at 1978 Draft
Played in the NHL 1978–88

Dave Hunter   Sudbury Wolves (OHA)
Selected 17th overall by Montreal at 1978 Draft
Played in the NHL 1979–89

Al Jensen   St. Catharines Fincups (OHA)
Selected 31st overall by Detroit at 1978 Draft
Played in the NHL 1980–87

Trevor Johansen   Toronto Marlboros (OHA)
Selected 12th overall by Toronto at 1977 Draft
Played in the NHL 1977–82

Mike Keating   St. Catharines Fincups (OHA)
Selected 26th overall by Rangers at 1977 Draft
Played in the NHL 1977–78

Brad Marsh   London Knights (OHA)
Selected 11th overall by Atlanta at 1978 Draft
Played in the NHL 1978–93

Dale McCourt   St. Catharines Fincups (OHA)
Selected 1st overall by Detroit at 1977 Draft
Played in the NHL 1977–84

Mark Plantery   St. Catharines Fincups (OHA)
Not drafted
Played in the NHL 1980–81

Rob Ramage   London Knights (OHA)
Selected 1st overall by Rockies at 1979 Draft
Played in the NHL 1979–94

Al Secord   St. Catharines Fincups (OHA)
Selected 16th overall by Boston at 1978 Draft
Played in the NHL 1978–90

Ric Seiling   St. Catharines Fincups (OHA)
Selected 14th overall by Buffalo at 1977 Draft
Played in the NHL 1977–87

Geoff Shaw   St. Catharines Fincups (OHA)
Not drafted
Did not play in the NHL

1978 WORLD JUNIOR CHAMPIONSHIPS CANADA, DECEMBER 22, 1977-- JANUARY 3, 1978

FINAL PLACINGS

GOLD MEDAL   Soviet Union
SILVER MEDAL   Sweden
BRONZE MEDAL   **CANADA**
Fourth Place   Czechoslovakia
Fifth Place   United States
Sixth Place   Finland
Seventh Place   West Germany
Eighth Place   Switzerland*

promoted from "B" pool in 1977; relegated to "B" pool for 1979

ALL-STAR TEAM

GOAL   Alexander Tyznych (Soviet Union)
DEFENCE   Risto Siltanen (Finland)
            Viacheslav Fetisov (Soviet Union)
FORWARD   Wayne Gretzky (Canada)
            Mats Naslund (Sweden)
            Anton Stastny (Czechoslovakia)

DIRECTORATE AWARDS

BEST GOALIE   Alexnader Tyzhnych (Soviet Union)
BEST DEFENCEMAN   Viacheslav Fetisov (Soviet Union)
BEST FORWARD   Wayne Gretzky (Canada)

COACH ERNIE "PUNCH" McLEAN

Although he got the nickname Punch because he was goofy, McLean lived up to the more physical interpretations of the moniker. While coaching the Estevan Bruins in the sixties and the New Westminster Bruins in the seventies, he trained his players to intimidate their opponents. In one practise drill, he stood two players back-to-back behind one goal. They skated along the boards and collided at full speed behind the other net. That, McLean felt, separated the men from the boys.

McLean was abrasive behind the Bruins' bench. His teams appeared in three successive Memorial Cups, and certainly his style wore off on his players. Once McLean pulled off the toupee of a linesmen after a missed offside call. He was suspended twenty-five games for punching a referee, and another time he accosted a linesmen in the hallway, grabbed him by the throat, and asked him if he'd like to pull his hair the way he had a Bruins player while breaking up a fight during the game. He threw a garbage can on the ice once to protest the officiating. The toss resulted in a five-game suspension.

McLean's survival-of-the-fittest mandate might well have been instilled in him years earlier when a plane he was flying in remote Saskatchewan crashed in the bush. His jaw was badly torn, and his left eye was dangling on his cheek. It took him twenty-seven hours to crawl four miles to help. He lost the eye, had fifty-seven splinters removed from his face, and needed seven operations over two years.

ASSEMBLING THE SQUAD

The Juniors held an initial assessment camp in the summer at the Bobby Orr-Mike Walton Hockey School in Haliburton, Ontario, where McLean and co-coaches Gus Bodnar and Orval Tessier made roster notes that would be amended frequently during the first half of the Canadian junior league season. Three coaches represented the major leagues — McLean the Western league, Bodnar in Ontario, and Tessier the Quebec juniors.

Initially, the invitees were distributed more or less evenly, fourteen from the OMJHL, fifteen from the WCHL, and twelve from the QMJHL. The forty-one were pared down to twenty-three, and then seven new Ontarians were added: Wayne Gretzky and Dan Lucas from the Soo, Pat Riggin and Brad Marsh from London, Tim Higgins and Bobby Smith of the 67's, and Joel Quenneville from Windsor. Pat Daley was added from the Quebec league. This distribution of talent infuriated Trois-Rivières coach Michel Bergeron, who felt that the QMJHL was not adequately represented. At the final camp in December, there were only eight players from the QMJHL — four of them

Bobby Smith wearing the innovative sweaters of 1978, which featured a distinctive blue maple leaf instead of the traditional red.

from Cornwall (which didn't count in the eyes of partisan Quebeckers). Only one, Dan Geoffrion, was a native of the province.

Coach Orval Tessier scoffed at the charges of regional favouritism: "I've had only four hours sleep in the last fifty, running all over Quebec defending Team Canada, and I don't like it at all. We were told there were to be no politics. No league or city club would be favoured in any way. No marketing was to be done in considering our selections. We can sympathize with any club that feels slighted, but we were not going to jeopardize our chances of winning the tournament."

Later, poor attendance affected the prestige of the tournament when not one French-Canadian was on the final team. For the Soviets' last game of the A Division round-robin against Czechoslovakia, a game that would decide one gold medal finalist, only 1,121 showed up at the Colisée in Quebec City, despite the lure of free beer and souvenirs.

The thirty-two Canadian players assembled for a final pre-tournament tryout on December 15, 1977, a day late because heavy storms in and around Montreal cancelled most players' flights into the training camp city. Once assembled, the boys received their sweaters, designed after the Canada Cup jerseys of 1976 but with one very striking difference: Canadian red was replaced by blue!

To help promote camaraderie, no players from the same junior team roomed together, and all players ate meals together. Four players had not yet arrived by the 16th. They preferred to play with their junior team, rather than practise with the tournament team. Their first exhibition game was on the 18th against Finland, in Cornwall. The following night they played the Czechs in Quebec City. Canada narrowly beat the smaller Finns 3–2 before hammering the Czechs 5–0. In two other pre-tournament games in Cornwall, the U.S. beat West Germany 5–2, and Sweden tied 5–5 with the Concordia University Stingers.

On the 19th, Team Canada beat Sweden 6–4 in Hull before a full house of 2,436. The game featured the Swedes playing in Hull Olympiques sweaters, as their yellow and blue national jerseys had been lost on the flight. The next night, Canada completed a perfect exhibition series by crushing the Russians 7–3 at the Forum in Montreal. In pre-tournament games, the Czechs won over the Quebec Remparts of the QMJHL 6–4; Finland beat Chicoutimi, of the same league, 12–6; the U.S. beat Cornwall 8–4; and a Cornwall-Hull team shut out the Germans 6–0.

THE UNDERAGE CONTROVERSY
GAINS MOMENTUM

This year marked another step in the history of hockey. Shortly after the championships, Mike Gartner signed with the Cincinnati Stingers of the WHA at the age of eighteen. He was lured not from the NHL (which didn't allow eighteen-year-olds) but from the OHL. The pirate league was demonstrating its intention of building a quality league at any legal or ethical cost. The NHL was in trouble — the WHA could undermine the NHL draft by signing the best players long before they ever became eligible to play in the NHL.

Further evidence of the dangers of the league occurred when Nelson Skalbania of the Indianapolis Racers signed Wayne Gretzky to a twenty-one-year personal services contract. Skalbania had seized the most cherished prize in the history of the draft. In response, the NHL changed its draft setup to include eighteen-year-olds and then did what had been considered unthinkable — it allowed four WHA teams to merge with the NHL. The juniors war was over, and in the process the NHL became much younger.

WAYNE GRETZKY

The Great One appeared in his first major international tournament, the World Juniors, at the age of sixteen, the youngest in the competition (Red Laurence was also sixteen when he represented Canada at the unofficial World Juniors in 1974.) Coach McLean confessed Gretzky was invited to camp only because he was leading the OHA in scoring while playing with the Soo Greyhounds. Almost a month later, when he rejoined the Soo, Gretzky was still leading the league in scoring.

Sixteen-year old Wayne Gretzky handles the puck as a member of the Soo Greyhounds in his only full year of junior hockey, 1977-78.

Torchy Schell, a former scout with the Leafs now covering the juniors as a member of the NHL Central Scouting bureau, tempered his praise for Gretzky: "He stick-handles and passes really well and knows what to do with the puck. But by the time he's eighteen, he may decide to be a doctor or something or find other interests. Mind you, if he continues playing, he'll attract a lot of attention."

Gretzky began playing when he was six, with the Nadrofsky Steelers in Brantford (Atom, 1967–72), then moved up to Peewee with the Turkstra Lumber (1972–74) and the Charcon Chargers (1974–75). He played one year (1976–77) with the Seneca Nationals in Metro Toronto Junior B, and was called up to play three games for the Peterborough Petes. The following year he joined the Soo. It was as a fourteen-year-old at the peewee championships in Quebec City that he first received national attention. His presence helped mollify the injured feelings of Quebeckers, who cheered wildly when he was introduced at these World Juniors.

SILVER MEDAL STRATEGY

Canada's bronze should have been a silver, but for a tactical error. Going into their final round robin of the championship series, Canada needed only a tie to finish ahead of Sweden. Canada jumped to a 2–0 lead midway through the first period. A win seemed likely but for the officiating of Russian Yuri Karandin. The Canadians kept hitting and then retaliating, and Karandin kept sending them to the penalty box. The Swedes scored three power-play goals and went on to win 6–5. After the game, retired Soviet coach Anatoli Tarasov asked Alan Eagleson why the Canadians didn't line up at the blue line and play to protect their win, a question the Eagle couldn't answer.

TOURNAMENT FORMAT

A round-robin format was used within each division. Each team played three games. The top two teams from each division advanced to a medal round, and the last two teams from each were grouped in a B pool. Another round robin was played with no first-round results carried over. The top two teams played a one-game final for gold.

THE OPPOSITION

CZECHOSLOVAKIA

Rene Andrejs, Marian Bezak, Vladimir Caldr, Ivan Cerny, Frantisek Cerny, Miroslav Frycer, Jan Hrabak, Jiri Hrdina, Jan Jasko, Arnold Kadlec, Eugen

Krajcovic, Miroslav Moc, Darius Rusnak, Jaromir Sindel, Pavel Skalicky, Anton Stastny, Ladislav Svozil, Vladimir Urban, Vlastimil Vajcner, Ondrej Weissman

FINLAND

Antti Heikkila, Arto Javanainen, Juha Jyrkkio, Risto Kankaanpera, Tero Kopynen, Tuomo Laukkanen, Pekka Laukkanen, Reijo Mansikka, Jukka Peitsoma, Rainer Risku, Reijo Ruotsalainen, Jorma Sevon, Risto Siltanen, Ilkka Sinisalo, Rauli Sohlman, Kai Suikkanen, Timo Susi, Harri Tuohimaa, Jouko Urvikko, Jari Viitala

SOVIET UNION

Pavel Ezovskin, Viacheslav Fetisov, Alexander Gerasimov, Alexander Gurjev, Alexei Kasatonov, Alexander Kozhevnikov, Sergei Makarov, Konstantin Makartsev, Sergei Mylnikov, Nikolai Narimanov, Sergei Paramanov, Viacheslav Ryanov, Victor Skurdjuk, Sergei Starikov, Anatoli Tarasov, Sergei Tuckmachev, Alexander Tyznych, Nikolai Varianov, Yuri Vozhakov, Vladimir Zhubkov

SWEDEN

Mikael Andersson, Bo Ericsson, Jan Eriksson, Bengt-Ake Gustafsson, Mats Hallin, Goran Henriksson, Dan Hermansson, Thomas Jonsson, Thomas Korrbrand, Pelle Lindbergh, Christer Lowdahl, Mats Naslund, Gunnar Persson, Tommy Samuelsson, Claes-Henrik Silfver, Conny Silfverberg, Ulf Skoglund, Thomas Steen, Anders Wallin, Ulf Zetterstrom

SWITZERLAND

Michael Braun, Claude Domeniconi, Daniel Dubois, Reto Durst, Philippe Favrod, Pierre Flotirant, Roger Geiger, Roland Gerber, Markus Graf, Pierre Houriet, Beat Lautenschlager, Rolf Leuenberger, Didier Mayor, Christian Patt, Hanspeter Sagesser, Roland Scheibli, Gerald Scheurer, Diego Ulrich, Marcel Wicks, Bernhard Wuthrich

WEST GERMANY

Karl Altmann, Johann Diepold, Michael Eggerbauer, Peter Eimannsberger, Bernd Engelbrecht, Thomas Gandorfer, Alexander Gross, Horst Heckelsmuller, Jorg Hiemer, Matthias Hoppe, Norbert Kafer, Sepp Klaus, Les Koch, Armin Lauer, Martin Muller, Miro Nentwich, Harry Pflugl, Manfred Schuster, Helmut Steiger, Gerhard Truntschka

UNITED STATES

Bret Bierken, Carl Bloomberg, Steve Blue, Bob Crawford, Dave Feamster, Mark Green, Ron Griffin, Kevin Hartzell, Ed Hospodar, Terry Jones, Paul Joswiak, Scott Lacy, Bart Larson, John Liprando, Jeff Lundgren, Mike McDougall, Jack McKinch, Steve Pepper, Steve Ulseth, Don Waddell

FINAL STANDINGS PRELIMINARY ROUND

GOLD DIVISION

	GP	W	L	T	GF	GA	P
Sweden	3	2	0	1	18	8	5
Soviet Union	3	2	1	0	31	11	4
Finland	3	1	1	1	26	15	3
Switzerland	3	0	3	0	3	44	0

Results

December 22	Cornwall	Soviet Union 18	Switzerland 1
	Chicoutimi	Finland 4	Sweden 4
December 23	Quebec City	Sweden 6	Soviet Union 3
	Chicoutimi	Finland 18	Switzerland 1
December 26	Cornwall	Sweden 8	Switzerland 1
	Montreal	Soviet Union 10	Finland 4

BLUE DIVISION

	GP	W	L	T	GF	GA	P
CANADA	3	3	0	0	23	6	6
Czechoslovakia	3	2	1	0	16	18	4
United States	3	1	2	0	16	18	2
West Germany	3	0	3	0	8	21	0

Results

December 22	Montreal	Canada 6	United States 3
	Quebec City	Czechoslovakia 5	West Germany 4
December 23	Cornwall	Canada 8	West Germany 0
	Hull	Czechoslovakia 8	United States 5
December 25	Montreal	Canada 9	Czechoslovakia 3
	Hull	United States 8	West Germany 4

FINAL STANDINGS CHAMPIONSHIP SERIES

A Division

	GP	W	L	T	GF	GA	P
Soviet Union	3	3	0	0	14	3	6
Sweden	3	2	1	0	8	11	4
CANADA	3	1	2	0	13	12	2
Czechoslovakia	3	0	3	0	5	14	0

Results

December 28	Quebec City	Soviet Union 3	Canada 2
	Montreal	Sweden 2	Czechoslovakia 1
December 31	Montreal	Canada 6	Czechoslovakia 3
	Quebec City	Soviet Union 5	Sweden 0
January 1	Montreal	Sweden 6	Canada 5
	Quebec City	Soviet Union 6	Czechoslovakia 1

B Division

	GP	W	L	T	GF	GA	P
United States	3	3	0	0	25	12	6
Finland	3	2	1	0	19	10	4
West Germany	3	1	2	0	12	12	2
Switzerland	3	0	3	0	4	26	0

Results

December 28	Chicoutimi	Finland 4	West Germany 1
	Cornwall	United States 11	Switzerland 1
December 30	Cornwall	Finland 9	Switzerland 1
	Hull	United States 6	West Germany 5
December 31	Hull	United States 8	Finland 6
	Cornwall	West Germany 6	Switzerland 2

GOLD MEDAL GAME

| January 3 | Montreal | Soviet Union 5 | Sweden 2 |

AGGREGATE STANDINGS

(ordered according to final placings)

	GP	W	L	T	GF	GA	GAA	SO	PIM
Soviet Union	7	6	1	0	50	16	2.29	1	84
Sweden	7	4	2	1	28	24	3.43	0	75
CANADA	6	4	2	0	36	18	3.00	1	52
Czechoslovakia	6	2	4	0	21	32	5.33	0	76
United States	6	4	2	0	41	30	5.00	0	90
Finland	6	3	2	1	45	25	4.17	0	61
West Germany	6	1	5	0	20	33	5.50	0	141
Switzerland	6	0	6	0	7	70	11.67	0	36

TEAM CANADA GAME SUMMARIES

December 22   *Canada 6*   *United States 3*

First Period

1. Canada, Daley (Ramage, Paterson)..4:58(pp)
2. Canada, Vaive (Daley) 17:12
3. Canada, McKegney (Gretzky, Babych)..18:53

    PENALTIES: Smyl (Can) 0:45, Lundgren (U.S.) 4:23, Ramage (Can) 19:45

Second Period

4. United States, Green (Lacy, Feamster) 4:22
5. United States, Green (McDougall)...19:12

    PENALTIES: Liprando (U.S.) 1:43

Third Period

6. United States, Liprando (Lundgren) ....1:53(pp)
7. Canada, Walter (Gartner) 4:59
8. Canada, Paterson (Hartsburg) 8:40
9. Canada, Gretzky (Hartsburg, Babych)..16:51

    PENALTIES: Walter (Can) 0:40, Babych (Can) 12:21, Ulseth (U.S.) 17:18, McCrimmon (Can) 19:47

Shots on Goal:

Canada	11	5	18	**34**
United States	6	14	10	**30**

In Goal:

    Canada — Jensen
    United States — Bloomberg/Joswiak (Joswiak [3 goals] replaced Bloomberg [3 goals] to start 2nd)

December 23   *Canada 8*   *West Germany 0*

First Period

1. Canada, McKegney (Gretzky) 8:37
2. Canada, Gretzky (Babych, McKegney) 8:52
3. Canada, Gretzky (Hartsburg)...11:22(pp)
4. Canada, Babych (Gretzky)..14:09

    PENALTIES: Heckelsmuller (WG) 10:32, McCrimmon (Can) 15:02

Second Period

5. Canada, Vaive (unassisted) 10:40
6. Canada, Walter (unassisted) 13:17
7. Canada, Gretzky (McKegney) 14:42
8. Canada, Gartner (Walter) 17:10

    PENALTIES: Gartner (Can) 3:19, Gandorfer (WG — double minor) 6:00

Third Period

No Scoring

> PENALTIES: Gandorfer (WG) 5:51, Vaive (Can) 9:11, Altmann (WG — misconduct) 13:18, Hartsburg (Can) 13:58

Shots on Goal:

Canada	26	20	15	**61**
West Germany	10	5	10	**25**

In Goal:

> Canada — Bernhardt
> West Germany — Hoppe

December 25   *Canada 9*   *Czechoslovakia 3*

First Period

1. Canada, Babych (Gretzky, McKegney).. 4:46
2. Canada, Gretzky (McKegney, Marsh).. 8:53
3. Canada, Walter (Smyl, Hartsburg).. 10:35
4. Czechoslovakia, Cerny (Vajcner, Jasko) 11:23
5. Canada, Tambellini (unassisted) 16:51
6. Czechoslovakia, Weissman (unassisted).. 18:55

> PENALTIES: Babych (Can) 1:46, Hartsburg (Can) 13:28, Smyl (Can) 19:21

Second Period

7. Canada, Gretzky (Babych, Young).. 3:08
8. Czechoslovakia, Hrdina (Cerny) 16:50
9. Canada, Tambellini (Gartner, Fraser) 17:23

> PENALTIES: Gartner (Can) 7:58, Svozil (Cze) 18:40

Third Period

10. Canada, Gretzky (Huber, McKegney) .... 2:36(pp)
11. Canada, Gartner (Fraser, Gretzky) 11:09
12. Canada, Hartsburg (Babych, Gretzky).. 15:56

> PENALTIES: Urban (Cze) 1:22, Kadlec (Cze) 8:11, Cerny (Cze) 16:40

Missed penalty shot: Steve Tambellini (Can) stopped by Jaromir Sindel (Cze)

Shots on Goal:

unknown

In Goal:

> Canada — Bernhardt
> Czechoslovakia — Sindel

December 28   *Soviet Union 3*   *Canada 2*

First Period

1. Canada, Daley (Paterson, Young) 10:39
2. Canada, Ramage (Tambellini) 12:16

    PENALTIES: Hartsburg (Can) 6:36, Makarov (Sov) 13:35

Second Period

3. Soviet Union, Kozhevnikov (Paramanov) 2:18
4. Soviet Union, Gurjev (Makarov, Fetisov) .... 12:23(pp)

    PENALTIES: Young (Can) 11:35, Huber (Can) 14:57, Paramanov (Sov) 18:05

Third Period

5. Soviet Union, Ryanov (Starikov, Varianov) 9:09

    PENALTIES: Ezovskin (Sov) 6:19, Can bench (served by Huber) 18:09

Shots on Goal:

Canada	11	6	8	25
Soviet Union	6	13	4	23

In Goal:

    Canada — Jensen
    Soviet Union — Tyznych

December 31   *Canada 6*   *Czechoslovakia 3*

First Period

1. Czechosloavkia, Bezak (Urban) 5:31
2. Canada, Vaive (Huber) 12:49

    PENALTIES: Gretzky (Can) 0:38

Second Period

3. Czechoslovakia, Moc (Vajcner, A. Stastny) 1:45
4. Canada, Gretzky (McCrimmon, Marsh) .... 10:50(pp)

    PENALTIES: Ramage (Can) 8:32, Frycer (Cz) 9:57, Svozil (Cz — misconduct) 10:50, Krajcovic (Cz) 13:09

Third Period

5. Canada, Smith (Walter, Ramage) 0:24
6. Canada, Smyl (Tambellini, McCrimmon) 14:34
7. Czechoslovakia, Frycer (I. Cerny) 16:20
8. Canada, Gartner (Smith, Daley) 18:07
9. Canada, Daley (Smith, Marsh) 19:13

    PENALTIES: Hartsburg (Can) 10:00, Moc (Cz) 16:30

Shots on Goal:

Canada	11	12	17	40
Czechoslovakia	9	8	8	25

In Goal:

Canada — Bernhardt
Czechoslovakia — Hrabak

January 1   **Sweden 6**   *Canada 5*

First Period

1. Canada, Babych (McKegney, Gretzky)..10:20(pp)
2. Canada, Walter (Smith, Gartner) 13:12
3. Sweden, Naslund (Steen, Hallin) ....15:29(pp)
4. Sweden, Hermansson (Eriksson, Naslund) 16:03

   PENALTIES: Hallin (Swe) 8:52, Smyl (Can) 14:33, Vaive (Can) 17:30, Marsh (Can) 19:52

Second Period

5. Sweden, Hermansson (Eriksson, Naslund) ....1:47(pp)
6. Sweden, Silfver (Hallin) 13:45

   PENALTIES: Hallin (Swe) 3:41, Gustafsson (Swe) 16:33, Ramage (Can) 16:47

Third Period

7. Canada, Babych (Smith, Gretzky) ....4:16(pp)
8. Canada, Babych (Walter, Gretzky) 9:36
9. Sweden, Hermansson (Jonsson, Naslund) ....13:59(pp)
10. Sweden, Lowdahl (Gustafsson)...19:28
11. Canada, Walter (Ramage, Marsh) 19:45

   PENALTIES: Jonsson (Swe) 4:13, Walter (Can) 4:19, Daley (Can) 13:23

Shots on Goal:

Canada	9	8	15	**32**
Sweden	14	15	13	**42**

In Goal:

Canada — Jensen
Sweden — Henriksson

TEAM CANADA FINAL STATISTICS
1978 WORLD JUNIOR CHAMPIONSHIPS
(National Junior All-Star Team)

			GP	G	A	A	PIM
9	F	Wayne Gretzky	6	8	9	17	2
20	F	Wayne Babych	6	5	5	10	4
14	F	Ryan Walter(C)	6	5	3	8	4
7	F	Tony McKegney	6	2	6	8	0
19	F	Mike Gartner	6	3	3	6	4

25	F	Pat Daley	6	3	2	5	2
4	D	Craig Hartsburg	6	1	4	5	8
15	F	Bobby Smith	3	1	4	5	0
10	F	Steve Tambellini	6	2	2	4	0
12	D	Rob Ramage	6	1	3	4	6
22	D	Brad Marsh	6	0	4	4	2
23	F	Rick Vaive	6	3	0	3	4
28	F	Rick Paterson	6	1	2	3	0
11	F	Stan Smyl	6	1	1	2	6
34	D	Brad McCrimmon	6	0	2	2	4
17	F	Willie Huber	6	0	2	2	2
16	D	Brian Young	6	0	2	2	2
29	F	Curt Fraser	5	0	2	2	0
31	G	Tim Bernhardt	3	0	0	0	0
1	G	Al Jensen	3	0	0	0	0

In Goal

	GP	W-L-T	MINS	GA	SO	AVG
Tim Bernhardt	3	3–0–0	180	6	1	2.00
Al Jensen	3	1–2–0	180	12	0	4.00

Coach   Ernie McLean
Assistants   Gus Bodnar / Orval Tessier

CANADIAN OFFICIALS AT THE 1978 WORLD JUNIOR CHAMPIONSHIPS

Doug Robb (referee)	5 games
Maurice Baril (linesman)	4 games
Louis Therrien (linesman)	4 games
Nelson Gagnon (linesman)	4 games
Serge Girard (linesman)	4 games
Denis Pierre Perreault (linesman)	2 games
Bob MacMillan (linesman)	3 games
Michel Stebin (linesman)	2 games
Jean Maheux (linesman)	2 games
Jacques Charbonneau (linesman)	1 game

TEAM CANADA ROSTER SUMMARY

Team Canada players	20	
Drafted Into NHL	19	(all but Gretzky)
Played in NHL	20	
Returning Players	4	(Huber, Jensen, Marsh, Ramage)

PLAYER REPRESENTATION BY LEAGUE

OHL	9	(Gartner, Gretzky, Hartsburg, Huber, Jensen, Marsh, McKegney, Ramage, Smith)
WHL	7	(Babych, Fraser, McCrimmon, Smyl, Tambellini, Walter, Young)
QMJHL	4	(Bernhardt, Daley, Paterson, Vaive)

PLAYER REPRESENTATION BY AGE

19-year-olds	12	(Babych, Bernhardt, Fraser, Huber, Jensen, Marsh, McKegney, Smith, Smyl, Tambellini, Walter, Young)
18-year-olds	7	(Daley, Gartner, Hartsburg, McCrimmon, Paterson, Ramage, Vaive)
16-year-olds	1	(Gretzky)

PLAYERS' CAREER PROFILES

Wayne Babych
Portland Winter Hawks (WHL)
Selected 3rd overall by St. Louis at 1978 Draft
Played in the NHL 1978–87

Tim Bernhardt
Cornwall Royals (QMJHL)
Selected 47th overall by Atlanta at 1978 Draft
Played in the NHL 1982–87

Pat Daley
Laval Nationals (QMJHL)
Selected 82nd overall by Winnipeg at 1979 Draft
Played in the NHL 1979–81

Curt Fraser
Victoria Cougars (WHL)
Selected 22nd overall by Vancouver at 1978 Draft
Played in the NHL 1978–90

Mike Gartner
Niagara Falls Flyers (OHL)
Selected 4th overall by Washington at 1979 Draft
Played in the NHL 1979–98

Wayne Gretzky
Sault Ste. Marie Greyhounds (OHL)
Not drafted
Played in the NHL 1979–98

Craig Hartsburg
Sault Ste. Marie Greyhounds (OHL)
Selected 6th overall by Minnesota at 1979 Draft
Played in the NHL 1979–89

Willie Huber
Hamilton Fincups (OHL)
Selected 9th overall by Detroit at 1978 Draft
Played in the NHL 1978–88

Al Jensen
Hamilton Fincups (OHL)
Selected 31st overall by Detroit at 1978 Draft
Played in the NHL 1980–87

Brad Marsh   London Knights (OHL)
                      Selected 11th overall by Atlanta at 1978 Draft
                      Played in the NHL 1978–93
Brad McCrimmon   Brandon Wheat Kings (WHL)
                      Selected 15th overall by Boston at 1979 Draft
                      Played in the NHL 1979–97
Tony McKegney   Kingston Canadians (OHL)
                      Selected 32nd overall by Buffalo at 1978 Draft
                      Played in the NHL 1978–91
Rick Paterson   Cornwall Royals (QMJHL)
                      Selected 46th overall by Chicago at 1978 Draft
                      Played in the NHL 1978–87
Rob Ramage   London Knights (OHL)
                      Selected 1st overall by Rockies at 1979 Draft
                      Played in the NHL 1979–94
Bobby Smith   Ottawa 67's (OHL)
                      Selected 1st overall by Minnesota at 1978 Draft
                      Played in the NHL 1978–93
Stan Smyl   New Westminster Bruins (WHL)
                      Selected 40th overall by Vancouver at 1978 Draft
                      Played in the NHL 1978–91
Steve Tambellini   Lethbridge Broncos (WHL)
                      Selected 15th overall by Islanders at 1978 Draft
                      Played in the NHL 1978–88
Rick Vaive   Sherbrooke Beavers (QMJHL)
                      Selected 5th overall by Vancouver at 1979 Draft
                      Played in the NHL 1979–92
Ryan Walter   Seattle Breakers (WHL)
                      Selected 2nd overall by Washington at 1978 Draft
                      Played in the NHL 1978–93
Brian Young   New Westminster Bruins (WHL)
                      Selected 63rd overall by Chicago at 1978 Draft
                      Played in the NHL 1980–81

1979 WORLD JUNIOR CHAMPIONSHIPS SWEDEN, DECEMBER 27, 1978-- JANUARY 3, 1979

FINAL PLACINGS

GOLD MEDAL	Soviet Union
SILVER MEDAL	Sweden
BRONZE MEDAL	Czechoslovakia
Fourth Place	Finland
Fifth Place	**CANADA**
Sixth Place	United States
Seventh Place	West Germany
Eighth Place	Norway*

promoted from "B" pool in 1978; relegated to "B" pool for 1980

ALL-STAR TEAM

GOAL	Pelle Lindbergh (Sweden)
DEFENCE	Ivan Cerny (Czechoslovakia)
	Alexei Kasatonov (Soviet Union)
FORWARD	Anatoli Tarasov (Soviet Union)
	Thomas Steen (Sweden)
	Vladimir Krutov (Soviet Union)

DIRECTORATE AWARDS

BEST GOALIE	Pelle Lindbergh (Sweden)
BEST DEFENCEMAN	Alexei Kasatonov (Soviet Union)
BEST FORWARD	Vladimir Krutov (Soviet Union)

COACH McLEAN RETURNS

After winning his second consecutive Memorial Cup in the team's fourth successive appearance in the finals, McLean volunteered to lead Canada's juniors again and Hockey Canada gladly took him up on the offer. McLean used his New Westminster Bruins as the core of the team, then added eight players whom he felt could step in to a close-checking system quickly. In so doing, he created debate about the makeup and organization of the team. This year, the latter system was implemented.

ASSEMBLING THE TEAM QUICKLY

The team played an exhibition game in Vancouver on December 18 against the Moscow Selects, then flew to Finland the next day to begin a three-game exhibition series before the championships. The game against the Selects was a 7–2 win before 12,650 fans at the Pacific Coliseum. McLean's strategy was particularly effective: "Other teams chase the Russians in their own zone," he explained. "If a check is missed, then the Russians quickly move the puck up ice and they're all over you. I believe that if you don't chase them, if you stand up at your own blue line and knock them down, they'll be less effective. . . . The Russians don't like to be hit. If you step into them, they don't like it and their offensive patterns become disorganized."

JUNIOR VIOLENCE

International hockey has long been seen as a way to confirm the superiority of Canadian hockey, to strengthen our status as world's best, and to determine where our strengths and weaknesses lie. No matter how well a team competes internationally, improvement is a benchmark of ambition, and performance is a confirmation of ability.

Shortly after the 1979 wjc, a bench-clearing, one-sided brawl occurred between the New Westminster Bruins and the Portland Winter Hawks. It was frightening in its violence. The Bruins cleared their benches during the third period of a lost game, but the Hawks remained on the bench. Seven players wound up in court on assault charges. They pleaded guilty and were granted conditional discharges. Charged were Boris Fistric, Bill Hobbins, Bruce Howes, Terry Kirkham, John Paul Kelly, Rob Roflick, and Richard Amann. All were suspended until December 1, 1979.

Judge James Shaw condemned the entire Canadian junior hockey system and suggested that the myopia of winning by violence in the short term was counter-productive developmentally in the larger scheme of things: "The

Yvan Joly of the Ottawa 67's was one of only two OHL players (the other was goalie Rollie Melanson) to play with the WHL all-stars that formed the majority of Canada's 1979 entry at the WJC.

entire system of hockey, as it exists in North America today, from midget to the NHL, the team owners, managers and, in particular, the coaches, must bear a large share of the responsibility," he commented. "These young men are manipulated, apparently happily, by the owners and coaches to do exactly what they are told." The result was that Canadian teams were outmatched when playing under international rules, which did not tolerate violence in the game.

Coach McLean had been at the eye of many a brawl-filled storm. The previous year he had been suspended for twenty-five games for his part in a violent game, and he once ran onto the ice in a display of temper that prompted a call for his suspension for the remainder of the season. He was ultimately fined $1,500.

TOURNAMENT FORMAT

The eight teams were divided into two four-team divisions and played a round-robin preliminary round within each. The top two countries from both divisions advanced to a round-robin finals pool, and the bottom four played a consolation round-robin. In the championship pool, each team played the other once, while in the consolation division, games played with other countries in the preliminary round were carried over, thus leaving each country to play two games in the consolation pool.

THE OPPOSITION

CZECHOSLOVAKIA

Juraj Bakos, Frantisek Cerny, Ivan Cerny, Miroslav Frycer, Jaroslav Horsky, Jan Hrabak, Jan Jasko, Vladimir Jerabek, Arnold Kadlec, Jiri Lala, Igor Liba, Pavol Norovsky, Dusan Pasek, Antonin Planovsky, Darius Rusnak, Pavel Setikovsky, Peter Slanina, Anton Stastny, Vlastimil Vajcner, Ondrej Weissmann

FINLAND

Timo Blomqvist, Juha Huikari, Jari Hytti, Kari Jalonen, Jarmo Jamalainen, Jari Jarvinen, Arto Javanainen, Juha Jyrkkio, Jari Kurri, Pekka Laukkanen, Jussi Lepisto, Jari Lindgren, Jarmo Makitalo, Juha Nurmi, Jari Paavola, Reijo Ruotsalainen, Rauli Sohlman, Kai Suikkanen, Timo Susi, Harri Tuohimaa

NORWAY

Trond Abrahamsen, Cato Andersen, Knut Andersen, Harald Bastiansen, Arne Billkvam, Bjorn D. Bratz, Tor H. Eikeland, Stephen Foyn, Frode Gaare, Geir Hansen, Tom Huse, Oysten Jarlsbo, Knut Johansen, Roy Johansen, Bjorn Kolsrud, Orjan Lovdahl, Tommy Skarberg, Frank Stromsnas, Petter Thoresen, Tor E. Torp

SOVIET UNION

Andrei Andreyev, Anatoli Antipov, Alexander Gerasimov, Vladimir Gerasimov, Victor Glushenkov, Vladimir Golovkov, Sergei Karpov, Alexei Kasatonov, Vladimir Krutov, Valeri Krylov, Glennady Kurdin, Igor Larionov, Nikolai Mazlov, Viacheslav Rianov, Dmitri Saprykin, Andrei Sidorenko, Yuri Strakhov, Anatoli Tarasov, Nikolai Varianov, Yuri Vozhakov

SWEDEN

Bjorn Akerblom, Mikael Andersson, Silvert Andersson, Jan-Ake Danielsson, Thomas Eriksson, Goran Henriksson, Tomas Jonsson, Lars Karlsson, Thomas Karrbrand, Pelle Lindbergh, Hakan Loob, Tommy Morth, Mats Naslund, Ove Olsson, Jan Remmelg, Tommy Samuelsson, Conny Silfverberg, Per Sjolander, Hakan Sodergren, Thomas Steen

UNITED STATES

Stuart Birenbaum, Aaron Broten, Neal Broten, Jeff Brownschidle, Dave Christian, Bobby Crawford, Gary DeGrio, Bryan Erickson, Jim Jetland, Peter Johnson, Mike LaBianca, John Liprando, Jeff Lundgren, Todd Mishler, Steve Murphy, Steve Palazzi, Mark Pettygrove, Mike Ramsey, Mike Stone, Steve Ulseth

WEST GERMANY

Jurgen Adams, Karl Altmann, Rainer Blum, Michael Eggerbauer, Alexander Gross, Klaus Haider, Gerhard Hegen, Willi Hofer, Georg Holzmann, Joachim Janzon, Bernhard Kopf, Harold Kreiss, Jurgen Lechl, Miro Nentwich, Peter Obressa, Harry Pflugel, Bernhard Seyller, Gunther Stauner, Helmut Steiger, Michael Tack

FINAL STANDINGS PRELIMINARY ROUND

Gold Division

	GP	W	L	T	GF	GA	P
Sweden	3	3	0	0	8	3	6
Finland	3	2	1	0	11	4	4
CANADA	3	1	2	0	7	6	2
West Germany	3	0	3	0	5	18	0

Results

December 27	Karlstad	Finland 3	Canada 1
	Karlstad	Sweden 5	West Germany 2
December 28	Karlstad	Canada 6	West Germany 2
	Karlskoga	Sweden 2	Finland 1
December 30	Karlskoga	Sweden 1	Canada 0
	Karlskoga	Finland 7	West Germany 1

Blue Division

	GP	W	L	T	GF	GA	P
Soviet Union	3	3	0	0	33	2	6
Czechoslovakia	3	2	1	0	10	15	4
United States	3	1	2	0	10	11	2
Norway	3	0	3	0	5	30	0

Results

December 27	Karlskoga	Soviet Union 17	Norway 0
	Karlskoga	Czechoslovakia 3	United States 2

December 28	Karlstad	Czechoslovakia 6	Norway 4
	Karlskoga	Soviet Union 7	United States 1
December 30	Karlstad	Soviet Union 9	Czechoslovakia 1
	Karlstad	United States 7	Norway 1

FINAL STANDINGS CONSOLATION ROUND

	GP	W	L	T	GF	GA	P
CANADA	3	3	0	0	22	6	6
United States	3	2	1	0	18	13	4
West Germany	3	1	2	0	14	14	2
Norway	3	0	3	0	2	23	0

Carry-over results

Canada 6	West Germany 2
United States 7	Norway 1

December 31	Karlstad	Canada 10	Norway 1
	Karlskoga	United States 8	West Germany 6
January 2	Karlskoga	Canada 6	United States 3
	Karlstad	West Germany 6	Norway 0

FINAL STANDINGS CHAMPIONSHIP ROUND

	GP	W	L	T	GF	GA	P
Soviet Union	3	2	0	1	13	9	5
Czechoslovakia	3	1	0	2	9	8	4
Sweden	3	1	1	1	11	10	3
Finland	3	0	3	0	9	15	0

Results

December 31	Karlstad	Soviet Union 4	Finland 2
	Karlskoga	Sweden 1	Czechoslovakia 1
January 2	Karlstad	Sweden 5	Finland 2
	Karlskoga	Czechoslovakia 2	Soviet Union 2
January 3	Karlskoga	Czechoslovakia 6	Finland 5
	Karlstad	Soviet Union 7	Sweden 5

AGGREGATE STANDINGS

(ordered according to final placings)

	GP	W	L	T	GF	GA	P	GAA	SO	PIM
Soviet Union	6	5	0	1	46	11	11	1.83	1	92
Sweden	6	4	1	1	19	13	9	2.17	1	81
Czechoslovakia	6	3	1	2	19	23	8	3.83	0	42*
Finland	6	2	4	0	20	19	4	3.17	0	99
CANADA	5	3	2	0	23	10	6	2.00	0	80
United States	5	2	3	0	21	23	4	4.60	0	73
West Germany	5	1	4	0	17	26	2	5.20	1	100
Norway	5	0	5	0	6	46	0	9.20	0	86

* won Fair Play Cup

TEAM CANADA GAME SUMMARIES

December 27   Finland 3   Canada 1

First Period

No Scoring

    PENALTIES: Susi (Fin) 18:26

Second Period

1. Canada, Lupul (Melnyk) 0:48
2. Finland, Jalonen (Ruotsalainen) 2:34
3. Finland, Makitalo (Kurri, Jarvinen) .... 12:58(pp)

    PENALTIES: Joly (Can) 3:29, Reardon (Can) 12:21

Third Period

4. Finland, Makitalo (unassisted) 19:43

    PENALTIES: Lepisto (Fin) 1:18, Kelly (Can) 14:09

Shots on Goal:

Canada	13	11	12	**36**
Finland	5	5	12	**22**

In Goal:

    Canada — Semenchuk
    Finland — Sohlman

December 28   Canada 6   West Germany 2

First Period

1. Canada, Ogrodnick (unassisted) .... 9:14(pp)
2. Canada, Irving (Ogrodnick) 16:46

    PENALTIES: Stauner (WGer) 8:58, Howes (Can) 12:14, Lupul (Can) 18:05

Second Period

3. Canada, Lupul (Allison)..6:01(pp)
4. Canada, Reardon (Hobbins) 6:45
5. West Germany, Haider (Seyller) ....18:21(pp)

> PENALTIES: Tack (WGer) 4:04, Kelly (Can) 7:40, Fistric (Can) & Stauner (WGer) 8:31, Hobbins (Can) 14:37, Stauner (WGer) 15:28, Kirkham (Can) 17:10

Third Period

6. Canada, Rausse (unassisted) 2:23
7. West Germany, Holzmann (unassisted) 3:11
8. Canada, Irving (Kirkham) 7:32

> PENALTIES: Kelly (Can) 12:04, Eggerbauer (WGer) 12:49, Steigner (WGer) 14:49, MacLeod (Can) 18:01, Kelly (Can) & Fistric (Can) 19:58

Shots on Goal:

Canada	14	16	15	**45**
West Germany	10	6	5	**21**

In Goal:

> Canada — Melanson
> West Germany — Hagen/Kopf

December 30   *Sweden 1*   *Canada 0*

First Period

No Scoring

> PENALTIES: Fistric (Can) 0:50, Jonsson (Swe) 11:52, Irving (Can) & Steen (Swe) 13:51, Danielsson (Swe) 15:09, Samuelsson (Swe) 16:24

Second Period

1. Sweden, Steen (Silfverberg)...19:42(pp)

> PENALTIES: Irving (Can) 12:01, Eriksson (Swe) 15:50, Fistric (Can) 18:56

Third Period

No Scoring

> PENALTIES: Karrbrand (Swe) 2:18, Steen (Swe) & MacLeod (Can) 3:57, Fistric (Can — double minor, misconduct) 10:46, Naslund (Swe) & McCrimmon (Can) 12:16, Eriksson (Swe) 14:10

Shots on Goal:

Canada	12	3	7	**22**
Sweden	7	13	10	**30**

In Goal:

> Canada — Semenchuk
> Sweden — Lindbergh

December 31   Canada 10   Norway 1

First Period

1. Canada, Ogrodnick (MacLeod) 6:57
2. Canada, Ogrodnick (Irving) .... 14:03(pp)
3. Canada, Kirkham (Irving, Allison)...14:22
4. Canada, Melnyk (MacLeod)... 19:32(pp)

PENALTIES: Reardon (Can) & Stromsnas (Nor) 7:58, Ogrodnick (Can) 11:40, Jarlsbo (Nor) 12:35, Kolsrud (Nor) 18:18

Second Period

5. Canada, Irving (unassisted) 2:14
6. Norway, Bastiansen (Lovdahl) 3:21
7. Canada, Joly (Howes) 4:41
8. Canada, Kirkham (McCrimmon) 18:33

PENALTIES: Kelly (Can) 8:29

Third Period

9. Canada, MacLeod (Propp) 2:36
10. Canada, Propp (Reardon) 11:15
11. Canada, Reardon (unassisted) 15:12

PENALTIES: Irving (Can) & Abrahamsen (Nor) 2:09, Allison (Can) 5:02, Bastiansen (Nor) 18:59

Shots on Goal:

Canada	18	17	22	**57**
Norway	9	8	4	21

In Goal:

Canada — Melanson
Norway — Stromsnas

January 2   Canada 6   United States 3

First Period

1. Canada, Joly (Brown)..16:43

PENALTIES: Allison (Can) 6:28, Erickson (U.S.) 10:13, Hobbins (Can) 18:04

Second Period

2. Canada, Propp (Lupul, Brown) 7:20
3. Canada, Irving (McCrimmon)... 12:32(pp)
4. Canada, Orleski (Allison) 14:15
5. Canada, McCrimmon (Allison) 14:31
6. United States, DeGrio (Ulseth) 14:54
7. United States, Christian (unassisted) 17:20
8. United States, N. Broten (A. Broten)...19:23(pp)

PENALTIES: Propp (Can) 1:29, Ramsey (U.S.) 5:33, Melnyk (Can) 6:15, Stone (U.S.) 10:54, Rausse (Can) 18:53, Liprando (U.S.) 19:42

Third Period

9.   Canada, Orleski (Rausse, Allison) 18:52

> PENALTIES: Ogrodnick (Can) 4:28, Pettygrove (U.S.) 8:26, Palazzi (U.S.) 11:00, Reardon (Can) 12:09, Mishler (U.S.) 12:57, Irving (Can) 15:43, Stone (U.S.) 19:40

Shots on Goal:

Canada	9	11	19	**39**
United States	8	9	14	**31**

In Goal:

> Canada — Semenchuk
> United States — Birenbaum/Jetland

TEAM CANADA FINAL STATISTICS
1979 WORLD JUNIOR CHAMPIONSHIPS
(New Westminster Bruins)

			GA	G	A	P	PIM
9	F	Randy Irving	5	4	2	6	8
12	F	Ray Allison	5	0	5	5	4
8	F	John Ogrodnick	5	3	1	4	4
19	F	Dave Orleski	5	3	0	3	0
18	F	Kent Reardon	5	2	1	3	6
15	F	Terry Kirkham	5	2	1	3	2
11	F	Brian Propp	5	2	1	3	2
7	F	Scott MacLeod	5	1	2	3	4
2	D	Brad McCrimmon	5	1	2	3	2
16	F	Yvan Joly	5	2	0	2	2
20	F	Gary Lupul	5	1	1	2	2
4	D	Larry Melnyk	5	1	1	2	2
10	F	Errol Rausse	5	1	1	2	2
3	D	Keith Brown	5	0	2	2	0
14	F	Bill Hobbins	5	0	1	1	4
5	D	Bruce Howes	5	0	1	1	2
21	D	Boris Fistric	5	0	0	0	22
17	F	John Paul Kelly(C)	5	0	0	0	10
30	G	Tom Semenchuk	3	0	0	0	0
1	G	Rollie Melanson	2	0	0	0	0

In Goal

	GP	W-L-T	MINS	GA	SO	AVG
Rollie Melanson	2	2—0—0	120	3	0	1.50
Tom Semenchuk	3	1—2—0	180	7	0	2.33

Coach   Ernie McLean
Assistant   Doug Sauter

CANADIAN OFFICIALS AT THE 1979 WORLD JUNIOR CHAMPIONSHIPS

Normand Caisse (referee)   4 games

TEAM CANADA ROSTER SUMMARY

Team Canada players   20
Drafted Into NHL   12 (all but Hobbins, Howes, Irving, Kirkham, Lupul,
                            MacLeod, Reardon, Semenchuk)
Played in NHL   12 (all but Fistric, Hobbins, Howes, Irving, Kirkham,
                            MacLeod, Reardon, Semenchuk)
Returning Players   1 (McCrimmon)

PLAYER REPRESENTATION BY LEAGUE

WHL   18 (all but Joly, Melanson)
OHL   2 (Joly, Melanson)

PLAYER REPRESENTATION BY AGE

19-year-olds   13 (Allison, Irving, Kelly, Kirkham, Lupul, MacLeod,
                            McCrimmon, Ogrodnick, Orleski, Propp, Rausse,
                            Reardon, Semenchuk)
18-year-olds   7 (Brown, Fistric, Hobbins, Howes, Joly, Melanson, Melnyk)

PLAYERS' CAREER PROFILES

Ray Allison   Brandon Wheat Kings (WHL)
                    Selected 18th overall by Hartford at 1979 Draft
                    Played in the NHL 1979–87
Keith Brown   Portland Winter Hawks (WHL)
                    Selected 7th overall by Chicago at 1979 Draft
                    Played in the NHL 1979–95
Boris Fistric   New Westminster Bruins (WHL)
                    Selected 46th overall by Detroit at 1979 Draft
                    Did not play in the NHL
Bill Hobbins   New Westminster Bruins (WHL)
                    Not drafted
                    Did not play in the NHL
Bruce Howes   New Westminster Bruins (WHL)
                    Not drafted
                    Did not play in the NHL
Randy Irving   New Westminster Bruins (WHL)
                    Not drafted
                    Did not play in the NHL

Yvan Joly   Ottawa 67's (OHL)
                          Selected 100th overall by Montreal at 1979 Draft
                          Played in the NHL 1979–83

John Paul Kelly   New Westminster Bruins (WHL)
                          Selected 50th overall by Los Angeles at 1979 Draft
                          Played in the NHL 1979–86

Terry Kirkham   New Westminster Bruins (WHL)
                          Not drafted
                          Did not play in the NHL

Gary Lupul   Victoria Cougars (WHL)
                          Not drafted
                          Played in the NHL 1979–86

Scott MacLeod   New Westminster Bruins (WHL)
                          Not drafted
                          Did not play in the NHL

Brad McCrimmon   Brandon Wheat Kings (WHL)
                          Selected 15th overall by Boston at 1979 Draft
                          Played in the NHL 1979–97

Rollie Melanson   Windsor Spitfires (OHA)
                          Selected 59th overall by Islanders at 1979 Draft
                          Played in the NHL 1980–92

Larry Melnyk   New Westminster Bruins (WHL)
                          Selected 78th overall by Boston at 1979 Draft
                          Played in the NHL 1980–90

John Ogrodnick   New Westminster Bruins (WHL)
                          Selected 66th overall by Detroit at 1979 Draft
                          Played in the NHL 1979–93

Dave Orleski   New Westminster Bruins (WHL)
                          Selected 79th overall by Montreal at 1979 Draft
                          Played in the NHL 1980–82

Brian Propp   Brandon Wheat Kings (WHL)
                          Selected 14th overall by Philadelphia at 1979 Draft
                          Played in the NHL 1979–94

Errol Rausse   Seattle Breakers (WHL)
                          Selected 24th overall by Washington at 1979 Draft
                          Played in the NHL 1979–82

Kent Reardon   New Westminster Bruins (WHL)
                          Not drafted
                          Did not play in the NHL

Tom Semenchuk   New Westminster Bruins (WHL)
                          Not drafted
                          Did not play in the NHL

1980 WORLD JUNIOR CHAMPIONSHIPS FINLAND, DECEMBER 27, 1979-- JANUARY 2, 1980

FINAL PLACINGS

GOLD MEDAL	Soviet Union
SILVER MEDAL	Finland
BRONZE MEDAL	Sweden
Fourth Place	Czechoslovakia
Fifth Place	CANADA
Sixth Place	West Germany
Seventh Place	United States
Eighth Place	Switzerland*

promoted from "B" pool in 1979; relegated to "B" pool for 1981

ALL-STAR TEAM

GOAL	Jari Paavola (Finland)
DEFENCE	Reijo Ruotsalainen (Finland)
	Tomas Jonsson (Sweden)
FORWARD	Hakan Loob (Sweden)
	Igor Larionov (Soviet Union)
	Vladimir Krutov (Soviet Union)

DIRECTORATE AWARDS

BEST GOALIE	Jari Paavola (Finland)
BEST DEFENCEMAN	Reijo Ruotsalainen (Finland)
BEST FORWARD	Vladimir Krutov (Soviet Union)

COACH MIKE KEENAN

Over the years, the Peterborough Petes have provided the NHL with dozens of players. The team has also provided many successful coaches. Mike Keenan was the third consecutive Petes coach (after Roger Neilson and Gary Green) to move up to the NHL. In the 1979–80 season, Keenan's one and only with Peterborough, the team came within one game of beating the Cornwall Royals for the Memorial Cup. In the summer of 1980, Keenan signed with the Sabres' AHL affiliate, the Rochester Americans, and from there the NHL became his port of call.

Keenan played junior hockey with the Oshawa Crushmen until 1968, then attended St. Lawrence University on a four-year scholarship. He had an unsuccessful tryout with the expansion Atlanta Flames. In 1973–74 he played for the farm team of the Vancouver Blazers of the WHA. In between, he went to the University of Toronto and played CIAU hockey under coach Tom Watt. The U of T Blues won the championship, and Keenan had found a coaching mentor.

From 1977 to 1979, Keenan coached the Oshawa Legionnaires of the Metro (Toronto) Junior B league to back-to-back championships, and when Gary Green left to coach the Washington Capitals in 1979, the Petes' vacancy was his. The transition for the players was initially rough. Green was softer spoken and emphasised hard-nosed hockey, while Keenan was in-your-face motivational and emphasised skating and strategy. Green was liked, Keenan respected. Both, however, were winners with the Petes.

ICING A TEAM

It was not until November 28, 1979, just a month before the tournament was set to begin, that Canada announced it would be sending a team to Helsinki for the World Junior Championships. The reticence had been monetary, as the initial cost for the trip had jumped from $23,000 to more than $50,000. However, donations from the three major junior leagues, as well as the CAHA, finally ensured the passage of a twenty-eight-man and five-official contingent to Finland. From the outset, the team promised to enhance its roster with juniors from other teams, and in the end the Petes added the talented Ottawa troika of Jim Fox, Yvan Joly, and Sean Simpson (who finished the season 1–2–4 in OHL scoring), as well as Dino Ciccarelli (London Knights), and defencemen Doug Crossman (Ottawa), Bill Kitchen (Ottawa), and Rick Lanz (Oshawa). In the team's only preparatory exhibition game for the WJC, they beat the U.S. national juniors 5–3 in Helsinki.

PETES' ALUMNI

The list of players the Petes have sent to the NHL is long and impressive, beginning with Wayne Gretzky, who played three games with the Petes as a minor midget call-up. (Thus the answer to the trivia question, "For what team did Gretzky play his first junior game?") Others to go on to greater hockey successes include Steve Yzerman, Bob Gainey, Craig Ramsay, Rick MacLeish, Tom Fergus, Bob Errey, Terry Carkner, Keith Acton, Ron Stackhouse, Mike Ricci, Mickey Redmond, Colin Campbell, Doug Halward, and Larry Murphy.

Rick LaFerriere, goalie of the Peterborough Petes, played four of the team's five games in Finland as Canada's representatives of the 1980 World Juniors.

CONDITIONING

Mike Keenan always made sure his teams did not lose games because of inferior conditioning. Tests done by a U of T physiologist during the 1979–80 Peterborough season found the players to be in superior shape to any of the NHL teams that had been tested, particularly in strength and the ability to perform at optimum levels under stress.

Keenan attributed the impressive test results to what he called micro-training, a program that consisted of ten exercises done for five to ten days every few months. He had been introduced to the idea by Tom Watt. For each drill, the player goes all out for thirty seconds, then rest for thirty seconds, then repeats the exercise. The ten exercises include: bench pressing, stair climbing (two at a time), stair bounding (two at a time, both feet together), arm curls, sit-ups, weight cleans (lifting from the floor to above the head), bench hopping, dynamic curls, dynamic leaps (jumping to the ground from a bench raised eighteen inches), and lateral weight raises.

TOURNAMENT FORMAT

Eight countries were placed in two divisions of four teams each. All teams played a round-robin format within each division, three games each. The top two advanced to a four-team medal round, the bottom two to a consolation round. Results from the preliminary round between teams that ended up in the same division in the next round were carried over, so no team played twice against any other in the tournament.

THE OPPOSITION

CZECHOSLOVAKIA

Zdenek Albrecht, Juraj Bakos, Ivan Beno, Jiri Dudacek, Petr Fiala, Jiri Hamal, Miloslav Horava, Otakar Janecky, Pavel Jiskra, Kamil Kaluzik, Igor Liba, Miroslav Majernik, Josef Metlicka, Dusan Pasek, Zdenek Pata, Pavel Setikovsky, Eduard Uvira, Oldrich Valek, Miroslav Venkrbec, Jan Vodila

FINLAND

Pekka Arbelius, Tony Arima, Timo Blomqvist, Harri Haapaniemi, Mika Helkearo, Juha Huikari, Kari Jalonen, Jari Jarvinen, Jouni Koutuaniemi, Jari Kurri, Ari Lahteenmaki, Jarmo Makitalo, Anssi Melametsa, Jari Munck, Jari Paavola, Reijo Ruotsalainen, Kari Suoraniemi, Ari Timosaari, Risto Tuomi, Pekka Tuomisto

SOVIET UNION

Alexei Bevz, Igor Bubenshikov, Dimitri Erastov, Victor Glushenkov, Vladimir Golovkov, Vladimir Krutov, Igor Larionov, Valeri Mikhailov, Igor Morozov, Andrei Morozov, Juri Nikitin, Igor Panin, Mikhail Panin, Evgeni Popikhin, Ildar Rakhmatullin, Dimitri Saprykin, Vladimir Shashov, Evgeni Shastin, Sergei Svetlov, Alexander Zybin

SWEDEN

Bjorn Akerblom, Peter Aslin, Anders Backstrom, Jan-Ake Danielsson, Peter Elander, Lars Eriksson, Lars Gunnar Pettersson, Tomas Jonsson, Lars Karlsson, Hakan Loob, Torbjorn Mattsson, Per Nilsson, Hakan Nordin, Roland Nyman, Ove Olsson, Matti Pauna, Thomas Rundqvist, Tommy Samulesson, Thomas Steen, Patrick Sundstrom

SWITZERLAND

Peter Baldinger, Hansruedi Eberle, Beat Eggiman, Mauro Foschi, Kenneth Green, Jakob Gross, Remo Gross, Gabriele Guschetti, Pius Kuonen, Henry Loher, Fausto Mazzoleni, Marcel Meier, Marco Muller, Marcel Niederer, Philippe Petey, Andreas Ritsch, Peter Schlagenhauf, Andreas Trumpler, Ludwig Waidacher, Bernhard Wist

UNITED STATES

John Anderson, Paul Brandrup, Bob Brooke, Scott Carlston, Mark Chiamp, Win Dahm, Glen De Mota, Lexi Doner, Bryan Erickson, Pat Ethier, Jim Gardner, Dave Jensen, Mike Lauen, Todd Lecy, Barry Mills, Brian Mullen, Venci Sebek, Scott Stoltzner, Julian Van Biesbrouck, Dan Vlaisavljevich

WEST GERMANY

Jurgen Adams, Manfred Ahne, Gerhard Alber, Christoph Augsten, Rainer Blum, Jurgen Breuer, Franco De Nobili, Michael Eggerbauer, Klaus Gotsch, Ulrich Hiemer, Wilhelm Hofer, Ralph Hoja, Georg Holzmann, Jurgen Lechl, Rainer Lutz, Anton Maidl, Peter Obressa, Michael Schmidt, Bernhard Seyller, Peter Zankl

FINAL STANDINGS PRELIMINARY ROUND

Gold Division

	GP	W	L	T	GF	GA	P
Soviet Union	3	3	0	0	16	6	6
Finland	3	2	1	0	22	4	4
CANADA	3	1	2	0	15	15	2
Switzerland	3	0	3	0	6	34	0

Results

December 27	Helsinki	Finland 2	Canada 1
	Higin Jaahalli	Soviet Union 6	Switzerland 0
December 28	Vantaa	Soviet Union 8	Canada 5
	Helsinki	Finland 19	Switzerland 1

| December 30 | Vantaa | Canada 9 | Switzerland 5 |
| | Helsinki | Soviet Union 2 | Finland 1 |

Blue Division

	GP	W	L	T	GF	GA	P
Sweden	3	2	0	1	20	10	5
Czechoslovakia	3	2	1	0	24	17	4
West Germany	3	1	2	0	10	20	2
United States	3	0	2	1	10	17	1

Results

December 27	Vantaa	Czechoslovakia 7	United States 3
	Vantaa	Sweden 5	West Germany 1
December 28	Vantaa	Sweden 5	United States 5
	Vantaa	Czechoslovakia 13	West Germany 4
December 30	Higin Jaahalli	West Germany 5	United States 2
	Helsinki	Sweden 10	Czechoslovakia 4

FINAL STANDINGS CONSOLATION ROUND

	GP	W	L	T	GF	GA	P
CANADA	3	3	0	0	19	8	6
West Germany	3	2	1	0	10	10	4
United States	3	1	2	0	13	14	2
Switzerland	3	0	3	0	12	22	0

Carry-Over Results

| Canada 9 | Switzerland 5 |
| West Germany 5 | United States 2 |

Results

January 1	Higin Jaahalli	Canada 4	United States 2
	Vantaa	West Germany 4	Switzerland 2
January 2	Helsinki	Canada 6	West Germany 1
	Vantaa	United States 9	Switzerland 5

FINAL STANDINGS MEDAL ROUND

	GP	W	L	T	GF	GA	P
Soviet Union	3	3	0	0	10	4	6
Finland	3	2	1	0	8	6	4
Sweden	3	1	2	0	13	9	2
Czechoslovakia	3	0	3	0	8	20	0

Carry-Over Results

Soviet Union 2	Finland 1
Sweden 10	Czechoslovakia 4

Results

January 1	Helsinki	Finland 3	Sweden 2
	Helsinki	Soviet Union 6	Czechoslovakia 2
January 2	Higin Jaahalli	Finland 4	Czechoslovakia 2
	Higin Jaahalli	Soviet Union 2	Sweden 1

AGGREGATE STANDINGS

(ordered according to final placings)

	GP	W	L	T	GF	GA	P	GAA	SO	PIM
Soviet Union	5	5	0	0	24	9	10	1.80	1	47*
Finland	5	4	1	0	29	8	8	1.60	0	66
Sweden	5	2	2	1	23	15	5	3.00	0	64
Czechoslovakia	5	2	3	0	28	27	4	5.40	0	84
CANADA	5	3	2	0	25	18	6	3.60	0	112
West Germany	5	2	3	0	15	28	4	5.60	0	110
United States	5	1	3	1	21	26	3	5.20	0	64
Switzerland	5	0	5	0	13	47	0	9.40	0	83

* won Fair Play Cup

TEAM CANADA GAME SUMMARIES

December 27   Finland 2   Canada 1

First Period

1. Finland, Ruotsalainen (Kurri, Jalonen) ....8:47(pp)

    PENALTIES: Crossman (Can) 7:48, Fenyves (Can) 14:02, Blomqvist (Fin) 18:49

Second Period

2. Canada, Bovair (unassisted) 19:59

    PENALTIES: Fenyves (Can) 4:51, Tuomi (Fin) 7:45, Bovair (Can) 10:49, Murphy (Can) 12:45, Smith (Can) 14:31, Lanz (Can) 17:44

Third Period

3. Finland, Ruotsalainen (Kurri) ....16:41(pp)

    PENALTIES: Gardner (Can) 8:43, Bovair (Can) & Ruotsalainen (Fin) 9:20, Murphy (Can) 10:43, Fenyves (Can) 14:35, Wiemer (Can) 16:05, Gardner (Can — misconduct) 16:27, Smith (Can — double minor) 16:35, Koutuaniemi (Fin) 18:49, Joly (Can) 18:55, Reeds (Can) & Ryder (Can — misconduct) & Suoraniemi (Fin — misconduct) 20:00

Shots on Goal:

Canada	6	5	8	19
Finland	15	18	9	42

In Goal:

Canada — LaFerriere
Finland — Paavola

December 28   *Soviet Union 8*   *Canada 5*

First Period

1. Soviet Union, Krutov (Larionov) 4:28
2. Soviet Union, Shastin (unassisted) 4:37
3. Soviet Union, Larionov (Krutov, Golovkov) 7:07
4. Soviet Union, Svetlov (Shastin, Glushenkov) .... 12:34(pp)
5. Canada, Ciccarelli (unassisted) 17:05

PENALTIES: Erastov (Sov) & Gardner (Can) 0:16, Larionov (Sov) 7:56, Kitchen (Can) 11:33, Rakhmatullin (Sov) & Smith (Can) 12:43, Kitchen (Can) 14:18, Smith (Can) 17:46

Second Period

6. Canada, Fox (Lanz) .... 7:07(pp)
7. Canada, Cirella (Ciccarelli) 8:18
8. Soviet Union, Krutov (Mikhailov) 18:02
9. Canada, Ciccarelli (Gardner) 19:17

PENALTIES: Krutov (Sov — major) 0:52, Popikhin (Sov) 6:25, Joly (Can) 8:35

Third Period

10. Soviet Union, Krutov (Mikhailov) 6:01
11. Soviet Union, Shashov (Panin) 11:52
12. Soviet Union, Svetlov (Golovkov) .... 17:07(pp)
13. Canada, Ciccarelli (Cirella) 18:26

PENALTIES: Beckon (Can) 9:01, Mikhailov (Sov) 13:14, Glushenkov (Sov) & Cirella (Can) & Ciccarelli (Can) 15:16, Lanz (Can) 18:46

Shots on Goal:

Canada	9	13	10	32
Soviet Union	8	5	14	27

In Goal:

Canada — LaFerriere
Soviet Union — Saprykin

December 30   *Canada 9*   *Switzerland 5*

First Period

1. Canada, Beckon (Wiemer) 1:16
2. Canada, Fox (Simpson)... 2:33
3. Canada, Wiemer (Ryder) 10:50
4. Canada, Bovair (Cirella) .... 12:32(sh)
5. Switzerland, Mazzoleni (Muller) .... 13:54(pp)

    PENALTIES: Fenyves (Can) 12:08, Bovair (Can) 13:20

Second Period

6. Switzerland, Kuonen (penalty shot)... 1:23
7. Canada, Smith (Crossman) 4:32
8. Canada, Hidi (Gardner) 18:42
9. Switzerland, Mazzoleni (J. Gross)... 19:50

    PENALTIES: none

Third Period

10. Switzerland, Trumpler (Mazzoleni) 1:54
11. Switzerland, Niederer (unassisted).. 3:35
12. Canada, Ciccarelli (Bovair)... 13:55
13. Canada, Ryder (Beckon) 17:46
14. Canada, Fox (Simpson).. 19:10(sh)

    PENALTIES: Kitchen (Can) 5:25, Ryder (Can) 18:15

Shots on Goal:

Canada	13	8	13	**34**
Switzerland	4	7	5	**16**

In Goal:

    Canada — Wright
    Switzerland — Green

January 1   *Canada 4*   *United States 2*

First Period

No Scoring

    PENALTIES: none

Second Period

1. Canada, Joly (Fox) 1:25
2. United States, Lauen (Doner) 3:52
3. Canada, Beckon (Wiemer) 4:03
4. United States, Mullen (unassisted) .... 5:55(pp)
5. Canada, Murphy (Fox) 14:04

    PENALTIES: Joly (Can) 5:05, LaFerriere (Can) 5:25, Doner (U.S.) 18:57

Third Period

6. Canada, Cirella (Bovair) 2:41

    PENALTIES: Sebek (U.S.) 6:10, Ryder (Can) 14:27, Brandrup (U.S.) 15:25, Kitchen (Can) 18:09

Shots on Goal:

Canada	10	12	12	**34**
United States	8	8	3	**19**

In Goal:

Canada — LaFerriere
United States — Chiamp

January 2   *Canada 6*   *West Germany 1*

First Period

1. Canada, Wiemer (Beckon) 0:35

    PENALTIES: Blum (WGer) 1:51, Lanz (Can) 15:25, Eggerbauer (WGer) 19:39

Second Period

2. Canada, Hidi (Gardner) .... 0:28(pp)
3. Canada, Reeds (Crossman, Gardner) .... 8:09(pp)
4. Canada, Ciccarelli (Cirella) .... 11:09(sh)
5. Canada, Joly (unassisted) 14:54

    PENALTIES: Cirella (Can) 3:11, Bovair (Can) 5:19, Hiemer (WGer) 6:08, Blum (WGer) 7:49, Bovair (Can) 10:44, Augsten (WGer) 12:10, DeNobili (WGer) 15:46, Kitchen (Can) 16:32, Seyller (WGer) 16:57

Third Period

6. Canada, Joly (Kitchen) 17:43
7. West Germany, Adams (Holzmann) 19:03

    PENALTIES: Seyller (WGer) 7:43, Hidi (Can) 8:52, Joly (Can) & Cirella (Can — misconduct) & Schmidt (WGer — misconduct) 12:12

Shots on Goal:

Canada	7	14	14	**35**
West Germany	5	3	4	**12**

In Goal:

Canada — LaFerriere
West Germany — Zankl

TEAM CANADA FINAL STATISTICS
1980 WORLD JUNIOR CHAMPIONSHIPS
(Peterborough Petes)

			GP	G	A	P	PIM
11	F	Dino Ciccarelli	5	5	1	6	2
10	F	Jim Fox	5	3	2	5	0
19	F	Carman Cirella	5	2	3	5	14
23	F	Terry Bovair	5	2	2	4	10
16	F	Dave Beckon	5	2	2	4	2
24	F	Jim Wiemer	5	2	2	4	2
4	F	Bill Gardner	5	0	4	4	14
9	F	Yvan Joly	5	3	0	3	8
12	F	Andre Hidi	5	2	0	2	2
8	F	Brad Ryder	4	1	1	2	14
3	D	Doug Crossman	5	0	2	2	2
21	F	Sean Simpson	5	0	2	2	0
5	D	Stuart Smith(A)	5	1	0	1	10
2	D	Larry Murphy	5	1	0	1	4
17	F	Mark Reeds(A)	5	1	0	1	2
6	D	Bill Kitchen	5	0	1	1	10
14	D	Rick Lanz(C)	5	0	1	1	6
22	D	Dave Fenyves(C/A)	5	0	0	0	8
1	G	Rick LaFerriere	4	0	0	0	2
30	G	Terry Wright	1	0	0	0	0

Captain Notes:

Fenyves captain vs. Finland, United States, West Germany
Lanz captian vs. Soviet Union, Switzerland

In Goal

	GP	W-L-T	MINS	GA	SO	AVG
Rick LaFerriere	4	2-2-0	240	13	0	3.25
Terry Wright	1	1-0-0	60	5	0	5.00

Coach   Mike Keenan
Assistant   Dick Todd

CANADIAN OFFICIALS AT THE 1980
WORLD JUNIOR CHAMPIONSHIPS

unknown

TEAM CANADA ROSTER SUMMARY

Team Canada players   20

Drafted Into NHL   14 (all but Bovair, Ciccarelli, Fenyves, Kitchen, Ryder, Wright)

Played in NHL   14 (all but Beckon, Bovair, Cirella, Ryder, Simpson, Wright)

Returning Players   1 (Joly)

PLAYER REPRESENTATION BY LEAGUE

OHL   20

PLAYER REPRESENTATION BY AGE

19-year-olds   13 (Bovair, Ciccarelli, Cirella, Crossman, Fenyves, Fox, Gardner, Hidi, Joly, Kitchen, Reeds, Smith, Wright)

18-year-olds   7 (Beckon, LaFerriere, Lanz, Murphy, Ryder, Simpson, Weimer)

PLAYERS' CAREER PROFILES

Dave Beckon   Peterborough Petes (OHL)
Selected 188th overall by Buffalo at 1980 Draft
Did not play in the NHL

Terry Bovair   Peterborough Petes (OHL)
Not drafted
Did not play in the NHL

Dino Ciccarelli   London Knights (OHL)
Not drafted
Played in the NHL 1980 to present

Carmen Cirella   Peterborough Petes (OHL)
Selected 108th overall by Detroit at 1979 Draft
Did not play in the NHL

Doug Crossman   Ottawa 67's (OHL)
Selected 112th overall by Chicago at 1979 Draft
Played in the NHL 1980–94

Dave Fenyves   Peterborough Petes (OHL)
Not drafted
Played in the NHL 1982–91

Jim Fox   Ottawa 67's (OHL)
Selected 10th overall by Los Angeles at 1980 Draft
Played in the NHL 1980–90

Bill Gardner   Peterborough Petes (OHL)
Selected 49th overall by Chicago at 1979 Draft
Played in the NHL 1980–89

Andre Hidi	Peterborough Petes (OHL)
	Selected 148th overall by Rockies at 1980 Draft
	Played in the NHL 1983–85
Yvan Joly	Ottawa 67's (OHL)
	Selected 100th overall by Montreal at 1979 Draft
	Played in the NHL 1979–83
Bill Kitchen	Ottawa 67's (OHL)
	Not drafted
	Played in the NHL 1981–85
Rick LaFerriere	Peterborough Petes (OHL)
	Selected 64th overall by Rockies at 1980 Draft
	Played one game in the NHL 1981–82
Rick Lanz	Oshawa Generals (OHL)
	Selected 7th overall by Vancouver at 1980 Draft
	Played in the NHL 1980–92
Larry Murphy	Peterborough Petes (OHL)
	Selected 4th overall by Los Angeles at 1980 Draft
	Played in the NHL 1980 to present
Mark Reeds	Peterborough Petes (OHL)
	Selected 86th overall by St. Louis at 1979 Draft
	Played in the NHL 1981–89
Brad Ryder	Peterborough Petes (OHL)
	Not drafted
	Did not play in the NHL
Sean Simpson	Ottawa 67's (OHL)
	Selected 141st overall by Chicago at 1980 Draft
	Did not play in the NHL
Stuart Smith	Peterborough Petes (OHL)
	Selected 39th overall by Hartford at 1979 Draft
	Played in the NHL 1979–83
Jim Wiemer	Peterborough Petes (OHL)
	Selected 83rd overall by Buffalo at 1980 Draft
	Played in the NHL 1982–94
Terry Wright	Peterborough Petes (OHL)
	Not drafted
	Did not play in the NHL

1981 WORLD JUNIOR CHAMPIONSHIPS WEST GERMANY, DECEMBER 27, 1980-- JANUARY 2, 1981

FINAL PLACINGS

GOLD MEDAL	Sweden
SILVER MEDAL	Finland
BRONZE MEDAL	Soviet Union
Fourth Place	Czechoslovakia
Fifth Place	West Germany
Sixth Place	United States
Seventh Place	CANADA
Eighth Place	Austria*

promoted from "B" pool in 1980; relegated to "B" pool for 1982

ALL-STAR TEAM

GOAL	Lars Eriksson (Sweden)
DEFENCE	Miloslav Horava (Czechoslovakia)
	Hakan Nordin (Sweden)
FORWARD	Ari Lahteenmaki (Finland)
	Patrik Sundstrom (Sweden)
	Jan Erixon (Sweden)

DIRECTORATE AWARDS

BEST GOALIE	Lars Eriksson (Sweden)
BEST DEFENCEMAN	Miloslav Horava (Czechoslovakia)
BEST FORWARD	Patrik Sundstrom (Sweden)

COACH BOB KILGER

Kilger was a promising junior with the Toronto Marlies whose career was cut short after a fight with Punch Imlach. He was exiled to the Oshawa Generals for two years, and never made it to the big tent. He became interested in staying in hockey as an official, and to that end attended the Bill Friday/Bruce Hood referee camp, graduating to the NHL camp and beginning as a trainee in the AHL. He was a referee in the NHL for eight years, and another two as linesman through the seventies, and all the while he acted as an assistant coach with the Cornwall Royals during their training camp. At the camp in September 1980 he became head coach of the Royals after incumbent Doug Carpenter accepted a job offer to coach the New Brunswick Hawks of the American Hockey League, and so began Kilger's eventual introduction to international hockey.

Coaches Mike Keenan and Jacques Lemaire were guests
at the 1981 summer camp, where off-ice instruction
and training complemented on-ice workouts.

THE TEAM

The team left for Germany on December 22 with twenty players, thirteen of whom were Cornwall Royals. Seven others were from other QMJHL teams: Corrado Micalef (Sherbrooke), Gilbert Delorme (Chicoutimi), Bill Campbell and Denis Cyr (Montreal), Guy Fournier (Shawinigan), and Jean-Marc Gaulin and Andre Chartrain (Sorel). Kilger dropped five Cornwall rookies to make room on the team for the others: Joe Mantione, Marc Lalonde, Steve Maloski, Gerard Peltier, and Sandy Mitchell. None had played on the Memorial Cup team the previous season. Two other Royals were also missing, Gilles Crepeau, who was over-age, and Dan Zavarise, who left the team. The trouble was, of course, that this was not an all-star team that could compete with the best from other hockey-playing nations. Seventh place was the result.

MONEY VS. PRESTIGE

Dave Branch, then the executive director of the Canadian Major Junior Hockey League, elucidated what he felt was the reason behind the Royals' poor showing: "These teams represent Canada, but they're not the best we have. Ideally, we'd like to send a true all-star team, comprised of the best players from throughout the country. But we just can't afford it." The costs were prohibitive. To send a true team would have cost $200,000. It cost the Royals $50,000, of which $20,000 came from the federal government. The national commitment just wasn't there, nor were there imaginative initiatives to come up with money in non-conventional ways.

On top of this, there was an internal battle between the CAHA and Hockey Canada. The CAHA had an agreement with the IIHF to send a team to the World Juniors each year, but it didn't really want to send a team unless it could do so properly. The CAHA feared, however, that if it backed away from the commitment, the IIHF would negotiate a similar agreement with Hockey Canada. The CAHA compromised its integrity by sending a less than superior team to the championships.

MARC CRAWFORD — TEAM CAPTAIN

Crawford was Cornwall's captain at the begining of the QMJHL season, but early on, coach and general manager Bob Kilger asked for the "C" back because he felt Crawford was taking too many bad penalties and developing a bad rapport with officials. For two months, the Royals didn't have a captain, though Crawford's attitude remained captainly throughout the season. In the team's last game before leaving for Germany, Kilger reinstated Crawford as the official team leader, citing a reversal in performance and demeanour.

The Nats held their summer camp in Kingston where a series of practises and scrimmages helped coaches evaluate potential candidates for the final camp in December.

7TH PLACE — THE DEBATE CONTINUES

The Cornwall Royals finished seventh at the 1981 WJC. Yet twelve of those players went on to play in the NHL, and two of them — Doug Gilmour and Dale Hawerchuk — have had careers worthy of the Hall of Fame. Why the poor finish?

The Royals had been Memorial Cup champs the previous spring, but the team that went to Germany was not the team that hoisted the Cup half a year earlier. Their win at the Memorial was by way of a significant upset of the Sherbrooke Beavers. Before going to Germany, the team had one game — a 9–4 win over a senior German club — to prepare. Other teams practised all year for the WJC. The seventh-place finish indicated that there must be a better way to participate in the premier junior tournament in the world.

Note: The Canadians and Americans were the only nations to wear face masks. This so impressed the IIHF that the use of masks became mandatory the following year.

TOURNAMENT FORMAT

A preliminary round robin was set up in two divisions of four nations each. The top two advanced to a medal round robin, the bottom two to a consolation round. If there were a tie in the standings, goal differential was the deciding factor. In the preliminary round, both Canada and Czechoslovakia had three points, but Canada finished third to the Czechs' second because of a poorer goal differential. (The teams had tied 3–3 in the round robin.)

THE COMPETITION

AUSTRIA

Ewald Brandstatter, Arno Cuder, Konrad Dorn, Manfred Frosch, Alexander Gruber, Dieter Haberl, Rudolf Hofer, Rupert Hopfer, Bernie Hutz, Robert Kasan, Herbert Keckeis, Wolfgang Kocher, Gunther Koren, Helmut Petrik, Andreas Philipp, Martin Platzer, Michael Salat, Gunther Stockhammer, Walter Wolf, Dietmar Zach

CZECHOSLOVAKIA

Vaclav Badoucek, Mojmir Bozik, Jiri Dudacek, Milan Eberle, Vaclav Furbacher, Jaroslav Hauer, Miloslav Horava, Frantisek Ibermajer, Thomas Jelinek, Milos Kraysel, Jaroslav Linc, Miroslav Majernik, Libor Martinek, Milan Razym, Vladimir Ruzicka, Antonin Stavjana, Vladimir Svitek, Eduard Uvira, Rostislav Vlach, Jan Vodila

FINLAND

Tony Arima, Timo Blomqvist, Risto Jalo, Pekka Jarvela, Timo Jutila, Veli-Pekka Kinnunen, Jouni Koutuaniemi, Jarmo Kuusisto, Ari Lahteenmaki, Heikki Leime, Anssi Melametsa, Jari Munck, Sakari Petajaaho, Arto Ruatonen, Juha Saarenoja, Jyrki Seppa, Arto Sirvio, Petri Skriko, Kari Takko, Ilmo Votila

SOVIET UNION

Ravil Juldachev, Andrei Khomutov, Sergei Kostiukin, Sergei Kudashov, Oleg Kudriavtsev, Konstantin Kurashev, Alexander Ledovsky, Yuri Nikitin, Sergei Odintsov, Andrei Ovchinikov, Mikhail Panin, Anatoli Semenov, Yuri Shipitsin, Igor Strelnov, Sergei Svetlov, Vladimir Tiurikov, Sergei Yashin, Mikhail Zakhorov, Sergei Zemchenko, Andrei Zemko

SWEDEN

Peter Andersson, Peter Aslin, Anders Bjorklund, Lars Eriksson, Jan Erixon, Mikael Granstedt, Roger Hagglund, Jan Ingman, Anders Jonsson, Peter

Madach, Dan Niklasson, Peter Nilsson, Hakan Nordin, Robert Nordmark, Jens Ohling, Martin Pettersson, Ove Pettersson, Peter Sundstrom, Patrik Sundstrom, Mikael Thelven

UNITED STATES

Andy Brickley, Bob Carpenter, Jim Chisholm, Cleon Daskalaskis, Pat Ethier, Dan Fishback, Mark Fusco, Jeff Grade, Steve Griffith, Mark Huglen, David Jensen, John Johannson, Keith Knight, Ed Lee, Craig Ludwig, Kelly Miller, Gregg Moore, Brian Mullen, Bob O'Connor, Greg Olson

WEST GERMANY

Jurgen Adams, Manfred Ahne, Christoph Augsten, Michael Betz, Franco De Nobili, Helmut de Raaf, Klaus Feistl, Klaus Gotsch, Dieter Hegen, Josef Heiss, Daniel Held, Ulrich Hiemer, Georg Holzmann, Franz Juttner, Rainer Lutz, Andreas Niederberger, Christoph Schodl, Robert Sterflinger, Ferdinand Strodl, Jens Tosse

FINAL STANDINGS

Gold Division

	GP	W	L	T	GF	GA	P
Soviet Union	3	3	0	0	31	5	6
Czechoslovakia	3	1	1	1	25	12	3
CANADA	3	1	1	1	17	11	3
Austria	3	0	3	0	6	51	0

Results

December 27	Kaufbeuren	Canada 3	Czechoslovakia 3
	Augsburg	Soviet Union 19	Austria 1
December 28	Landsberg	Soviet Union 7	Canada 3
	Fussen	Czechoslovakia 21	Austria 4
December 30	Landsberg	Canada 11	Austria 1
	Fussen	Soviet Union 5	Czechoslovakia 1

Blue Division

	GP	W	L	T	GF	GA	P
Sweden	3	3	0	0	19	6	6
Finland	3	2	1	0	17	9	4
West Germany	3	1	2	0	13	17	2
United States	3	0	3	0	5	22	0

Results

December 27	Fussen	Sweden 7	West Germany 3
	Landsberg	Finland 8	United States 1
December 28	Obertsdorf	Finland 8	West Germany 6
	Augsburg	Sweden 10	United States 2
December 30	Kempten	Sweden 2	Finland 1
	Kaufbeuren	West Germany 4	United States 2

CONSOLATION ROUND

	GP	W	L	T	GF	GA	P
West Germany	3	3	0	0	20	9	6
United States	3	2	1	0	16	9	4
CANADA	3	1	2	0	20	15	2
Austria	3	0	3	0	4	27	0

Carry-Over Results

| Canada 11 | Austria 1 |
| West Germany 4 | United States 2 |

Results

December 31	Landsberg	United States 7	Canada 3
	Fussen	West Germany 9	Austria 1
January 2	Kaufbeuren	West Germany 7	Canada 6
	Fussen	United States 7	Austria 2

CHAMPIONSHIP ROUND

	GP	W	L	T	GF	GA	P
Sweden	3	2	0	1	8	6	5
Finland	3	1	1	1	13	11	3
Soviet Union	3	1	2	0	10	10	2
Czechoslovakia	3	0	1	2	10	14	2

Carry-Over Results

| Sweden 2 | Finland 1 |
| Soviet Union 5 | Czechoslovakia 1 |

Results

December 31	Kaufbeuren	Finland 6	Soviet Union 3
	Oberstdorf	Sweden 3	Czechoslovakia 3
January 2	Augsburg	Sweden 3	Soviet Union 2
	Landsberg	Finland 6	Czechoslovakia 6

AGGREGATE STANDINGS

(ordered according to final standings)

	GP	W	L	T	GF	GA	GAA	SO	PIM
Sweden	5	4	0	1	25	11	2.20	0	44*
Finland	5	3	1	1	29	18	3.60	0	66
Soviet Union	5	3	2	0	36	14	2.80	0	62
Czechoslovakia	5	1	1	3	34	21	4.20	0	46
West Germany	5	3	2	0	29	24	4.80	0	122
United States	5	2	3	0	19	27	5.40	0	86
CANADA	5	1	3	1	26	25	5.00	0	74
Austria	5	0	5	0	9	67	13.40	0	56

* won Fair Play Cup

TEAM CANADA GAME SUMMARIES

December 27   Canada 3   Czechoslovakia 3

First Period

1. Czechoslovakia, Ruzicka (Badoucek) 0:42

    PENALTIES: Kirk (Can) 13:30

Second Period

2. Canada, Eatough (Fournier) .... 12:54(pp)
3. Canada, Hawerchuk (Kirk) .... 13:52(pp)

    PENALTIES: Campbell (Can) 4:06, Gaulin (Can) 5:49, Bozik (Cze) 9:38, Arniel (Can) 10:47, Vlach (Cze) 11:25, Badoucek (Cze) 12:47, Arthur (Can) 19:21

Third Period

4. Czechoslovakia, Eberle (Bozik) 4:38
5. Czechoslovakia, Vodila (Svitek) 5:05
6. Canada, Chartrain (Campbell) 7:13

    PENALTIES: none

Shots on Goal:

Canada	23
Czechoslovakia	28

In Goal:

> Canada — Micalef
> Czechoslovakia — Furbacher

December 28   *Soviet Union 7*   *Canada 3*

First Period

1. Canada, Kirk (Hawerchuk) 3:44
2. Soviet Union, Semenov (Panin) .... 5:07(sh)
3. Soviet Union, Juldachev (Semenov) 7:42
4. Soviet Union, Yashin (unassisted) 14:41

PENALTIES: Kirk (Can) 1:01, Khomutov (Sov) 4:51, Eatough (Can) 8:15, Calder (Can) & Zakhorov (Sov) 10:06, Zakhorov (Sov) 14:54, Eatough (Can) 15:03

Second Period

5. Soviet Union, Zemchenko (Juldachev) .... 3:03(pp)
6. Soviet Union, Strelnov (Kudashov, Zemko) 16:01
7. Soviet Union, Kudashov (Zakhorov) 19:13

PENALTIES: Kirk (Can) 1:44, Ovchinikov (Sov) 9:21, Arniel (Can) 17:02

Third Period

8. Soviet Union, Zakhorov (Yashin, Shipitsin) 4:20
9. Canada, Hawerchuk (Kirk) .... 6:05(pp)
10. Canada, Gaulin (unassisted) 8:51

PENALTIES: Semenov (Sov) 5:17, Hawerchuk (Can) 11:30, Ovchinikov (Sov) 16:05

Shots on Goal:

Canada	7	6	17	**30**
Soviet Union	12	9	8	**29**

In Goal:

Canada — Micalef/Graovac (Graovac [one goal] replaced Micalef [6 goals] to start 3rd)
Soviet Union — Nikitin

December 30   *Canada 11*   *Austria 1*

First Period

1. Canada, Fournier (Chartrain) 18:06

PENALTIES: Savard (Can) 8:39, Petrik (Aus) 13:37, Petrik (Aus) 18:24

Second Period

2. Canada, Boimistruck (Hawerchuk) .... 7:59(pp)
3. Canada, Cyr (Savard) .... 11:11(pp)
4. Canada, Delorme (Eatough, Crawford) 12:35
5. Canada, Gaulin (unassisted) 14:05

PENALTIES: Kirk (Can) 4:56, Dorn (Aus) 7:35, Hutz (Aus) 11:07

Third Period

6. Canada, Boimistruck (unassisted) 2:53
7. Canada, Arniel (Eatough, Crawford) 7:50

8. Canada, Hawerchuk (Arthur)..10:56
9. Austria, Hofer (Haberl)..12:37
10. Canada, Cyr (unassisted) 14:43
11. Canada, Hawerchuk (unassisted)...............................15:20
12. Canada, Kirk (Cyr)...19:23

PENALTIES: none

Shots on Goal:

Canada   67
Austria   16

In Goal:

Canada — Graovac
Austria — Cuder/Philipp

December 31   *United States 7*   *Canada 3*

First Period

1. United States, Chisholm (Carpenter)...........................6:24(pp)
2. United States, Knight (Carpenter) 6:53
3. Canada, Kirk (Hawerchuk)..10:24

PENALTIES: Boimistruck (Can — double minor) & Lee (U.S. — double minor) 0:24, Arthur (Can) 4:44, Grade (U.S.) 7:00, Gaulin (Can) & Ludwig (U.S.) 9:05

Second Period

4. Canada, Arniel (Kirk) 8:41
5. United States, Lee (unassisted)...................................10:38
6. Canada, Chartrain (Fournier) 18:43
7. United States, Johannson (Mullen).............................19:01

PENALTIES: Arthur (Can) & Carpenter (U.S.) 4:42, Arthur (Can) & Mullen (U.S.) 14:22

Third Period

8. United States, Carpenter (Griffith) 1:37
9. United States, Carpenter (Lee) 14:06
10. United States, Carpenter (Griffith) 16:51

PENALTIES: Ethier (U.S.) 4:17, Calder (Can) 7:35, Carpenter (U.S.) 11:18

Shots on Goal:

unknown

In Goal:

Canada — Micalef
United States — O'Connor

January 2　　　　West Germany 7　　Canada 6

First Period

1. West Germany, Lutz (Held) .... 2:58(pp)
2. West Germany, Gotsch (Strodl) 4:15
3. West Germany, Hegen (Sterflinger) 6:53
4. West Germany, Augsten (Betz) 7:47
5. West Germany, Hegen (Gotsch) 11:07
6. Canada, Arniel (unassisted) 15:46
7. Canada, Calder (Hawerchuk) 18:03

PENALTIES: Kirk (Can) 1:31, Lutz (WGer) 4:24, Eatough (Can) 11:07, Holzmann (WGer) 13:29, Crawford (Can ---- double minor) & Feistl (WGer ---- misconduct) & Holzmann (WGer) 17:29, Eatough (Can ---- misconduct) & Holzmann (WGer) 19:29

Second Period

8. Canada, Boimistruck (Savard) 9:38
9. Canada, Crawford (Arniel) 10:22
10. West Germany, Hegen (Schodl) 10:52
11. Canada, Kirk (Hawerchuk) 11:05
12. West Germany, Strodl (Hiemer) 16:06

PENALTIES: Boimistruck (Can — double minor) & Adams (WGer — double minor) & Holzmann (WGer — misconduct) 1:29, Arthur (Can) 13:59, Halliday (Can) & Hegen (WGer) 20:00

Third Period

13. Canada, Hawerchuk (Arthur) 15:59

PENALTIES: Chartrain (Can) 11:06, Kirk (Can — double minor) & Hiemer (WGer) 15:18

Shots on Goal:

unknown

In Goal:

Canada — Graovac/Micalef (Micalef [4 goals] replaced Graovac [3 goals] at 6:53 of 1st)
West Germany — de Raaf

TEAM CANADA FINAL STATISTICS
1981 WORLD JUNIOR CHAMPIONSHIPS
(Cornwall Royals)

			GP	G	A	P	PIM
10	F	Dale Hawerchuk	5	5	5	10	2
24	F	John Kirk	5	4	3	7	14
22	F	Scott Arniel	5	3	1	4	4
20	D	Fred Boimistruck	5	3	0	3	8
8	F	Andre Chartrain	5	2	1	3	2

12	F	Denis Cyr	5	2	1	3	0
27	F	Jeff Eatough	5	1	2	3	16
11	F	Marc Crawford(C)	5	1	2	3	4
16	F	Guy Fournier	5	1	2	3	0
18	F	Jean-Marc Gaulin	5	2	0	2	4
3	D	Fred Arthur	5	0	2	2	10
7	D	Robert Savard	5	0	2	2	2
5	D	Eric Calder	5	1	0	1	4
4	D	Gilbert Delorme	5	1	0	1	0
21	D	Bill Campbell	5	0	1	1	2
2	F	Craig Halliday	5	0	0	0	2
9	F	Doug Gilmour	5	0	0	0	0
14	F	Roy Russell	5	0	0	0	0
30	G	Corrado Micalef	4	0	0	0	0
1	G	Tom Graovac	3	0	0	0	0

In Goal

	GP	W–L–T	MINS	GA	SO	AVG
Tom Graovac	3	1–0–0	87	5	0	3.45
Corrado Micalef	4	0–3–1	213	20	0	5.63

Goalie Notes:

1. Graovac [one goal] replaced Micalef [6 goals] to start 3rd, December 28 vs. Soviet Union
2. Micalef [4 goals] replaced Graovac [3 goals] at 6:53 of 1st, January 2 vs. West Germany

Coach Bob Kilger
Assistant Fred Martell

CANADIAN OFFICIALS AT THE 1981 WORLD JUNIOR CHAMPIONSHIPS

Jim Lever (referee)   4 games

TEAM CANADA ROSTER SUMMARY

Team Canada players   20
Drafted Into NHL   14 (all but Chartrain, Graovac, Halliday, Kirk, Russell, Savard)
Played in NHL   12 (all but Campbell, Chartrain, Fournier, Graovac, Halliday, Kirk, Russell, Savard)
Returning players   none

PLAYER REPRESENTATION BY LEAGUE

QMJHL   20

PLAYER REPRESENTATION BY AGE

19-year-olds	4	(Arthur, Crawford, Cyr, Graovac, Kirk, Micalef, Russell)
18-year-olds	7	(Arniel, Boimistruck, Chartrain, Delorme, Fournier, Gaulin, Halliday)
17-year-olds	4	(Calder, Eatough, Gilmour, Hawerchuk, Russell)
16-year-olds	1	(Campbell)

PLAYERS' CAREER PROFILES

Scott Arniel	Cornwall Royals (QMJHL) Selected 22nd overall by Winnipeg at 1981 Draft Played in the NHL 1981–92
Fred Arthur	Cornwall Royals (QMJHL) Selected 8th overall by Hartford at 1980 Draft Played in the NHL 1980–83
Fred Boimistruck	Cornwall Royals (QMJHL) Selected 43rd overall by Toronto at 1980 Draft Played in the NHL 1981–83
Eric Calder	Cornwall Royals (QMJHL) Selected 45th overall by Washington in 1981 Draft Played in the NHL 1981–83
Bill Campbell	Montreal Juniors (QMJHL) Selected 47th overall by Philadelphia at 1982 Draft Did not play in the NHL
Andre Chartrain	Sorel Black Hawks (QMJHL) Not drafted Did not play in the NHL
Marc Crawford	Cornwall Royals (QMJHL) Selected 70th overall by Vancouver at 1980 Draft Played in the NHL 1981–87
Denis Cyr	Montreal Juniors (QMJHL) Selected 13th overall by Calgary at 1980 Draft Played in the NHL 1980–86
Gilbert Delorme	Chicoutimi Sagueneens (QMJHL) Selected 18th overall by Montreal at 1981 Draft Played in the NHL 1981–90
Jeff Eatough	Cornwall Royals (QMJHL) Selected 80th overall by Buffalo at 1981 Draft Played in the NHL 1981–82
Guy Fournier	Shawinigan Cataractes (QMJHL) Selected 65th overall by Winnipeg at 1980 Draft Did not play in the NHL

Jean-Marc Gaulin   Sorel Black Hawks (QMJHL)
Selected 53rd overall by Quebec at 1981 Draft
Played in the NHL 1982–86

Doug Gilmour   Cornwall Royals (QMJHL)
Selected 134th overall by St. Louis at 1982 Draft
Played in the NHL 1983 to present

Tom Graovac   Cornwall Royals (QMJHL)
Not drafted
Did not play in the NHL

Craig Halliday   Cornwall Royals (QMJHL)
Not drafted
Did not play in the NHL

Dale Hawerchuk   Cornwall Royals (QMJHL)
Selected 1st overall by Winnipeg at 1981 Draft
Played in the NHL 1981–97

John Kirk   Cornwall Royals (QMJHL)
Not drafted
Did not play in the NHL

Corrado Micalef   Sherbrooke Beavers (QMJHL)
Selected 44th overall by Detroit at 1981 Draft
Played in the NHL 1981–86

Roy Russell   Cornwall Royals (QMJHL)
Not drafted
Did not play in the NHL

Robert Savard   Cornwall Royals (QMJHL)
Not drafted
Did not play in the NHL

1982 WORLD JUNIOR CHAMPIONSHIPS UNITED STATES, DECEMBER 22, 1981-- JANUARY 2, 1982

(some games played in Canada)

FINAL PLACINGS

GOLD MEDAL	**CANADA**
SILVER MEDAL	Czechoslovakia
BRONZE MEDAL	Finland
Fourth Place	Soviet Union
Fifth Place	Sweden
Sixth Place	United States
Seventh Place	West Germany
Eighth Place	Switzerland*

promoted from "B" pool in 1981; relegated to "B" pool for 1983

ALL-STAR TEAM

GOAL	Mike Moffat (Canada)
DEFENCE	Gord Kluzak (Canada)
	Ilya Biakin (Soviet Union)
FORWARD	Mike Moller (Canada)
	Petri Skriko (Finland)
	Vladimir Ruzicka (Czechoslovakia)

DIRECTORATE AWARDS

BEST GOALIE	Mike Moffat (Canada)
BEST DEFENCEMAN	Gord Kluzak (Canada)
BEST FORWARD	Petri Skriko (Finland)

COACH DAVE KING

The name Dave King is synonymous with Canadian hockey internationally. King began as an assistant coach at the University of Saskatchewan in 1974 while teaching at a Saskatoon high school. He coached the Saskatoon Quakers (Junior B), went to the Canada Games in 1975, and became head coach of the Saskatoon Jays in 1976. He was bench boss for the Billings Bighorns in the WHL, and won coach-of-the-year honours in his second year there.

Then he moved on to the University of Saskatchewan Huskies, where he again won coach-of-the-year. "I guess I got the national job because as a university coach it was easier for me to get time off," the self-effacing King said. "It would be impossible for a major junior coach to take a month off and work with the national team."

Advising him from the three junior leagues were Murray Costello of the CHA, Sherry Bassin of the OHL, George Lariviere of the QMJHL. Other advisors were Jim Gregory of the NHL and Bob Strumm, general manager of the Regina Pats of the WHL. The six men collectively chose the players to invite to camp.

A NEW LOGO

Team Canada's jerseys for 1982 changed dramatically from the previous design. Conceived by Ric Freeborn, the new design featured a hockey stick with letters spelling Canada down the outside of the stick and three receding maple leafs on the inside of the shaft.

A NEW INITIATIVE

This was a watershed year for hockey in Canada, particularly the development of young players. The CAHA introduced a new mandate called "Program of Excellence," which, in the context of the World Juniors, meant that for the first time, the team representing Canada would be made up of the finest twenty players younger than twenty as of December 31, 1981. This all-star team would have two preparatory camps before the tournament began.

The first camp was held from August 23 to 31 at Queen's University in Kingston, Ontario, before the players' regular junior league camps opened. The tryouts featured tough twice-a-day workouts, fitness tests, dry land training, and a daily Red and White scrimmage. Coach King had a chance to make some initial assessments and projections about talent, and he could decide which kinds of players he would take with him to Minnesota. The first camp also featured "guest" coaches Jacques Lemaire and Mike Keenan, both of whom offered King and the players advice and opinions. Lemaire, fresh from a two-year term as playing-coach in Switzerland, inculcated the juniors with the importance of skating and handling the puck.

The camp opened amid internal controversy in Canadian amateur hockey. The CAHA, the governing body for all amateur hockey in Canada, wanted to control the World Junior Championships, particularly who was invited to camp. It was funded by the federal government, and argued that its mandate demanded control. This control extended to inviting players from Canadian and American colleges and universities for tryouts.

The Canadian Major Junior Hockey Leagues, however, felt they had all the finest young players in the country. They thought they should control the invite list, and the list would not include college and university players. The CAHA won the day, and invited forty-seven players, thirteen of whom were playing in post-secondary institutions.

THE PLAYERS

The second camp opened December 17, just prior to the championships, and featured a few exhibition games in Winnipeg to mold the team and make a few last-minute roster decisions. Of the twenty-eight players invited to this camp, only twenty would remain four days later, after final cuts. The team ended its schedule with a 12–2 drubbing of Central Amateur Senior Hockey Selects in Carman, Manitoba on December 20.

The best laid plans are often mutated by destiny, fate, bad luck, or whatever effects unplanned change on those who plan carefully. Brian Bellows was clearly the best player Team Junior Canada was going to have. He had the size, maturity, and skill to lead, and he was certain to be the first selection overall at the 1982 entry draft. But after separating his shoulder November 1, he hadn't played a game. He went to the final camp in December knowing he'd miss at least the first two games of the tournament, and wound up not playing at all on doctors' orders. Tony Tanti, another great junior, also missed the tournament due to injury.

As usual, politics also had a hand in forming the team. Brent Sutter was advised by his agent not to play, and Ken Yaremchuk of Portland and Randy Velischek of Providence College were refused a leave of absence by their clubs. The Winnipeg Jets were impressed by what they saw of Scott Arniel early in the season, but sent him back to junior (Cornwall) in time for him to be with the national team, realizing that three weeks without a teenager would be a small sacrifice for the more experienced player they'd have returning to the NHL in January.

The final cuts, always the most difficult, were made just before the team's opening game against Finland on December 22 in Winnipeg: Dave Berry (University of Denver), Rick Chernomaz (Victoria, WHL), Luc Dufour (Chicoutimi, QMJHL), Jean-Marc Gaulin (Hull, QMJHL), Mitch Lamoureux (Oshawa, OHL), John Newberry (University of Wisconsin), Randy Boyd (Ottawa, OHL), Al MacInnis (Kitchener, OHL), Ron Meighan (Niagara Falls, OHL), Mike Sands (Sudbury, OHL), Eric Calder (Cornwall, OHL), and Yves Courteau (Laval, QMJHL).

The next day, Bruce Eakin of Saskatoon and Garth Butcher of Regina were added to the roster to replace Bellows and Tanti.

A 3-3 tie with the Czechs on the last day of the 1982 tournament,
on January 2, gave Canada its first gold medal in WJC play.

INTERNATIONAL DRAFTING

In 1981, NHL teams began to draft European players. The 1982 WJC featured no fewer than fifteen players from Czechoslovakia, Finland, and Sweden. The World Juniors was clearly becoming a significant tournament; it was being scouted more heavily each year, and the quality of play was improving as the NHL began to move in a more international direction.

International picks included: Jiri Dudacek (Czechoslovakia, 17th overall by Buffalo), Hannu Virta (Finland, 38th overall by Buffalo), Dieter Hegen (West Germany, 46th by Montreal), Peter Madach (Sweden, 78th overall by Calgary), Kjell Dahlin (Sweden, 82nd overall by Montreal), Anders Wikberg (Sweden, 83rd overall by Buffalo), Peter Aslin (Sweden, 125th overall by St. Louis), Peter Nilsson (Sweden, 127th overall by Winnipeg), Risto Jalo (Finland, 131st overall by Washington), Vladimir Svitek (Czechoslovakia, 137th overall by Philadelphia), Heikki Leime (Finland, 143rd overall by Buffalo), Teppo Virta (Finland, 147th overall by Islanders), Petri Skriko (Finland, 157th overall by Vancouver), Robert Nordmark (Sweden, 191st overall by Detroit), Kari Takko (Finland, 200th overall by Quebec). None among this number went on to great things in the NHL, but the change had begun. The stage was set for future great Europeans to leave their mark in the world's premier league.

KING'S STRATEGY

There are always two teams on the ice, and this means there are always two sets of considerations: what your own team does, and what you expect the other team to do. King made it clear from the beginning that although all twenty players on Team Canada were stars in their own league, each was now one of twenty equals in the national dressing room. Check your egos at the door.

For the opposition, King used a 2–1–2 system of forecheck and containment. The Canadian forwards could then effectively shut down the middle of the ice, forcing the other team to the boards when coming out of their zone. This was the key to thwarting any attack because Europeans are used to playing in the huge middle of the large ice and are not as comfortable playing along the boards.

In the deciding game, the Czechs could do little besides mock the Canadians. Whenever a Canuck skated by their bench, Czechs taunted the champions with calls of "Hit. Hit. Dump it in. Canadian hockey." The psychology backfired — the Canadians won.

BASSIN'S STRATEGY

Motivation, spirit, pride, determination. These words describe great characteristics anyone would want to possess in any job. In the deciding game, trailing 2–1 after two periods, Sherry Bassin found a gold medal and brought it into the dressing room. Twenty minutes of hockey, and each player could have one — if he earned it. Seven minutes later, they were leading 3–2 and hung on for a 3–3 tie. Every player could hold a medal.

*Canada trailed 1-0 and 2-1 in the gold medal game
against the Czechs before scoring twice early in the third
and hanging on for the tie to ensure first place.*

OUR HOME AND NATIVE LAND

Team Canada won the gold medal on January 2, 1982, with a 3–3 tie against second-place Czechoslovakia in tiny Graham Arena in Rochester, Minnesota. After the hugs and handshakes, they stood at the blue line ready to listen to O Canada. It never came. There was no recording in the building. Realizing this, the team started singing, sans music. Thus began a yearly tradition. Not one member of this team went on to perform at la Scala or the Met, but no death scene from La Boheme or Aida could possibly match the emotional or dramatic power of such an out-of-tune, heartfelt rendering of our national anthem!

TOURNAMENT FORMAT

All teams were placed in one division and played a round-robin series of games. Tie games would not go into overtime, and ties in the standings were broken first by results between the tied teams. (That is how the fourth-place Soviets finished ahead of Sweden in the final standings.)

THE OPPOSITION

CZECHOSLOVAKIA

Vaclav Badoucek, Mojmir Bozik, Ivan Dornic, Jiri Dudacek, Milan Eberle, Vaclav Furbacher, Peter Harazin, Jaroslav Hauer, Tomas Jelinek, Peter Kasik, Ludwig Kopecky, Frantisek Musil, Kamil Precechtel, Pavel Prorok, Petr Rosol, Vladimir Ruzicka, Karel Soudek, Antonin Stavjana, Vladimir Svitek, Rostislav Vlach

FINLAND

Hannu Henriksson, Risto Jalo, Pekka Jarvela, Hannu Jarvenpaa, Timo Jutila, Markus Lehto, Heikki Leime, Jari Munck, Harri Nystrom, Jose Pekkala, Sakari Petajaaho, Simo Saarinen, Arto Sirvio, Petri Skriko, Raimo Summanen, Kari Takko, Jukka Tammi, Esa Tommila, Hannu Virta, Teppo Virta

SOVIET UNION

Evgeny Belov, Ilya Biakin, Andrei Karpin, Viacheslav Khalisov, Sergei Kuchin, Sergei Kudiashov, Konstantin Kurashev, Sergei Odintzov, Sergei Priakhin, Evgeny Roshin, Vitali Samoilov, Anatoli Semenov, Yuri Shipitsin, Evgeny Shtepa, Oleg Starkov, Igor Stelnov, Vladimir Tiurikov, Leonid Trukhno, Mikhail Vasiliev, Sergei Yashin

SWEDEN

Peter Andersson, Peter Aslin, Jonas Bergqvist, Lennart Dahlberg, Kjell Dahlin, Per-Erik Eklund, Mikael Hjaelm, Jens Johansson, Anders Jonsson, Ake Liljebjorn, Martin Linse, Mats Lusth, Peter Madach, Peter Nilsson, Robert Nordmark, Jens Ohling, Ove Pettersson, Magnus Roupe, Ulf Samulesson, Anders Wickberg

SWITZERLAND

Andreas Beutler, Fredy Bosch, Patrice Brasey, Urs Burkart, Jorg Eberle, Philippe Giachino, Pierre Girardin, Yvan Griga, Bruno Hidber, Eric Jeandupeux, Richard Jost, Willy Kohler, Ludwig Lemmenmeier, Cedric Lengacher, Jurg Marton, Thomas Meyer, Peter Moser, Yvar Schwartz, Sergio Soguel, Renato Tosio, Roman Waeger

UNITED STATES

Jon Casey, Chris Chelios, Rich Erdall, Kevin Foster, Scott Fusco, Dan Gerarden, Chris Guy, Tom Herzig, Phil Housley, Tony Kellin, Tom Kurvers, Charlie Lundeen, Mark Maroste, Dan McFall, Cory Millen, Kelly Miller, Mike O'Connor, Bill Schafhauser, Tim Thomas, John Vanbiesbrouck

WEST GERMANY

Michael Betz, Thomas Borntraeger, Boris Capla, Hans-Georg Eder, Klaus Faistl, Robert Hammerle, Dieter Hegen, Josef Heiss, Ulrich Hiemer, Franz Juttner, Franz Kummer, Edgar Lill, Andreas Niederberger, Helmut Patzner, Alexander Schnoell, Peter Stankovic, Robert Sterflinger, Jens Tosse, Joe Wassereck, Peter Wiegl

FINAL STANDINGS

	GP	W	L	T	GF	GA	P	GAA	SO	PIM
CANADA	7	6	0	1	45	14	13	2.00	1	68*
Czechoslovakia	7	5	1	1	44	17	11	2.43	1	95
Finland	7	5	2	0	47	29	10	4.14	0	102
Soviet Union	7	4	3	0	42	25	8	3.57	1	128
Sweden	7	4	3	0	42	26	8	3.71	1	124
United States	7	2	5	0	28	34	4	4.86	0	114
West Germany	7	1	6	0	19	56	2	8.00	0	113
Switzerland	7	0	7	0	15	81	0	11.57	0	107

* won Fair Play Cup

RESULTS

December 22	Winnipeg	Canada 5	Finland 1
	Kenora	Sweden 17	Switzerland 0
	Duluth	Soviet Union 12	West Germany 3
	Duluth	Czechoslovakia 6	United States 4
December 23	Winnipeg	Canada 3	Sweden 2
	Brandon	Finland 14	Switzerland 2
	Duluth	United States 8	West Germany 1
	Duluth	Czechoslovakia 3	Soviet Union 2
December 26	Winnipeg	Canada 7	Soviet Union 0
	Grand Rapids	United States 6	Switzerland 3
	Brainerd	Sweden 5	West Germany 1
	Virginia	Czechoslovakia 5	Finland 1
December 27	Bloomington	Canada 5	United States 4
	Bloomington	Sweden 6	Czechoslovakia 4
	International Falls	Soviet Union 11	Switzerland 4
	St. Cloud	Finland 8	West Germany 4
December 29	Bloomington	Canada 11	West Germany 3
	Bloomington	Czechoslovakia 16	Switzerland 0
	Bloomington	Soviet Union 7	United States 0

December 30	Burnsville	Finland 9	Sweden 6
December 31	New Ulm	Czechoslovakia 7	West Germany 1
	Bloomington	Finland 6	Soviet Union 3
	Bloomington	Sweden 4	United States 2
January 1	Minneapolis	Canada 11	Switzerland 1
January 2	Rochester	Canada 3	Czechoslovakia 3
	Mankato	West Germany 6	Switzerland 5
	Bloomington	Soviet Union 7	Sweden 2
	Bloomington	Finland 8	United States 4

TEAM CANADA GAME SUMMARIES

December 22   *Canada 5*   *Finland 1*

First Period

1. Canada, Cyr (Eakin, M. Morrison)..6:58
2. Canada, M. Moller (Habscheid, Butcher)...................................11:26(pp)
3. Canada, Wilson (Strueby, D. Morrison)..19:58

   PENALTIES: Jalo (Fin) 10:37, Eakin (Can) 17:18

Second Period

4. Canada, M. Moller (Habscheid)..0:59
5. Finland, Jarvenpaa (Jutila) ....10:50(sh)

   PENALTIES: Rioux (Can) 6:59, Leime (Fin) 9:39

Third Period

6. Canada, Eakin (Wilson)..18:13

   PENALTIES: Henriksson (Fin) 15:23

Shots on Goal:

| Canada | 15 | 13 | 8 | **35** |
| Finland | 8 | 13 | 14 | **36** |

In Goal:

Canada — Moffat
Finland — Takko

December 23   *Canada 3*   *Sweden 2*

First Period

1. Sweden, Hjaelm (Bergqvist) 9:57

   PENALTIES: K. Dahlin (Swe) 13:14

Second Period

2.   Canada, Butcher (Arniel) 6:55

PENALTIES: Murray (Can) 1:02, Samuelsson (Swe) & Lemay (Can) 10:15, Andersson (Swe) & Cyr (Can) 16:10

Third Period

3.   Sweden, Andersson (Dahlin, Roupe) .... 10:46(pp)
4.   Canada, Murray (unassisted) 11:55
5.   Canada, Wilson (Butcher) 14:41

PENALTIES: Strueby (Can) 4:05, Strueby (Can) 9:21, R. Moller (Can) 9:35

Shots on Goal:

Canada	11	6	11	**28**
Sweden	8	14	12	**34**

In Goal:

Canada — Caprice
Sweden — Aslin

December 26   *Canada 7*   *Soviet Union 0*

First Period

1.   Canada, Eakin (Strueby, R. Moller) 3:40
2.   Canada, M. Morrison (Eakin) 7:58

PENALTIES: Kurashev (Sov) 5:25, M. Moller (Can) 9:35, Semenov (Sov) & Kuchin (Sov) 10:59

Second Period

3.   Canada, Cyr (M. Morrison) .... 2:15(pp)

PENALTIES: Biakin (Sov) 2:00, Tiurikov (Sov) 3:23, Lemay (Can) 10:56

Third Period

4.   Canada, Boutilier (M. Morrison, Eakin) .... 7:12(pp)
5.   Canada, Habscheid (M. Moller, Arniel) 8:40
6.   Canada, M. Moller (Boutilier, R. Moller) 12:32
7.   Canada, Arniel (M. Moller, Habscheid) 17:35

PENALTIES: Stelnov (Sov) 6:43, Vasiliev (Sov) 14:42

Shots on Goal:

Canada	11	14	11	**36**
Soviet Union	8	7	6	**21**

In Goal:

Canada — Moffat
Soviet Union — Samoilov

December 27   *Canada 5*   *United States 4*

First Period

1. United States, Millen (Lundeen, Miller) 4:48
2. United States, Herzig (Kellin, Miller) 14:48

PENALTIES: Murray (Can) 1:40, Maroste (U.S.) 14:58

Second Period

3. Canada, Arniel (Habscheid, Boutilier) 1:24
4. Canada, Cyr (Nylund, M. Morrison) 3:43
5. Canada, Wilson (unassisted) 5:06
6. United States, McFall (Foster, Lundeen) .... 10:02(pp)
7. Canada, Rioux (M. Moller, Murray) .... 19:40(pp)

PENALTIES: Foster (U.S.) 1:56, Eakin (Can) 7:36, Boutilier (Can) 8:56, Lundeen (U.S.) 10:59, Cyr (Can) 13:53, Schafhauser (U.S.) 19:32

Third Period

8. Canada, Habscheid (M. Moller) 0:26
9. United States, Chelios (Maroste, Kurvers) .... 4:29(pp)

PENALTIES: Cyr (Can) 2:39, Arniel (Can) & Lundeen (U.S.) 4:59, Wilson (Can) 7:30, Wilson (Can) 15:47

Shots on Goal:

Canada	12	15	7	**34**
United States	8	15	13	**36**

In Goal:

Canada — Caprice
United States — Vanbiesbrouck

December 29   *Canada 11*   *West Germany 3*

First Period

1. Canada, Arniel (M. Moller, Patrick) 0:17
2. Canada, Murray (unassisted) 1:33
3. Canada, Arniel (M. Moller, Habscheid) 4:40
4. Canada, Nylund (Cyr) 9:33

PENALTIES: Cyr (Can) 15:03, Betz (WGer) 19:51

Second Period

5. Canada, Lemay (Rioux, Nylund) 1:10
6. Canada, Murray (Boutilier, Rioux) 8:16
7. Canada, D. Morrison (Strueby) 10:28
8. West Germany, Hegen (Kummer) 10:43
9. Canada, Cyr (M. Morrison, Eakin) 14:17
10. West Germany, Hegen (Betz) 19:59

PENALTIES: none

Third Period

11. Canada, Murray (Rioux, Butcher) .... 6:07(pp)
12. Canada, Habscheid (Arniel, Kluzak) 6:41
13. Canada, Eakin (Murray) 11:58
14. West Germany, Patzner (Tosse) 12:17

PENALTIES: Patrick (Can) 3:44, Niederberger (WGer) 5:02, Kluzak (Can) 7:56, Kluzak (Can) 18:01

Shots on Goal:

Canada	20	25	14	**59**
West Germany	5	4	2	**11**

In Goal:

Canada — Moffat
West Germany — Heiss/Borntraeger (Borntraeger [3 goals] replaced Heiss [8 goals] to start 3rd)

January 1 *Canada 11* *Switzerland 1*

First Period

1. Canada, Rioux (Cyr, Nylund) 2:43
2. Canada, Lemay (M. Morrison, Murray) 6:48
3. Canada, M. Morrison (Cyr, Eakin) 13:03
4. Canada, M. Morrison (Cyr, Eakin) 19:35

PENALTIES: none

Second Period

5. Canada, Habscheid (M. Moller, Patrick) 0:13
6. Switzerland, Moser (Jeandupeux, Jost) .... 3:35(pp)
7. Canada, Arniel (M. Moller, R. Moller) 8:32
8. Canada, Wilson (Strueby, D. Morrison) 18:20

PENALTIES: Boutilier (Can) 2:06, Burkart (Swi) 12:14, Giachino (Swi) 15:40

Third Period

9. Canada, M. Moller (Arniel, Habscheid) 11:17
10. Canada, Rioux (Murray) 13:39
11. Canada, Eakin (M. Morrison, Cyr) 14:33
12. Canada, Habscheid (M. Moller, Arniel) 15:44

PENALTIES: Arniel (Can) 5:48, Patrick (Can) 9:07, M. Moller (Can) & Schwartz (Swi) 16:37, Wilson (Can) & Griga (Swi) 16:46

Shots on Goal:

Canada	15	20	17	**52**
Switzerland	9	8	5	**22**

In Goal:

Canada — Caprice
Switzerland — Tosio

| January 2 | Canada 3 | Czechoslovakia 3 |

First Period

1. Czechoslovakia, Ruzicka (Stavjana) .... 18:53(pp)
2. Canada, Boutilier (Cyr, Eakin) 19:28

PENALTIES: Rioux (Can) 6:22, M. Moller (Can) & Kasik (Cze) 13:52, Furbacher (Cze) 16:38, Habscheid (Can) 17:15

Second Period

3. Czechoslovakia, Vlach (Eberle) 19:16

PENALTIES: Patrick (Can) 0:21, Cyr (Can) & Bozik (Cze) 5:19, Badoucek (Cze) 12:39

Third Period

4. Canada, Habscheid (Arniel) 4:36
5. Canada, M. Moller (Strueby, Boutilier) 12:41
6. Czechoslovakia, Dudacek (Precechtel) 15:30

PENALTIES: Cze bench 16:37

Shots on Goal:

| Canada | 5 | 5 | 9 | **19** |
| Czechoslovakia | 13 | 16 | 12 | **41** |

In Goal:

Canada — Moffat
Czechoslovakia — Furbacher

TEAM CANADA FINAL STATISTICS
1982 WORLD JUNIOR CHAMPIONSHIPS

			GP	G	A	P	PIM
26	F	Mike Moller	7	5	9	14	6
16	F	Marc Habschied	7	6	6	12	2
14	F	Scott Arniel	7	5	6	11	4
24	F	Bruce Eakin	7	4	7	11	4
19	F	Paul Cyr	7	4	6	10	12
17	F	Mark Morrison	7	3	7	10	0
21	F	Troy Murray(C)	7	4	4	8	4
7	F	Pierre Rioux	7	3	3	6	4
5	D	Paul Boutilier	7	2	4	6	4
20	F	Carey Wilson	7	4	1	5	6
11	F	Todd Strueby	7	0	5	5	4
10	D	Garth Butcher	7	1	3	4	0
3	D	Gary Nylund	7	1	3	4	0
23	F	Dave Morrison	7	1	2	3	0
2	D	Randy Moller	7	0	3	3	2
12	F	Moe Lemay	7	2	0	2	4

9	D	James Patrick	7	0	2	2	6
4	D	Gord Kluzak	7	0	1	1	4
30	G	Mike Moffat	4	0	0	0	0
1	G	Frank Caprice	3	0	0	0	0

In Goal

	GP	W-L-T	MINS	GA	SO	AVG
Mike Moffat	4	3—0—1	240	7	1	1.75
Frank Caprice	3	3—0—0	180	7	0	2.33

Coach Dave King
Assistants Michel Morin/Doug Sauter

CANADIAN OFFICIALS AT THE 1982 WORLD JUNIOR CHAMPIONSHIPS

Dan Cournoyer (referee)	4 games
Ron Renneberg (referee)	4 games
Greg Hilker (linesman)	7 games
Jim Petschenig (linesman)	7 games
Ken Skingle (linesman)	7 games

TEAM CANADA ROSTER SUMMARY

Team Canada players	20
Drafted Into NHL	20
Played in NHL	20
Returning Players	1 (Arniel)

PLAYER REPRESENTATION BY LEAGUE

OHL	4	(Caprice, Lemay, Moffat, D. Morrison)
WHL	10	(Butcher, Cyr, Eakin, Habscheid, Kluzak, M. Moller, R. Moller, M. Morrison, Nylund, Strueby)
QMJHL	3	(Arniel, Boutilier, Rioux)
U.S. COLLEGE	2	(Murray, Patrick)
OTHER*	1	(Wilson)

* Finnish League

PLAYER REPRESENTATION BY AGE

19-year-olds	10	(Arniel, Caprice, Eakin, Lemay, Moffat, M. Moller, D. Morrison, Murray, Rioux, Wilson)
18-year-olds	9	(Boutilier, Butcher, Cyr, Habscheid, R. Moller, M. Morrison, Nylund, Patrick, Strueby)
17-year-olds	1	(Kluzak)

PLAYERS' CAREER PROFILES

Scott Arniel   Cornwall Royals (QMJHL)
                   Selected 22nd overall by Winnipeg at 1981 Draft
                   Played in the NHL 1981–92

Paul Boutilier   Sherbrooke Beavers (QMJHL)
                   Selected 21st overall by Islanders at 1981 Draft
                   Played in the NHL 1981–89

Garth Butcher   Regina Pats (WHL)
                   Selected 10th overall by Vancouver at 1981 Draft
                   Played in the NHL 1981–95

Frank Caprice   London Knights (OHL)
                   Selected 178th overall by Vancouver at 1981 Draft
                   Played in the NHL 1982–88

Paul Cyr   Victoria Cougars (WHL)
                   Selected 9th overall by Buffalo at 1982 Draft
                   Played in the NHL 1982–92

Bruce Eakin   Saskatoon Blades (WHL)
                   Selected 204th overall by Calgary at 1981 Draft
                   Played in the NHL 1981–86

Marc Habscheid   Saskatoon Blades (WHL)
                   Selected 113th overall by Edmonton at 1981 Draft
                   Played in the NHL 1981–92

Gord Kluzak   Billings Bighorns (WHL)
                   Selected 1st overall by Boston at 1982 Draft
                   Played in the NHL 1982–91

Moe Lemay   Ottawa 67's (OHL)
                   Selected 105th overall by Vancouver at 1981 Draft
                   Played in the NHL 1981–89

Mike Moffat   Kingston Canadians (OHL)
                   Selected 165th overall by Boston at 1980 Draft
                   Played in the NHL 1981–84

Mike Moller   Lethbridge Broncos (WHL)
                   Selected 41st overall by Buffalo at 1980 Draft
                   Played in the NHL 1980–87

Randy Moller   Lethbridge Broncos (WHL)
                   Selected 11th overall by Quebec at 1981 Draft
                   Played in the NHL 1981–95

Dave Morrison   Peterborough Petes (OHL)
                   Selected 34th overall by Los Angeles at 1980 Draft
                   Played in the NHL 1980–85

Mark Morrison   Victoria Cougars (WHL)
                   Selected 51st overall by Rangers at 1981 Draft
                   Played in the NHL 1981–84

Troy Murray University of North Dakota Fighting Sioux (WCHA)
      Selected 57th overall by Chicago at 1980 Draft
      Played in the NHL 1981–96

Gary Nylund Portland Winter Hawks (WHL)
      Selected 3rd overall by Toronto at 1982 Draft
      Played in the NHL 1982–93

James Patrick University of North Dakota Fighting Sioux (WCHA)
      Selected 9th overall by Rangers at 1981 Draft
      Played in the NHL 1983 to present

Pierre Rioux Shawinigan Cataractes (QMJHL)
      Not drafted
      Played in the NHL 1982–83

Todd Strueby Saskatoon Blades (WHL)
      Selected 29th overall by Edmonton at 1981 Draft
      Played in the NHL 1981–84

Carey Wilson HIFK Helsinki
      Selected 67th overall by Chicago at 1980 Draft
      Played in the NHL 1983–93

1983 WORLD JUNIOR CHAMPIONSHIPS SOVIET UNION, DECEMBER 26, 1982-- JANUARY 4, 1983

FINAL PLACINGS

GOLD MEDAL	Soviet Union
SILVER MEDAL	Czechoslovakia
BRONZE MEDAL	**CANADA**
Fourth Place	Sweden
Fifth Place	United States
Sixth Place	Finland
Seventh Place	West Germany
Eighth Place	Norway*

promoted from "B" pool in 1982; relegated to "B" pool for 1984

ALL-STAR TEAM

GOAL	Matti Rautiainen (Finland)
DEFENCE	Ilya Biakin (Soviet Union)
	Simo Saarinen (Finland)
FORWARD	Tomas Sandstrom (Sweden)
	Vladimir Ruzicka (Czechoslovakia)
	German Volgin (Soviet Union)

DIRECTORATE AWARDS

BEST GOALIE	Dominik Hasek (Czechoslovakia)
BEST DEFENCEMAN	Ilya Biakin (Soviet Union)
BEST FORWARD	Tomas Sandstrom (Sweden)

COACH DAVE KING

Canada's gold medal in 1982 was our first in the World Juniors since the tournament began in 1977. Through the Program of Excellence, teams were learning how to win, and there was no reason for tampering with success. In the summer of 1982, after the gold at the juniors, King took his university Huskies to the finals for the second year in a row, then was assistant coach to the Canadian team that won a bronze at the World Championships in Helsinki.

He was offered two coaching jobs by NHL teams, the Edmonton Oilers and the Minnesota North Stars, but turned both down so he could focus on Sarajevo '84: "The most important thing to me is the Olympic program," he commented. "It has been on my mind for such a long time. Ever since I got into coaching, the epitome has been the Olympic team — that's what I've been shooting for. I've set my goals and all my thoughts on that." As players have to prepare, so, too, does a coach. The '83 World Juniors were part of King's Olympic preparations, and he wasn't about to jeopardize his dream.

THE ROSTER

The team invited twenty-six juniors to Toronto for a camp December 18–19, during which four cuts were made. They travelled to Vierumaki, Finland, for two exhibition games against the Finnish juniors on December 21 and 22, and continued their pre-tournament training until Christmas Day, when they took a train to Leningrad for their first game the next night against West Germany.

The nascent junior program was reliant upon the whims of NHL teams. Scotty Bowman, a pretty good hockey man, knew that to release Dave Andreychuk and Paul Cyr from the Sabres for three weeks could only benefit the players' development, and thus the club allowed them to leave. Despite having two injured goalies — Don Edwards and Reggie Lemelin — the Flames loaned goaler Mike Vernon. Fifteen years later, he is still a force in the league. One can't help but think Calgary did right by him. Glen Sather of Edmonton played Scrooge and refused to release Marc Habscheid, who played only 345 NHL games in eleven seasons.

The four last-minute cuts from camp were Doug Gilmour (Cornwall, OHL), Norm Schmidt (Oshawa, OHL), Bob Errey (Peterborough, OHL), and Andre Villeneuve (Chicoutimi, QMJHL). Gilmour is the most notable name. Like Wayne Gretzky in 1978, Doug Gilmour was not on the original list of twenty-six. He made the grade because he was leading the OHL in scoring, and an invitation to the league's leading point-getter was requisite. In the end, King opted to leave him at home, not the first time Gilmour had been

Steve Yzerman's spectacular NHL career began with the Peterborough Petes where he was selected to play for the World Juniors in 1983.

slighted. A few months earlier, he was drafted by St. Louis in the 7th round, hardly a flattering selection for a player who scored 119 points in the OHL the previous season.

In all, four players from the winning team the year before played in Leningrad — Paul Boutilier, James Patrick, Mark Morrison, and Paul Cyr. The coaches formed a consensus as to how the team should be selected: skating ability, versatility, and agility. A player who possessed those qualities, they felt, could overcome any deficiencies.

MISSION STATEMENT: *Returning for the Gold*

PRE-TOURNAMENT VS. FINLAND

As part of the preparation, Dave King put the team through a gruelling regimen to ready the boys for the tournament and the difficulties they'd face living in the Soviet Union for two weeks. After the Leaf game at the Gardens on December 18, the team had an 11:00 p.m. practise, the second one of the day. They got up for an 8:30 skate the next morning, and later in the day made the all-night flight to Finland. After a two-hour bus trip to Vierumaki, they had a gruelling two-hour practise, and the next day another two-hour skate in the morning before playing the Finns — a 3–1 loss — that night. The next night, a fresher and better adjusted team won 5–3. Two more days of intense practise and fine-tuning prepared the team for a Christmas train ride to their title defence in Leningrad.

INJURIES: NOT AN EXCUSE BUT A CONCERN

Perseverence came to team Canada by having to deal with injuries that wouldn't go away. In the games against Finland, Dale Derkatch had pneumonia, Larry Trader had a bad back, Mike Sands a groin pull, Steve Yzerman a knee injury, and Paul Boutilier an eye infection. In the tournament, Mario Lemieux and Paul Cyr were hurt. All overcame their physical battles (injuries heal), though they did have an adverse effect on performance.

"INTELLIGENCE IS THE ABILITY TO ADJUST"

So saith coach King prior to leaving for pre-perestroika U.S.S.R. Start with the bigger ice and weak European officiating, and move to the difficulty of eighteen-year-old kids adjusting to the culture shock and playing at Christmastime, and the chances of repeating as world champions seemed remote.

Mind games were a Soviet trademark. At first, the Soviets were willing to grant the 35-man Canadian delegation only twenty-five visas. They scheduled Canada's first three games against lesser opponents in a smaller rink — the Sports Arena — before setting the critical game against the Soviets in Junilejny Arena. The Canadians were not given time to practise once in what would be an unfamiliar rink. Previous experience told of last-minute cancelled practises or team buses not showing, little things to throw the Canadians off their game.

They arrived in Leningrad, and Customs officials ordered all luggage not in anyone's possession seized, held, and searched. Canada's equipment and clothing were taken away at midnight, Christmas night. Team GM Sherry Bassin told a Soviet official that if the luggage was not returned promptly, Canada would withdraw from the tournament. The luggage was restored some three hours later after a late-night rendez-vous at a warehouse.

THE GAMES

After taking two silly penalties in the opener against West Germany, then two more in the first two periods against the Americans, Dave Andreychuk was benched for the third period of the game. King gave him encouragement against the Finns next time out by putting him on one wing and Steve Yzerman on the other, centring Mario Lemieux. Andreychuk responded with two goals, and Canada won 6–3.

Canada lost to the Soviets 7–3 and the Swedes 5–2. The team had a slim chance for a silver medal heading into the final game against Norway — if they could score sixteen goals. Canada stormed the Norwegians, outshooting them 66–6, but could only score thirteen times. Coach King even pulled goalie Vernon in the last minute, but the team scored only once. It was all a moot point, however, as the Finns went down 5–3.

The 1983 summer evaluation camp featured prospects
for both the World Junior team and the under-18 team
in a series of rigourous practises and intense scrimmages.

TOURNAMENT FORMAT

All eight teams were placed in one division and played a round robin. In the case of a tie in the standings, the winner of the head-to-head match was placed above the loser. Goal differential would be the next deciding factor if a tie in the standings persisted.

THE OPPOSITION

CZECHOSLOVAKIA

Miroslav Blaha, Roman Bozek, Milan Cerny, Libor Dolana, Vaclav Furbacher, Dominik Hasek, Ernest Hornak, Milos Hrubes, Jiri Jiroutek, Jiri Jonak, Vladimir Kames, Petr Klima, Ludwig Kopecky, Lumir Kotala, Jaromir Latal, Frantisek Musil, Kamil Prachar, Petr Rosol, Vladimir Ruzicka, Antonin Stavjana

FINLAND

Raimo Helminen, Hannu Henriksson, Juha Jaaskelainen, Hannu Jarvenpaa, Iiro Jarvi, Timo Jutila, Jouni Kalliokoski, Kari Kanervo, Risto Kurkinen, Pekka Laksola, Mika Lartama, Matti Rautiainen, Christian Ruuttu, Simo Saarinen, Ville Siren, Markku Tiinus, Esa Tikkanen, Keijo Tutti, Jouni Vuorinen, Jali Wahlsten

NORWAY

Christian Arnesen, Lars Bergseng, Lars Cato Svendsen, Karl Erik Ulseth, Jarl Eriksen, Rune Eriksen, Jon Fjeld, Jarl Friis, Rune Gulliksen, Ingar Gundersen, Tommi Hansen, Geir Hoff, Truls Kristiansen, Erik Nerell, Jon Neumann, Paul Ole Wideroe, Olle Peter Studstrud, Kim Sogaard, William Steinsland, Paul Thoresen

SOVIET UNION

Sergei Ageikin, Ilya Biakin, Igor Boldin, Alexander Chernykh, Sergei Goloshumov, Sergei Gorbunov, Andrei Karpin, Viacheslav Khalizov, Sergei Kharin, Andrei Martemianov, Andrei Matytsin, Sergei Nemchinov, Arkadi Obukhov, Sergei Priakhin, Evgeny Shtepa, Valeri Shyraev, Oleg Starkov, Vladimir Tiurikov, Leonid Trukhno, German Volgin

SWEDEN

Tommy Albelin, Peter Andersson, Jacob Bergman, Kjell Dahlin, Per-Erik Eklund, Roger Eliasson, Jacob Gustavsson, Per Hedenstrom, Mikael Hjaelm, Erik Holmberg, Jens Johansson, Jan Karlsson, Mats Kihlstrom, Tommy Lehman, Thomas Ljungberg, Jon Lundstrom, Magnus Roupe, Ulf Samuelsson, Tomas Sandstrom, Anders Wickberg

UNITED STATES

Tom Barrasso, Chris Cichoski, Ron Duda, Rich Erdall, Tony Granato, Scott Harlow, Jim Johannson, Tony Kellin, Brian Lawton, Mark Maroste, Dan McFall, Kelly Miller, Andy Otto, Peter Sawkins, Vensy Sebek, Chris Seychel, Tim Thomas, John Vanbiesbrouck, Arnie Vargas, Rick Zombo

WEST GERMANY

Florian Aeger, Markus Berwanger, Harald Birk, Hans-Georg Eder, Georg Franz, Engelbert Grzesiczek, Rainer Guck, Josef Heiss, Franz Ibelherr, Axel Kammerer, Walter Kirchmaier, Georg Kisslinger, Uwe Krupp, Andreas Niederberger, Robert Sterflinger, Bernhard Truntschka, Bernd Wagner, Joe Wassereck, Peter Weigl, Alfred Weiss

FINAL STANDINGS

	GP	W	L	T	GF	GA	P	GAA	SO	PIM
Soviet Union	7	7	0	0	50	15	14	2.14	0	82
Czechoslovakia	7	5	1	1	43	22	11	3.14	1	121
CANADA	7	4	2	1	39	24	9	3.43	2	101
Sweden	7	4	3	0	35	23	8	3.29	0	92
United States	7	3	4	0	28	29	6	4.14	0	88
Finland	7	3	4	0	35	29	6	4.14	0	92
West Germany	7	1	6	0	14	46	2	6.57	0	60*
Norway	7	0	7	0	13	69	0	9.86	0	90

* won Fair Play Cup

RESULTS

(all games played at Leningrad)

December 26	Canada 4	West Germany 0
	Soviet Union 10	Norway 1
	Finland 6	Sweden 4
	Czechoslovakia 6	United States 4
December 27	Canada 4	United States 2
	Soviet Union 4	Czechoslovakia 3
	Sweden 4	West Germany 2
	Finland 10	Norway 2
December 29	Canada 6	Finland 3
	Soviet Union 12	West Germany 2
	Czechoslovakia 9	Norway 2
	Sweden 4	United States 1

December 30	Soviet Union 7	Canada 3
	Czechoslovakia 4	Sweden 2
	West Germany 4	Norway 2
	United States 4	Finland 2
January 1	Canada 7	Czechoslovakia 7
	Finland 9	West Germany 1
	Sweden 15	Norway 3
	Soviet Union 5	United States 3
January 2	Sweden 5	Canada 2
	Soviet Union 7	Finland 2
	Czechoslovakia 9	West Germany 0
	United States 8	Norway 3
January 4	Canada 13	Norway 0
	Soviet Union 5	Sweden 1
	Czechoslovakia 5	Finland 3
	United States 6	West Germany 5

TEAM CANADA GAME SUMMARIES

December 26   *Canada 4*   *West Germany 0*

First Period

No Scoring

> PENALTIES: Sterflinger (WGer) 2:25, Derkatch (Can) 6:07, Sterflinger (WGer) 9:28, Andreychuk (Can) 19:26

Second Period

1. Canada, Turgeon (Andreychuk) .... 1:35(pp)
2. Canada, Andreychuk (Eagles) 9:05
3. Canada, Verbeek (Eagles) .... 11:06(sh)

> PENALTIES: Weigl (WGer) 0:26, Lemieux (Can) 2:36, Andreychuk (Can) 9:50

Third Period

4. Canada, Turgeon (Lemieux, Trader).. 1:28

> PENALTIES: Flatley (Can) 3:59, Weigl (WGer) 8:25, Eagles (Can) 12:38, Verbeek (Can) 14:21

Shots on Goal:

unknown

In Goal:

Canada — Sands
West Germany — Heiss

December 27   Canada 4   United States 2

First Period

1. United States, Otto (Thomas) 7:34
2. United States, Erdall (unassisted)... 10:40(pp)
3. Canada, Flatley (Trader) .... 15:34(pp)
4. Canada, Boutilier (Cyr, Morrison) .... 16:56(pp)

   PENALTIES: Andreychuk (Can) 3:43, U.S. bench 5:14, Cirella (Can) 9:47, Granato (U.S.) 14:08, Kellin (U.S.) 15:14, Leeman (Can) 18:25

Second Period

5. Canada, Sherven (Lemieux) 13:38

   PENALTIES: Andreychuk (Can) 14:19

Third Period

6. Canada, Flatley (Boutilier) 10:40

   PENALTIES: Seychel (U.S.) 13:10, Tanti (Can) 18:38

Shots on Goal:

unknown

In Goal:

Canada — Vernon
United States — Vanbiesbrouck

December 29   Canada 6   Finland 3

First Period

1. Canada, Yzerman (unassisted) 4:54
2. Canada, Andreychuk (unassisted) 9:42
3. Canada, Morrison (unassisted) 9:59
4. Finland, Jarvi (Helminen) 11:57

   PENALTIES: Jutila (Fin) & Cyr (Can) 0:36, Laksola (Fin) & Cyr (Can) 6:07, Siren (Fin) 13:52, Andreychuk (Can) 15:41

Second Period

5. Canada, Shaw (Leeman) .... 11:15(pp)
6. Finland, Jarvi (unassisted) 12:15

   PENALTIES: Lemieux (Can) 3:37, Can bench 5:49, Trader (Can) 8:41, Henriksson (Fin) 10:37, Jarvenpaa (Fin) 18:11

Third Period

7. Finland, Saarinen (unassisted) 2:41
8. Canada, Turgeon (Sherven) 14:23
9. Canada, Andreychuk (Lemieux) 16:49

   PENALTIES: Cirella (Can) 18:41

Shots on Goal:

unknown

In Goal:

Canada — Sands
Finland — Rautiainen

December 30   Soviet Union 7   Canada 3

First Period

1. Soviet Union, Nemchinov (Kharin, Biakin) 14:43
2. Soviet Union, Trukhno (unassisted) 15:05
3. Soviet Union, Shtepa (Prakhin) .... 16:00(sh)

PENALTIES: Flatley (Can) 4:44, Biakin (Sov) & Trader (Can) 6:07, Trukhno (Sov) 15:17, Patrick (Can) 19:27, Shaw (Can) & Trukhno (Sov) 19:57

Second Period

4. Soviet Union, Gorbunov (Biakin, Boldin) 1:07
5. Soviet Union, Nemchinov (Ageikin) 2:59
6. Soviet Union, Trukhno (Starkov) 9:49
7. Canada, Eagles (unassisted) 10:34

PENALTIES: Turgeon (Can) 3:30, Trader (Can) 5:08, Volgin (Sov) 6:31, Andreychuk (Can) 7:27, Biakin (Sov) 13:36, Boutilier (Can) 19:03

Third Period

8. Canada, Yzerman (unassisted) 10:28
9. Soviet Union, Volgin (unassisted) .... 11:15(pp)
10. Canada, Derkatch (Sherven) 16:56

PENALTIES: Trukhno (Sov — high-sticking major) 3:53, Lemieux (Can) 6:59, Cirella (Can) 11:03, Cyr (Can — major, misconduct) & Prakhin (Sov — major) 12:14, Verbeek (Can) 18:16

Shots on Goal:

unknown

In Goal:

Canada — Sands/Vernon (Vernon [one goal] replaced Sands [6 goals] to start 3rd)
Soviet Union — Karpin

January 1   Canada 7   Czechoslovakia 7

First Period

1. Czechoslovakia, Klima (Kames, Latal) 12:07
2. Canada, Morrison (Leeman, Verbeek) .... 14:08(pp)

PENALTIES: Latal (Cze) 1:02, Trader (Can) 3:14, Ruzicka (Cze) 13:18, Hasek (Cze) 18:00

Second Period

3. Czechoslovakia, Ruzicka (unassisted) 0:56
4. Czechoslovakia, Hornak (Klima, Kames) 2:48
5. Canada, Cyr (Patrick, Verbeek) 3:13
6. Canada, Flatley (Tanti, Derkatch) 4:14
7. Czechoslovakia, Rosol (Ruzicka) 6:16
8. Czechoslovakia, Hornak (Jonak, Ruzicka) .... 9:42(pp)
9. Czechoslovakia, Dolana (Jiroutek) 9:51
10. Canada, Turgeon (Eagles) 13:34
11. Canada, Morrison (Cyr) 14:05
12. Canada, Leeman (Tanti, Derkatch) 17:52
13. Czechoslovakia, Ruzicka (Dolana) 19:24

PENALTIES: Musil (Cze) 7:01, Yzerman (Can) 7:27, Andreychuk (Can) 7:54, Prachar (Cze) & Turgeon (Can) 15:04

Third Period

14. Canada, Verbeek (Eagles, Turgeon) 16:02

PENALTIES: Jonak (Cze) 9:35, Klima (Cze) & Tanti (Can) 15:20

Shots on Goal:

Canada   **44**
Czechoslovakia   **29**

In Goal:

Canada — Vernon/Sands (Sands [no goals] replaced Vernon [7 goals] to start 3rd)
Czechoslovakia — Hasek

January 2   *Sweden 5*   *Canada 2*

First Period

1. Sweden, Hjaelm (Wikberg) .... 13:47(pp)
2. Sweden, Anderson (Lehman, Roupe) 15:09
3. Sweden, Sandstrom (unassisted) 18:25

PENALTIES: Turgeon (Can) 12:58, Patrick (Can) & Holmberg (Swe) 17:32

Second Period

4. Sweden, Lehman (Dahlin) 5:27
5. Canada, Derkatch (Tanti) 8:51

PENALTIES: Turgeon (Can) 6:03, Anderson (Swe) 12:25

Third Period

6. Canada, Lemieux (Sherven) 7:56
7. Sweden, Sandstrom (unassisted) 19:21

PENALTIES: Karlsson (Swe) 9:38

Shots on Goal:

unknown

In Goal:

Canada — Sands
Sweden — Gustavsson

January 4   *Canada 13*   *Norway 0*

First Period

1. Canada, Lemieux (Andreychuk, Boutilier) 1:28
2. Canada, Boutilier (Morrison, Cyr) 9:50
3. Canada, Andreychuk (Lemieux, Yzerman) 10:40
4. Canada, Derkatch (Patrick) 19:33
5. Canada, Lemieux (Andreychuk) 19:41

   PENALTIES: Flatley (Can) 1:42, Lemieux (Can) 13:58, Kristiansen (Nor) 15:37

Second Period

6. Canada, Trader (Derkatch) .... 7:52(pp)
7. Canada, Lemieux (Andreychuk, Yzerman) 8:50
8. Canada, Andreychuk (Lemieux) 13:06
9. Canada, Lemieux (Boutilier, Vernon) 13:22
10. Canada, Flatley (Tanti, Derkatch) 17:05
11. Canada, Andreychuk (Yzerman, Trader) .... 19:33(sh)

   PENALTIES: Verbeek (Can) 5:34, Eriksen (Nor) 7:28, Hoff (Nor) 18:07

Third Period

12. Canada, Eagles (Shaw, Turgeon) .... 2:46(pp)
13. Canada, Trader (Andreychuk) .... 19:25(ea)

   PENALTIES: Bergseng (Nor) 0:51, Thoresen (Nor) & Lemieux (Can) 12:27, Thoresen (Nor) & Tanti (Can) 19:07

Shots on Goal:

Canada	**66**
Norway	**6**

In Goal:

Canada — Vernon
Norway — Eriksen/Hansen (Hansen [8 goals] replaced Eriksen [5 goals] to start 3rd)

TEAM CANADA FINAL STATISTICS
1983 WORLD JUNIOR CHAMPIONSHIPS

			GP	G	A	P	PIM
15	F	Dave Andreychuk	7	6	5	11	14
24	F	Mario Lemieux	7	5	5	10	10

12	F	Dale Derkatch	7	3	4	7	2
10	F	Sylvain Turgeon	7	4	2	6	8
8	F	Mike Eagles	7	2	4	6	2
17	F	Mark Morrison	7	3	2	5	0
3	D	Larry Trader	7	2	3	5	8
5	D	Paul Boutilier	7	2	3	5	2
14	F	Steve Yzerman	7	2	3	5	2
20	F	Pat Flatley	7	4	0	4	6
18	F	Pat Verbeek	7	2	2	4	6
19	F	Paul Cyr	7	1	3	4	19
21	F	Gord Sherven	7	1	3	4	0
11	F	Toni Tanti	7	0	4	4	6
4	D	Gary Leeman	7	1	2	3	2
7	D	Brad Shaw	7	1	1	2	2
9	D	James Patrick(C)	7	0	2	2	4
30	G	Mike Vernon	4	0	1	1	0
2	D	Joe Cirella	7	0	0	0	6
1	G	Mike Sands	5	0	0	0	0

In Goal

	GP	W–L–T	MINS	GA	SO	AVG
Mike Vernon	4	2–0–0	180	10	1	3.33
Mike Sands	5	2–2–1	240	14	1	3.50

Goalie Notes:

1. Vernon [one goal] replaced Sands [6 goals] to start 3rd, December 30 vs. Soviet Union
2. Sands [no goals] replaced Vernon [7 goals] to start 3rd, January 1 vs. Czechoslovakia

Coach Dave King
Assistants Michel Morin/Doug Sauter

CANADIAN OFFICIALS AT THE 1983 WORLD JUNIOR CHAMPIONSHIPS

Sandy Proctor (referee) 6 games

TEAM CANADA ROSTER SUMMARY

Team Canada players 20
Drafted Into NHL 20
Played in NHL 19 (all but Derkatch)
Returning Players 4 (Boutilier, Cyr, Morrison, Patrick)

PLAYER REPRESENTATION BY LEAGUE

OHL	8	(Andreychuk, Cirella, Eagles, Sands, Shaw, Tanti, Trader, Verbeek, Yzerman)
WHL	4	(Cyr, Derkatch, Leeman, Morrison)
QMJHL	3	(Boutilier, Lemieux, Turgeon)
NHL	2	(Andreychuk, Vernon)
U.S. COLLEGE	3	(Flatley, Patrick, Sherven)

PLAYER REPRESENTATION BY AGE

19-year-olds	13	(Andreychuk, Boutilier, Cirella, Cyr, Eagles, Flatley, Morrison, Patrick, Sands, Sherven, Tanti, Trader, Vernon)
18-year-olds	4	(Derkatch, Leeman, Shaw, Verbeek)
17-year-olds	3	(Lemieux, Turgeon, Yzerman)

PLAYERS' CAREER PROFILES

Dave Andreychuk	Buffalo Sabres (NHL)
	last Junior team: Oshawa Generals (OHL)
	Selected 16th overall by Buffalo at 1982 Draft
	Played in the NHL 1982 to present
Paul Boutilier	St. Jean Beavers (QMJHL)
	Selected 21st overall by Islanders at 1981 Draft
	Played in the NHL 1981–89
Joe Cirella	Oshawa Generals (OHL)
	Selected 5th overall by Rockies at 1981 Draft
	Played in the NHL 1981–96
Paul Cyr	Victoria Cougars (WHL)
	Selected 9th overall by Buffalo at 1982 Draft
	Played in the NHL 1982–92
Dale Derkatch	Regina Pats (WHL)
	Selected 140th overall by Edmonton at 1983 Draft
	Did not play in the NHL
Mike Eagles	Kitchener Rangers (OHL)
	Selected 116th overall by Quebec at 1981 Draft
	Played in the NHL 1982 to present
Pat Flatley	University of Wisconsin Badgers (NCAA)
	Selected 21st overall by Islanders at 1982 Draft
	Played in the NHL 1983–97
Gary Leeman	Regina Pats (WHL)
	Selected 24th overall by Toronto at 1982 Draft
	Played in the NHL 1982–97

Mario Lemieux   Laval Voisins (QMJHL)
Selected 1st overall by Pittsbugh at 1984 Draft
Played in the NHL 1984–97

Mark Morrison   Victoria Cougars (WHL)
Selected 51st overall by Rangers at 1981 Draft
Played in the NHL 1981–84

James Patrick   University of North Dakota Fighting Sioux (NCAA)
Selected 9th overall by Rangers at 1981 Draft
Played in the NHL 1983 to present

Mike Sands   Sudbury Wolves (OHL)
Selected 31st overall by Minnesota at 1981 Draft
Played in the NHL 1984–87

Brad Shaw   Ottawa 67's (OHL)
Selected 86th overall by Detroit at 1982 Draft
Played in the NHL 1985–95

Gord Sherven   University of North Dakota Fighting Sioux (WCHA)
Selected 197th overall by Edmonton at 1981 Draft
Played in the NHL 1983–88

Tony Tanti   Oshawa Generals (OHL)
Selected 12th overall by Chicago at 1981 Draft
Played in the NHL 1981–92

Larry Trader   London Knights (OHL)
Selected 86th overall by Detroit at 1981 Draft
Played in the NHL 1982–88

Sylvain Turgeon   Hull Olympiques (QMJHL)
Selected 2nd overall by Hartford at 1983 Draft
Played in the NHL 1983–95

Pat Verbeek   Sudbury Wolves (OHL)
Selected 43rd overall by New Jersey at 1982 Draft
Played in the NHL 1982 to present

Mike Vernon   Calgary Flames (NHL)
last Junior team: Calgary Wranglers (WHL)
Selected 56th overall by Calgary at 1981 Draft
Played in the NHL 1982 to present

Steve Yzerman   Peterborough Petes (OHL)
Selected 4th overall by Detroit at 1983 Draft
Played in the NHL 1983 to present

1984 WORLD JUNIOR CHAMPIONSHIPS SWEDEN, DECEMBER 25, 1983-- JANUARY 3, 1984

FINAL PLACINGS

GOLD MEDAL   Soviet Union
SILVER MEDAL   Finland
BRONZE MEDAL   Czechoslovakia
Fourth Place   **CANADA**
Fifth Place   Sweden
Sixth Place   United States
Seventh Place   West Germany
Eighth Place   Switzerland*

promoted from "B" pool in 1983; relegated to "B" pool for 1985

ALL-STAR TEAM

GOAL   Evgeny Belosheikin (Soviet Union)
DEFENCE   Alexei Gusarov (Soviet Union)
    Frantisek Musil (Czechoslovakia)
FORWARD   Petr Rosol (Czechoslovakia)
    Raimo Helminen (Finland)
    Nikolai Borschevsky (Soviet Union)

DIRECTORATE AWARDS

BEST GOALIE   Alan Perry (United States)
BEST DEFENCEMAN   Alexei Gusarov (Soviet Union)
BEST FORWARD   Raimo Helminen (Finland)

COACH BRIAN KILREA

Dave King, who had won a gold and bronze as junior coach, was devoting all his time and energy to the upcoming Olympic Winter Games in Sarajevo. The junior job, therefore, was offered to Kilrea, one of the most respected hockey men in the country.

Kilrea was the nephew of three NHL uncles — Hector, Wally, and Ken — and his brief time in the NHL was highlighted when he scored the first goal in the history of the Los Angeles Kings, at the Long Beach Arena. He began coaching the Ottawa 67's in 1974, and in the next ten years won five OHL championships and a Memorial Cup. He was voted coach of the year in both 1981 and 1982, and never had a losing season with Ottawa. After this season, he became an assistant coach to Al Arbour with the Islanders, and assumed he was being groomed for the head job. Two years later, he found he was wrong, and returned to Ottawa, where he has been ever since. He is now the winningest coach in the history of the OHL.

THE PLAYERS

Because this was an Olympic year, there were a few wrinkles in the way the team was put together. Coach Kilrea invited twenty-eight players to a training camp in Ottawa from December 17 to 19. He named twenty to the final roster. The NHL, as always, played both friend and foe as far as player loans went. The Leafs let number one goalie Ken Wregget go, but five bona fide stars had already made such an impact in the NHL that teams couldn't justify sending them away for experience and maturity: Bob Errey, Scott Stevens, Brian Bellows, Sylvain Turgeon, and Pat Verbeek were all eligible to play (under twenty as of December 31, 1983), but none would have benefited from the competition. Dave King's Olympic team loaned Dave Gagner, J.J. Daigneault, and Craig Redmond, feeling the extra tournament pressure would be a perfect tuneup for the show in Sarajevo.

The most notable absentee was Mario Lemieux, who sent a letter to all Quebec teams and coach Kilrea saying he had no intention of representing his country in Sweden at the World Junior Championships. He claimed he wanted to spend time with his family, but admitted he was upset by the way Dave King had treated him the year before: "I don't have a good relationship with King," Lemieux said. "I only played three games out of seven last year, only a couple of shifts a game. The coach did not talk to me at all when I was there." This was the first in a long list of international no-shows for Lemieux, who was subsequently suspended from league play for the duration of the WJC. The QMJHL argued that by refusing to play he was violating his junior contract.

Two other players of interest were seventeen-year-old Kirk Muller and eighteen-year-old Russ Coutnall. Along with Gagner and Daigneault, they were among a select number of players who took part in both a World Junior Championship and an Olympics in the same year.

THE CUTS

The young Nats finished their Canadian-based training with a sound 10–3 exhibition win over the 67s in Ottawa, leaving the coaches with the daunting task of having to trim the roster by four players before the team flew to Sweden the next day.

The game on December 19 put Diduck and Evason on the team. Craig Redmond was out with an injury, and the Vancouver Canucks refused to loan Michel Petit. Paul Lawless (Windsor, OHL) and Murray Craven (Medicine Hat, WHL) were the first to go. Sergio Momesso (Shawinigan, QMJHL), Alan Kerr (Seattle, WHL), Doug Bodger (Kamloops, WHL), and goalie Luc Guenette (Quebec City, QMJHL) were the final cuts before the team left for Stockholm.

THE SECOND ROSTER IN THE NHL

Canada is blessed with more hockey talent than any other nation. When the WJC comes around each year, Canada's best young players are all in the NHL. The team that represents the country officially is always the second-best Canada can provide. For instance, consider the eligible players for the WJC who were already regulars in the NHL: Brian Bellows, Sylvain Turgeon, Pat Verbeek, Steve Yzerman, Murray Craven, Lane Lambert, Bob Errey, Andrew McBain, Dan Quinn, Adam Creighton, Paul Lawless, Nevin Markwart, Gord Kluzak, Scott Stevens, and Richard Kromm.

THE EXHIBITIONS

The Canadians played two games in Sweden to recover from jet lag. They also had to get used to the larger ice surface and European officiating, perennial difficulties facing any Canadian team playing in Europe. They lost the first game 5–4 at the Linkoping Ishall, a close score despite having 13 penalties to Sweden's four. Afterwards, they learned that the Leafs had loaned Gary Leeman to the team, and that J.J. Daigneault and Dave Gagner would join them after playing for the Canadian Olympic team at the Izvestia tournament in Moscow. In the second game, they blew a 5–1 lead and had to rally for a 7–6 win over a Swedish team called HV71 (after a local weapons factory) at the Rosenloundhallen in Jonkoping. The two games accomplished what had been hoped for, and the team set out to the real McCoy, intent on improving upon their bronze medal the previous year.

J.J. Daigneault scores in Canada's 6-0 win over Germany at Nykoping,
Sweden. For three years, the juniors wore the innovative Cooperall pants instead
of the traditional combination of knee-length pants and shin pads.

FAKING AN INJURY HOCKEY ESPIONAGE?

Sometimes a soft player will be accused of exaggerating the extent of an injury. But how about a doctor? In Canada's game against Finland on Christmas night, forward Gary Lacey injured his wrist. He was in pain but played the next day against the Americans. He visited a Swedish doctor, who told him there was a hairline fracture. He put a cast on Lacey, who missed the rest of the tournament. When he returned to Canada, he had the wrist X-rayed again. No fracture was discovered, only calcium deposits. The cast came off, and he scored two goals for the Marlies in a 5–3 loss to London that night.

TOURNAMENT FORMAT

The format was simple: all countries were placed in one standing, and each played every other nation once. First place won gold, second silver, third bronze, and ties would be decided by results against the tying teams.

THE OPPOSITION

CZECHOSLOVAKIA

Petr Briza, Libor Dolana, Petr Holubar, Ernest Hornak, Milos Hrubes, Jiri Jiroutek, Vladimir Kames, Kamil Kastak, Petr Klima, Lumir Kotala, Frantisek Musil, Jiri Paska, Stanislav Pavelec, Ivo Pesat, Jozef Petho, Michal Pivonka, Petr Rosol, Martin Strida, Petr Svoboda, Igor Talpas

FINLAND

Ari Haanpaa, Erik Hamalainen, Raimo Helminen, Iiro Jarvi, Janne Karelius, Esa Keskinen, Pekka Laksola, Harri Laurila, Mikko Makela, Reijo Mikkolainen, Jarmo Myllys, Joel Paunio, Tommy Pohja, Christian Ruuttu, Vesa Salo, Ville Siren, Ari Suutari, Esa Tikkanen, Jari Torkki, Jarmo Uronen

SOVIET UNION

Evgeny Belosheikin, Igor Boldin, Nikolai Borschevsky, Alexander Chernykh, Alexei Cherviak, Evgeny Chizamin, Alexei Gusarov, Yuri Khimilev, Vasili Lamenev, Alexander Lisenko, Andrei Lomakin, Igor Martinov, Oleg Mikulchik, Sergei Nemchinov, Alexander Semak, Sergei Shendelev, Alexander Smirnov, Mikhail Tatarinov, Igor Viazimkin, Sergei Vostrikov

SWEDEN

Tommy Albelin, Peter Andersson, Mikael Andersson, Lars Bystrom, Henrik Cedergren, Per Forsberg, Jacob Gustavsson, Anders Huss, Jens Johansson, Jan Karlsson, Mats Kihlstrom, Tommy Lehman, Jon Lundstrom, Niklas Mannberg, Jorgen Marklund, Ulf Nilsson, Ulf Samuelsson, Tomas Sandstrom, Roland Westin, Mikael Wikstrom

SWITZERLAND

Markus Bleuer, Andreas Caduff, Andrea Cahenzli, Daniel Dubois, Rene Gehri, Marc Heitzmann, Felix Hollenstein, Andreas Jurt, Bernhard Lauber, Markus Maef, Thomas Mueller, Patrik Mueller, Philipp Neuenschwander, Patrice Niederhausen, Guido Pfosi, Martin Rauch, Jean-Luc Rod, Christof Ruefenacht, Pascal Speck, Dino Stecher

UNITED STATES

Paul Ames, Al Bourbeau, Wally Chapman, Bob Curtis, Clark Donatelli, Mike Golden, Tony Granato, Kevin Hatcher, Jim Johansson, Brian Johnson, Brian Jopling, Mark LaVarre, Stephen Leach, Craig Mack, Todd Okerlund, Alan Perry, Scott Sandelin, Gary Suter, Alfie Turcotte, Marty Wiitala

WEST GERMANY

Fritz Brunner, Peter Draisaitl, Sven Erhart, Thomas Frohlich, Frank Gentges, Jorg Hanft, Franz Ibelherr, Axel Kammerer, Michael Komma, Rupert Meister, Klaus Pillmaier, Gunther Preuss, Christian Reuter, Michael Rumrich, Udo Schmid, Robert Sterflinger, Bernhard Truntschka, Bernd Wagner, Alfred Weiss, Tauno Zobel

FINAL STANDINGS

	GP	W	L	T	GF	GA	P	GAA	SO	PIM
Soviet Union	7	6	0	1	50	17	13	2.43	0	62
Finland	7	6	1	0	44	21	12	3.00	0	103
Czechoslovakia	7	5	2	0	51	24	10	3.43	0	91
CANADA	7	4	2	1	39	17	9	2.43	2	97
Sweden	7	3	4	0	27	28	6	4.00	0	104
United States	7	2	5	0	32	38	4	5.43	0	114
West Germany	7	1	6	0	12	54	2	7.71	0	74
Switzerland	7	0	7	0	16	72	0	10.23	0	44*

* won Fair Play Cup

RESULTS

December 25	Nykoping	Finland 4	Canada 2
	Norrkoping	Soviet Union 14	Switzerland 2
	Nykoping	Czechoslovakia 6	West Germany 1
	Norrkoping	Sweden 4	United States 1
December 26	Nykoping	Canada 5	United States 2
	Nykoping	Sweden 5	Switzerland 2
	Norrkoping	Soviet Union 9	West Germany 1
	Norrkoping	Finland 8	Czechoslovakia 7
December 28	Norrkoping	Canada 12	Switzerland 0
	Nykoping	Soviet Union 3	Finland 1
	Nykoping	Sweden 11	West Germany 2
	Norrkoping	Czechoslovakia 10	United States 1

December 29	Nykoping	Canada 7	West Germany 0
	Nykoping	Czechoslovakia 13	Switzerland 2
	Norrkoping	Finland 4	Sweden 1
	Norrkoping	Soviet Union 7	United States 4
December 31	Norrkoping	Canada 6	Sweden 2
	Nykoping	Soviet Union 6	Czechoslovakia 4
	Norrkoping	West Germany 4	Switzerland 3
	Nykoping	Finland 7	United States 2
January 2	Norrkoping	Canada 3	Soviet Union 3
	Nykoping	Finland 12	Switzerland 4
	Nykoping	Czechoslovakia 5	Sweden 2
	Norrkoping	United States 10	West Germany 2
January 3	Nykoping	Czechoslovakia 6	Canada 4
	Nykoping	Finland 8	West Germany 2
	Norrkoping	Soviet Union 8	Sweden 2
	Norrkoping	United States 12	Switzerland 3

TEAM CANADA GAME SUMMARIES

December 25   *Finland 4*   *Canada 2*

First Period

1. Finland, Helminen (Haanpaa) 1:11
2. Finland, Pohja (Haanpaa) 1:31
3. Finland, Helminen (Ruuttu) .... 4:01(sh)
4. Canada, MacLean (unassisted) .... 14:21(pp)

   PENALTIES: Tikkanen (Fin) 3:08, Byers (Can) 5:43, Pohja (Fin) & Paterson (Can) 8:39, Heath (Can) 9:56, Tikkanen (Fin) 13:47, Cote (Can) 16:40

Second Period

5. Finland, Torkki (Ruuttu, Paunio) .... 6:56(pp)

   PENALTIES: Cassidy (Can) 4:58, Pohja (Fin) 7:04, Paterson (Can) 9:59, Diduck (Can) 13:08, Pohja (Fin) 15:20, Lacey (Can) 17:51

Third Period

6. Canada, Derkatch (Leeman) 11:29

   PENALTIES: Paunio (Fin) 2:08, MacLean (Can) 7:52, Diduck (Can) 8:52, Laurila (Fin) 9:27, Derkatch (Can) 14:35, Salo (Fin) 18:46

Shots on Goal:

| Canada | 9 | 6 | 14 | **29** |
| Finland | 14 | 8 | 6 | **28** |

In Goal:

Canada — Wregget
Finland — Myllys

December 26   Canada 5   United States 2

First Period

1. Canada, Muller (Leeman) 2:04
2. Canada, Courtnall (Evason, Leeman) 7:04
3. Canada, Derkatch (Byers) 7:27

PENALTIES: Johnson (U.S.) 7:39, Heath (Can) 11:48

Second Period

4. United States, Granato (Johansson) 2:03
5. United States, Turcotte (unassisted) .... 7:01 (pp)
6. Canada, MacLean (Muller) 9:59
7. Canada, Evason (Heath) 11:22

PENALTIES: Cote (Can) 6:16, Lacey (Can) 18:30

Third Period

No Scoring

PENALTIES: MacLean (Can) 3:19, Curtis (U.S.) 17:37

Shots on Goal:

Canada	16	17	20	53
United States	7	8	4	19

In Goal:

Canada — Bester
United States — Perry

December 28   Canada 12   Switzerland 0

First Period

1. Canada, Courtnall (Daigneault) 9:35

PENALTIES: Heath (Can) 1:33

Second Period

2. Canada, Evason (unassisted) 1:56
3. Canada, Derkatch (Hodgson) 3:02
4. Canada, Courtnall (Leeman) .... 8:13 (pp)
5. Canada, Courtnall (MacLean, Heath) 18:15
6. Canada, Gagner (Courtnall) 18:29
7. Canada, Gagner (unassisted) 18:38
8. Canada, Evason (Courtnall) 19:23

PENALTIES: Dubois (Swi) 7:08, Leeman (Can) 10:08, Gehri (Swi) 13:51

Third Period

9. Canada, MacLean (Leeman) 0:43
10. Canada, Evason (Courteau) 7:09
11. Canada, MacLean (Muller) 14:45

12. Canada, Heath (Muller) 16:47

  PENALTIES: Heath (Can) 1:17, Hodgson (Can) 11:43

Shots on Goal:

Canada	16	25	22	63
Switzerland	4	6	2	12

In Goal:

  Canada — Bester
  Switzerland — Stecher

December 29 Canada 7 West Germany 0

First Period

1. Canada, Byers (Shaw, Hodgson) 0:36

  PENALTIES: Truntschka (WGer) 3:26, Cote (Can — major) 18:51

Second Period

2. Canada, Gagner (Courtnall) 10:11
3. Canada, Leeman (unassisted) 11:07
4. Canada, Hodgson (unassisted) 11:39
5. Canada, Courtnall (Gagner, Daigneault) 15:54
6. Canada, Courtnall (unassisted) 16:07

  PENALTIES: Sterflinger (WGer) 6:49, Cassidy (Can) 11:40

Third Period

7. Canada, Courtnall (Leeman) 19:11

  PENALTIES: Hanft (WGer) & Leeman (Can) 11:29

Shots on Goal:

Canada	10	20	17	47
West Germany	3	9	5	17

In Goal:

  Canada — Wregget
  West Germany — Meister

December 31 Canada 6 Sweden 2

First Period

1. Sweden, Huss (Samuelsson, Cedergren) .... 4:06(pp)

  PENALTIES: Kihlstrom (Swe) 1:10, Byers (Can) 3:25, Muller (Can) 4:35,
  Daigneault (Can) & Muller (Can — misconduct) 5:04, Leeman (Can) 15:31,
  Sandstrom (Swe) 16:09, Cedergren (Swe) 19:04

Second Period

2. Sweden, Sandstrom (unassisted) 4:13

3. Canada, Derkatch (Hodgson, Leeman) 8:53
4. Canada, Heath (Shaw, Cote) .... 11:47(pp)
5. Canada, Derkatch (Hodgson) 16:42

PENALTIES: Lundstrom (Swe) 5:27, Kihlstrom (Swe) 10:12, Paterson (Can) 12:26, Gagner (Can) 17:18

Third Period

6. Canada, MacLean (Leeman) .... 5:00(pp)
7. Canada, Gagner (Heath, Cassidy).. 6:31
8. Canada, Evason (unassisted) 18:27

PENALTIES: Karlsson (Swe) 4:22, Paterson (Can) 12:04, Cote (Can) 13:12, Derkatch (Can) & Sandstrom (Swe) & Samuelsson (Swe — misconduct) 19:52, Sandstrom (Swe) & Samuelsson (Swe — misconduct) 20:00

Shots on Goal:

Canada	4	8	15	27
Sweden	13	12	10	35

In Goal:

Canada — Wregget
Sweden — Gustavsson

January 2   *Canada 3*   *Soviet Union 3*

First Period

1. Canada, Leeman (Courtnall) 9:17
2. Canada, MacLean (Paterson, Heath) 15:39

PENALTIES: MacLean (Can) 1:43, Martinov (Sov) 7:23

Second Period

3. Soviet Union, Viazimkin (Semak) 6:11
4. Soviet Union, Borschevsky (Gusarov) 12:48
5. Canada, Muller (MacLean, Heath) .... 18:16(pp)
6. Soviet Union, Boldin (Semak) 19:16

PENALTIES: Gagner (Can) 0:39, Belosheikin (Sov — served by Shendelev) 7:04, Shendelev (Sov) 18:01

Third Period

No Scoring

PENALTIES: Leeman (Can) 3:00

Shots on Goal:

Canada	15	10	12	37
Soviet Union	17	7	6	30

In Goal:

Canada — Wreggett
Soviet Union — Belosheikin

January 3   *Czechoslovakia 6*   *Canada 4*

First Period

1. Canada, MacLean (Heath) ....6:51(pp)
2. Czechoslovakia, Dolana (Talpas) 16:18
3. Canada, Heath (Gagner) 16:27

    PENALTIES: Svoboda (Cze) & Heath (Can) 4:08, Talpas (Cze) 6:40, Muller (Can) 7:24, Muller (Can) 11:18, Klima (Cze) & Musil (Cze) 18:55

Second Period

4. Czechoslovakia, Rosol (Svoboda) 2:40
5. Canada, Leeman (Courtnall) 14:17

    PENALTIES: Hodgson (Can) 6:11, Leeman (Can) 12:11, Rosol (Cze) 15:55, Heath (Can) 19:55

Third Period

6. Czechoslovakia, Dolana (Kames) 13:43
7. Czechoslovakia, Kotala (Petho, Jiroutek) 14:06
8. Czechoslovakia, Kames (unassisted) 14:54
9. Canada, Evason (Courtnall)..15:10
10. Czechoslovakia, Kames (unassisted) ....19:25(en)

    PENALTIES: Rosol (Cze) 3:41, Cote (Can) 16:34, Paterson (Can) & Rosol (Cze) 19:23, Kames (Cze) 19:25

Shots on Goal:

Canada	11	8	9	**28**
Czechoslovakia	15	10	15	**40**

In Goal:

    Canada — Wregget
    Czechoslovakia — Briza

TEAM CANADA FINAL STATISTICS
1984 WORLD JUNIOR CHAMPIONSHIPS

			GP	G	A	P	PIM
9	F	Russ Courtnall(C)	7	7	6	13	0
19	D	Gary Leeman	7	3	8	11	10
8	F	John MacLean	7	7	2	9	6
12	F	Randy Heath	7	3	6	9	12
11	F	Dean Evason	7	6	1	7	0
17	F	Dave Gagner	7	4	2	6	4
26	F	Dale Derkatch	7	5	0	5	4
10	F	Kirk Muller	7	2	3	5	16
16	F	Dan Hodgson	7	1	4	5	4
20	F	Lyndon Byers	6	1	1	2	4
3	D	J.J. Daigneault	7	0	2	2	2

4	D	Brad Shaw(A)	7	0	2	2	0
22	D	Sylvain Cote	7	0	1	1	13
5	D	Mark Paterson	7	0	1	1	10
6	D	Bruce Cassidy	7	0	1	1	4
21	F	Yves Courteau	7	0	1	1	0
23	D	Gerald Diduck	7	0	0	0	4
27	F	Gary Lacey	5	0	0	0	4
1	G	Ken Wregget	5	0	0	0	0
30	G	Allan Bester	2	0	0	0	0

In Goal

	GP	W-L-T	MINS	GA	SO	AVG
Allan Bester	2	1–0–0	120	0	1	1.00
Ken Wregget	5	2–2–1	300	14	1	2.80

Coach Brian Kilrea
Assistants Terry Simpson/Georges Lariviere

CANADIAN OFFICIALS AT THE 1984 WORLD JUNIOR CHAMPIONSHIPS

none

TEAM CANADA ROSTER SUMMARY

Team Canada players   20
Drafted Into NHL   19 (all but Lacey)
Played In NHL   18 (all but Derkatch, Lacey)
Returning Players   3 (Derkatch, Leeman, Shaw)

PLAYER REPRESENTATION BY LEAGUE

OHL	7	(Bester, Cassidy, Lacey, MacLean, Muller, Paterson, Shaw)
WHL	7	(Byers, Courtnall, Derkatch, Diduck, Evason, Heath, Hodgson)
QMJHL	2	(Cote, Courteau)
NHL	2	(Leeman, Wregget)
OTHER*	2	(Daigneault, Gagner)

* *Canadian Olympic team*

PLAYER REPRESENTATION BY AGE

19-year-olds	13	(Bester, Byers, Courteau, Derkatch, Evason, Gagner, Heath, Lacey, Leeman, MacLean, Paterson, Shaw, Wregget)
18-year-olds	5	(Cassidy, Courtnall, Daigneult, Diduck, Hodgson)
17-year-olds	2	(Cote, Muller)

PLAYERS' CAREER PROFILES

Allan Bester   Brantford Alexanders (OHL)
Selected 48th overall by Toronto at 1983 Draft
Played in the NHL 1983–96

Lyndon Byers   Regina Pats (WHL)
Selected 39th overall by Boston at 1982 Draft
Played in the NHL 1983–93

Bruce Cassidy   Ottawa 67's (OHL)
Selected 18th overall by Chicago at 1983 Draft
Played in the NHL 1983–90

Sylvain Cote   Quebec Remparts (QMJHL)
Selected 11th overall by Hartford at 1984 Draft
Played in the NHL 1984 to present

Yves Courteau   Laval Voisins (QMJHL)
Selected 23rd overall by Detroit at 1982 Draft
Played in the NHL 1984–87

Russ Courtnall   Victoria Cougars (WHL)
Selected 7th overall by Toronto at 1983 Draft
Played in the NHL 1983 to present

J.J. Daigneault   Canadian Olympic Team
Selected 10th overall by Vancouver at 1984 Draft
Played in the NHL 1984 to present

Dale Derkatch   Regina Pats (WHL)
Selected 140th overall by Edmonton at 1983 Draft
Did not play in the NHL

Gerald Diduck   Lethbridge Broncos (WHL)
Selected 16th overall by Islanders at 1983 Draft
Played in the NHL 1984 to present

Dean Evason   Kamloops Junior Oilers (WHL)
Selected 89th overall by Washington at 1982 Draft
Played in the NHL 1983–96

Dave Gagner   Canadian Olympic Team
Selected 12th overall by Rangers at 1983 Draft
Played in the NHL 1984 to present

Randy Heath   Portland Winter Hawks (WHL)
Selected 33rd overall by Rangers at 1983 Draft
Played in the NHL 1984–86

Dan Hodgson   Prince Albert Raiders (WHL)
Selected 85th overall by Toronto at 1983 Draft
Played in the NHL 1985–89

Gary Lacey   Toronto Marlboros (OHL)
Not drafted
Did not play in the NHL

Gary Leeman   Toronto Maple Leafs (NHL)
last Junior team: Regina Pats (WHL)
Selected 24th overall by Toronto at 1982 Draft
Played in the NHL 1982–97

John MacLean   Oshawa Generals (OHL)
Selected 6th overall by New Jersey at 1983 Draft
Played in the NHL 1983 to present

Kirk Muller   Guelph Platers (OHL)
Selected 2nd overall by New Jersey at 1984 Draft
Played in the NHL 1984 to present

Mark Paterson   Ottawa 67's (OHL)
Selected 31st overall by Hartford at 1982 Draft
Played in the NHL 1982–86

Brad Shaw   Ottawa 67's (OHL)
Selected 86th overall by Detroit at 1982 Draft
Played in the NHL 1985–95

Ken Wregget   Toronto Maple Leafs (NHL)
last Junior team: Lethbridge Broncos (WHL)
Selected 45th overall by Toronto at 1982 Draft
Played in the NHL 1983 to present

1985 WORLD JUNIOR CHAMPIONSHIPS FINLAND, DECEMBER 23, 1984-- JANUARY 1, 1985

FINAL PLACINGS

GOLD MEDAL	**CANADA**
SILVER MEDAL	Czechoslovakia
BRONZE MEDAL	Soviet Union
Fourth Place	Finland
Fifth Place	Sweden
Sixth Place	United States
Seventh Place	West Germany
Eighth Place	Poland*

promoted from "B" pool in 1984; relegated to "B" pool for 1986

ALL-STAR TEAM

GOAL	Timo Lehkonen (Finland)
DEFENCE	Bobby Dollas (Canada)
	Mikhail Tatarinov (Soviet Union)
FORWARD	Mikko Makela (Finland)
	Michal Pivonka (Czechoslovakia)
	Esa Tikkanen (Finland)

DIRECTORATE AWARDS

BEST GOALIE	Craig Billington (Canada)
BEST DEFENCEMAN	Vesa Salo (Finland)
BEST FORWARD	Michal Pivonka (Czechoslovakia)

COACH TERRY SIMPSON

Simpson was named coach on October 17, 1984, but his seemingly quick rise had taken many a hard-working year. Like so many others before him, he was a player manque. He played four years of junior hockey with Estevan and a year with the Jacksonville Rockets of the Eastern League.

He was player-coach for an intermediate team in Shellbrook, Saskatchewan, in the mid-sixties while hoping to become an electrical engineer. The electrical stuff became less and less important as his team won five provincial championships, and his Drumheller Miners won the Allan Cup in 1968.

Simpson was offered the job of coaching the Prince Albert Raiders, then a Tier II team looking for an interim coach. He wound up staying fourteen years. In the first decade, the team won eight league championships and four Centennial Cups as Tier II Junior A champs. Thanks to Simpson, the team moved to Junior A in the Western Hockey League, the premier junior level in Canada. Simpson was chosen coach of the year the previous season while also acting as assistant to World Junior head coach Brian Kilrea at the 1984 Championships. An important trend was being set: the assistant from one World Junior becomes head coach the next. Apprenticeship and experience for the coaching staff is important.

THE INVITATIONS AND CAMP

Forty-six prospects were invited to the December camp, which began in Belleville on December 10 and moved to Ottawa three days later. The team left for Finland one week later. Coach Simpson had one week and two exhibition games against OHL teams to evaluate and pare the roster to twenty players. The final team had two friendlies in Finland before beginning the tournament on December 23.

As usual, the best junior players invited were the second-best available. The best were already in the NHL. This year, not able to go were Mario Lemieux, Steve Yzerman, Sylvain Cote, Sylvain Turgeon, Dan Quinn, and Craig Redmond. On the positive side, the Sabres loaned Adam Creighton to the team. There were also a few notables absent because of injuries: Fabian Joseph of the Marlies and Guy Rouleau of Longueuil. Jeff Brown hurt his shoulder early and was sent home.

THE CUTTING PROCESS

In Belleville, ten players were released in the morning and ten more in the afternoon. The next day, the final roster was more or less set. Cut were: Todd

*Canada and Finland played to a 4-4 tie at the 1985 World Juniors,
thanks to Mikko Makela's power-play goal early in the third period.*

Gill (Windsor, OHL), Mike Millar (Hamilton, OHL), Terry Carkner (Peterborough, OHL), Sergio Momesso (Shawinigan, QMJHL), Patrick Roy (Granby, QMJHL), Terry Zaporzan (Kelowna, WHL), Al Conroy (Medicine Hat, WHL), Bob Halkidis (London, OHL), Don Biggs (Oshawa, OHL), Jim Sandlak (London, OHL), Gord Walker (Kamloops, WHL), Brian Wilks (Kitchener, OHL), Bruce Cassidy (Ottawa, OHL), Jeff Reese (London, OHL), Gary Johnson (Medicine Hat, WHL), Shawn Burr (Kitchener, OHL), Craig Duncanson (Sudbury, OHL), Graeme Bonar (Sault Ste. Marie), Brian Benning (Portland, WHL), Doug Trapp (Regina, WHL), Claude Gosselin (Quebec, QMJHL), and Scott Mellanby (Wisconsin), Emmanuel Viveiros (Prince Albert, WHL), Dave Latta (Kitchener, OHL), Dave Lowry (London, OHL).

In two exhibition games, the junior nationals beat the Hamilton Steel Hawks 7–3, and the next night they beat the Ottawa 67's 9–3. After the games, coach Simpson made a goalie change, deciding to keep American collegian Norm Foster and returning Gary Johnson to Medicine Hat. Gary Roberts, a late invitee, was also sent back to his club in Ottawa.

As usual, Simpson and GM Sherry Bassin were criticized for cutting Gary Roberts. Bassin quipped, "It's like Mark Twain used to say. 'When I was 14 I couldn't believe how stupid my father was and when I was 21 I couldn't believe how much he'd learned in the last seven years.' 'How could you leave this guy off?' 'What about this guy?' Then we won. It's amazing how smart we became in seventeen days."

Dave Goertz of Prince Albert made the final cut but did not play in Helsinki because of an injury in the exhibition games. He was replaced at the last minute by Jim Sandlak of the London Knights, who had been cut the previous week.

MIDGET PROGRAM

December 1984 was another watershed period in the development of hockey in Canada. At this time a national midget team was set to play its first series of exhibition games, ten in all, against the finest from the Soviet Union. The under-17 level was augmented the next year by an under-18 group, thus ensuring the proper development of players from the midget level to junior and on to the NHL.

GOLD MEDAL DEJA VU

When Canada won the gold in Minnesota in 1982, the final game was against the Czechs, and they needed a tie to ensure first place. A 3–3 finish after withstanding a last-minute flurry from the Czechs ensured victory then, and in 1985 the situation was the same. Canada's last game was against Czechoslovakia, and because of a better goals for/against figure, Canada knew going into the game a tie would mean gold.

The key to success was Wendel Clark. Clark delivered the most famous hit in the history of the tournament when he hammered Soviet defenceman Mikhail Tatarinov out of consciousness, the game, and the tournament. Coach Terry Simpson had converted Clark, a defenceman with Saskatoon, to a forward, but in this game against the Czechs, he put Wendel back on defence for the first two periods because of injuries to his blue line corps. In the third, he gambled again and put Clark up on the wing, and it was Clark who tied the game for Canada at 13:43 of the third to ensure a tie and the gold medal.

The Czechs removed their goalie, Dominik Hasek, but couldn't win any of the important draws in the final minute to press the Canadian net. The Canadians watched from the stands as the Soviets beat the Finns 6–5 in the final game of the tournament. If the Finns had beaten the Russians by eight goals, they would have had twelve points and won the gold by goals differential. That, though, was not likely to happen.

The 1985 WJC saw a number of international stars establish themselves: Hasek for the Czechs; Esa Tikkanen for Finland; Valeri Kamensky and Igor Kravchuk for the Soviets; Craig Janney and Mike Richter for the Americans. But with Canada's win in the 1984 Canada Cup and a gold medal showing at the Spengler Cup just days before, the red and white maple leaf was certainly once again right where it should be — at the top of the world hockey heap.

Brian Bradley (#8) moves in on the Czech goal while Canadian forward-defenceman Wendel Clark (#6) watches the play develop.

TOURNAMENT FORMAT

All eight teams were placed in one standings, and a simple round robin schedule was adopted. In the case of a tie in the standings between two teams, the result of the game between those two would be the first tie-breaker. Goal differential was the second decider. The Soviets won the bronze despite finishing with the same number of points as fourth-place Finland because the Russians won the head-to-head game 6–5.

THE OPPOSITION

CZECHOSLOVAKIA

Ales Flasar, Leo Gudas, Eduard Hartmann, Dominik Hasek, Stanislav Horansky, Marian Horvath, Drahomir Kadlec, Tomas Kapusta, Kamil Kastak, Robert Kron, Vojtech Kucera, Jiri Kucera, Jiri Latal, Ladislav Lubina, Tomas Mares, Stanislav Medrik, Michal Pivonka, Petr Prajzler, Jaroslav Sevcik, Michal Tomek

FINLAND

Kari-Pekka Friman, Ari Haanpaa, Erik Hamalainen, Iiro Jarvi, Esa Keskinen, Harri Laurila, Timo Lehkonen, Mikko Makela, Mikko Mustala, Jarmo Myllys, Timo Norppa, Ossi Piitulainen, Vesa Ruotsalainen, Vesa Salo, Eerik Sjoblom, Ari Suutari, Arto Taipola, Esa Tikkanen, Jari Torkki, Kari Tuiskula

POLAND

Wladyslaw Balakowicz, Zbigniew Bryjak, Wlodzimierz Cieslik, Miroslaw Copija, Ludwik Czapka, Adam Dolinski, Adam Golinski, Jacek Kurowski, Marek Litwin, Jerzy Matras, Ryszard Mroz, Wojiech Musial, Ireneusz Pacula, Mariusz Puzio, Marek Stebnicki, Janusz Syposz, Roman Szewczyk, Miroslaw Tomasik, Jaroslaw Wajda, Robert Walczewski

SOVIET UNION

Evgeny Belosheikin, Oleg Bratash, Alexander Chernykh, Vladimir Elovikov, Anatoli Fedotov, Alexei Grischenko, Valeri Kamensky, Ravil Khaidarov, Igor Kravchuk, Yuri Lynov, Igor Nikitin, Sergei Novoselov, Andrei Popogayev, Oleg Posmetjev, Igor Rasko, Alexander Semak, Sergei Sverzhov, Mikhail Tatarinov, Pavel Torgayev, Andrei Vakrushev

SWEDEN

Peter Andersson, Mikael Andersson, Goran Arnmark, Peter Berntsson, Arto Blomsten, Lars Bystrom, Leif Carlsson, Christian Due-Boije, Eddy Eriksson, Tommy Eriksson, Lennart Hermansson, Stefan Jonsson, Reine Karlsson, Ulf Konradsson, Stefan Larsson, Sam Lindestahl, Mats Lundstrom, Ulf Nilsson, Stefan Nilsson, Fredrik Olausson, Harri Tiala

UNITED STATES

Chris Biotti, Al Bourbeau, Clark Donatelli, Greg Dornbach, David Espe, Perry Florio, Brian Hannon, Craig Janney, Brian Johnson, Bill Kopecky, Steve Leach, Brian Leetch, Jay Octeau, Alan Perry, Mike Richter, Jeff Rohlicek, Scott Schneider, Eric Weinrich, Doug Wieck, Scott Young

WEST GERMANY

Klaus Birk, Andreas Brockmann, Michael Flemming, Georg Franz, Frank Gentges, Thomas Groger, Raimond Hilger, Toni Krinner, Uwe Krupp, Rene Ledock, Rupert Meister, Christian Reuter, Thomas Riedel, Peter Romberg, Udo Schmid, Jurgen Stortz, Richard Trojan, Andreas Volland, Sepp Wassermann, Oliver Weissenberger

FINAL STANDINGS

	GP	W	L	T	GF	GA	P	GAA	SO	PIM
CANADA	7	5	0	2	44	14	12	2.00	2	110
Czechoslovakia	7	5	0	2	32	13	12	1.86	0	88
Soviet Union	7	5	2	0	38	17	10	2.43	1	120
Finland	7	4	1	2	42	20	10	2.86	1	66*
Sweden	7	3	4	0	32	26	6	3.71	1	146
United States	7	2	5	0	23	37	4	5.23	0	114
West Germany	7	0	6	1	9	44	1	6.29	0	98
Poland	7	0	6	1	10	59	1	8.14	0	78

* won Fair Play Cup

RESULTS

December 23	Helsinki	Canada 8	Sweden 2
	Vantaa	Soviet Union 10	Poland 0
	Turku	Finland 9	West Germany 0
	Turku	Czechoslovakia 9	United States 1
December 25	Turku	Canada 12	Poland 1
	Vantaa	Soviet Union 12	West Germany 1
	Helsinki	Czechoslovakia 4	Sweden 3
	Turku	Finland 7	United States 4
December 26	Helsinki	Canada 6	West Germany 0
	Espoo	Czechoslovakia 6	Poland 2
	Turku	Finland 5	Sweden 3
	Turku	Soviet Union 4	United States 2
December 28	Turku	Canada 7	United States 5
	Turku	Soviet Union 5	Sweden 1
	Vantaa	Czechoslovakia 7	West Germany 3
	Helsinki	Finland 11	Poland 2

December 29	Turku	Canada 5	Soviet Union 0
	Turku	Sweden 11	Poland 0
	Helsinki	Czechoslovakia 1	Finland 1
	Helsinki	United States 2	West Germany 1
December 31	Helsinki	Canada 4	Finland 4
	Turku	Sweden 5	West Germany 1
	Turku	Czechoslovakia 3	Soviet Union 1
	Helsinki	United States 6	Poland 2
January 1	Helsinki	Canada 2	Czechoslovakia 2
	Vantaa	West Germany 3	Poland 3
	Helsinki	Soviet Union 6	Finland 5
	Vantaa	Sweden 7	United States 3

TEAM CANADA GAME SUMMARIES

December 23   *Canada 8*   *Sweden 2*

First Period

1. Canada, Richer (unassisted)...10:14

   PENALTIES: Creighton (Can) 1:13, Andersson (Swe) 6:16, S. Nilsson (Swe) & Beukeboom (Can) 10:56, Clark (Can) 13:09, Jackson (Can) 15:57, Dollas (Can) 18:00

Second Period

2. Sweden, Karlsson (Andersson, Bystrom) 4:32
3. Canada, Creighton (unassisted) 9:44
4. Canada, Lemieux (unassisted) ....14:21(pp)

   PENALTIES: Andersson (Swe) 2:18, Andersson (Swe) 13:00, Hermansson (Swe) & Dollas (Can) 15:07, Odelein (Can) 16:34

Third Period

5. Canada, Clark (Hodgson)..5:03(pp)
6. Canada, Bradley (unassisted) 5:37
7. Sweden, Andersson (unassisted) ....7:35(pp)
8. Canada, Creighton (unassisted) 15:19
9. Canada, Lemieux (unassisted) 17:05
10. Canada, Corson (Creighton, Berry)..18:01

   PENALTIES: Andersson (Swe) 4:54, Lemieux (Can) 6:55, Eriksson (Swe) 7:49, Beukeboom (Can) 10:10

Shots on Goal:

Canada	7	12	9	**28**
Sweden	9	8	6	**23**

In Goal:

Canada — Billington
Sweden — Lindestahl

December 25   *Canada 12*   *Poland 1*

First Period

1. Canada, Beukeboom (Creighton, Jackson) 0:51
2. Poland, Bryjak (Stebnicki, Syposz) 4:09
3. Canada, Jackson (Bradley, Creighton) 5:10

PENALTIES: Odelein (Can) 2:05, Richer (Can) 9:33, Bryjak (Pol) 12:19, Miner (Can) 17:11

Second Period

4. Canada, Johnston (Corson) 2:16
5. Canada, Bradley (Dollas, Beaudoin) .... 3:57(pp)
6. Canada, Creighton (Jackson, Bradley) .... 4:22(pp)
7. Canada, Lemieux (Gratton) 11:09

PENALTIES: Mroz (Pol) 2:29, Stebnicki (Pol) 3:26, Golinski (Pol) 14:35, Beaudoin (Can) 19:03

Third Period

8. Canada, Corson (Richer) .... 1:34(pp)
9. Canada, Richer (Beaudoin, Corson) 9:48
10. Canada, Clark (Creighton) 11:04
11. Canada, Bradley (Jackson, Odelein) 14:33
12. Canada, Hodgson (Beaudoin, Gratton) 15:29
13. Canada, Corson (Richer) .... 17:47(pp)

PENALTIES: Dolinski (Pol) 1:26, Miner (Can) 11:13, Puzio (Pol) 12:31, Wajda (Pol) 16:58

Shots on Goal:

Canada	14	22	11	**47**
Poland	6	4	8	**18**

In Goal:

Canada — Foster
Poland — Wajda

December 26   *Canada 6*   *West Germany 0*

First Period

1. Canada, Creighton (unassisted) 10:37

PENALTIES: Dollas (Can) 7:55, Clark (Can) 15:46

Second Period

2. Canada, Bradley (Clark) .... 13:48(pp)

   PENALTIES: Volland (WGer) 1:50, Schmid (WGer) 3:29, Gratton (Can) 7:10, Hilger (WGer) 12:44

Third Period

3. Canada, Gratton (Hodgson) 2:57
4. Canada, Hodgson (Odelein) 6:00
5. Canada, Hodgson (Odelein) 8:10
6. Canada, Bradley (Miner)... 18:30(pp)

   PENALTIES: Hilger (WGer) 0:22, Clark (Can) 10:08, Bradley (Can) 13:37, Ledock (WGer) 17:03

Shots on Goal:

Canada	13	16	12	41
West Germany	11	2	6	19

In Goal:

Canada — Foster

West Germany — Weissenberger/Meister [5 goals] replaced Weissenberger [one goal] to start 2nd)

December 28   *Canada 7*   *United States 5*

First Period

1. Canada, Gratton (Miner) 2:12
2. United States, Donatelli (Hannon) 7:34
3. United States, Janney (Rohlicek) 15:54
4. Canada, Odelein (Dollas)... 16:40
5. Canada, Creighton (Bradley) 17:20

   PENALTIES: Rohlicek (U.S.) 4:22, Odelein (Can) & Wieck (U.S.) 7:28, Dollas (Can) 13:33, Lemieux (Can) 17:54

Second Period

6. United States, Kopecky (Dornbach, Young) 6:51
7. United States, Bourbeau (Hannon).. 19:37

   PENALTIES: Sandlak (Can) 16:45

Third Period

8. Canada, Clark (Odelein)... 0:28
9. Canada, Creighton (unassisted) 6:38
10. Canada, Richer (unassisted).. 8:01
11. Canada, Creighton (Jackson, Bradley) 9:44
12. United States, Bourbeau (Hannon)....................................... 16:56(pp)

   PENALTIES: Gratton (Can) 16:09

Shots on Goal:

Canada	11	9	18	**38**
United States	11	11	9	**31**

In Goal:

Canada — Billington
United States — Perry

December 29   Canada 5   Soviet Union 0

First Period

1. Canada, Bassen (Clark) 12:50
2. Canada, Hodgson (Gratton, Lemieux) 13:25

PENALTIES: Jackson (Can) 1:27, Sandlak (Can) 15:45

Second Period

No Scoring

PENALTIES: Johnston (Can) 4:48, Dollas (Can) 6:40, Miner (Can) 8:37, Bassen (Can) 14:05

Third Period

3. Canada, Creighton (Richer)...6:19(pp)
4. Canada, Hodgson (Lemieux) 7:29
5. Canada, Bradley (Jackson) 8:11

PENALTIES: Semak (Sov) 5:50, Bassen (Can) 8:55, Sverzhov (Sov) 9:40, Lemieux (Can) 15:23, Chernykh (Sov) & Miner (Can) 19:00

Shots on Goal:

Canada	4	8	10	**22**
Soviet Union	8	3	6	**17**

In Goal:

Canada — Billington
Soviet Union — Belosheikin/Bratash (Bratash [no goals] replaced Belosheikin [5 goals] at 8:11 of 3rd)

December 31   Canada 4   Finland 4

First Period

1. Canada, Bradley (Jackson) 6:47
2. Canada, Bassen (Jackson)...12:26
3. Finland, Makela (Laurila, Tikkanen) 15:22

PENALTIES: Torkki (Fin) & Creighton (Can) 1:41, Sandlak (Can) 7:04, Odelein (Can) 11:44

145

Second Period

4. Canada, Richer (Corson, Odelein) 2:51
5. Finland, Haanpaa (Jarvi) 6:13
6. Canada, Johnston (unassisted) 12:50
7. Finland, Keskinen (unassisted) 17:41

> PENALTIES: Corson (Can) & Tikkanen (Fin) 0:34, Miner (Can) 3:49, Clark (Can) 13:14, Torkki (Fin) 18:09

Third Period

8. Finland, Makela (Keskinen) .... 5:08(pp)

> PENALTIES: Miner (Can) & Makela (Fin) 2:20, Beaudoin (Can) 3:57, Jackson (Can) & Suutari (Fin) 5:33, Gratton (Can — minor, misconduct) 11:53, Jackson (Can) & Haanpaa (Fin) 19:50

Shots on Goal:

Canada	10	11	6	27
Finland	16	6	6	28

In Goal:

Canada — Billington
Finland — Lehkonen

January 1   *Canada 2*   *Czechoslovakia 2*

First Period

No Scoring

> PENALTIES: Bassen (Can) & Mares (Cze) 4:32, Gudas (Cze) 14:45

Second Period

1. Czechoslovakia, Lubina (Mares) 13:57
2. Canada, Sandlak (unassisted) 14:33

> PENALTIES: Bassen (Can) 3:09, Jackson (Can) 5:13, Flasar (Cze) 7:42, Clark (Can) 9:22, Berry (Can) 17:02

Third Period

3. Czechoslovakia, Pivonka (unassisted) 12:22
4. Canada, Clark (Bradley) 13:43

> PENALTIES: Dollas (Can) 4:00

Shots on Goal:

Canada	10	9	7	26
Czechoslovakia	14	4	10	28

In Goal:

Canada — Billington
Czechoslovakia — Hasek

TEAM CANADA FINAL STATISTICS
1985 WORLD JUNIOR CHAMPIONSHIPS

			GP	G	A	P	PIM
11	F	Adam Creighton(A)	7	8	4	12	4
8	F	Brian Bradley	7	7	5	12	2
12	F	Jeff Jackson	7	1	7	8	10
16	F	Dan Hodgson(C)	7	5	2	7	0
23	F	Stephane Richer	7	4	3	7	2
6	F	Wendel Clark	7	4	2	6	10
9	F	Shayne Corson	7	3	3	6	2
7	D	Selmar Odelein	7	1	5	6	8
21	F	Claude Lemieux	6	3	2	5	6
24	F	Dan Gratton	7	2	3	5	16
19	D	Yves Beaudoin	7	0	3	3	4
14	F	Bob Bassen	7	2	0	2	8
10	F	Greg Johnston	7	2	0	2	2
5	D	Bobby Dollas	7	0	2	2	12
3	D	John Miner	7	0	2	2	12
26	F	Jim Sandlak	5	1	0	1	6
25	D	Jeff Beukeboom	3	1	0	1	4
2	D	Brad Berry	7	0	1	1	2
1	G	Craig Billington	5	0	0	0	0
30	G	Norm Foster	2	0	0	0	0

In Goal

	GP	W–L–T	MINS	GA	SO	AVG
Norm Foster	2	2–0–0	120	1	1	0.50
Craig Billington	5	3–0–2	300	13	1	2.60

Coach   Terry Simpson
Assistant   Ron Lapointe

CANADIAN OFFICIALS AT THE 1985
WORLD JUNIOR CHAMPIONSHIPS

Richard Trottier (referee)   5 games

TEAM CANADA ROSTER SUMMARY

Team Canada players   20
Drafted Into NHL   19 (all but Bassen)
Played in NHL   20
Returning Players   1 (Hodgson)

PLAYER REPRESENTATION BY LEAGUE

OHL   8   (Beukeboom, Billington, Bradley, Corson, Gratton, Jackson, Johnston, Sandlak)

WHL   5   (Bassen, Clark, Hodgson, Miner, Odelein)

QMJHL   3   (Beaudoin, Lemieux, Richer)

NHL   2   (Creighton, Dollas)

U.S. COLLEGE   2   (Berry, Foster)

PLAYER REPRESENTATION BY AGE

19-year-olds   13   (Bassen, Beaudoin, Berry, Beukeboom, Bradley, Creighton, Dollas, Foster, Hodgson, Jackson, Johnston, Lemieux, Miner)

18-year-olds   7   (Billington, Clark, Corson, Gratton, Odelein, Richer, Sandlak)

PLAYERS' CAREER PROFILES

Bob Bassen
Medicine Hat Tigers (WHL)
Not drafted
Played in the NHL 1985 to present

Yves Beaudoin
Shawinigan Cataractes (QMJHL)
Selected 203rd overall by Washington at 1983 Draft
Played in the NHL 1985–88

Brad Berry
University of North Dakota Fighting Sioux (WCHA)
Selected 29th overall by Winnipeg at 1983 Draft
Played in the NHL 1985–94

Jeff Beukeboom
Sault Ste. Marie Greyhounds (OHL)
Selected 19th overall by Edmonton at 1983 Draft
Played in the NHL 1985 to present

Craig Billington
Belleville Bulls (OHL)
Selected 23rd overall by New Jersey at 1984 Draft
Played in the NHL 1985 to present

Brian Bradley
London Knights (OHL)
Selected 52nd overall by Calgary at 1983 Draft
Played in the NHL 1985 to present

Wendel Clark
Saskatoon Blades (WHL)
Selected 1st overall by Toronto at 1985 Draft
Played in the NHL 1985 to present

Shayne Corson
Hamilton Steel Hawks (OHL)
Selected 8th overall by Montreal at 1984 Draft
Played in the NHL 1985 to present

Adam Creighton Buffalo Sabres (NHL)
last Junior team: Ottawa 67's (OHL)
Selected 11th overall by Buffalo at 1983 Draft
Played in the NHL 1983 to present

Bobby Dollas Winnipeg Jets (NHL)
last Junior team: Laval Nationals (QMJHL)
Selected 14th overall by Winnipeg at 1983 Draft
Played in the NHL 1983 to present

Norm Foster Michigan State University Spartans (CCHA)
Selected 222nd overall by Boston at 1983 Draft
Played in the NHL 1990–92

Dan Gratton Oshawa Generals (OHL)
Selected 10th overall by Los Angeles at 1985 Draft
Played in the NHL 1987–88

Dan Hodgson Prince Albert Raiders (WHL)
Selected 85th overall by Toronto at 1983 Draft
Played in the NHL 1985–89

Jeff Jackson Hamilton Steel Hawks (OHL)
Selected 28th overall by Toronto at 1983 Draft
Played in the NHL 1984–92

Greg Johnston Toronto Marlboros (OHL)
Selected 42nd overall by Boston at 1983 Draft
Played in the NHL 1983–92

Claude Lemieux Verdun Juniors (QMJHL)
Selected 26th overall by Montreal at 1983 Draft
Played in the NHL 1983 to present

John Miner Regina Pats (WHL)
Selected 229th overall by Edmonton at 1983 Draft
Played 14 games in the NHL 1987–88

Selmar Odelein Regina Pats (WHL)
Selected 21st overall by Edmonton at 1984 Draft
Played in the NHL 1985–89

Stephane Richer Granby Bisons (QMJHL)
Selected 29th overall by Montreal at 1984 Draft
Played in the NHL 1984 to present

Jim Sandlak London Knights (OHL)
Selected 4th overall by Vancouver at 1985 Draft
Played in the NHL 1985–96

1986 WORLD JUNIOR CHAMPIONSHIPS CANADA, DECEMBER 26, 1985-- JANUARY 4, 1986

FINAL PLACINGS

GOLD MEDAL	Soviet Union
SILVER MEDAL	**CANADA**
BRONZE MEDAL	United States
Fourth Place	Czechoslovakia
Fifth Place	Sweden
Sixth Place	Finland
Seventh Place	Switzerland*
Eighth Place	West Germany**

promoted from "B" pool in 1985
**relegated to "B" pool for 1987*

ALL-STAR TEAM

GOAL	Evgeny Belosheikin (Soviet Union)
DEFENCE	Sylvain Cote (Canada)
	Mikhail Tatarinov (Soviet Union)
FORWARD	Shayne Corson (Canada)
	Igor Viazmikin (Soviet Union)
	Michal Pivonka (Czechoslovakia)

DIRECTORATE AWARDS

BEST GOALIE	Evgeny Belosheikin (Soviet Union)
BEST DEFENCEMAN	Mikhail Tatarinov (Soviet Union)
BEST FORWARD	Jim Sandlak (Canada)

COACH TERRY SIMPSON

Winner of the gold medal the previous winter, coach Simpson and assistant Ron Lapointe were confirmed as returnees on March 27, 1985, for the 1986 championships to be held in Hamilton, Ontario. Hosting the tournament would seem like a sure advantage, but Simpson knew travel to another country helped the team every bit as much as home ice. Team Canada always relied on its players to come together as a group quickly. Such camaraderie is much easier to accomplish in a foreign country, where nothing is familiar except the company and friendship of your teammates. Spending Christmas day in Canada with their families would be more enjoyable than spending time with twenty guys in an hotel room, but it didn't necessarily help mold the players into a competitive unit.

SUMMER AND PRE-TOURNAMENT CAMPS

Some forty-four players were invited to initial tryouts in Belleville from July 20–27 as a first step in making the final World Junior team. Forty players reconvened in December for final tryouts while playing two exhibition games, December 22 against Sweden in Kingston (6–4 win) and December 23 against Finland in Peterborough (5–2 win).

After the exhibtion play, coach Simpson made his final cuts: James Gasseau (Drummondville, QMJHL), Steve Finn (Laval, QMJHL), Dave Manson (Prince Albert, WHL), Tony Hrkac (Canadian Olympic team), Bob Joyce (University of North Dakota), Graeme Bonar (Sault Ste. Marie, OHL). Canada now had its twenty players for the tournament.

In other exhibition games that night, a group of OHL Selects beat Sweden 8–7, and the Guelph Platers beat the Czechs 8–6 in the final warmups. The WJC began two days later in Hamilton.

CUTTING TONY HRKAC

The last-minute trimming of Hrkac from the junior roster created a bit of a furor but it pointed to the huge difference between a key player for the juniors and an oustanding prospect for the NHL. Hrkac would be a key player for Dave King at the 1988 Olympics, two years hence, and many felt Hrkac would benefit enormously by playing with the juniors. He had size, speed, and scoring touch, but his skills needed refining and fine-tuning.

Coach Terry Simpson, however, didn't have time to be concerned with fine-tuning a future great. He was concerned with a player's abilities in the next two weeks. What could he do *now*? How could he contribute *today* and

*Canada's Juniors played the local Hamilton Steel Hawks in an
exhibition, giving coach Terry Simpson a chance to evaluate his players*

fit in with *these* players? In these regards Hrkac was found wanting. The
difference is critical. It may seem a coach makes a bad move cutting a player
who goes on to great things in the NHL. But what a veteran in the NHL
can do has little to do with what a nineteen-year-old can do during a very
short tournament.

COMPLAINTS

The Swedes, Finns, and Soviets ganged up on Canadian organizers, complain-
ing about long bus rides to games and practices. They said Canada would have
an advantage if most of their games were played at Copps Coliseum in
Hamilton. Although the Canucks seemed to have all these breaks, they failed
to win gold. Hardships create victory as often as they inhibit it.

GOLD MEDAL SHOWDOWN

The Canada-Russia game was the sixth for both teams in the tournament,
and with perfect 5–0 records, it was the gold medal game. Canada had a
superior goals differential, so a tie or win would mean gold. A loss meant
silver. Ten players on the Soviet team had been on last year's squad, hammered

5–0 by Canada. To Russians, money was always the great inspirer, and before the game players were promised $700 to spend as they wished in Canada if they beat the home team. If they lost, they got nary a dime.

The Soviets were the better team, winning 4–1, but they weren't physically battered the way they had been the previous year. They incorporated soccer tactics into their game, diving without pride and writhing in mock injury whenever a check of significance was delivered. Six times the Russian trainer Oleg Kuchenov came out onto the ice to revivify slain players. Three of those players recovered so fully they didn't even have to leave the ice. The Canadians were short-handed seven times to the Soviets' two, which took the steam out of Canada's aggressive play. In the end, the Canadians lost to a better team, but a team whose play was unworthy of the title of World Junior champions.

Canadian players wore the Cooperall
pants for the last time at the 1986 WJC.

ROUND-ROBIN ARITHMETIC

The current format for the World Juniors is more exciting than that used in the seventies and eighties because a semi-finals and finals elimination set-up is clear and decisive. A round-robin set-up is often nebulous. After Canada's loss to Russia, for instance, it still had to play the Czechs (a 5–3 loss) in a game that meant nothing to the final standings. The last day decided the bronze medal in what turned out to be a math test. Going into the final day, the United States, Sweden, Finland, and Czechoslovakia were all in contention for third place. In the case of a tie between two teams, the deciding factor was the game between the two. But, in the case of a tie between three or more teams, head-to-head results would be the deciding factor.

On the last day, the Americans and Czechs won, the Swedes and Finns lost. Thus, the U.S., Sweden, and the Czechs were tied for third place. The Americans, with victories over both the Czechs (5–2) and Sweden (5–1) won the bronze medal. Oddly, at this stage, head-to-head results between Czechoslovakia and Sweden did not decide fourth. Instead, overall goal differential was the deciding factor. Thus, Czechoslovakia (30 goals for, 20 against, for +10) was placed above Sweden (26–23, +3), even though the Swedes beat the Czechs 3–2 in the round-robin.

ATTENDANCE

For the twenty-eight games played in Hamilton and environs, a tournament record 154,172 fans attended these World Junior Championships.

TOURNAMENT FORMAT

The World Juniors continued to adhere to a simple one division, round-robin formula. No overtime or extra games would be played.

THE OPPOSITION

CZECHOSLOVAKIA

Tomas Kapusta, Kamil Kastak, Richard Kolar, Dusan Kralik, Robert Kron, Jiri Kucera, Jaroslav Landsman, Jiri Latal, Roman Lipovsky, Ladislav Lubina, Michal Madl, Stanislav Medrik, Lubos Pazler, Michal Pivonka, Josef Reznicek, Tomas Srsen, Oldrich Svoboda, Radek Toupal, David Volek, Rudolf Zaruba

FINLAND

Kari-Pekka Friman, Mikko Haapakoski, Timo Iljina, Jouni Kantola, Jarmo Kekalainen, Ville Kentala, Teppo Kivela, Jari Korpisalo, Timo Kulonen, Mikko Laaksonen, Timo Lehkonen, Pentti Lehtosaari, Sakari Lindfors, Jyrki Lumme, Petri Matikainen, Lasse Nieminen, Kimmo Nurro, Vesa Ruotsalainen, Antti Tuomenoska, Sami Wahlsten

SOVIET UNION

Evgeny Belosheikin, Oleg Bratash, Evgeny Davydov, Anatoli Fedotov, Alexander Galcheniuk, Sergei Gapeenko, Valeri Kamensky, Ravil Khajdarov, Vladimir Konstantinov, Andrei Kovalev, Igor Kravchuk, Igor Monaenkov, Igor Nikitin, Yuri Nikonov, Sergei Osipov, Sergei Selianin, Alexander Semak, Mikhail Tatarinov, Pavel Torgayev, Igor Viazmikin

SWEDEN

Mikael Andersson, Tony Barthelsson, Tomas Bjurh, Robert Burakowski, Ulf Dahlen, Christian Due-Boije, Per Edlund, Stefan Falk, Hans Goran Elo, Stefan Jansson, Carl Johansson, Mikael Johansson, Roger Johansson, Sam Lindestahl, Anders Lindstrom, Mats Lundstrom, Roger Ohman, Fredrik Olausson, Joakim Persson, Fredrik Stillman

SWITZERLAND

Beat Aebischer, Jean-Jacques Aeschlimann, Marius Boesch, Martin Bruderer, Beat Cattaruzza, Filippo Celio, Manuele Celio, Gilles Dubois, Andreas Fischer, Martin Hofacker, Peter Jaks, Dino Kessler, Andre Kunzi, Beat Nuspliger, Andreas Schneeberger, Roger Thony, Bruno Vollmer, Thomas Vrabec, Raymond Walder, Thomas Wiedmer

UNITED STATES

Chris Biotti, Greg Brown, Jim Carson, Tom Chorske, Greg Dornbach, Craig Janney, Mike Kelfer, Steve Leach, Brian Leetch, Lane MacDonald, Max Middendorf, Scott Paluch, Alan Perry, David Quinn, Paul Ranheim, Mike Richter, Dan Shea, Eric Weinrich, Mike Wolak, Scott Young

WEST GERMANY

Klaus Birk, Andreas Brockmann, Christian Gelzinus, Thomas Groeger, Toni Krinner, Rene Ledock, Andreas Lupzig, Klaus Merk, Klaus Micheller, Dan Nowak, Christian Ott, Marco Rentzsch, Christian Reuter, Michael Schmidt, Stefan Steinecker, Rindolf Sternkopf, Richard Trojan, Andreas Volland, Josef Wassermann, Thomas Werner

FINAL STANDINGS

	GP	W	L	T	GF	GA	P	GAA	SO	PIM
Soviet Union	7	7	0	0	42	14	14	2.00	1	84
CANADA	7	5	2	0	54	21	10	3.00	0	90
United States	7	4	3	0	35	26	8	3.71	0	74
Czechoslovakia	7	4	3	0	30	20	8	2.86	1	76

Sweden	7	4	3	0	26	23	8	3.29	2	98
Finland	7	3	4	0	31	23	6	3.14	0	54*
Switzerland	7	1	6	0	19	54	2	7.71	0	108
West Germany	7	0	7	0	9	65	0	9.29	0	117

won Fair Play Cup

RESULTS

December 26	Hamilton	Canada 12	Switzerland 1
	London	Soviet Union 7	United States 3
	Orillia	Sweden 2	Finland 0
	Newmarket	Czechoslovakia 9	West Germany 3
December 27	Kitchener	Canada 18	West Germany 2
	St. Catharines	Finland 9	Switzerland 2
	Oshawa	Soviet Union 6	Sweden 1
	Hamilton	United States 5	Czechoslovakia 2
December 29	Hamilton	Canada 5	United States 2
	Guelph	Soviet Union 7	Switzerland 3
	Stratford	Sweden 3	Czechoslovakia 2
	Toronto	Finland 7	West Germany 2
December 30	Hamilton	Canada 9	Sweden 2
	Dundas	Czechoslovakia 7	Switzerland 2
	Kitchener	Soviet Union 10	West Germany 0
	Oshawa	Finland 7	United States 5
January 1	Toronto	Canada 6	Finland 5
	London	Soviet Union 4	Czechoslovakia 3
	Hamilton	United States 4	West Germany 1
	Oakville	Sweden 7	Switzerland 1
January 2	Hamilton	Soviet Union 4	Canada 1
	Brantford	Czechoslovakia 2	Finland 0
	Georgetown	Sweden 10	West Germany 0
	Niagara Falls	United States 11	Switzerland 3
January 4	Hamilton	Czechoslovakia 5	Canada 3
	Hamilton	United States 5	Sweden 1
	Brantford	Switzerland 7	West Germany 1
	Hamilton	Soviet Union 4	Finland 3

TEAM CANADA GAME SUMMARIES

December 26　　　Canada 12　　　Switzerland 1

First Period

1. Canada, Sandlak (Nieuwendyk, Corson) 0:11
2. Canada, Sandlak (Nieuwendyk) 4:19
3. Canada, Sandlak (Nieuwendyk, Roberts) .... 11:11(pp)

　　PENALTIES: Aebischer (Swi — served by Wiedmer) 9:54, S. Cote (Can) 12:21, Vollmer (Swi) 16:37

Second Period

4. Switzerland, Thony (unassisted)... 5:20
5. Canada, Roberts (Laxdal) 7:27
6. Canada, Murphy (A. Cote)... 12:59
7. Canada, Murphy (Carkner) 18:15

　　PENALTIES: Nuspliger (Swi) 0:04, Viveiros (Can) 1:39, Nuspliger (Swi) & Conroy (Can) 7:25, Stapleton (Can) 8:30, Laxdal (Can) 13:41, Stapleton (Can) 14:07, Corson (Can) 15:33

Third Period

8. Canada, Mellanby (A. Cote) 0:36
9. Canada, Roberts (S. Cote) 3:25
10. Canada, Mellanby (Robitaille).. 9:12
11. Canada, Corson (Sandlak) 10:05
12. Canada, Douris (Murphy, Corson) .... 17:04(pp)
13. Canada, Conroy (A. Cote) 18:53

　　PENALTIES: Nuspliger (Swi) 15:20

Shots on Goal:

Canada	19	8	22	**49**
Switzerland	2	12	0	**14**

In Goal:

Canada — Billington
Switzerland — Aebischer/Boesch (Boesch [4 goals] replaced Aebischer [8 goals] at 8:53 of 3rd)

December 27　　　Canada 18　　　West Germany 2

First Period

1. Canada, Nieuwendyk (Sandlak, Carkner)....................................... 3:01(pp)
2. Canada, Greenlaw (Douris, Murphy)... 4:07
3. Canada, Stapleton (Mellanby) .... 8:29(sh)
4. Canada, Sandlak (Corson) 12:25
5. Canada, Douris (Murphy, Robitaille) .... 15:05(pp)
6. Canada, Conroy (Mellanby).. 16:24

7. Canada, Douris (Murphy) .... 19:30(pp)

    PENALTIES: Steinecker (WGer) 2:01, Roberts (Can) 7:47, Corson (Can) 8:58, Wassermann (WGer) 13:29, Ledock (WGer) 17:55

Second Period

8. Canada, Roberts (Conroy) 0:41
9. Canada, Stapleton (Robitaille, Mellanby) 4:09
10. West Germany, Sternkopf (unassisted) 12:13
11. Canada, Mellanby (Stapleton, Robitaille) 13:45
12. Canada, Nieuwendyk (Corson, Moylan) 15:43
13. Canada, Roberts (Conroy, Laxdal) 19:25
14. West Germany, Krinner (Micheller) 19:51

    PENALTIES: Micheller (WGer) 5:08, Mellanby (Can) 16:27

Third Period

15. Canada, Laxdal (Carkner) 0:24
16. Canada, Mellanby (unassisted) 2:40
17. Canada, Greenlaw (Murphy) 8:10
18. Canada, Mellanby (Stapleton) 9:06
19. Canada, Moylan (Nieuwendyk, Roberts) .... 13:31(pp)
20. Canada, Murphy (unassisted) 17:29

    PENALTIES: Sternkopf (WGer — misconduct) 9:01, Ledock (WGer) & Douris (Can) 10:51, Reuter (WGer) 13:08, Mellanby (Can) 13:53, Micheller (WGer) & Greenlaw (Can) 15:27, Micheller (WGer) 18:54, Nieuwendyk (Can) 19:43

Shots on Goal:

Canada	20	15	17	52
West Germany	8	8	4	20

In Goal:

Canada — Burke
West Germany — Merk/Schmidt (Schmidt [11 goals] replaced Merk [7 goals] to start 2nd)

December 29   *Canada 5*   *United States 2*

First Period

1. Canada, Conroy (Corson) .... 4:48(sh)
2. United States, Leetch (Shea, Paluch) 14:00

    PENALTIES: Sandlak (Can) 3:39, Sandlak (Can) & Weinrich (U.S.) 13:22, Roberts (Can) & Young (U.S. — double minor) 18:56

Second Period

3. Canada, Corson (Nieuwendyk, A. Cote) 8:28
4. United States, Leetch (unassisted) 14:11
5. Canada, Corson (Nieuwendyk, Sandlak) 18:18

    PENALTIES: Nieuwendyk (Can) & Kelfer (U.S.) 5:39, A. Cote (Can) 11:26

Third Period

6. Canada, Stapleton (Mellanby, Robitaille) 9:00
7. Canada, Nieuwendyk (Sandlak) .... 11:21(pp)

PENALTIES: Paluch (U.S.) 9:37

Shots on Goal:

Canada	11	18	9	38
United States	9	9	5	23

In Goal:

Canada — Billington
United States — Richter

December 30   Canada 9   Sweden 2

First Period

1. Canada, Murphy (unassisted) 4:16
2. Canada, Nieuwendyk (Sandlak, Corson) 6:51
3. Canada, Nieuwendyk (S. Cote, Corson) 12:17
4. Canada, Robitaille (Viveiros, Odelein) 13:13

PENALTIES: Laxdal (Can) 0:03, Due-Boije (Swe) 0:40, Greenlaw (Can) 8:22, Stapleton (Can) 16:34

Second Period

5. Canada, Roberts (Conroy) 3:59
6. Sweden, M. Johansson (Persson) 14:03
7. Canada, Viveiros (Murphy, Greenlaw) 19:12

PENALTIES: Murphy (Can) 0:50, Ohman (Swe) & Conroy (Can) 1:01

Third Period

8. Canada, Greenlaw (Murphy) 6:04
9. Sweden, Persson (Olausson, M. Johansson) 7:07
10. Canada, Conroy (Roberts, Laxdal) 12:51
11. Canada, Corson (Sandlak, Nieuwendyk) 14:43

PENALTIES: C. Johansson (Swe) 1:49

Shots on Goal:

Canada	18	16	14	48
Sweden	6	9	9	24

In Goal:

Canada — Billington
Sweden — Lindestahl/Elo (Elo [no goals] replaced Lindstahl [9 goals] at 14:43 of 3rd)

January 1   Canada 6   Finland 5

First Period

1. Finland, Kantola (Kivela, Laaksonen) .... 8:30(pp)
2. Canada, Corson (Sandlak) 11:37

    PENALTIES: Corson (Can) 7:51, Ruotsalainen (Fin) 12:28, Tuomenoska (Fin) 16:00

Second Period

3. Finland, Kekalainen (Nieminen, Wahlsten) 3:06
4. Canada, A. Cote (Murphy, Douris) .... 4:16(pp)
5. Canada, Roberts (Moylan, Laxdal) 5:43
6. Finland, Lehtosaari (Kantola, Kivela) 7:10
7. Canada, Sandlak (unassisted) .... 10:44(pp)
8. Canada, Robitaille (Murphy) .... 11:08(pp)
9. Finland, Laaksonen (Kivela, Kantola) .... 15:58(pp)

    PENALTIES: Ruotsalainen (Fin) 3:56, S. Cote (Can) 7:29, Korpisalo (Fin) 9:03, Nurro (Fin) 9:34, Odelein (Can) 14:04, A. Cote (Can) 17:50

Third Period

10. Canada, S. Cote (Carkner, Stapleton) 7:44
11. Finland, Lehtosaari (Tuomenoska) 8:00

    PENALTIES: Sandlak (Can) 0:49, Kivela (Fin) 4:09, Odelein (Can) 12:55, Douris (Can) 16:08

Shots on Goal:

Canada	20	13	15	**48**
Finland	7	13	5	**25**

In Goal:

    Canada — Burke
    Finland — Lehkonen

January 2   Soviet Union 4   Canada 1

First Period

1. Canada, Corson (S. Cote) 6:36
2. Soviet Union, Semak (Fedotov) .... 18:30(pp)

    PENALTIES: A. Cote (Can) 3:20, Laxdal (Can) 11:13, Sandlak (Can) 17:10

Second Period

3. Soviet Union, Osipov (Kamensky) 2:05

    PENALTIES: Nieuwendyk (Can) 2:39, Konstantinov (Sov) 4:02, Odelein (Can) 12:01, Selianin (Sov) 18:24, Sandlak (Can) 18:58

Third Period

4. Soviet Union, Khajdarov (Semak, Nikonov) 6:20
5. Soviet Union, Viazmikin (unassisted) 8:16

    PENALTIES: Roberts (Can) 13:59

Shots on Goal:

Canada	11	5	13	**29**
Soviet Union	13	8	8	**29**

In Goal:

Canada — Billington
Soviet Union — Belosheikin

January 4 Czechoslovakia 5 Canada 3

First Period

1. Czechoslovakia, Kastak (Pivonka, Reznicek) ....5:54(pp)
2. Czechoslovakia, Kapusta (Kolar) 11:57
3. Canada, Corson (Conroy) 14:55

PENALTIES: Sandlak (Can) 3:55, Lubina (Cze) 13:35

Second Period

4. Czechoslovakia, Kucera (Toupal, Lubina) 15:12

PENALTIES: Pivonka (Cze) 4:39, Pivonka (Cze) 7:58, Volek (Cze) 9:38, Douris (Can) 10:31, Conroy (Can) 11:37, Kucera (Cze) & Mellanby (Can) 11:59, Medrik (Cze) 12:39

Third Period

5. Czechoslovakia, Pivonka (Medrik, Kastak) ....3:38(pp)
6. Czechoslovakia, Kucera (Lubina, Toupal) 5:37
7. Canada, Robitaille (S. Cote) 10:27
8. Canada, Douris (Murphy) 13:01

PENALTIES: Sandlak (Can) 1:55, Pivonka (Cze) & Sandlak (Can) 9:34, Robitaille (Can) 10:39

Shots on Goal:

Canada	14	6	14	**34**
Czechoslovakia	10	16	10	**36**

In Goal:

Canada — Billington
Czechoslovakia — Landsman

TEAM CANADA FINAL STATISTICS
1986 WORLD JUNIOR CHAMPIONSHIPS

			GP	G	A	P	PIM
9	F	Shayne Corson	7	7	7	14	6
14	F	Joe Murphy	7	4	10	14	2
26	F	Jim Sandlak(C)	7	5	7	12	16
19	F	Joe Nieuwendyk	7	5	7	12	6
12	F	Gary Roberts	7	6	3	9	6

20	F	Scott Mellanby	7	5	4	9	6
27	F	Al Conroy	7	4	4	8	6
15	F	Luc Robitaille	7	3	5	8	2
10	F	Peter Douris	7	4	2	6	6
25	F	Mike Stapleton	7	3	3	6	6
24	F	Alain Cote	7	1	4	5	6
8	F	Derek Laxdal	7	1	4	5	6
21	D	Sylvain Cote	7	1	4	5	4
22	F	Jeff Greenlaw	7	3	1	4	4
2	D	Terry Carkner	7	0	4	4	0
5	D	Dave Moylan	7	1	2	3	0
3	D	Emanuel Viveiros	7	1	1	2	2
7	D	Selmar Odelein	7	0	1	1	6
1	G	Craig Billington	5	0	0	0	0
30	G	Sean Burke	2	0	0	0	0

In Goal

	GP	W-L-T	MINS	GA	SO	AVG
Craig Billington	5	3–2–0	300	14	0	2.80
Sean Burke	2	2–0–0	120	7	0	3.50

Coach Terry Simpson
Assistant Michel Parizeau

CANADIAN OFFICIALS AT THE 1986 WORLD JUNIOR CHAMPIONSHIPS

Dennis Pottage (referee)	5 games
John Willsie (referee)	3 games
Charles Biehn (linesman)	7 games
Doug Brousseau (linesman)	7 games
Dan Emerson (linesman)	7 games
Ron Rost (linesman)	7 games

TEAM CANADA ROSTER SUMMARY

Team Canada players	20
Drafted Into NHL	19 (all but Conroy)
Played In NHL	19 (all but Moylan)
Returning Players	5 (Billington, Corson, S. Cote, Odelein, Sandlak)

PLAYER REPRESENTATION BY LEAGUE

OHL	8	(Billington, Burke, Carkner, Corson, Moylan, Roberts, Sandlak, Stapleton)
WHL	4	(Conroy, Laxdal, Odelein, Viveiros)
QMJHL	1	(Robitaille)
NHL	2	(A. Cote, S. Cote)
U.S. COLLEGE	3	(Mellanbly, Murphy, Nieuwendyk)
OTHER*	2	(Douris, Greenlaw)

Canadian National Team

PLAYER REPRESENTATION BY AGE

19-year-olds	15	(Billington, Carkner, Conroy, Corson, S. Cote, Douris, Laxdal, Mellanby, Nieuwendyk, Odelein, Roberts, Robitaille, Sandlak, Stapleton, Viveiros)
18-year-olds	4	(Burke, A. Cote, Moylan, Murphy)
17-year-olds	1	(Greenlaw)

PLAYERS' CAREER PROFILES

Craig Billington	Belleville Bulls (OHL)
	Selected 23rd overall by New Jersey at 1984 Draft
	Played in the NHL 1984 to present
Sean Burke	Toronto Marlboros (OHL)
	Selected 24th overall by New Jersey at 1985 Draft
	Played in the NHL 1987 to present
Terry Carkner	Peterborough Petes (OHL)
	Selected 14th overall by Rangers at 1984 Draft
	Played in the NHL 1986 to present
Al Conroy	Medicine Hat Tigers (WHL)
	Not drafted
	Played in the NHL 1991–94
Shayne Corson	Hamilton Steel Hawks (OHL)
	Selected 9th overall by Montreal at 1984 Draft
	Played in the NHL 1985 to present
Alain Cote	Boston Bruins (NHL)
	last Junior team: Quebec Ramparts (QMJHL)
	Selected 31st overall by Boston at 1985 Draft
	Played in the NHL 1985–94
Sylvain Cote	Hartford Whalers (NHL)
	last Junior team: Quebec Ramparts (QMJHL)
	Selected 11th overall by Hartford at 1984 Draft
	Played in the NHL 1984 to present

Peter Douris   Canadian National Team
Selected 30th overall by Winnipeg at 1984 Draft
Played in the NHL 1985–98

Jeff Greenlaw   Canadian National Team
Selected 19th overall by Washington at 1986 Draft
Played in the NHL 1986–94

Derek Laxdal   Brandon Wheat Kings (WHL)
Selected 151st overall by Toronto at 1984 Draft
Played in the NHL 1984–91

Scott Mellanby   University of Wisconsin Badgers (WCHA)
Selected 27th overall by Philadelphia at 1984 Draft
Played in the NHL 1985 to present

Dave Moylan   Sudbury Wolves (OHL)
Selected 77th overall by Buffalo at 1985 Draft
Did not play in the NHL

Joe Murphy   Michigan State University Spartans (CCHA)
Selected 1st overall by Detroit at 1986 Draft
Played in the NHL 1986 to present

Joe Nieuwendyk   Cornell University Big Red (ECAC)
Selected 27th overall by Calgary at 1985 Draft
Played in the NHL 1986 to present

Selmar Odelein   Regina Pats (WHL)
Selected 21st overall by Edmonton at 1984 Draft
Played in the NHL 1985–89

Gary Roberts   Ottawa 67's (OHL)
Selected 12th overall by Calgary at 1984 Draft
Played in the NHL 1986 to present

Luc Robitaille   Hull Olympiques (QMJHL)
Selected 171st overall by Los Angeles at 1984 Draft
Played in the NHL 1986 to present

Jim Sandlak   London Knights (OHL)
Selected 4th overall by Vancouver at 1985 Draft
Played in the NHL 1985–96

Mike Stapleton   Cornwall Royals (OHL)
Selected 132nd overall by Chicago at 1984 Draft
Played in the NHL 1986 to present

Emanuel Viveiros   Prince Albert Raiders (WHL)
Selected 106th overall by Edmonton at 1984 Draft
Played in the NHL 1985–88

1987 WORLD JUNIOR CHAMPIONSHIPS CZECHOSLOVAKIA, DECEMBER 26, 1986-- JANUARY 4, 1987

FINAL PLACINGS

GOLD MEDAL	Finland
SILVER MEDAL	Czechoslovakia
BRONZE MEDAL	Sweden
Fourth Place	CANADA
Fifth Place	United States
Sixth Place	Soviet Union
Seventh Place	Poland*
Eighth PLace	Switzerland**

* promoted from "B" pool in 1986
** relegated to "B" pool for 1988

ALL-STAR TEAM

GOAL	Sam Lindstahl (Sweden)
DEFENCE	Jiri Latal (Czechoslovakia)
	Brian Leetch (United States)
FORWARD	Ulf Dahlen (Sweden)
	Juraj Jurik (Czechoslovakia)
	Scott Young (United States)

DIRECTORATE AWARDS

BEST GOALIE	Markus Ketterer (Finland)
BEST DEFENCEMAN	Calle Johansson (Sweden)
BEST FORWARD	Robert Kron (Czechoslovakia)

COACH BERT TEMPLETON

The man called Dirty Bert, Crazy Bert, and Bramalea Bert, the man who coached the Hamilton Fincups at the 1977 World Juniors, was back to boss the World Junior bench for Canada in Czechoslovakia in 1987.

Between national assignments, Templeton had coached for the Niagara Falls Flyers and for the 1982–83 season moved to the North Bay Centennials, where he had been ever since.

THE CAMP AND EXHIBITION

Training camp opened December 14 at the Orleans Recreation Complex near Ottawa, an ideal venue because it had an international-size ice surface. Two nights later, the Nats played the first of back-to-back games against the bolstered Hull Olympiques, losing the first game 7–4 and winning the next night 7–3. "I've never placed a lot of emphasis on exhibition games," coach Templeton said. "I wanted to test them, see them tired and ugly, and make sure we're taking the best twenty players."

The first cuts were Benoit Brunet (Hull, QMJHL), Jeff Waver (Hamilton, OHL), and Rocky Dundas (Spokane, WHL). Added to the team were two NHLers, Steve Chiasson on loan from Detroit and Yvon Corriveau from Washington. The two final cuts were the toughest for the coach: Daniel Vincelette (who was suffering from a minor groin injury) and Ken Priestlay, whose presence wasn't needed after Templeton learned that Steve Nemeth would remain in Europe after the Canadian Olympic team had finished competing in the Izvestia tournament and join the juniors in Switzerland for two exhibition games.

DAVE DRAPER

In many competing countries, the World Junior coach was a high school or league coach who was supported by the national program to scout and train the team full-time. In Europe, international games were of paramount importance. In Canada, NHL preparation took precedence.

Dave Draper was the first scout the juniors employed, and his job was important in determining who should be invited to camp. Attitude was as important as skill, Draper thought. A player's contribution to the dressing-room was as important as his on-ice abilities. "If the player is *sent* rather than being asked, and then comes with the wrong attitude," Draper explained, "it can prove very disruptive. Ultimately, the player has to be very keen and realize it could be a learning experience and beneficial experience for his career."

Pierre Turgeon scores Canada's sixth of seven first period goals against
Wlodzimierz Krauzowicz en route to an 18-3 clobbering of Poland.

FORESHADOWING OF A BRAWL

International rules of hockey don't accept fighting or violence as part of the
game. The Brawl at Piestany will go down as the darkest hour of World Junior
hockey, but an incident earlier in the tournament that was almost as bad has
since been forgotten.

During the warm-up to the Canada-United States game, two U.S. players
— Bob Corkum and one other — were apparently lined up well inside the
Canadian half of the ice. Goalie Shawn Simpson took a light swipe at Corkum's ankle to notify the American of his territorial gaffe, and a melee
ensued. Fights were numerous, and the two coaches had to come out onto
the ice to control their teams. Match penalties were assessed to Steve
Chiasson of Canada and Mike Hartman of the States, and both missed their
next game, as well. Tournament officials interpreted the incident as an
aberration and learned nothing from the brawl.

THE BRAWL

Almost always, the ultimate game at any international competition is Canada vs. the Soviets. Such was not the case in Czechoslovakia. When the two teams met on the last day of competition, Canada was in medal contention; the Russians were completely out. If Canada had won by five goals, it would have won gold. A win by fewer goals would have guaranteed a silver.

The problem began with referee Hans Roenning of Norway, a man not suited for such an important game. The previous year, he had received the lowest rating of all officials at the tournament. He let many infractions go by both teams, and by 13:53 of the second period, with Canada winning 4–2 and in control, a brawl erupted. Russian Pavel Kostichkin slashed Theo Fleury, and everyone on the ice joined the fray. Russian players — notably Evgeny Davydov — were the first to leave their bench, and Canadian coach Bert Templeton accused his Russian counterpart, Vladimir Vasiliev, of opening the door for his bench to empty. (Vasiliev was fired shortly after the tournament.)

After about ten minutes, the officials (Roenning, linesmen Peter Pomoell of Finland and Julian Gorski of Poland) left the ice, and the building operator turned the stadium's lights on and off to try to stem the fighting. The players eventually dispersed and went to their dressing-rooms, and the IIHF held an emergency meeting at which time it was decided to suspend the game. Fighting carried an automatic game misconduct, and the officials thought all players should be expelled. Of the nine committee members at the meeting, only Canada's Dennis McDonald wanted the game to continue. The Canadians came home without a medal and without an official win over the Soviets.

After the tournament, the IIHF suspended all the players on both teams for eighteen months and all the coaches for three years. That fall, the players' suspensions were rescinded, but the coaches' sentences remained. The player most affected was Canadian Steve Nemeth, who didn't even fight. On loan from the Olympic team, he was not allowed to play in a series of exhibition games against the Moscow Selects two months later. He was sent back to junior and did not play at the 1988 Games in Calgary.

TOURNAMENT FORMAT

All eight nations were placed in one group and played a single round-robin schedule. Because of the Canada-Russia brawl, both nations were disqualified from medal contention. Even though Canada had nine points in six games and Sweden had nine points in seven games, Sweden was awarded the bronze.

Krauzowicz stops Turgeon on this attempt, but was pulled after 20 minutes in favour of Grzegorz Wojakiewicz who allowed 11 goals in the final two periods.

THE OPPOSITION

CZECHOSLOVAKIA

Roman Andrys, Ales Badal, Radomir Brazda, Martin Hostak, Juraj Jurik, Tomas Kapusta, Robert Kron, Frantisek Kucera, Jiri Latal, Roman Lipovsky, Ladislav Lubina, Ivan Matulik, Roman Nemcicky, Petr Pavlas, Lubos Pazler, Rudolf Pejchar, Karol Rusznak, Robert Svoboda, Oldrich Svoboda, Lubomir Vaclavicek

FINLAND

Marko Allen, Mikko Haapokoski, Markus Ketterer, Marko Kiuru, Teppo Kivela, Timo Kulonen, Mikko Laaksonen, Jari Laukkanen, Pentti Lehtosaari, Jukka Marttila, Petri Matikainen, Janne Ojanen, Jari Parviainen, Kari Rosenberg, Jukka Seppo, Jyrki Silius, Pekka Tirkkonen, Antti Tuomenoska, Sami Wahlsten, Sami Wikstrom

POLAND

Marek Adamek, Damian Adamus, Ryszard Bielak, Ryszard Borecki, Andrzej Husse, Janusz Janikowski, Jacek Jankowski, Jedrzej Kasperczyk, Wlodzimierz Krauzowicz, Wlodzimierz Krol, Jacek Kubowicz, Jerzy Merta, Zbigniew

Niedospial, Zbigniew Raszewski, Krzysztof Ruchala, Marek Trybus, Grzegorz Wojakiewicz, Jacek Zamojski, Piotr Zdunek, Robert Zymankows

SOVIET UNION

Evgeny Davydov, Sergei Fedorov, Alexander Galcheniuk, Valery Ivannikov,
Alexander Kerch, Vladimir Konstantinov, Pavel Kostichkin, Vladimir
Malakhov, Dmitri Medvedev, Alexander Mogilny, Igor Monaenkov, Vadim
Mosatov, Sergei Osipov, Valeri Popov, Vadim Privalov, Sergei Shesterikov,
Andrei Smirnov, Dmitri Tsygurov, Anton Zagorodny, Valeri Zelepukin

SWEDEN

Hakan Ahlund, Roger Akerstrom, Johan Borg, Ulf Dahlen, Par Edlund, Tomaz
Ericsson, Rickard Franzen, Niklas Gallstedt, Johan Garpenlov, Anders Gozzi,
Roger Hansson, Jonas Heed, Calle Johansson, Roger Johansson, Orjan Lindmark,
Sam Lindstahl, Roger Ohman, Ulf Sandstrom, Tomas Sjogren, Bo Svanberg

SWITZERLAND

Beat Aebischer, Jean-Jacques Aeschlimann, Peter Baertschi, Daniel Buenzli,
Marco Dazzi, Ruben Fontana, Olivier Hoffmann, Christian Hofstetter, Andre
Kuenzi, Martin Lang, Romeo Mattioni, Peter Meier, Toni Nyffenegger, Reto
Pavoni, Achim Pleschberger, Luigi Riva, Laurent Stehlin, Roger Thoeni,
Bruno Vollmer, Raymond Walder

UNITED STATES

Chris Biotti, Greg Brown, Adam Burt, Dave Capuano, Todd Copeland, Bob
Corkum, Lee Davidson, Tom Fitzgerald, Mike Hartman, Pat Jablonski, Mike
Kelfer, Ed Krayer, Brian Leetch, Marty Nanne, Mike Posma, Bobby Reynolds,
Robb Stauber, Darren Turcotte, Mike Wolak, Scott Young

FINAL STANDINGS

	GP	W	L	T	GF	GA	P	GAA	SO	PIM
Finland	7	5	1	1	45	23	11	3.29	0	89
Czechoslovakia	7	5	2	0	36	23	10	3.29	0	46*
Sweden	7	4	2	1	45	11	9	1.57	4	76
CANADA	6	4	1	1	41	23	9	3.83	0	108†
United States	7	4	3	0	42	30	8	4.29	0	106
Soviet Union	6	2	3	1	27	20	5	3.33	1	124†
Poland	7	1	6	0	21	80	2	11.42	0	115
Switzerland	7	0	7	0	15	62	0	8.86	0	74

* won Fair Play Cup

† because the game did not count, no penalties were assessed as a result of the brawl that suspended the
Canada-Soviet Union match of January 4, 1987

RESULTS

December 26	Topolcany	Canada 6	Switzerland 4
	Trencin	Soviet Union 7	Poland 3
	Nitra	Czechoslovakia 4	Sweden 3
	Piestany	Finland 4	United States 1
December 27	Trencin	Canada 6	Finland 6
	Piestany	Soviet Union 8	Switzerland 0
	Topolcany	Sweden 15	Poland 0
	Nitra	United States 8	Czechoslovakia 2
December 29	Nitra	Czechoslovakia 5	Canada 1
	Piestany	Sweden 8	Switzerland 0
	Topolcany	Finland 5	Soviet Union 4
	Trencin	United States 15	Poland 2
December 30	Nitra	Canada 18	Poland 3
	Piestany	Sweden 5	Finland 0
	Trencin	Czechoslovakia 5	Soviet Union 3
	Topolcany	United States 12	Switzerland 6
January 1	Piestany	Canada 6	United States 2
	Nitra	Soviet Union 3	Sweden 3
	Trencin	Finland 12	Switzerland 1
	Topolcany	Czechoslovakia 9	Poland 2
January 2	Trencin	Canada 4	Sweden 3
	Piestany	Czechoslovakia 8	Switzerland 1
	Nitra	Finland 13	Poland 3
	Topolcany	United States 4	Soviet Union 2
January 4	Piestany	Canada 4 (suspended by brawl)	Soviet Union 2
	Nitra	Finland 5	Czechoslovakia 3
	Topolcany	Poland 8	Switzerland 3
	Trencin	Sweden 8	United States 0

TEAM CANADA GAME SUMMARIES

December 26   *Canada 6*   *Switzerland 4*

First Period

1. Canada, Elynuik (McLlwain) 0:31
2. Canada, McLlwain (Latta) 6:45
3. Canada, Elynuik (McLlwain) 7:24
4. Canada, McLlwain (unassisted) .... 12:20(sh)
5. Switzerland, Kuenzi (unassisted) .... 12:52(pp)

6. Canada, Nemeth (Metcalfe) 15:36
7. Switzerland, Walder (unassisted) 16:41

PENALTIES: Metcalfe (Can) 1:53, Hawgood (Can) 8:55, Sanipass (Can) 11:37

Second Period

8. Canada, McLlwain (Latta) 13:22
9. Switzerland, Mattioni (Walder) .... 18:32(pp)

PENALTIES: Thoeni (Swi) 0:58, Metcalfe (Can) 2:17, Wesley (Can) 4:19, Vollmer (Swi) 11:19, Hofstetter (Swi) & Roy (Can) 11:45, Aeschlimann (Swi) & Joseph (Can — double minor) & Keane (Can) 18:08

Third Period

10. Switzerland, Nyffenegger (Kuenzi) 4:23

PENALTIES: Roy (Can) 2:10, Pleschberger (Swi) 14:52

Shots on Goal:

unknown

In Goal:

Canada — Waite
Switzerland — Aebischer

December 27   *Canada 6*   *Finland 6*

First Period

1. Canada, Latta (unassisted) 9:07

PENALTIES: Sanipass (Can) 3:11, Can bench 9:07, Allen (Fin) 9:31, Keane (Can) 12:04, Silius (Fin) 15:14, Tuomenoska (Fin) 15:55

Second Period

2. Canada, Latta (Elynuik) 0:22
3. Finland, Seppo (unassisted) .... 7:29(pp)
4. Finland, Kiuru (Kulonen, Seppo) .... 9:15(sh)
5. Finland, Ojanen (Laaksonen) 11:53
6. Canada, Corriveau (unassisted) 14:24
7. Finland, Kivela (unassisted) 15:16
8. Finland, Seppo (Tirkkonen) 18:07

PENALTIES: Corriveau (Can) 5:46, Laukkanen (Fin) 7:37, Huffman (Can) 8:42, Latta (Can) 18:20, Tirkkonen (Fin) 19:57

Third Period

9. Canada, Turgeon (Nemeth, Chiasson) .... 1:23(pp)
10. Canada, Chiasson (Elynuik) 11:12
11. Canada, Shanahan (Metcalfe) 11:35
12. Finland, Wahlsten (Lehtosaari, Kivela) 14:43

PENALTIES: Haapokoski (Fin) & Latta (Can) 0:50, Laaksonen (Fin) 18:03

Shots on Goal:

unknown

In Goal:

Canada — Simpson
Finland — Ketterer

December 29   Czechoslovakia 5   Canada 1

First Period

1. Czechoslovakia, Lubina (Hostak) 0:14

    PENALTIES: Fleury (Can) 4:21, Kron (Cze) 4:57, Roy (Can) 12:20, Chiasson (Can) 15:46, Hostak (Cze) 19:07

Second Period

2. Czechoslovakia, Hostak (unassisted) 10:26
3. Canada, Hawgood (unassisted) 17:06

    PENALTIES: Corriveau (Can) 3:29, Hawgood (Can) 4:41

Third Period

4. Czechoslovakia, Latal (Jurik) 2:54
5. Czechoslovakia, Lubina (Hostak) 13:56
6. Czechoslovakia, Kron (Kapusta) .... 18:36(pp)

    PENALTIES: Chiasson (Can) 16:26, Latta (Can) 16:51, Metcalfe (Can) & Brazda (Cze) 19:19

Missed penalty shot: Ladislav Lubina (Cz) stopped by Shawn Simpson (Can) at 12:24 of 1st

Shots on Goal:

Canada	6	8	4	**18**
Czechoslovakia	7	13	15	**35**

In Goal:

Canada — Simpson
Czechoslovakia — Svoboda

December 30   Canada 18   Poland 3

First Period

1. Canada, Nemeth (Hawgood) 7:50
2. Canada, Sanipass (Fleury) 13:30
3. Canada, Shanahan (Metcalfe, Nemeth) 13:43
4. Canada, Fleury (Sanipass) 15:22
5. Canada, Metcalfe (Elynuik) 16:17
6. Canada, Turgeon (unassisted) 16:53

7. Canada, Sanipass (Huffman)......................................18:05

PENALTIES: Latta (Can) & Borecki (Pol) 3:25, Sanipass (Can) 4:27, Chiasson (Can) 9:14

Second Period

8. Poland, Niedospial (unassisted) ....2:46(pp)
9. Canada, Fleury (Sanipass) ....6:17(pp)
10. Canada, Elynuik (Latta) 6:58
11. Canada, Nemeth (Shanahan) 13:55
12. Canada, Turgeon (Joseph, Corriveau) 16:55
13. Canada, Wesley (Fleury) 18:09

PENALTIES: Borecki (Pol) 0:45, Nemeth (Can) 1:07, Janikowski (Pol) 5:20, Metcalfe (Can) 8:15

Third Period

14. Canada, Corriveau (unassisted) 0:35
15. Poland, Merta (Raszewski)......................................5:55
16. Canada, Elynuik (Nemeth) 6:53
17. Canada, Shanahan (Nemeth, Metcalfe) 10:05
18. Canada, Latta (Shanahan, Elynuik) 11:17
19. Canada, Chiasson (Latta) 12:24
20. Canada, Joseph (unassisted)....................................14:25
21. Poland, Kasperczyk (Adamek, Krol) ....17:47(pp)

PENALTIES: Raszewski (Pol) 2:01, Elynuik (Can) 16:16, Wesley (Can) 16:25

Shots on Goal:

Canada	21	14	18	53
Poland	11	5	6	22

In Goal:

Canada — Simpson/Waite (Waite [3 goals] replaced Simpson [no goals] to start 2nd)

Poland — Krauzowicz/Wojakiewicz (Wojakiewicz 11 goals] replaced Krowzowicz [7 goals] to start 2nd)

January 1　　　　　*Canada 6*　　　　　*United States 2*

First Period

1. Canada, McLlwain (Elynuik)....................................3:21(pp)
2. Canada, Sanipass (Fleury, Keane) 5:03
3. Canada, Nemeth (Roy)..15:33(pp)
4. United States, Turcotte (Davidson)..............................19:24

PENALTIES: Chiasson (Can — match penalty) & Hartman (U.S. — match penalty) 00:00, Posma (U.S.) 2:15, Huffman (Can) 7:25, Nemeth (Can) 13:05, Jablonski (U.S.) 14:07, Latta (Can) 17:07

Second Period

5. United States, Young (Leetch) 0:33
6. Canada, Elynuik (Latta, McLlwain) 7:48

    PENALTIES: Hawgood (Can) 8:11, Joseph (Can) 13:10, Leetch (U.S.) 13:49

Third Period

7. Canada, Wesley (Shanahan).. 4:27
8. Canada, Elynuik (Latta) .... 19:00(pp)

    PENALTIES: Joseph (Can) 1:07, Joseph (Can) 9:28, Shanahan (Can) 12:36, Corkum (U.S.) 18:29

Shots on Goal:

Canada	10	14	7	31
United States	5	7	12	24

In Goal:

Canada — Waite
United States — Jablonski

January 2   *Canada 4*   *Sweden 3*

First Period

1. Canada, Latta (McLlwain) .... 3:53(pp)
2. Canada, Metcalfe (unassisted) 12:58

    PENALTIES: Sjogren (Swe) 3:18, Shanahan (Can) 4:09, Johansson (Swe) & Metcalfe (Can) 15:29, Turgeon (Can) 19:09

Second Period

3. Sweden, Franzen (Sjogren, Hansson) 2:20
4. Canada, Hawgood (Wesley).. 18:18(pp)

    PENALTIES: Metcalfe (Can) 6:09, Svanberg (Swe) 6:28, Johansson (Swe) & Sanipass (Can) 16:31, Akerstrom (Swe) 18:05, Latta (Can) 19:41

Third Period

5. Sweden, Sandstrom (Sjogren) 3:58
6. Sweden, Dahlen (Hansson, Ohman) .... 15:46(pp)
7. Canada, Shanahan (Hawgood, Metcalfe) 18:10

    PENALTIES: Joseph (Can) 12:16, McLlwain (Can) 15:10, Joseph (Can) 18:31, Svanberg (Swe) 18:59

Missed penalty shot: Tomas Sandstrom (Sweden) stopped by Jimmy Waite at 18:31 of 3rd

Shots on Goal:

Canada	5	4	6	15
Sweden	16	8	12	36

In Goal:

Canada — Waite
Sweden — Lindstahl

January 4   Canada 4   Soviet Union 2

(suspended by brawl — statistics from this game do not count)

First Period

1. Canada, Fleury (Keane, Sanipass) 4:34
2. Soviet Union, Shesterikov (Zelepukin) 4:45
3. Canada, Latta (Hawgood) 15:32
4. Canada, Fleury (unassisted) 18:47

     PENALTIES: Fleury (Can) 9:05, Wesley (Can) & Davydov (Sov) 13:55

Second Period

5. Soviet Union, Kostichkin (Tsygurov) 11:13
6. Canada, Nemeth (unassisted) 12:08

     PENALTIES: Malakhov (Sov) 0:47, Popov (Sov) 3:02, Popov (Sov) & Monaenkov (Sov) & Sanipass (Can) & Fleury (Can) 6:04, Davydov (Sov) 7:25, Hawgood (Can) 9:15, Latta (Can) & Davydov (Sov) 10:51

Brawl erupted at 13:53 of 2nd — game suspended

Shots on Goal:

unknown

In Goal:

Canada — Waite

Soviet Union — Ivannikov

TEAM CANADA FINAL STATISTICS
1987 WORLD JUNIOR CHAMPIONSHIPS

			GP	G	A	P	PIM
15	F	Pat Elynuik	6	6	5	11	2
22	F	David Latta	6	4	6	10	12
19	F	Steve Nemeth(A)	6	4	4	8	4
14	F	Dave McLlwain	6	4	4	8	2
18	F	Brendan Shanahan	6	4	3	7	4
16	F	Scott Metcalfe(A)	6	2	5	7	12
12	F	Everett Sanipass	6	3	2	5	8
10	F	Theoren Fleury	6	2	3	5	2
2	D	Greg Hawgood	6	2	2	4	6
20	F	Pierre Turgeon	6	3	0	3	2
4	D	Steve Chiasson(C)	6	2	1	3	16
9	F	Yvon Corriveau	6	2	1	3	4
3	D	Glen Wesley	6	2	1	3	4
5	D	Chris Joseph	6	1	1	2	14
21	F	Stephane Roy	6	0	1	1	6

6	D	Kerry Huffman	6	o	1	1	4
11	F	Mike Keane	6	o	1	1	4
8	D	Luke Richardson	6	o	o	o	o
1	G	Shawn Simpson	4	o	o	o	o
30	G	Jimmy Waite	3	o	o	o	o

In Goal

	GP	W–L–T	MINS	GA	SO	AVG
Jimmy Waite	3	2–0–0	160	10	o	3.75
Shawn Simpson	4	2–1–1	200	13	o	3.90

Goalie Notes:

1. Waite [3 goals] replaced Simpson [no goals] to start 2nd, December 30 vs. Poland

Coach   Bert Templeton
Assistant   Pat Burns

CANADIAN OFFICIALS AT THE 1987 WORLD JUNIOR CHAMPIONSHIPS

Richard Trottier (referee)   4 games

TEAM CANADA ROSTER SUMMARY

Team Canada players	20
Drafted Into NHL	19 (all but Keane)
Played In NHL	19 (all but Simpson)
Returning Players	None

PLAYER REPRESENTATION BY LEAGUE

OHL	7	(Huffman, Latta, McLlwain, Metcalfe, Richardson, Shanahan, Simpson)
WHL	6	(Elynuik, Fleury, Hawgood, Joseph, Keane, Wesley)
QMJHL	4	(Roy, Sanipass, Turgeon, Waite)
NHL	2	(Chiasson, Corriveau)
OTHER*	1	(Nemeth)

Canadian Olympic team

PLAYER REPRESENTATION BY AGE

19-year-olds	9	(Chiasson, Corriveau, Elynuik, Keane, Latta, McLlwain, Metcalfe, Nemeth, Roy)
18-year-olds	6	(Fleury, Hawgood, Huffman, Sanipass, Simpson, Wesley)
17-year-olds	5	(Joseph, Richardson, Shanahan, Turgeon, Waite)

PLAYERS' CAREER PROFILES

Steve Chiasson   Detroit Red Wings (NHL)
last Junior team: Guelph Platers (OHL)
Selected 50th overall by Detroit at 1985 Draft
Played in the NHL 1986 to present

Yvon Corriveau   Washington Capitals (NHL)
last Junior team: Toronto Marlboros (OHL)
Selected 19th overall by Washington at 1985 Draft
Played in the NHL 1985–94

Pat Elynuik   Prince Albert Raiders (WHL)
Selected 8th overall by Winnipeg at 1986 Draft
Played in the NHL 1987–96

Theoren Fleury   Moose Jaw Warriors (WHL)
Selected 166th overall by Calgary at 1986 Draft
Played in the NHL 1988 to present

Greg Hawgood   Kamloops Blazers (WHL)
Selected 202nd overall by Boston at 1986 Draft
Played in the NHL 1987 to present

Kerry Huffman   Guelph Platers (OHL)
Selected 20th overall by Philadelphia at 1986 Draft
Played in the NHL 1986–96

Chris Joseph   Seattle Thunderbirds (WHL)
Selected 5th overall by Pittsburgh at 1987 Draft
Played in the NHL 1987 to present

Mike Keane   Moose Jaw Warriors (WHL)
Not drafted
Played in the NHL 1988 to present

David Latta   Kitchener Rangers (OHL)
Selected 15th overall by Quebec at 1985 Draft
Played in the NHL 1985–91

Dave McLlwain   North Bay Centennials (OHL)
Selected 172nd overall by Pittsburgh at 1986 Draft
Played in the NHL 1987 to present

Scott Metcalfe   Kingston Canadians (OHL)
Selected 20th overall by Edmonton at 1985 Draft
Played in the NHL 1987–90

Steve Nemeth   Canadian Olympic Team
Selected 196th overall by Rangers at 1985 Draft
Played in the NHL 1987–88

Luke Richardson   Peterborough Petes (OHL)
Selected 7th overall by Toronto at 1987 Draft
Played in the NHL 1987 to present

Stephane Roy	Granby Bisons (QMJHL) Selected 51st overall by Minnesota at 1985 Draft Played in the NHL 1987–88
Everett Sanipass	Verdun Canadians (QMJHL) Selected 14th overall by Chicago at 1986 Draft Played in the NHL 1986–91
Brendan Shanahan	London Knights (OHL) Selected 2nd overall by New Jersey at 1987 Draft Played in the NHL 1987 to present
Shawn Simpson	Sault Ste. Marie Greyhounds (OHL) Selected 60th overall by Washington at 1986 Draft Did not play in the NHL
Pierre Turgeon	Granby Bisons (QMJHL) Selected 1st overall by Buffalo at 1987 Draft Played in the NHL 1987 to present
Jimmy Waite	Chicoutimi Sagueneens (QMJHL) Selected 8th overall by Chicago at 1987 Draft Played in the NHL 1988 to present
Glen Wesley	Portland Winter Hawks (WHL) Selected 3rd overall by Boston at 1987 Draft Played in the NHL 1987 to present

1988 WORLD JUNIOR CHAMPIONSHIPS SOVIET UNION, DECEMBER 26, 1987-- JANUARY 4, 1988

FINAL PLACINGS

GOLD MEDAL	**CANADA**
SILVER MEDAL	Soviet Union
BRONZE MEDAL	Finland
Fourth Place	Czechoslovakia
Fifth Place	Sweden
Sixth Place	United States
Seventh Place	West Germany*
Eighth Place	Poland**

promoted from "B" pool in 1987
**relegated to "B" pool for 1989*

ALL-STAR TEAM

GOAL	Jimmy Waite (Canada)
DEFENCE	Greg Hawgood (Canada)
	Teppo Numminen (Finland)
FORWARD	Theoren Fleury (Canada)
	Alexander Mogilny (Soviet Union)
	Petr Hrbek (Czechoslovakia)

DIRECTORATE AWARDS

BEST GOALIE	Jimmy Waite (Canada)
BEST DEFENCEMAN	Teppo Numminen (Finland)
BEST FORWARD	Alexander Mogilny (Soviet Union)

COACH DAVE CHAMBERS

Chambers had been coaching in a variety of leagues since 1972. His one consistent quality was his ability to win. He began as coach at the University of Saskatchewan, then moved to Ohio State University, where he earned his Ph.D. in physical education. He coached York University from 1972–77, winning coach of the year honours in 1975 and 1977. He coached the Marlies for one season (1979–80) and was coach of the year there, too. He returned to York and won the CIAU title in 1985. Then he took a year's leave of absence as athletic director at York to give his all to the national junior program.

He also coached the Italian national team in 1978 and 1981–83, winning the B pool at the 1981 World Championships that promoted the Italians to the world-class A pool. He coached part of 1981–82 with the Bern Bears in Switzerland, but quit in frustration because the part-time Swiss players lacked commitment to the team. He was behind the Spengler Cup bench in 1984 and again in gold-winning 1986, and acted as under-18 bench boss in 1985–86. By the time he hit the Canadian juniors in 1988, Chambers had enough national, international, and junior experience to make him the most qualified man for the job.

THE TEAM

Only four players were returnees from the previous, brawl-violated tournament, but four was all that was needed to make this a series of revenge and justification. What should have been Canada's last year was, at all costs, going to be ours this time around. Goalie Jimmy Waite, captain Theoren Fleury, and Greg Hawgood and Chris Joseph were back to prove a point. Their suspensions had been lifted by the IIHF the previous October, and they were ready.

The team was strengthened by the NHL additions of Rob Brown from Pittsburgh and Wayne McBean from L.A. Practises were held in Orleans, where an international-size rink made for superior preparations for the team. In their only exhibition game in Canada, the young Nats beat the Hull Olympiques (coached by Alain Vigneault) 6–3. They left the following morning for Finland. Last minute cuts included Benoit Brunet (Hull, for the second consecutive year), Daniel Marois (Verdun), Stephane Giguere (St. Jean), Jim Hrivnak (Merrimack College), and Bryan Deasley (University of Michigan).

The team landed in Helsinki and played two exhibitions before heading to Russia. The first was a jet-lagged 2–1 loss to the junior Finns. The next night there was a wild 11–7 shootout win over Kouvola, a team from the Finnish elite league. Then it was on to Moscow, where Olympian Chris Joseph had waited after the end of the Izvestia tournament to join the Canadian national juniors.

Captain Theoren Fleury and mates celebrate gold in '88 to make up for a lost medal in '87.

ODDS AND ENDS

The public address announcer, in an attempt to be thorough, called out at the appropriate time throughout the game: "Canada's penalty is over and Canada is at full strength." Adam Graves's reaction: "Strange, isn't it?"

CULTURE

After beating the Russians 3–2 New Year's Day, in what amounted to be the gold medal game, the Canadians visited their Embassy for some burgers and fries. The next day was a day off for the team and coach Chambers took them on a tour of Moscow that included the University of Moscow, KGB headquarters, and Novodevichy Convent, an historic section of old Moscow. The team saw the famous Moscow Circus that night and pounded the West Germans 8–1 the next.

The anticlimactic 9–1 win over Poland — technically the gold medal game — was played at the huge Olympiisky Arena in Moscow. It seats 28,000. Total attendance that day was . . . 120!

1987: CANADA'S YEAR

Canada won the Canada Cup again in 1987, then followed with a dramatic win in the Spengler Cup by the Olympic team, and closed the year with the World Junior win. Back on top of the hockey world.

TOURNAMENT FORMAT

All eight teams were placed in one division, and a round-robin was played. Czechoslovakia placed fourth and Sweden fifth because of goal differential (they tied 5–5 in the round robin). In another complex tie break, sixth, seventh, and eighth places were decided by goal differential:

United States	3–4, 6–4 = 9–8 (+1)
West Germany	4–6, 6–3 = 10–9 (+1)
Poland	3–6, 4–3 = 7–9 (−2)

The U.S. was placed above the Germans based on the earlier 6–4 win, thus finalizing the order.

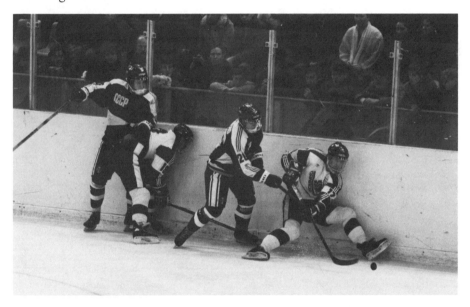

In what turned out to be the most important game of the tournament, Canada beat the Soviet Union 3-2 to avenge the Piestany brawl of the previous year and win the gold medal.

THE OPPOSITION

CZECHOSLOVAKIA

Zdenko Ciger, Radek Gardon, Pavel Gross, Roman Horak, Petr Hrbek, Juraj Jurik, Robert Kisela, Frantisek Kucera, Karel Mimochodek, Roman Nemcicky, Petr Pavlas, Rudolf Pejchar, Robert Reichel, Karel Smid, Roman Svacina, Pavel Taborsky, Milan Tichy, Pavel Valko, Ondrej Vosta, Josef Zajic

FINLAND

Harri Aho, Tero Arkiomaa, Kari Harila, Ari Hilli, Juha Jokiharju, Markku Jokinen, Marko Kiuru, Arto Kulmala, Marko Lapinkoski, Jukka Marttila, Teppo Numminen, Janne Ojanen, Timo Peltomaa, Petri Pulkkinen, Mika Rautio, Vesa Savolainen, Jukka Seppo, Pekka Tirkkonen, Tero Toivola, Mika Tuovinen

POLAND

Marek Batkiewicz, Janusz Janikowski, Jedrzej Kasperczyk, Mariusz Kieca, Marek Koszowski, Wlodzimierz Krol, Krzysztof Kuzniecow, Zbigniew Niedospial, Krzystaf Niedziolka, Czeslaw Niedzwiedz, Dariusz Olejowski, Jacek Plachta, Tadeusz Pulavski, Janusz Strzempek, Andrzej Szlapka, Wojciech Tkacz, Marek Trybus, Slovomir Weloch, Jacek Zamojski, Tomasz Zmudzinski

SOVIET UNION

Vladimir Aleksushin, Igor Chibirev, Igor Dorofeev, Sergei Fedorov, Alexei Ivashkin, Ulvis Katlaps, Pavel Kostichkin, Dmitri Kristich, Uriy Krivohija, Igor Malyhin, Alexander Mogilny, Evgeny Muhin, Sergei Petrenko, Syanislav Ranfilenkov, Andrei Rasolko, Alexei Sheblanov, Andrei Sidorov, Sergei Sorokin, Hariy Vitolinish, Valeri Zelepukin

SWEDEN

Fredrik Andersson, Patrik Carnbeck, Per Djoos, Patrik Eriksson, Tomas Forslund, Richard Franzen, Johan Garpenlov, Patrik Hofbauer, Peter Larsson, Petri Liimatainen, Per Ljustereng, Per Lundell, Stefan Nilsson, Stefan Nilsson (I), Stefan Nilsson (II), Markus Okerblom, Richard Persson, Leif Rohlin, Ola Rosander, Tomas Sjoegren

UNITED STATES

Ted Crowley, Lee Davidson, Joe Day, Kevin Dean, Ted Donato, David Emma, Jason Glickman, John LeClair, Rob Mendel, Kip Miller, Kris Miller, Mike Modano, Damian Rhodes, Jeremy Roenick, Steve Scheifele, Mathieu Schneider, Randy Skarda, Mike Sullivan, Darren Turcotte, Carl Young

WEST GERMANY

Tobias Abstreiter, Lutz Bongers, Thomas Brandl, Alfred Burghard, Markus Flemming, Peter Franke, Lorenz Funk, Frank Hirtreiter, Ernst Kopf, Christian Lukes, Andreas Lupzig, Joern Mayr, Gunter Oswald, Michael Pohl, Andreas Pokorny, Jurgen Rumrich, Heinz Schiffl, Thomas Schinko, Stefan Sinner, Jurgen Trattner

FINAL STANDINGS

	GP	W	L	T	GF	GA	P	GAA	SO	PIM
CANADA	7	6	0	1	37	16	13	2.29	0	88
Soviet Union	7	6	1	0	44	18	12	2.57	0	92
Finland	7	5	1	1	36	20	11	3.00	1	70*
Czechoslovakia	7	3	3	1	36	23	7	3.29	0	84
Sweden	7	3	3	1	36	24	7	3.43	1	114
United States	7	1	6	0	28	46	2	6.57	0	160
West Germany	7	1	6	0	18	47	2	6.71	0	82
Poland	7	1	6	0	12	53	2	7.57	0	84

* won Fair Play Cup

RESULTS

(all games played at Moscow)

December 26	Canada 4	Sweden 2
	Soviet Union 6	Czechoslovakia 4
	Finland 6	West Germany 0
	Poland 4	United States 3
December 28	Canada 4	Czechoslovakia 2
	Sweden 13	Poland 0
	Soviet Union 6	Finland 2
	United States 6	West Germany 4
December 29	Canada 4	Finland 4
	Sweden 5	West Germany 1
	Czechoslovakia 6	Poland 1
	Soviet Union 7	United States 3
December 31	Canada 5	United States 4
	Czechoslovakia 7	West Germany 4
	Soviet Union 4	Sweden 2
	Finland 9	Poland 1
January 1	Canada 3	Soviet Union 2
	West Germany 6	Poland 3
	Czechoslovakia 5	Sweden 5
	Finland 8	United States 6
January 3	Canada 8	West Germany 1
	Finland 5	Sweden 2
	Soviet Union 7	Poland 2
	Czechoslovakia 11	United States 1

January 4	Canada 9	Poland 1
	Soviet Union 12	West Germany 2
	Finland 2	Czechoslovakia 1
	Sweden 7	United States 5

TEAM CANADA GAME SUMMARIES

December 26 *Canada 4* *Sweden 2*

First Period

1. Canada, Dimaio (unassisted) 11:14
2. Canada, Brown (Recchi) 15:25
3. Sweden, Garpenlov (Nilsson) 16:09

   PENALTIES: Graves (Can) 1:55, Franzen (Swe) 8:12, Eriksson (Swe) 16:34

Second Period

No Scoring

   PENALTIES: Brown (Can) 1:32, Dimaio (Can) 5:19, Persson (Swe) 8:03, Nilsson (Swe) 16:05

Third Period

4. Canada, Currie (Kennedy) .... 7:15(pp)
5. Canada, Fleury (Hull) 7:58
6. Sweden, Larsson (Persson, Sjoegren) .... 14:04(pp)

   PENALTIES: Nilsson (Swe) 2:06, Djoos (Swe) 6:50, Larsson (Swe) 8:31, Kennedy (Can) 10:17, McCrady (Can) 13:42, Carnbeck (Swe) 14:26

Shots on Goal:

| Canada | 13 | 10 | 12 | **35** |
| Sweden | 10 | 3 | 7 | **20** |

In Goal:

Canada — Waite
Sweden — Hofbauer

December 28 *Canada 4* *Czechoslovakia 2*

First Period

1. Canada, Sakic (Kennedy) 3:07
2. Czechoslovakia, Jurik (Kisela) .... 11:05(pp)
3. Canada, Brown (Hawgood, Babe) 11:27

   PENALTIES: Graves (Can) 0:46, Laniel (Can) 4:26, Ciger (Cze) 6:38, Sakic (Can) 8:14, Joseph (Can) 9:13, Pederson (Can) 17:40, Mimochodek (Cze) 18:12

Second Period

4. Czechoslovakia, Ciger (Hrbek) .... 9:21 (pp)

     PENALTIES: Currie (Can) 5:17, Desjardins (Can) 8:19, McCrady (Can) 12:54, Mimochodek (Cze) 13:36, Hawgood (Can) 18:31

Third Period

5. Canada, Graves (unassisted) .... 8:47 (sh)
6. Canada, Fleury (Brown) .... 10:29 (pp)

     PENALTIES: Reichel (Cze) 1:06, Pavlas (Cze) 4:37, McBean (Can) 7:10, Vosta (Cze) 8:37, Dimaio (Can) 11:40, Desjardins (Can) 16:03, Fleury (Can) 19:05

Shots on Goal:

Canada	16	7	6	**29**
Czechoslovakia	13	4	9	**26**

In Goal:

Canada — Waite

Czechosovakia — Pejchar

December 29   *Canada 4*   *Finland 4*

First Period

1. Finland, Jokiharju (unassisted) 9:33
2. Canada, Hull (unassisted) 17:48
3. Finland, Jokiharju (Arkiomaa) 19:19

     PENALTIES: Fleury (Can) 4:15, Ojanen (Fin) 5:38, Harila (Fin) 7:13, Ojanen (Fin) 12:18, Desjardins (Can) 19:28

Second Period

4. Canada, Sakic (Babe) 7:38
5. Finland, Tirkkonen (Seppo) 9:19
6. Canada, Kennedy (unassisted) 13:52
7. Canada, Currie (Fleury, Hawgood) 19:26

     PENALTIES: Waite (Can) 4:35, Babe (Can) & Kennedy (Can) 9:27, Peltomaa (Fin) 9:45, Aho (Fin) 14:35

Third Period

8. Finland, Numminen (unassisted) 0:48

     PENALTIES: none

Shots on Goal:

Canada	4	9	4	**17**
Finland	12	8	15	**35**

In Goal:

Canada — Waite

Finland — Rautio

December 31   *Canada 5*   *United States 4*

First Period

1. United States, Miller (unassisted) .... 12:05(pp)
2. Canada, Currie (unassisted)... 13:44(pp)
3. Canada, Kennedy (Hawgood)... 18:43
4. United States, Modano (Day)... 19:19

   PENALTIES: Dimaio (Can) 10:56, Day (U.S.) 13:16

Second Period

5. Canada, Fleury (Currie) 0:12
6. Canada, Brown (Hawgood) 3:16
7. Canada, Joseph (Laniel)... 13:06(pp)

   PENALTIES: Joseph (Can) 0:42, Glickman (U.S.) 11:11, Laniel (Can) 14:15, McCrady (Can) 16:12, Donato (U.S.) 17:05, Babe (Can) 19:34

Third Period

8. United States, Miller (Davidson) .... 0:16(pp)
9. United States, Donato (Roenick) .... 11:42(pp)

   PENALTIES: Pederson (Can) & Miller (U.S.) & Scheifele (U.S.) 5:45, Hull (Can) 9:47, Emma (U.S.) 14:28

Shots on Goal:

Canada	14	13	9	36
United States	10	2	13	25

In Goal:

Canada — Waite
United States — Glickman

January 1   *Canada 3*   *Soviet Union 2*

First Period

1. Canada, Fleury (Joseph) .... 8:12(pp)
2. Canada, Linden (Hawgood) 10:12

   PENALTIES: Malyhin (Sov) 0:39, Malyhin (Sov) 7:26, Laniel (Can) 11:29, Recchi (Can) 18:47

Second Period

3. Soviet Union, Vitolinish (Katlaps, Dorofeev) .... 6:55(pp)
4. Canada, Laniel (Pederson) .... 11:45(pp)
5. Soviet Union, Zelepukin (Kristich) 12:13

   PENALTIES: Joseph (Can) 6:38, Vitolinish (Sov) 10:49, Mogilny (Sov) 13:50, Joseph (Can) 14:49, Hawgood (Can) 16:13

Third Period

No Scoring

   PENALTIES: none

Shots on Goal:

Canada	8	4	4	**16**
Soviet Union	6	17	17	**40**

In Goal:

Canada — Waite
Soviet Union — Sheblanov

January 3   Canada 8   *West Germany 1*

First Period

1. Canada, Brown (unassisted)..14:54

   PENALTIES: Mayr (WGer) 1:34, Babe (Can) 17:24

Second Period

2. Canada, Graves (Hawgood) ....4:51(pp)
3. Canada, Hull (Currie, Fleury)...6:20
4. Canada, Graves (Laniel)...6:54
5. Canada, Graves (Recchi)...10:37
6. Canada, Currie (Hawgood) 18:27

   PENALTIES: Sinner (WGer) 4:00, Sinner (WGer) 8:33, Hawgood (Can) & Kennedy (Can) 11:02

Third Period

7. Canada, Sakic (unassisted)..2:33(sh)
8. Canada, Brown (Pederson) 7:28
9. West Germany, Lupzig (Schiffl, Schinko) 17:08

   PENALTIES: Dimaio (Can) 1:02, Babe (Can) 8:25, Rumrich (WGer) 18:07

Shots on Goal:

Canada	15	25	10	**50**
West Germany	7	6	10	**23**

In Goal:

Canada — Waite
West Germany — Franke

January 4   Canada 9   *Poland 1*

First Period

1. Canada, Fleury (Hawgood, Joseph) ....3:39(pp)
2. Poland, Koszowski (Olejowski) ....12:06(pp)
3. Canada, Fleury (Currie) 14:09

   PENALTIES: Pol bench (served by Trybus) 2:29, Babe (Can) 5:57, Recchi (Can) 11:48, Plachta (Pol) 16:42

Second Period

4. Canada, Graves (Recchi)...19:35

    PENALTIES: Zmudzinski (Pol) 3:29, Tkacz (Pol) 5:45, McCrady (Can) 9:13

Third Period

5. Canada, Brown (unassisted)...3:10(pp)
6. Canada, Hawgood (Recchi, McCrady) 5:15
7. Canada, Kennedy (unassisted) 12:52
8. Canada, Pederson (Brown)..14:58
9. Canada, Kennedy (Sakic) 17:09
10. Canada, McBean (Recchi) 18:59

    PENALTIES: Tkacz (Pol) 1:15, Plachta (Pol) 9:47, Koszowski (Pol) & Dimaio (Can)
    17:37

Shots on Goal:

Canada	10	18	24	52
Poland	9	7	2	18

In Goal:

Canada — Waite

Poland — Kieca

TEAM CANADA FINAL STATISTICS
1988 WORLD JUNIOR CHAMPIONSHIPS

			GP	G	A	P	PIM
4	D	Greg Hawgood	7	1	8	9	6
9	F	Theoren Fleury(C)	7	6	2	8	4
16	F	Rob Brown	7	6	2	8	2
26	F	Dan Currie	7	4	3	7	2
20	F	Sheldon Kennedy	7	4	2	6	6
15	F	Adam Graves	7	5	0	5	4
8	F	Mark Recchi	7	0	5	5	4
19	F	Joe Sakic	7	3	1	4	2
12	F	Jody Hull	7	2	1	3	2
5	D	Chris Joseph	7	1	2	3	8
3	D	Marc Laniel	7	1	2	3	6
14	F	Mark Pederson	7	1	2	3	4
17	F	Warren Babe	7	0	2	2	10
18	F	Rob Dimaio	7	1	0	1	10
7	D	Wayne McBean	7	1	0	1	2
10	F	Trevor Linden	7	1	0	1	0
6	D	Scott McCrady	7	0	1	1	8
21	D	Eric Desjardins	7	0	0	0	6
29	G	Jimmy Waite	7	0	0	0	2

In Goal

	GP	W–L–T	MINS	GA	SO	AVG
Jimmy Waite	7	6–0–1	419	16	0	2.29
Jeff Hackett	did not play					

Coach   Dave Chambers
Assistant   Ken Hitchcock/Jean Begin

CANADIAN OFFICIALS AT THE 1988 WORLD JUNIOR CHAMPIONSHIPS

Dave Lynch (referee)   4 games

TEAM CANADA ROSTER SUMMARY

Team Canada players	19
Drafted Into NHL	19
Played In NHL	17 (all but Laniel, McCrady)
Returning Players	4 (Fleury, Hawgood, Joseph, Waite)

PLAYER REPRESENTATION BY LEAGUE

OHL	4	(Curry, Graves, Hull, Laniel)
WHL	9	(Dimaio, Fleury, Hawgood, Kennedy, Linden, McCrady, Pederson, Recchi, Sakic)
QMJHL	2	(Desjardins, Waite)
NHL	4	(Babe, Brown, Joseph, McBean)

PLAYER REPRESENTATION BY AGE

19-year-olds	11	(Babe, Brown, Currie, Dimaio, Fleury, Graves, Hawgood, Laniel, McCrady, Pederson, Recchi)
18-year-olds	7	(Desjardins, Hull, Joseph, Kennedy, McBean, Sakic, Waite)
17-year-olds	1	(Linden)

PLAYERS' CAREER PROFILES

Warren Babe   Minnesota North Stars (NHL)
                     Last Junior team: Kamloops Blazers (WHL)
                     Selected 12th overall by Minnesota at 1986 Draft
                     Played in the NHL 1987–91

Rob Brown
　　　　　　　Pittsburgh Penguins (NHL)
　　　　　　　Last Junior team: Kamloops Blazers (WHL)
　　　　　　　Selected 67th overall by Pittsburgh at 1986 Draft
　　　　　　　Played in the NHL 1987 to present

Dan Currie
　　　　　　　Sault Ste. Marie Greyhounds (OHL)
　　　　　　　Selected 84th overall by Edmonton at 1986 Draft
　　　　　　　Played in the NHL 1990–94

Eric Desjardins
　　　　　　　Granby Bisons (QMJHL)
　　　　　　　Selected 38th overall by Montreal at 1987 Draft
　　　　　　　Played in the NHL 1988 to present

Rob Dimaio
　　　　　　　Medicine Hat Tigers (WHL)
　　　　　　　Selected 118th overall by Islanders at 1987 Draft
　　　　　　　Played in the NHL 1988 to present

Theoren Fleury
　　　　　　　Moose Jaw Warriors (WHL)
　　　　　　　Selected 166th overall by Calgary at 1987 Draft
　　　　　　　Played in the NHL 1988 to present

Adam Graves
　　　　　　　Windsor Spitfires (OHL)
　　　　　　　Selected 22nd overall by Detroit at 1986 Draft
　　　　　　　Played in the NHL 1987 to present

Greg Hawgood
　　　　　　　Kamloops Blazers (WHL)
　　　　　　　Selected 202nd overall by Boston at 1986 Draft
　　　　　　　Played in the NHL 1987 to present

Jody Hull
　　　　　　　Peterborough Petes (OHL)
　　　　　　　Selected 18th overall by Hartford at 1987 Draft
　　　　　　　Played in the NHL 1988 to present

Chris Joseph
　　　　　　　Edmonton Oilers (NHL)
　　　　　　　Last Junior team: Seattle Thunderbirds (WHL)
　　　　　　　Selected 5th overall by Pittsburgh at 1987 Draft
　　　　　　　Played in the NHL 1987 to present

Sheldon Kennedy
　　　　　　　Swift Current Broncos (WHL)
　　　　　　　Selected 80th overall by Detroit at 1988 Draft
　　　　　　　Played in the NHL 1989 to present

Marc Laniel
　　　　　　　Oshawa Generals (OHL)
　　　　　　　Selected 62nd overall by New Jersey at 1986 Draft
　　　　　　　Did not play in the NHL

Trevor Linden
　　　　　　　Medicine Hat Tigers (WHL)
　　　　　　　Selected 2nd overall by Vancouver at 1988 Draft
　　　　　　　Played in the NHL 1988 to present

Wayne McBean
　　　　　　　Los Angeles Kings (NHL)
　　　　　　　Last Junior team: Medicine Hat Tigers (WHL)
　　　　　　　Selected 4th overall by Los Angeles at 1987 Draft
　　　　　　　Played in the NHL 1987–94

Scott McCrady
　　　　　　　Medicine Hat Tigers (WHL)
　　　　　　　Selected 35th overall by Minnesota at 1987 Draft
　　　　　　　Did not play in the NHL

Mark Pederson   Medicine Hat Tigers (WHL)
Selected 15th overall by Montreal at 1986 Draft
Played in the NHL 1989–94

Mark Recchi   Kamloops Blazers (WHL)
Selected 67th overall by Pittsburgh at 1988 Draft
Played in the NHL 1988 to present

Joe Sakic   Swift Current Broncos (WHL)
Selected 15th overall by Quebec at 1987 Draft
Played in the NHL 1988 to present

Jimmy Waite   Chicoutimi Sagueneens (QMJHL)
Selected 8th overall by Chicago at 1987 Draft
Played in the NHL 1988 to present

1989 WORLD JUNIOR CHAMPIONSHIPS UNITED STATES, DECEMBER 26, 1988-- JANUARY 4, 1989

FINAL PLACINGS

GOLD MEDAL — Soviet Union
SILVER MEDAL — Sweden
BRONZE MEDAL — Czechoslovakia
Fourth Place — **CANADA**
Fifth Place — United States
Sixth Place — Finland
Seventh Place — Norway*
Eighth Place — West Germany**

promoted from "B" pool in 1988
**relegated to "B" pool for 1990*

ALL-STAR TEAM

GOAL — Alexei Ivashkin (Soviet Union)
DEFENCE — Rickard Persson (Sweden)
Milan Tichy (Czechoslovakia)
FORWARD — Niklas Eriksson (Sweden)
Pavel Bure (Soviet Union)
Jeremy Roenick (United States)

DIRECTORATE AWARDS

BEST GOALIE — Alexei Ivashkin (Soviet Union)
BEST DEFENCEMAN — Rickard Persson (Sweden)
BEST FORWARD — Pavel Bure (Soviet Union)

COACH TOM WEBSTER

Webster began his hockey life as a player, and although many an NHL coach started by playing, he was the only man with experience in the big leagues to coach the national junior team.

He played for a decade in the NHL and WHA, then coached Adirondack from 1979 to 1981. From there he went to Springfield (1981–82), Tulsa (1982–84), and Salt Lake City of the IHL (1984–85). He moved back to Canada to coach the Windsor Spitfires from 1985 to 1989.

His second season with Tulsa was incredible. The team went bankrupt midway through the year, but rather than abandon all hope they moved to Denver and played the last twenty-seven games of their season on the road. They made the playoffs and swept the Indianapolis Checkers to win the CHL championship. After he coached Canada's juniors, Webster was offered the head coaching job with Los Angeles. He stayed with the Kings for three years.

His years with the Spits were interrupted in 1986–87, when he took over as coach of the New York Rangers. However, he developed a serious ear problem that prevented him from flying, so he resigned as coach. He returned to Windsor, had an operation to correct the ear problem and resumed his coaching career, though not in the NHL.

THE ROSTER

As usual, the under-20 Canadians playing in the NHL would have made a gold medal team — but they were unavailable. This year's list included Brendan Shanahan, Joe Sakic, Pierre Turgeon, Dave Archibald, Luke Richardson, Wayne McBean, Chris Joseph, Jody Hull, Trevor Linden, Jimmy Waite, and Curtis Leschyshyn. Cornwall Royals goalie Rick Tabaracci and Jason Muzzatti of Michigan State were the only invitees to turn the Nats down.

The players arrived at camp in Calgary on December 14 and had eight days to impress before coach Webster had to finalize his roster. Cuts at camp included Brent Grieve (Oshawa), Kevin Miehm (Oshawa), Russ Romaniuk (University of North Dakota), Mike Griffith (Ottawa), Eric Dubois (Laval), Peter Ing (London), and Jeff Harding (of the NHL Flyers). The team lost its first exhibition game 6–4 to the University of Calgary on December 16, but beat the Swedish national team 7–5 two days later. Both games were played at the Father David Bauer arena in Calgary. A few days later, the Swedes beat Canada 7–1.

The win by the U of C team was especially sweet for the players because although Canada produces the vast majority of NHLers, the universities are rarely, if ever, scouted by the pros. Considered inferior and non-competitive,

Mike Ricci (#9, Peterborough) provided the team with grit and leadership throughout the '89 tournament and was selected 4th overall by Philadelphia in the Entry Draft the following year.

CIAU hockey has always provided high quality skill for those who wish to gain a serious education. For those students to beat Canada's finest juniors, admittedly roughly-hewn at this stage of preparation, was thrilling.

December 22 was final roster day, and that meant heartbreak for three players: goaler Danny Lorenz (Seattle, WHL), defenceman Brian Collinson (Toronto, OHL), and forward Scott Pearson (Niagara Falls, OHL). Only Pearson went on to play in the NHL.

GOLD MEDAL DECISION

The Russians won the gold medal by virtue of a 3–2 win over Sweden in the round robin. (Both countries had finished with 6–1 records.) However, there was a bit of intrigue in the game. The Swedes felt they had scored the tying goal only to discover that there were *two* pucks on the ice! Referee Dave Piotrowski of the U.S. disallowed the goal, the Swedes protested, and the final score was 3–2. The next day, the IIHF directorate supported Piotrowski's decision after watching video highlights from the game, concluding that the puck seemed to have come from someone on the ice rather than in the stands!

CAPITALISM

The tournament was held in Anchorage, on U.S. soil, so it was all the more appealing to players from behind the Iron Curtain. Two — Roman Kontsek of the Czechs and Sergei Gomolyako of the Soviets — were arrested for shoplifting from a local department store. They were not charged. Kontsek was suspended by his Federation for the series and was suspended by the IIHF for eighteen months. Gomolyako, the Russians assured one and all, would be dealt with upon his return home. Gulp.

TOURNAMENT FORMAT

All eight countries were placed in a single division and played a round-robin schedule. The first factor in breaking a tie between two nations was the result of the head-to-head game in the round robin, which is how the Soviets beat Sweden for the gold. The second determining factor was goal differential (goals against subtracted from goals for), which is how the Czechs beat Canada for the bronze. The teams tied 2–2 in the round robin, but the Czechs were a +17 (36 goals scored, 19 goals allowed) while Canada was just +8 (31–23).

THE OPPOSITION

CZECHOSLOVAKIA

Martin Bakula, Josef Beranek, Vladimir Buril, Zdenko Ciger, Jiri Cihlar, Radek Gardon, Bobby Holik, Petr Hrbek, Jaroslav Kames, Roman Kontsek, Martin Maskarinec, Robert Reichel, Lubos Rob, Milan Tichy, Roman Turek, Jan Varholik, Roman Veber, Jiri Vykoukal, Pavol Zubek, Peter Zubek

FINLAND

Petri Aaltonen, Mika Alatalo, Henry Eskelinen, Veli-Pekka Kautonen, Marko Kiuru, Karri Kivi, Petro Koivunen, Juha Lampinen, Marko Lapinkoski, Janne Leppanen, Jouko Myrra, Sami Nuutinen, Rauli Raitanen, Timo Saarikoski, Keijo Sailynoja, Teemu Selanne, Teemu Sillanpaa, Mika Stromberg, Mika Valila, Juha Virenius

NORWAY

Glenn Asland, Bjorn Berg Larsen, Magnus Christoffersen, Ole-Eskild Dahlstrom, Tom Erik Olsen, Jan Erik Smithurst, Klas Forfang, Mattis Haakensen,

Tommy Jakobsen, Stig Johansen, Espen Kjell Knutsen, Rune Kraft, Kent Inge Kristiansen, Pal Kristiansen, Remo Martinsen, Magne Nordnes, Oystein Olsen, Christian Olsvik, Marius Rath, Bjornar Sorensen

SOVIET UNION

Pavel Bure, Boris Bykovsky, Sergei Fedorov, Alexander Godynyuk, Sergei Gomalyako, Victor Gordiuk, Igor Ivanov, Alexei Ivashkin, Dmitri Kristich, Igor Malykhin, Maxim Mikhailovsky, Alexander Mogilny, Roman Oksiuta, Stanislav Panfilenkov, Andrei Sidorov, Sergei Sorokin, Vladimir Tsyplakov, Alexandr Yudin, Dmitri Yushkevich, Sergei Zubov

SWEDEN

Markus Akerblom, Niklas Andersson, Jan Bergman, Stefan Claesson, Stefan Elvenes, Patrik Erickson, Niklas Eriksson, Peter Hammarstrom, Magnus Jansson, Pierre Johnsson, Jonas Karlsson, Patric Kjellberg, Petri Liimatainen, Torbjorn Lindberg, Stefan Ornskog, Rickard Persson, Ola Rosander, Daniel Rydmark, Tommy Soderstrom, Mattias Svedberg

UNITED STATES

Tony Amonte, Adam Burt, Neil Carnes, Peter Ciavaglia, Ted Crowley, Tom Dion, David Emma, Jason Glickman, Bill Guerin, Steve Heinze, Shaun Kane, Mike Lappin, John LeClair, Mike Modano, Tom Pederson, Mark Richards, Barry Richter, Jeremy Roenick, Joe Sacco, Rodger Sykes

WEST GERMANY

Tobias Abstreiter, Thomas Brandl, Christian Curth, Lorenz Funk, Reinhard Haider, Rolf Hammer, Peter Heima, Raphael Krueger, Wolfgang Kummer, Christian Lukes, Jorg Mayr, Gunther Oswald, Andreas Ott, Reemt Pyka, Michael Raubal, Jurgen Schulz, Stefan Sinner, Roland Timoschuk, Stefan Urban, Bernd Zimmer

FINAL STANDINGS

	GP	W	L	T	GF	GA	P	GAA	SO	PIM
Soviet Union	7	6	1	0	51	14	12	2.00	2	78
Sweden	7	6	1	0	39	14	12	2.00	1	78
Czechoslovakia	7	4	2	1	36	19	9	2.71	0	80
CANADA	7	4	2	1	31	23	9	3.29	0	110
United States	7	3	3	1	41	25	7	3.57	0	74
Finland	7	2	4	1	29	37	5	5.29	0	98
Norway	7	1	6	0	14	56	2	8.00	0	56*
West Germany	7	0	7	0	13	66	0	9.43	0	79

* won Fair Play Cup

RESULTS

December 26	Fire Lake	Canada 7	Norway 1
	Anchorage	Sweden 5	Czechoslovakia 3
	Anchorage	Soviet Union 15	West Germany 0
	Anchorage	Finland 5	United States 5
December 27	Anchorage	Czechoslovakia 7	Norway 1
	Anchorage	Soviet Union 4	United States 2
December 28	Anchorage	Canada 7	West Germany 4
	Anchorage	Sweden 6	Finland 2
December 29	Anchorage	Canada 5	United States 1
	Anchorage	Soviet Union 3	Sweden 2
	Fire Lake	Finland 9	Norway 3
	Fire Lake	Czechoslovakia 11	West Germany 1
December 30	Anchorage	Soviet Union 10	Norway 0
	Anchorage	United States 5	Czechoslovakia 1
December 31	Anchorage	Sweden 5	Canada 4
	Anchorage	Finland 5	West Germany 3
January 1	Anchorage	Canada 2	Czechoslovakia 2
	Fire Lake	Soviet Union 9	Finland 3
	Fire Lake	Sweden 9	Norway 1
	Anchorage	United States 15	West Germany 3
January 2	Anchorage	Czechoslovakia 5	Soviet Union 3
	Anchorage	United States 12	Norway 4
January 3	Anchorage	Canada 4	Finland 3
	Anchorage	Sweden 9	West Germany 0
January 4	Anchorage	Soviet Union 7	Canada 2
	Fire Lake	Norway 4	West Germany 2
	Fire Lake	Czechoslovakia 7	Finland 2
	Anchorage	Sweden 3	United States 1

TEAM CANADA GAME SUMMARIES

December 26   Canada 7   Norway 1

First Period

1. Canada, Savage (Shannon) 4:00
2. Norway, Asland (Dahlstrom) 4:57
3. Canada, Ricci (Foster, Gelinas) .... 11:03(pp)

   PENALTIES: K. Kristiansen (Nor) & Kennedy (Can) 0:20, Loewen (Can) 5:56, Smithurst (Nor) 9:49, Dahlstrom (Nor) 18:27

Second Period

4. Canada, Desjardins (Cassels, Gelinas) 0:29
5. Canada, Foster (Kennedy) .... 15:15(pp)

PENALTIES: Loewen (Can) 2:15, Gelinas (Can) 6:21, Gelinas (Can) 18:06, Asland (Nor) 13:32

Third Period

6. Canada, Shannon (Cimetta, Savage) 7:59
7. Canada, Murphy (unassisted) .... 10:45(sh)
8. Canada, Cimetta (Savage)... 12:53

PENALTIES: Brind'Amour (Can) 2:11, Kennedy (Can) 8:54, Racine (Can) 9:43, Loewen (Can) 13:08, Racine (Can) 19:05

Shots on Goal:

unknown

In Goal:

Canada — Fiset
Norway — Martinsen

December 28   *Canada 7*   *West Germany 4*

First Period

1. Canada, McIntyre (Loewen) 6:09
2. Canada, Lambert (Cassels) .... 18:41(pp)
3. Canada, Leach (Foster)... 19:58

PENALTIES: Murphy (Can) 9:32, Oswald (WGer) & Murphy (Can) 15:31, Mayr (WGer) 18:29

Second Period

4. West Germany, Funk (Mayr) 5:51
5. Canada, Cimetta (Savage) 16:20

PENALTIES: Kennedy (Can) 8:22, Brandl (WGer) 16:29

Third Period

6. Canada, Ricci (Brind'Amour, Leach) 1:20
7. Canada, Brind'Amour (Lambert, Leach) 6:24
8. West Germany, Oswald (Sinner, Mayr) ....7:14(pp)
9. West Germany, Funk (Pyka).....................................8:35(pp)
10. Canada, Loewen (Lambert, Cassels) 14:10
11. West Germany, Hammer (Brandl, Mayr) .... 19:16(pp)

PENALTIES: Kennedy (Can) 1:42, Murphy (Can) 7:06, Kennedy (Can) 7:46, Cimetta (Can) 9:01, Shannon (Can) 10:25, Sinner (WGer) & Ricci (Can) 15:51, Cassels (Can) 16:45, Desjardins (Can) 17:39

Shots on Goal:

Canada	17	11	14	**42**
West Germany	6	11	11	**28**

In Goal:

Canada — Morschauser
West Germany — Haider

December 29   Canada 5   United States 1

First Period

1. Canada, Savage (unassisted) 5:56
2. Canada, Ricci (Foster) 13:48

PENALTIES: Guerin (U.S.) 0:30, Lambert (Can) 1:57, Smith (Can) 15:14, Kane (U.S.) 18:35

Second Period

3. Canada, Savage (Cimetta) 11:13
4. Canada, Kennedy (Desjardins, Savage) .... 18:13(pp)

PENALTIES: Shannon (Can) 6:09, Emma (U.S.) & Veilleux (Can) 8:24, LeClair (U.S.) 17:58

Third Period

5. United States, Roenick (Dion, Modano) 4:11
6. Canada, Cimetta (Leach) 7:25

PENALTIES: none

Shots on Goal:

Canada	2	13	12	**27**
United States	7	7	8	**22**

In Goal:

Canada — Fiset
United States — Glickman/Richards (Richards [one goal] replaced Glickman [4 goals] to start 3rd)

December 31   Sweden 5   Canada 4

First Period

1. Canada, Cimetta (Savage, Desjardins) 8:12

PENALTIES: Shannon (Can) 5:34, Leach (Can) 11:57

Second Period

2. Canada, Kennedy (Smith, Cassels) 12:22
3. Sweden, Jansson (Kjellberg) 13:05
4. Sweden, Persson (Svedberg, Akerblom) 15:29
5. Canada, Ricci (Cassels) .... 18:49(pp)

PENALTIES: Ricci (Can) & Kjellberg (Swe) 5:55, McIntyre (Can) 10:12, Elvenes (Swe) 17:02

Third Period

6. Sweden, Persson (Erickson) .... 2:40(pp)
7. Canada, Cimetta (Ricci) 15:23
8. Sweden, Akerblom (Lindberg) 16:59
9. Sweden, Akerblom (Rosander) 19:33

   PENALTIES: Ricci (Can) 2:15, Rosander (Swe) 4:09, Loewen (Can) 8:03, Cimetta (Can) & Desjardins (Can) 19:43

Shots on Goal:

Canada	4	7	7	18
Sweden	12	14	12	38

In Goal:

Canada — Fiset
Sweden — Karlsson

January 1   *Canada 2*   *Czechoslovakia 2*

First Period

1. Czechoslovakia, Holik (Reichel, Cihlar) .... 5:20(pp)

   PENALTIES: Gelinas (Can) 4:15, Brind'Amour (Can) 6:36, Tichy (Cze) 9:32, Kennedy (Can) 9:40, Pe. Zubek (Cze) 14:28, Shannon (Can) 18:00, Bakula (Cze) 18:47

Second Period

2. Canada, Cimetta (Desjardins) 4:02
3. Czechoslovakia, Holik (Reichel) 15:32

   PENALTIES: Bakula (Cze) 13:03, Kennedy (Can) 20:00

Third Period

4. Canada, Cimetta (Ricci, Kennedy) .... 19:28(ea/pp)

   PENALTIES: Veilleux (Can) 4:45, Shannon (Can) 6:46, Vykoukal (Cze) 9:39, Gelinas (Can) 16:45, Ciger (Cze) & Murphy (Can) 18:38, Bakula (Cze) 19:08

Shots on Goal:

Canada	10	11	5	26
Czechoslovakia	8	14	5	27

In Goal:

Canada — Fiset
Czechoslovakia — Turek

January 3   *Canada 4*   *Finland 3*

First Period

No Scoring

   PENALTIES: Loewen (Can) 7:55, Koivunen (Fin) 11:04, Foster (Can) & Leppanen (Fin) 13:07, Sillanpaa (Fin) 14:05

Second Period

1. Finland, Stromberg (Saarikoski, Alatalo)..4:46
2. Finland, Selanne (Nuutinen)...9:58
3. Canada, Savage (Kennedy, Brind'Amour)..................................15:22(pp)

   PENALTIES: Savage (Can) & Selanne (Fin) 1:13, Leppanen (Fin) 5:29, Savage (Can) 11:21, Virenius (Fin — served by Raitanen) 14:24, McIntyre (Can) 16:08, Kautonen (Fin) 19:14, Stromberg (Fin) 19:24

Third Period

4. Canada, Brind'Amour (Kennedy, Desjardins) ....1:01(pp)
5. Canada, Kennedy (unassisted)...5:19
6. Finland, Selanne (Kautonen, Virenius) 16:30
7. Canada, Cassels (Shannon, Brind'Amour).......................................17:46

   PENALTIES: Fin bench 1:54, Loewen (Can) 6:20, Smith (Can) 8:15

Shots on Goal:

Canada	11	11	12	**34**
Finland	14	9	6	**29**

In Goal:

Canada — Fiset
Finland — Virenius

January 4　　　*Soviet Union 7*　　　*Canada 2*

First Period

1. Soviet Union, Kristich (Panfilenkov)...9:08
2. Canada, Cassels (Cimetta, Shannon)..18:41

   PENALTIES: Gomolyako (Sov) 10:11, Veilleux (Can) 14:43, Desjardins (Can) 15:45, Kristich (Sov) 16:18

Second Period

3. Soviet Union, Mogilny (Fedorov) 0:20
4. Soviet Union, Sidorov (unassisted) 1:33
5. Soviet Union, Mogilny (unassisted) 3:41
6. Soviet Union, Mogilny (Fedorov) ....8:01(pp)
7. Soviet Union, Oksiuta (Gordiuk, Ivanov)...................................8:52(pp)
8. Canada, Ricci (Leach, Cimetta) 18:30

   PENALTIES: Foster (Can) 6:05, Racine (Can) 7:03, Veilleux (Can) 19:10

Third Period

9. Soviet Union, Fedorov (Bure, Mogilny)....................................0:50(pp)

   PENALTIES: Zubov (Sov) 15:10, Lambert (Can) 17:23

Shots on Goal:

Canada	10	7	10	**27**
Soviet Union	10	22	10	**42**

In Goal:

Canada — Fiset/Morschauser (Morschauser [one goal] replaced Fiset
[6 goals] at 8:52 of 2nd)
Soviet Union — Ivashkin

TEAM CANADA FINAL STATISTICS
1989 WORLD JUNIOR CHAMPIONSHIPS

			GP	G	A	P	PIM
27	F	Rob Cimetta	7	7	4	11	4
18	F	Reginald Savage	7	4	5	9	4
26	F	Mike Ricci	7	5	2	7	6
21	F	Sheldon Kennedy(A)	7	3	4	7	14
25	F	Andrew Cassels	7	2	5	7	2
20	F	Rod Brind'Amour	7	2	3	5	4
6	D	Eric Desjardins(C)	7	1	4	5	6
28	F	Jamie Leach	7	1	4	5	2
22	F	Darrin Shannon	7	1	3	4	10
4	D	Corey Foster	7	1	3	4	4
24	D	Daniel Lambert	7	1	2	3	4
10	F	Darcy Loewen	7	1	1	2	12
7	F	Martin Gelinas	7	0	2	2	8
14	F	Rob Murphy	7	1	0	1	8
8	F	John McIntyre	7	1	0	1	4
5	D	Geoff Smith	7	0	1	1	4
2	D	Steve Veilleux	7	0	0	0	8
16	D	Yves Racine	7	0	0	0	6
29	G	Stephane Fiset	6	0	0	0	0
1	G	Gus Morschauser	2	0	0	0	0

In Goal

	GP	W–L–T	MINS	GA	SO	AVG
Stephane Fiset	6	3–2–1	329	18	0	3.27
Gus Morschauser	2	1–0–0	92	5	0	3.30

Goalie Notes:

1. Morschauser [one goal] replaced Fiset [6 goals] at 8:52 of 2nd, January 4 vs. Soviet Union

Coach   Tom Webster
Assistant Alain Vigneault

CANADIAN OFFICIALS AT THE 1989
WORLD JUNIOR CHAMPIONSHIPS

George McCorry (referee)   6 games
Brad Watson (linesman)   4 games
Jay Sharrers (linesman)   5 games

TEAM CANADA ROSTER SUMMARY

Team Canada players   20
Drafted Into NHL   20
Played in the NHL   18 (all but Morschauser, Veilleux)
Returning Players   2 (Desjardins, Kennedy)

PLAYER REPRESENTATION BY LEAGUE

OHL	8	(Cassels, Cimetta, Foster, Leach, McIntyre, Morschauser, Ricci, Shannon)
WHL	3	(Kennedy, Lambert, Loewen)
QMJHL	5	(Fiset, Gelinas, Racine, Savage, Veilleux)
NHL	2	(Desjardins, Murphy)
U.S. COLLEGE	2	(Brind'Amour, Smith)

PLAYER REPRESENTATION BY AGE

19-year-olds	13	(Cassels, Desjardins, Foster, Kennedy, Leach, Loewen, McIntyre, Morschauser, Murphy, Racine, Shannon, Smith, Veilleux)
18-year-olds	6	(Brind'Amour, Cimetta, Fiset, Gelinas, Lambert, Savage)
17-year-olds	1	(Ricci)

PLAYERS' CAREER PROFILES

Rod Brind'Amour   Michigan State University Spartans (CCHA)
Selected 9th overall by St. Louis at 1988 Draft
Played in the NHL 1988–97

Andrew Cassels   Ottawa 67's (OHL)
Selected 17th overall by Montreal at 1987 Draft
Played in the NHL 1989 to present

Rob Cimetta   Toronto Marlboros (OHL)
Selected 18th overall by Boston at 1988 Draft
Played in the NHL 1988–92

Eric Desjardins   Montreal Canadiens (NHL)
Last Junior team: Granby Bisons (QMJHL)
Selected 38th overall by Montreal at 1987 Draft
Played in the NHL 1988 to present

Stephane Fiset   Victoriaville Tigers (QMJHL)
Selected 24th overall by Quebec at 1988 Draft
Played in the NHL 1989 to present

Corey Foster   Peterborough Petes (OHL)
Selected 12th overall by New Jersey at 1988 Draft
Played in the NHL 1988–97

Martin Gelinas   Hull Olympiques (QMJHL)
Selected 7th overall by Los Angeles at 1988 Draft
Played in the NHL 1988 to present

Sheldon Kennedy   Swift Current Broncos (WHL)
Selected 80th overall by Detroit at 1988 Draft
Played in the NHL 1989–97

Dan Lambert   Swift Current Broncos (WHL)
Selected 106th overall by Quebec at 1989 Draft
Played in the NHL 1990–92

Jamie Leach   Niagara Falls Thunder (OHL)
Selected 47th overall by Pittsburgh at 1987 Draft
Played in the NHL 1989–94

Darcy Loewen   Spokane Chiefs (WHL)
Selected 55th overall by Buffalo at 1988 Draft
Played in the NHL 1989–94

John McIntyre   Guelph Platers (OHL)
Selected 49th overall by Toronto at 1987 Draft
Played in the NHL 1989–95

Gus Morschauser   Kitchener Rangers (OHL)
Selected 197th overall by Vancouver at 1989 Draft
Did not play in the NHL

Rob Murphy   Vancouver Canucks (NHL)
Last Junior team: Drummondville Voltigeurs (QMJHL)
Selected 24th overall by Vancouver at 1987 Draft
Played in the NHL 1987–94

Yves Racine   Victoriaville Tigers (QMJHL)
Selected 11th overall by Detroit at 1987 Draft
Played in the NHL 1989 to present

Mike Ricci   Peterborough Petes (OHL)
Selected 4th overall by Philadelphia at 1990 Draft
Played in the NHL 1990 to present

Reg Savage   Victoriaville Tigers (QMJHL)
Selected 15th overall by Washington at 1988 Draft
Played in the NHL 1990–94

Darrin Shannon   Windsor Spitfires (OHL)
Selected 4th overall by Pittsburgh at 1988 Draft
Played in the NHL 1988 to present

Geoff Smith   University of North Dakota Fighting Sioux WCHA)
Selected 63rd overall by Edmonton at 1987 Draft
Played in the NHL 1989 to present

Steve Veilleux   Trois-Rivieres Draveurs (QMJHL)
Selected 45th overall by Vancouver at 1987 Draft
Did not play in the NHL

1990 WORLD JUNIOR CHAMPIONSHIPS FINLAND, DECEMBER 26, 1989-- JANUARY 4, 1990

FINAL PLACINGS

GOLD MEDAL	**CANADA**
SILVER MEDAL	Soviet Union
BRONZE MEDAL	Czechoslovakia
Fourth Place	Finland
Fifth Place	Sweden
Sixth Place	Norway
Seventh Place	United States
Eighth Place	Poland*

promoted from "B" pool in 1989; relegated to "B" pool for 1991

ALL-STAR TEAM

GOAL	Stephane Fiset (Canada)
DEFENCE	Alexander Godynyuk (Soviet Union)
	Jiri Slegr (Czechoslovakia)
FORWARD	Dave Chyzowski (Canada)
	Jaromir Jagr (Czechoslovakia)
	Robert Reichel (Czechoslovakia)

DIRECTORATE AWARDS

BEST GOALIE	Stephane Fiset (Canada)
BEST DEFENCEMAN	Alexander Godynyuk (Soviet Union)
BEST FORWARD	Robert Reichel (Czechoslovakia)

COACH GUY CHARRON

What Guy Charron knew about winning certainly did not come from his time as a player in the NHL. His first year was with Montreal, in 1969–70, the only time the Habs had missed the playoffs in forty-one years. He went to Detroit where for five years the team didn't qualify. He joined Kansas City for three more non-playoff years and finished his skating career with Washington for five more years. Career totals: 734 regular season NHL games; zero playoff games.

In 1977, he played for Canada at the World Championships, and two years later he was team captain. He fell in love with the international experience and sought to expand his portfolio. He became a player/assistant coach with Arosa of the Swiss league and then became coach of the Quebec Remparts of the QMJHL. He was hired August 9, 1984, as an assistant to Dave King with the national team and Hockey Canada, where he remained for five years. King praised Charron: "We had a number of people apply for the job. Guy's resume was very impressive. He had distinguished himself in the NHL. He played in Europe. He coached major junior hockey. He has an outstanding personality and a great deal of enthusiasm. . . . Guy gives us a great image and presence in Quebec. That's important."

QMJHL president Gilles Courteau cancelled an exhibition game between Charron's national junior team and a group of Quebec all-stars because Courteau felt Charron was anti-francophone and pro-anglophone. Courteau was red-faced a short time later when Canada won gold. The tournament MVP was Quebec goalie Stephane Fiset.

THE TEAM

Players convened on December 12 at the Elizabeth Manley Complex in Gloucester, Ontario, just outside Ottawa, for five days of work and try-outs. They then flew to Finland, where they had nine days in Vierumaki to prepare for the big show, including two exhibition games against a Finnish club team, K-Reipas. They played the Czech national team on December 24 (a 3–1 loss). Also included in the regimen were two-a-day workouts that left the players exhausted but better prepared.

Vierumaki was a significant experience for the team. Dan Ratushny noted, "We were five to a cabin two hours from Helsinki with not much to do. It was the first Christmas away from home for a lot of guys and we got to know each other pretty well." Competing for a team is always a greater motivation than competing for yourself, as this gold-medal team soon discovered.

One player the team hoped to acquire was Martin Gelinas who was playing with the Edmonton Oilers. Coach Charron was prepared to take Gelinas to Finland even as a last-minute addition to the team, but Glen Sather would not release the future star. The Islanders loaned Dave Chyzowski to the young Nats (he had been selected second overall at the 1989 draft, behind only Mats Sundin).

The most talked about player at camp was Eric Lindros. He was the second sixteen-year-old to play at the World Juniors for Canada, the first being Wayne

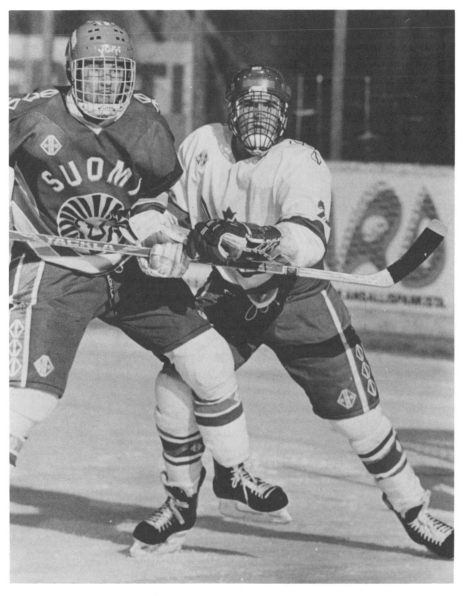

Canada's Dan Ratushny and Vesa Viitakoski of Finland fight for position.

Gretzky. He had been drafted by the Soo Greyhounds of the OHL in the midget draft but refused to report because there was no university in the Soo. The OHL was a little red-faced. It had always advocated the importance of education for its players, yet seemed to be preventing a player's education. The most promising young player was threatening to play outside the OHL, a public-relations nightmare for the world's most prestigious junior league. OHL regulations prohibited first-round choices from being traded, so Lindros was playing for Detroit Compuware in Tier II.

In the end, the league adopted what was called the Lindros Rule. For the first time, teams were allowed to trade first-round draft choices. The day after the juniors left for Finland, the trade was finalized. The Oshawa Generals acquired Lindros for goalie Mike Lenarduzzi, forwards Jason Denomme and Mike DeCoff, second-round draft choices in 1990 and 1991, and around $80,000 cash.

FINAL CUTS

Coach Charron made a few unpopular cuts during the final days of training camp in Gloucester. The Nats edged the Belleville Bulls 3–2 in an exhibition game and then released Owen Nolan (Cornwall), John Slaney (Cornwall), and Adam Bennett (Sudbury), as well as Kevin Cheveldayoff, who was on loan from the Islanders, though injuries had prevented him from playing. The morning the team left for Helsinki, the final six players were given the bad news. Gone were Scott Thornton (Belleville), Jason Marshall (Olympic team), Mike Sillinger (Regina), Brent Thompson (Medicine Hat), Jarrod Skalde (Oshawa), and Todd Bojcun (Peterborough). With that, Charron took his twenty man roster to Finland. Two weeks later they won gold.

19:59

On the penultimate day of the tournament, the Swedes beat a stunned Canadian team 5–4. They scored three goals in a ninety-six-second span. Russia had no losses and one tie. Canada's loss meant the Soviets had the inside track on gold. The next day, a miracle occurred. To win gold, Canada had to beat the Czechs and Sweden had to beat the Russians. The Canadians were doing their part, leading the Czechs 2–1 in the third period. But the team kept hearing reports from the bench that the Russians were up 5–3 on the Swedes. Then Tre Kronor scored a late goal and Patrick Englund scored for Sweden at 19:59 of the third! When the Canadians found out, the bench erupted, but there was still 2:36 left in their game, now a gold-medal game. When the buzzer sounded they had won the gold medal, partly because of

*Canada's Stu Barnes gets an open ice hook from a Finn during a
3-3 tie which saw Canada lose a one-goal lead on three occasions.*

their success, partly because of the tournament format, and partly because
of Englund, Canada's 21st player!

While the Canadians were whooping it up in the dressing room, the Soviets
were launching an official protest, claiming they had a video that confirmed
the Swedish goal was scored after the third period had ended. The protest
was to no avail — the video proved the puck crossed the line before the clock
hit 00:00. Canada's gold was confirmed.

TOURNAMENT FORMAT

All eight teams played a simple round-robin in one division. A tie in the
standings between two teams was broken first by the result of the game
between the two (which is how Canada beat the Soviet Union for gold, and
also why Finland was placed above Sweden in the final table). In a continuing
tie, goal differential would decide the placings.

THE OPPOSITION

CZECHOSLOVAKIA

Petr Bares, Milos Holan, Bobby Holik, Robert Horyna, Jaromir Jagr, Ladislav Karabin, Petr Kuchyna, Miroslav Mach, Jiri Malinsky, Martin Prochazka, Robert Reichel, Lubos Rob, Jiri Slegr, Richard Smehlik, Roman Turek, Marian Uharcek, Jan Varholik, Jiri Vykoukal, Peter Zubek, Pavol Zubek

FINLAND

Petri Aaltonen, Mika Alatalo, Henry Eskelinen, Jonas Hemming, Veli-Pekka Kautonen, Janne Kekalainen, Karri Kivi, Petro Koivunen, Janne Laukkanen, Sami Nuutinen, Toni Porkka, Tommi Pullola, Rauli Raitanen, Pasi Raty, Keijo Sailynoja, Teemu Sillanpaa, Mika Stromberg, Harri Suvanto, Mika Valila, Vesa Viitakoski

NORWAY

Vegar Barlie, Henrik Buskoven, Ole-Eskild Dahlstrom, Geir Dalene, Tommie Eriksen, Mattis Haakensen, Rene Hansen, Tommy Jacobsen, Stig Johansen, Espen Knutsen, Pal Kristiansen, Trond Magnussen, Per Martinsen, Svein-Enok Norstebo, Tom-Erik Olsen, Marius Rath, Jan-Tore Ronningen, Peter Samuelsen, Bjornar Sorensen, Lasse Syversen

POLAND

Wojciech Baca, Mariusz Czerkawski, Adam Fras, Maciej Funiok, Slawomir Furca, Dariusz Garbocz, Dariusz Karamuz, Jacek Kuc, Piotr Matlakiewicz, Janusz Misterka, Maciej Pachucki, Piotr Sadlocha, Andrzej Secemski, Jerzy Sobera, Wojciech Sosinski, Rafal Sroka, Jacek Szlapka, Leszek Trybus, Ryszard Tyrala, Wojciech Winiarski

SOVIET UNION

Pavel Bure, Viacheslav Butsayev, Alexander Godynyuk, Victor Gordiyuk, Igor Ivanov, Jan Kaminsky, Alexander Karpovtsev, Andrei Kovalenko, Viacheslav Kozlov, Alexei Kudashov, Sergei Martynyuk, Evgeny Namestnikov, Roman Oksiuta, Sergei Poljakov, Andrei Potaichuk, Sergei Tertyshny, Sergei Tkachenko, Dmitri Yushkevich, Alexei Zhamnov, Sergei Zubov

SWEDEN

Niklas Andersson, Henrik Andersson, Henrik Bjorkman, Niklas Brannstrom, Patric Englund, Joacim Esbjors, Patrik Juhlin, Jonas Leven, Nicklas Lidstrom, Torbjorn Lindberg, Fredrik Nilsson, Henrik Nilsson, Mattias Olsson, Joakim Persson, Patrik Ross, Daniel Rydmark, Osmo Soutokorva, Mats Sundin, Per-Johan Svensson, Marcus Thuresson

UNITED STATES

Tony Amonte, Marc Beran, Jeff Blaeser, Mike Boback, Brian Bruininks, Keith Carney, Ted Crowley, Ted Drury, Rob Gaudreau, Bill Guerin, Sean Hill, Chuck Hughes, Shaun Kane, Jim Larkin, Cory Laylin, Barry Richter, Bryan Smolinski, Jeff Stolp, Jason Zent, Doug Zmolek

FINAL STANDINGS

	GP	W	L	T	GF	GA	P	GAA	SO	PIM
CANADA	7	5	1	1	36	18	11	2.57	1	84
Soviet Union	7	5	1	1	50	23	11	3.29	1	98
Czechoslovakia	7	5	2	0	51	17	10	2.43	0	82
Finland	7	4	2	1	32	21	9	3.00	0	76
Sweden	7	4	2	1	38	29	9	4.14	1	68*
Norway	7	2	5	0	25	51	4	7.29	0	108
United States	7	1	6	0	22	37	2	5.29	0	78
Poland	7	0	7	0	7	65	0	9.29	0	68*

* won Fair Play Cup

RESULTS

December 26	Turku	Canada 3	United States 2
	Kerava	Soviet Union 11	Poland 0
	Kauniainen	Sweden 4	Norway 3
	Helsinki	Czechosloavkia 7	Finland 1
December 27	Kauniainen	Soviet Union 12	Norway 2
	Helsinki	Czechoslovakia 7	United States 1
December 28	Kauniainen	Canada 12	Poland 0
	Turku	Finland 5	Sweden 2
December 29	Kerava	Canada 6	Norway 3
	Turku	Soviet Union 3	Finland 2
	Kauniainen	Czechoslovakia 11	Poland 1
	Helsinki	Sweden 6	United States 5
December 30	Kauniainen	Czechoslovakia 13	Norway 2
	Helsinki	Soviet Union 7	United States 3
December 31	Helsinki	Canada 3	Finland 3
	Turku	Sweden 14	Poland 0
January 1	Helsinki	Canada 6	Soviet Union 4
	Turku	Czechoslovakia 7	Sweden 2
	Helsinki	Finland 8	Norway 2
	Kerava	United States 3	Poland 2

January 2	Helsinki	Soviet Union 8	Czechoslovakia 5
	Kerava	Norway 6	United States 5
January 3	Helsinki	Sweden 5	Canada 4
	Helsinki	Finland 7	Poland 1
January 4	Turku	Canada 2	Czechoslovakia 1
	Helsinki	Soviet Union 5	Sweden 5
	Turku	Norway 7	Poland 3
	Helsinki	Finland 6	United States 3

TEAM CANADA GAME SUMMARIES

December 26 *Canada 3* *United States 2*

First Period

No Scoring

    PENALTIES: Larkin (U.S.) 16:58

Second Period

1. Canada, Barnes (unassisted)...12:16
2. United States, Gaudreau (Boback) 16:33

    PENALTIES: Carney (U.S.) 7:07, Needham (Can) 12:37

Third Period

3. Canada, Haller (Barnes) ....1:10(pp)
4. United States, Drury (unassisted) 5:30
5. Canada, Chyzowski (unassisted) 6:12

    PENALTIES: Boback (U.S.) 0:17, Plavsic (Can) 3:19

Shots on Goal:

| Canada | 8 | 7 | 11 | **26** |
| United States | 14 | 12 | 9 | **35** |

In Goal:

    Canada — Fiset

    United States — Hughes

December 28 *Canada 12* *Poland 0*

First Period

1. Canada, Pellerin (Norris)..0:18
2. Canada, Craig (Draper) 5:04
3. Canada, Haller (Needham)..5:42
4. Canada, Ratushny (unassisted) ....13:50(sh)
5. Canada, Lindros (unassisted) 15:34

6. Canada, Craig (Haller) 16:47
7. Canada, Norris (Barnes) 17:27

> PENALTIES: Ratushny (Can) 2:43, Garbocz (Pol) 9:21, Furca (Pol) 9:55, Haller (Can) 13:16, Rice (Can) 19:26

Second Period

8. Canada, Chyzowski (Needham) 3:46

> PENALTIES: Sobera (Pol) 4:15, Rice (Can) 10:03, Ratushny (Can) 18:04

Third Period

9. Canada, Walz (Brisebois, Needham) 1:04
10. Canada, Chyzowski (unassisted) 4:02
11. Canada, Needham (Walz)... 13:36(pp)
12. Canada, Needham (unassisted) .... 17:50(pp)

> PENALTIES: Funiok (Pol) 1:56, Norris (Can) 5:09, Draper (Can) 6:42, Brisebois (Can) 8:29, Pachucki (Pol) 13:25, Sosinski (Pol) 16:07, Lindros (Can) 18:13, Barnes (Can) & Winiarski (Pol) 19:30

Shots on Goal:

unknown

In Goal:

Canada — Fiset
Poland — Karamuz/Baca (Baca [7 goals] replaced Karamuz [5 goals] at 15:42 of 1st)

December 29   Canada 6   Norway 3

First Period

1. Canada, Chyzowski (Needham) 0:59
2. Canada, Lindros (Manderville)...................................... 1:43

> PENALTIES: Plavsic (Can) & Rice (Can) 5:28, Lindros (Can) 11:14, Hansen (Nor) 15:03

Second Period

3. Norway, Barlie (Knutsen) 10:51
4. Canada, Brisebois (Walz) 12:45
5. Norway, Johansen (unassisted) 13:39
6. Canada, Rice (Herter)... 14:14
7. Norway, Rath (Knutsen) .... 15:21(pp)

> PENALTIES: Jacobsen (Nor) 4:12, Nor bench 6:25, Lindros (Can) 16:06, Rice (Can) 18:22

Third Period

8. Canada, Barnes (Norris) 0:42
9. Canada, Ratushny (Chyzowski) 5:55

> PENALTIES: Haller (Can) 6:08, Eriksen (Nor) 9:08, Lindros (Can) 13:15, Haller (Can) & Jacobsen (Nor) 13:51

Shots on Goal:

unknown

In Goal:

Canada — Fiset

Norway — Haakensen

December 31   *Canada 3*   *Finland 3*

First Period

1. Canada, Rice (Manderville) 10:08
2. Finland, Koivunen (unassisted) 17:51

PENALTIES: Rice (Can) & Eskelinen (Fin) 5:40

Second Period

3. Canada, Chyzowski (Ricci) .... 2:35(pp)
4. Finland, Viitakoski (Aaltonen) 5:43
5. Canada, Manderville (Malganus) 11:38
6. Finland, Koivunen (Valila) 13:02

PENALTIES: Raitanen (Fin) 1:45, Barnes (Can) & Suvanto (Fin) 5:05, Brisebois (Can) 14:48

Third Period

No Scoring

PENALTIES: Kautonen (Fin) 1:03, Pellerin (Can) 9:46, Plavsic (Can) 16:17

Shots on Goal:

unknown

In Goal:

Canada — Fiset

Finland — Eskelinen

January 1   *Canada 6*   *Soviet Union 4*

First Period

1. Soviet Union, Oksiuta (Kozlov) .... 11:09(pp)
2. Soviet Union, Kudashov (Zhamnov) 14:23
3. Soviet Union, Butsayev (Kovalenko, Bure) 15:47
4. Canada, Brisebois (Chyzowski, Ricci) .... 16:29(pp)
5. Canada, Needham (Brisebois, Barnes) .... 17:18(pp)

PENALTIES: Godynyuk (Sov) 3:16, Potaichuk (Sov) 4:37, Herter (Can) 10:21, Kovalenko (Sov) 15:47, Zhamnov (Sov) 17:04

Second Period

6. Canada, Chyzowski (Ratushny) 10:25

7.   Canada, Chyzowski (Plavsic, Norris) 12:39
8.   Canada, Walz (Draper) 17:00

   PENALTIES: Rice (Can) 7:18, Namestnikov (Sov) 8:38, Barnes (Can) 15:06, Karpovtsev (Sov) 15:19

Third Period

9.   Canada, Pellerin (Haller, Ratushny) 8:15
10. Soviet Union, Bure (Butsayev, Kovalenko) .... 14:48(pp)

   PENALTIES: Craig (Can) 13:01

Shots on Goal:

   unknown

In Goal:

   Canada — Fiset
   Soviet Union — Tkachenko

January 3   *Sweden 5*   *Canada 4*

First Period

1.   Sweden, Brannstrom (Esbjors, Rydmark) .... 3:44(pp)
2.   Canada, Chyzowski (Ricci) .... 5:03(pp)
3.   Sweden, Olsson (Rydmark) 12:17
4.   Canada, Lindros (unassisted) 17:13

   PENALTIES: Plavsic (Can) 1:46, Ross (Swe) 3:53, Olsson (Swe) & Rice (Can) 9:32

Second Period

No Scoring

   PENALTIES: Lindros (Can) 8:19, Craig (Can) 10:19, Olsson (Swe — double minor) 11:41

Third Period

5.   Canada, Lindros (Chyzowski) 3:14
6.   Canada, Chyzowski (Barnes, Norris) 4:32
7.   Sweden, Brannstrom (Rydmark) .... 8:28(pp)
8.   Sweden, Englund (unassisted) 9:40
9.   Sweden, Olsson (unassisted) 10:04

   PENALTIES: Rice (Can) 7:35

Shots on Goal:

   unknown

In Goal:

   Canada — Fiset
   Sweden — Persson

| January 4 | Canada 2 | Czechoslovakia 1 |

First Period

1. Czechoslovakia, Reichel (Jagr) 19:11

   PENALTIES: Slegr (Cze) 1:21, Craig (Can) 3:28, Lindros (Can) 7:51, Mach (Cze) 10:35, Craig (Can) 12:39, Karabin (Cze) 14:36, Smehlik (Cze) 16:32, Lindros (Can) 19:46

Second Period

2. Canada, Craig (Walz) 7:28
3. Canada, Norris (Ricci, Chyzowski) 16:03

   PENALTIES: Slegr (Cze) 8:53, Brisebois (Can) 13:14

Third Period

No Scoring

   PENALTIES: Haller (Can) 5:15, Draper (Can) 7:00, Chyzowski (Can) 10:55

Shots on Goal:

unknown

In Goal:

Canada — Fiset
Czechoslovakia — Turek

TEAM CANADA FINAL STATISTICS
1990 WORLD JUNIOR CHAMPIONSHIPS

			GP	G	A	P	PIM
16	F	Dave Chyzowski(A/C)	7	9	4	13	2
14	F	Mike Needham	7	3	4	7	2
28	F	Stu Barnes	7	2	4	6	6
10	F	Dwayne Norris	7	2	4	6	2
13	F	Wes Walz	7	2	3	5	0
88	F	Eric Lindros	7	4	0	4	14
6	D	Kevin Haller	7	2	2	4	8
24	D	Patrice Brisebois	7	2	2	4	6
2	D	Dan Ratushny(C/A)	7	2	2	4	4
9	F	Mike Ricci(A/C)	5	0	4	4	0
15	F	Mike Craig	7	3	0	3	8
21	F	Kent Manderville	7	1	2	3	0
12	F	Steve Rice	7	2	0	2	16
18	F	Scott Pellerin	7	2	0	2	2
19	F	Kris Draper	7	0	2	2	4
7	D	Adrien Plavsic	7	0	1	1	8
5	D	Jason Herter	7	0	1	1	2
4	D	Stewart Malgunas	7	0	1	1	0
29	G	Stephane Fiset	7	0	0	0	0

Captain Notes:

Ricci captain vs. Finland, Czechoslovakia
Ratushny captain vs. United States, Norway, Sweden
Chyzowski captain vs. Poland, Soviet Union

In Goal

	GP	W–L–T	MINS	GA	SO	AVG
Stephane Fiset	7	5–1–1	420	18	1	2.57
Trevor Kidd	did not play					

Coach   Guy Charron
Assistants   Dick Todd / Perry Pearn

CANADIAN OFFICIALS AT THE 1990 WORLD JUNIOR CHAMPIONSHIPS

Kevin Muench (referee)   5 games

TEAM CANADA ROSTER SUMMARY

Team Canada players   19
Drafted Into NHL   19
Played In NHL   19
Returning Players   2   (Fiset, Ricci)

PLAYER REPRESENTATION BY LEAGUE

OHL	4	(Craig, Lindros, Ricci, Rice)
WHL	5	(Barnes, Haller, Malgunas, Needham, Walz)
QMJHL	2	(Brisebois, Fiset)
NHL	1	(Chyzowski)
U.S. COLLEGE	5	(Herter, Manderville, Norris, Pellerin, Ratushny)
IHL	1	(Plavsic)
OTHER*	1	(Draper)

Canadian National team

PLAYER REPRESENTATION BY AGE

19-year-olds	11	(Barnes, Fiset, Haller, Herter, Malgunas, Needham, Norris, Pellerin, Plavsic, Ratushny, Walz)
18-year-olds	7	(Brisebois, Chyzowski, Craig, Draper, Manderville, Ricci, Rice)
16-year-olds	1	(Lindros)

PLAYERS' CAREER PROFILES

Stu Barnes Tri-City Amercians (WHL)
Selected 4th overall by Winnipeg at 1989 Draft
Played in the NHL 1991 to present

Patrice Brisebois Laval Titans (QMJHL)
Selected 30th overall by Montreal at 1989 Draft
Played in the NHL 1990 to present

Dave Chyzowski New York Islanders (NHL)
Last Junior team: Kamloops Blazers (WHL)
Selected 2nd overall by Islanders at 1989 Draft
Played in the NHL 1989 to present

Mike Craig Oshawa Generals (OHL)
Selected 28th overall by Minnesota at 1989 Draft
Played in the NHL 1990 to present

Kris Draper Canadian National Team
Selected 62nd overall by Winnipeg at 1989 Draft
Played in the NHL 1990 to present

Stephane Fiset Victoriaville Tigers (QMJHL)
Selected 24th overall by Quebec at 1988 Draft
Played in the NHL 1989 to present

Kevin Haller Regina Pats (WHL)
Selected 14th overall by Buffalo at 1989 Draft
Played in the NHL 1989 to present

Jason Herter University of North Dakota Fighting Sioux (WCHA)
Selected 8th overall by Vancouver at 1989 Draft
Played in the NHL 1995–96

Eric Lindros Oshawa Generals (OHL)
Selected 1st overall by Quebec at 1991 Draft
Played in the NHL 1992 to present

Stewart Malgunas Seattle Thunderbirds (WHL)
Selected 66th overall by Detroit at 1990 Draft
Played in the NHL 1993 to present

Kent Manderville Cornell University Big Red (ECAC)
Selected 24th overall by Calgary at 1989 Draft
Played in the NHL 1991 to present

Mike Needham Kamloops Blazers (WHL)
Selected 126th overall by Pittsburgh at 1989 Draft
Played in the NHL 1991–94

Dwayne Norris Michigan State University Spartans (CCHA)
Selected 127th overall by Quebec at 1990 Draft
Played in the NHL 1993–96

Scott Pellerin University of Maine Black Bears (HE)
Selected 47th overall by New Jersey at 1989 Draft
Played in the NHL 1992 to present

Adrien Plavsic   Peoria Rivermen (IHL)
                        Selected 30th overall by St. Louis at 1988 Draft
                        Played in the NHL 1989 to present
Dan Ratushny   Cornell University Big Red (ECAC)
                        Selected 25th overall by Winnipeg at 1989 Draft
                        Played in the NHL 1992–93
Mike Ricci   Peterborough Petes (OHL)
                        Selected 4th overall by Philadelphia at 1990 Draft
                        Played in the NHL 1990 to present
Steve Rice   Kitchener Rangers (OHL)
                        Selected 20th overall by Rangers at 1989 Draft
                        Played in the NHL 1990 to present
Wes Walz   Lethbridge Hurricanes (WHL)
                        Selected 57th overall by Boston at 1989 Draft
                        Played in the NHL 1989–96

1991 WORLD JUNIOR CHAMPIONSHIPS CANADA, DECEMBER 26, 1990-- JANUARY 4, 1991

FINAL PLACINGS

GOLD MEDAL	**CANADA**
SILVER MEDAL	Soviet Union
BRONZE MEDAL	Czechoslovakia
Fourth Place	United States
Fifth Place	Finland
Sixth Place	Sweden
Seventh Place	Switzerland*
Eighth Place	Norway**

promoted from "B" pool in 1990
**relegated to "B" pool for 1992*

ALL-STAR TEAM

GOAL	Pauli Jaks (Switzerland)
DEFENCE	Dimitri Yushkevich (Soviet Union)
	Scott Lachance (United States)
FORWARD	Mike Craig (Canada)
	Eric Lindros (Canada)
	Martin Rucinsky (Czechoslovakia)

DIRECTORATE AWARDS

BEST GOALIE	Pauli Jaks (Switzerland)
BEST DEFENCEMAN	Jiri Slegr (Czechoslovakia)
BEST FORWARD	Eric Lindros (Canada)

COACH DICK TODD

Todd was in his eleventh season as head coach of the Peterborough Petes, OHL champs three times and Memorial Cup winners the previous season. As was the hope of Canadian Hockey, coaches as well as players grew within the national system. So, having been assistant coach the previous season at the World Juniors in 1989–90, he was promoted to head coach for the championships in Saskatoon.

Todd began in hockey in 1973 as a trainer with the Peterborough Petes when Roger Neilson was head coach. But from day one, his duties were more complex. He did everything from scouting with Neilson to selling ads for the team program, learning about coaching and running a hockey team from top to bottom. Neilson had coached Todd as a ten-year-old baseball player on a team that won a Canadian championship in 1964. Todd went on to sign with the Pittsburgh Pirates, but a torn rotator cuff ended his major league field of dreams.

Todd took over as general manager and coach for the Petes midway through the 1981–82 season, replacing Dave Dryden, and almost instantly instilled in the team a winning attitude through skill, enthusiasm, and hard work.

MOTIVATION

The team slogan "Stay focused and enjoy it" was created by team psychologist Dr. Wayne Halliwell, who spent two weeks with the team.

CANADA AS HOST NATION

For the third time, Canada hosted the World Junior Championships in 1991. (Canada earned a bronze medal in Quebec in 1978 and a silver in Hamilton in 1986.) Once the country had been awarded the tournament, though, fierce national competition raged to decide which city would win hosting honours. The decision was made by the Canadian International Hockey Committee after lobbying from two camps, Hamilton and Saskatoon. (Ottawa and Halifax expressed interest, but that was as far as their bids went.) It seemed Hamilton would win the day after guaranteeing a profit of $750,000 for the national program.

Then Saskatoon promised a cool million-dollar profit and was supported by the huge uranium company Cameco, which guaranteed to make up any shortfall. Combined with Saskatoon's impressive hosting of the Brier that same winter, its bid won the day. The tournament was highly successful, but ended $100,000 short of the million-dollar guarantee. True to its word, Cameco made up the difference.

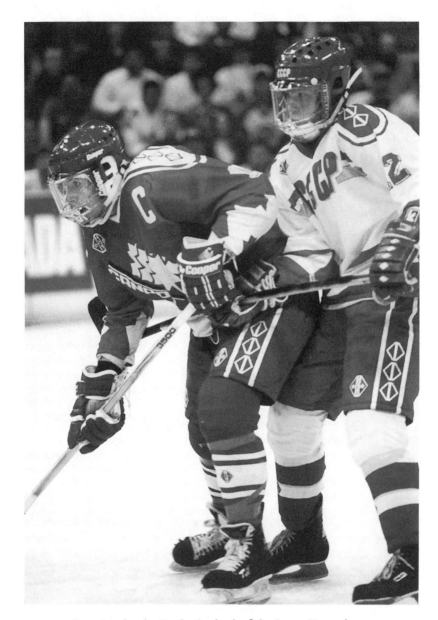

*Steve Rice battles Sandis Ozolinsh of the Soviet Union during
Canada's dramatic 3-2 win on the last day of the tournament
to give Canada the gold medal to the Soviets' silver.*

THE TWO TRAINING CAMPS

There was an evaluation camp in August for the forty-five invitees to showcase
their talents and give the coaching staff some idea of what they had to work
with. The final crunch came December 13–19 in Kindersley, Saskatchewan,

though the final twenty-two-man roster (twenty skaters and two goalies) didn't officially have to be named until Christmas Day, one day prior to the tournament's opening.

The team learned that two NHLers — Keith Primeau of Detroit and Owen Nolan of Quebec — would be loaned to the team only if they were guaranteed spots. Todd and his staff said thanks, but no thanks, and the camp opened without them. Nineteen-year-old Mats Sundin was doing well with the Quebec Nordiques and was not released by the team to play for Sweden. The Czechs, too, were hurt by the NHL. Not available to the junior team were Robert Reichel (Calgary), Jaromir Jagr (Pittsburgh), Bobby Holik (Hartford), and Petr Nedved (Vancouver), all regulars with the big league teams.

Team Canada began with twice-a-day workouts and augmented these with four exhibition games. On December 16, they played the Swift Current Broncos, coached by the nefarious Graham James, and won 4–2. On December 17, they played in Kindersley against the University of Saskatchewan, and on December 21 they tied the Finnish juniors 3–3 in Hanna, Alberta. The next night, they beat Sweden's junior team 5–2 in Red Deer, Alberta, the final tuneup before the tournament opened on Boxing Day.

Players invited to camp who did not make the team included: Yanick Degrace (Trois-Rivieres, QMJHL), Mike Torchia (Kitchener, OHL), Adam Bennett (Sudbury, OHL), Drake Berehowsky (Kingston, OHL), Adam Foote (Sault Ste. Marie, OHL), Darryl Sydor (Kamloops, WHL), Brent Thompson (Medicine Hat, WHL), Yanic Perreault (Trois-Rivieres, QMJHL), Jarrod Skalde (Belleville, OHL), Patrick Poulin (St.-Hyacinthe, QMJHL), Geoff Sanderson (Swift Current, WHL), Scott Scissons, Saskatoon, WHL). These players alone could have formed the nucleus of a second Canadian entry in the WJC and stood as good a chance as any of winning. But Todd decided to mold his team around speed and fitness rather than size, and this showed players such as Foote and Berehowsky in a slightly lesser light.

Of the twenty-two who made the final team and played in Saskatoon, all were drafted by NHL teams and all have played or continue to play in the NHL. Of the thirteen players who were cut from camp, every one except goalie Yanick Degrace made it to the NHL.

HOCKEY'S PERESTROIKA

In December 1990, the NHL and the Soviet Ice Hockey Federation were in negotiations that would ensure transfer of players to NHL teams. As a result, security was tight around games featuring the Soviets and Czechs. The NHL's Board of Governors agreed to fine any team $250,000 for tampering if they tried to convince a player to defect or sign a contract under the table.

KRIS DRAPER

Draper has the rare distinction of scoring his first goal in junior hockey *after* scoring his first goal in the NHL and AHL. From midget hockey in Toronto, Draper joined Dave King's Canadian National Team for two seasons. He began the 1990–91 season with the Winnipeg Jets, where he scored. After an injury, he was sent to Moncton for two weeks of rehabilitation, where he also scored. He was recalled by the Jets, then demoted to the junior team in Ottawa that had obtained his rights from Hamilton. He played the balance of the season before and after the World Juniors with the 67's.

Gold medal glory...a Canadian tradition!

FATE SMILES ON CANADA AGAIN

As was the case the year before when Sweden tied the Russians at 19:59 to give Canada a chance for a gold medal, this year's tournament also came down to a non-Canadian game to determine the country's shot at a gold medal. Finland played the Soviets in a game in which a Soviet victory would eliminate Canada from gold medal contention; a tie or loss would give them a chance. Up 5–4 with two minutes to go, the Russians looked like they'd eliminate the Canucks. But they were called for too many men at 17:57. The Finns pulled goalie Pasi Kulvalainen and tied the game at 19:45. Then Jarkko Varvio took a quick shot that slipped between the pads of Sergei Sviagin.

The die was cast, then, for the next game between Canada and the Soviets. A Canadian win meant gold; a tie silver; a loss fourth place. Before the game, someone wrote on the dressing-room bulletin board, "God is a Canadian." After John Slaney scored with just 5:13 remaining to give Canada a 3–2 win, a few words were added: "who goes to Finland for the occasional holiday." Slaney jumped so high after scoring he sprained his ankle and didn't play the rest of the game. It didn't matter. He had done his job, and Canada won a gold medal for the second straight year.

THE OFFICIALS' STORY

The World Juniors provided a chance for young players and officials to shine. Canada's contingent of officials included one referee, Blaine Angus, and two linesmen, Mike Hasenfratz and Jeff Gardiner (Angus is now in the NHL). The selection process was far more complex for officials than for players. The CAHA submitted to the IIHF a list of two referees and six linesmen one year in advance, a list compiled by Dennis Pottage, the CAHA's referee-in-chief and a one-time WJC ref. The IIHF referees' committee met and chose the officials from all the lists from all IIHF member countries. Even though Hasenfratz was a referee in Canada, his name had been submitted as a linesman, and that was his position in Saskatoon. On-ice officials learn of their duties for the tournament schedule only the night before games are played. A list of assignments is slipped under their hotel room door; if they see their name, they know they're working. If not, they have a day off.

TURNING A PROFIT FOR CANADIAN HOCKEY

Cities that hosted games at these WJC all received a royalty based on gate receipts (attendance) and all made a profit over and above their expenses and $10,000 fee to the CAHA to host the games. Prince Albert earned $15,000, which went to the WHL Raiders; Rosetown earned about $6,000 toward the town's minor hockey association from hosting the Czech-Norway game; Moose Jaw's $10,000 profit went toward the Warriors' scholarship fund; North Battleford made $10,000; Yorkton took in $3,000, a bit disappointing, from the Soviet-Swiss (mis)match; Humboldt put its $6,000 toward local minor hockey; and Kindersley put its $5,000 toward minor hockey as well.

TOURNAMENT FORMAT

The eight teams were pooled in one division to play a round-robin tournament. In case of a tie in the standings, head-to-head results were the deciding factor. On the last day of the championships, Canada and the Soviet Union were tied for first and set to play each other.

The official rule book explains: "Where two or more teams have equal points, their positions will be determined by the results of the games played between such teams. If the goal system has to be applied, then firstly the goals scored against will be deducted from the goals scored for, the team having the greatest surplus taking precedence; if equality still exists, then dividing the goals scored by the goals against, the team having the greatest quotient taking precedence. If equality still exists, then all games played will count as long as the teams in equality have played with the same opponents."

THE OPPOSITION

CZECHOSLOVAKIA

Jaroslav Brabec, Roman Cechmanek, Ivan Droppa, Martin Hamrlik, Milan Hnilicka, Milos Holan, Branislav Janos, Jiri Kuntos, Jaromir Kverka, Patrik Luza, Martin Madovy, Jiri Malinsky, Roman Meluzin, Tomas Mikolasek, Jaroslav Modry, Zigmund Palffy, Martin Prochazka, Martin Rucinsky, Jiri Slegr, Martin Straka, Josef Stumpel, Masrian Uharchek

FINLAND

Kim Ahlroos, Mika Alatalo, Mikael Granlund, Tommi Gronlund, Janne Gronvall, Marko Jantunen, Erik Kakko, Petri Kalteva, Tommy Kiviaho, Toni Koivunen, Petteri Koskimaki, Pasi Kuivalainen, Tero Lehtera, Jere Lehtinen, Niko Marttila, Sami Nuutinen, Tommi Pullola, Teemu Sillanpaa, Jarkko Varvio, Vesa Viitakoski, Mika Yli-Maenpaa, Juha Ylonen

NORWAY

Karl Andersen, Vegar Barlie, Kim Fagerhoi, Rune Fjeldstad, Jarle Gundersen, Terje Haukali, Arve Jansen, Thomas Johansson, Christian Kjelsberg, Espen Knutsen, Morten Kristoffersen, Anders Larsen, Jo-Espen Leibnitz, Svein-Enok Norstebo, Eivind Olsen, Jan-Tore Ronningen, Peter Samuelsen, Michael Smithurst, Oyvind Sor, Robert Sundt, Erik Tveten, Per-Odvar Walbye

SOVIET UNION

Egor Bachkatov, Sergei Berezin, Pavel Bure, Jan Kaminsky, Valeri Karpov, Darius Kasparaitis, Konstantin Korotkov, Viacheslav Kozlov, Alexei Kudashov, Sergei Martinyuk, Boris Mironov, Mitri Motkov, Evgeny Namestnikov, Sandis Ozolinsh, Oleg Petrov, Sergei Sviagin, Sergei Tkachenko, Mikhail Volkov, Dimitri Yushkevich, Sergei Zholtok, Alexei Zhitnik, Sergei Zolotov

SWEDEN

Bjorn Ahlstrom, Eric Andersson, Niklas Andersson, Henric Bjorkman, Thomas Carlsson, Peter Ekelund, Jorgen Eriksson, Nichlas Falk, Khristian Gahn, Anders Huusko, Eric Huusko, Peter Jacobsson, Stefan Ketola, Ove Molin, Fredrik Nilsson, Mikael Nylander, Stefan Nyman, Mattias Olsson, Thomas Rhodin, Tommy Salo, Marcus Thuresson, Rolf Wanhainen

SWITZERLAND

Rene Ackermann, Raoul Baumgartner, Marco Bayer, Thomas Burillo, Arthur Camenzind, Nicola Celio, Harry Derungs, Marco Ferrari, Marco Fischer, Noel Guyaz, Axel Heim, Simon Hochuli, Pauli Jaks, Olivier Keller, Andy Krapf, Daniel Meier, Didier Princi, Andy Rufener, Bjorn Schneider, Bernhard Schuemperli, Daniel Sigg, Nando Wieser

UNITED STATES

Brent Brekke, Tony Burns, Mike Doers, Ted Drury, Mike Dunham, Bryan Ganz, Chris Gotziaman, Mike Heinke, Chris Imes, Craig Johnson, Trent Klatt, Ken Klee, Scott Lachance, Bill Lindsay, Aaron Miller, Ian Moran, Pat Neaton, Derek Plante, Brian Rolston, Jim Storm, Keith Tkachuk, Doug Weight

FINAL STANDINGS

	GP	W	L	T	GF	GA	P	GAA	SO	PIM
CANADA	7	5	1	1	40	18	11	2.57	1	56*
Soviet Union	7	5	1	1	44	15	11	2.14	1	129
Czechoslovakia	7	5	2	0	44	19	10	2.71	1	64
United States	7	4	2	1	45	19	9	2.71	1	68
Finland	7	3	3	1	35	30	7	4.29	0	78
Sweden	7	3	4	0	32	29	6	4.14	1	110
Switzerland	7	1	6	0	5	48	2	6.86	0	82
Norway	7	0	7	0	8	75	0	0.71	0	70

* won Fair Play Cup

RESULTS

December 26	Saskatoon	Canada 6	Switzerland 0
	Rosetown	Czechoslovakia 11	Norway 3
	Saskatoon	Finland 8	Sweden 5
	Prince Albert	Soviet Union 4	United States 2

December 27	Saskatoon	Canada 4	United States 4
	Regina	Sweden 4	Czechoslovakia 3
December 28	Moose Jaw	Finland 7	Switzerland 1
	Saskatoon	Soviet Union 13	Norway 0
December 29	Regina	Canada 10	Norway 1
	Saskatoon	Soviet Union 5	Sweden 1
	Kindersley	Czechoslovakia 10	Switzerland 0
	North Battleford	United States 6	Finland 3
December 30	Regina	Canada 7	Sweden 4
	Saskatoon	Czechoslovakia 5	United States 1
December 31	Saskatoon	Finland 10	Norway 2
	Yorkton	Soviet Union 10	Switzerland 1
January 1	Saskatoon	Canada 5	Finland 1
	Regina	United States 19	Norway 1
	Saskatoon	Sweden 6	Switzerland 1
	Regina	Soviet Union 5	Czechoslovakia 3
January 2	Saskatoon	Czechoslovakia 6	Canada 5
	Humboldt	United States 5	Sweden 2
January 3	Regina	Soviet Union 5	Finland 5
	Saskatoon	Switzerland 2	Norway 1
January 4	Saskatoon	Canada 3	Soviet Union 2
	Prince Albert	Sweden 10	Norway 0
	Saskatoon	Czechoslovakia 6	Finland 1
	Regina	United States 8	Switzerland 0

TEAM CANADA GAME SUMMARIES

December 26   *Canada 6*   *Switzerland 0*

First Period

1. Canada, Sevigny (Lindros)... 1:00
2. Canada, Manderville (Lindros)...4:13(pp)

PENALTIES: Heim (Swi) 3:39, Sigg (Swi) 15:22, Bayer (Swi) 18:59

Second Period

3. Canada, Falloon (Brisebois) 17:10
4. Canada, Lindros (Craig, Marshall) 19:53

PENALTIES: Marshall (Can) 5:36, Guyaz (Swi) 13:30

Third Period

5. Canada, Sillinger (Lindros, Manderville) 2:39
6. Canada, Sillinger (Lindros, Manderville) 16:41

PENALTIES: Sevigny (Can) 0:08

Shots on Goal:

Canada	17	21	11	**49**
Switzerland	9	3	8	**20**

In Goal:

Canada — Kidd

Switzerland — Jaks

December 27   *Canada 4*   *United States 4*

First Period

1. Canada, Falloon (Draper, Johnson)... 2:07
2. United States, Drury (Lindsay, Rolston) 5:27
3. United States, Tkachuk (Weight, Lachance)..................................... 17:03
4. United States, Storm (Johnson, Klatt) 18:01

    PENALTIES: Craig (Can) 7:37, Doers (U.S.) 13:00, Drury (U.S.) 19:20

Second Period

5. Canada, Lindros (Snell, Brisebois) .... 13:21(pp)

    PENALTIES: Gotziaman (U.S.) 13:05, Tkachuk (U.S.) & Lindros (Can) 16:32

Third Period

6. Canada, Rice (Slaney) 7:13
7. United States, Weight (unassisted) 10:29
8. Canada, Craig (Lindros, Snell) .... 15:37(pp)

    PENALTIES: Klee (U.S.) 14:43

Shots on Goal:

Canada	6	9	10	**25**
United States	7	7	7	**21**

In Goal:

Canada — Kidd

United States — Heinke

December 29   *Canada 10*   *Norway 1*

First Period

1. Canada, Johnson (Manderville, Falloon) 8:05
2. Canada, May (Johnson, Brisebois)... 14:53
3. Canada, Lindros (Craig, Sevigny)... 16:53
4. Canada, Thornton (Lapointe, Craigwell)... 19:44

    PENALTIES: Olsen (Nor) 4:31, Ronningen (Nor) 4:54, Slaney (Can) 12:07

Second Period

5. Canada, Lindros (Brisebois, Harlock) 7:11

6. Canada, Craigwell (Lapointe, Thornton)..12:25
7. Canada, Rice (Manderville, Snell)..14:14
8. Canada, Johnson (Falloon, Manderville)......................................19:24

PENALTIES: Sevigny (Can) 1:03, Haukali (Nor) 16:47

Third Period

9. Canada, Thornton (unassisted) 0:17
10. Norway, Tveten (Smithurst, Knutsen) 3:55
11. Canada, Sillinger (unassisted)..12:45

PENALTIES: May (Can) 0:52

Shots on Goal:

Canada	15	14	12	41
Norway	7	4	7	18

In Goal:

Canada — Potvin

Norway — Kristoffersen

December 30   *Canada 7*   *Sweden 4*

First Period

1. Canada, Craig (Snell, Lindros) 0:34
2. Sweden, E. Huusko (Falk, A. Huusko) 2:21
3. Sweden, Nylander (unassisted)..4:39(sh)
4. Canada, Sevigny (Marshall, Craig)..9:50(pp)
5. Sweden, A. Huusko (Falk)...19:34
6. Sweden, E. Andersson (Thuresson) 19:58

PENALTIES: N. Andersson (Swe) 2:53, Dykhuis (Can) 6:00, Ketola (Swe) 6:05, A. Huusko (Swe) 8:08, Marshall (Can) 13:07

Second Period

7. Canada, Lindros (Craig) 8:20

PENALTIES: Falloon (Can) 1:04, Nylander (Swe) 2:05, Nylander (Swe) & Lapointe (Can) 6:29

Third Period

8. Canada, Rice (unassisted) 6:40
9. Canada, Craig (Dykhuis, Lindros) 8:04
10. Canada, Johnson (Falloon, Manderville)...................................16:58
11. Canada, Thornton (Draper) ....19:23(sh)

PENALTIES: Sevigny (Can) & N. Andersson (Swe) 12:40, Harlock (Can) 19:08, Falk (Swe — misconduct) 19:23

Shots on Goal:

Canada	14	11	9	34
Sweden	10	3	5	18

In Goal:

Canada — Potvin/Kidd (Kidd [no goals] replaced Potvin [4 goals] to start 2nd)
Sweden — Wanhainen/Salo (Salo [5 goals] replaced Wanhainen [2 goals] at 17:06 of 1st)

January 1   Canada 5   Finland 1

First Period

1. Canada, Sillinger (Rice, Draper) 1:34
2. Canada, Brisebois (Craigwell, Lapointe) .... 7:14(pp)
3. Canada, Craig (unassisted) .... 18:14(sh)
4. Canada, Sevigny (Harlock, Sillinger) 19:31

PENALTIES: Alatalo (Fin) 5:15, Sillanpaa (Fin) & Lindros (Can) 7:00, Viitakoski (Fin) 8:11, Pullola (Fin) 12:57, Brisebois (Can) 14:11, Slaney (Can) 16:28

Second Period

5. Finland, Kiviaho (Koskimaki) 17:58

PENALTIES: Rice (Can) 7:48, Marshall (Can) 9:12, Craig (Can) 11:43, Ylonen (Fin) & Kiviaho (Fin) & Sevigny (Can) & Lindros (Can) 19:46

Third Period

6. Canada, Draper (Brisebois, Dykhuis) 0:56

PENALTIES: Alatalo (Fin — misconduct) 0:56, Craig (Can) 17:55, Kalteva (Fin) 19:36

Shots on Goal:

Canada	15	10	12	**37**
Finland	14	14	2	**30**

In Goal:

Canada — Kidd
Finland — Kuivalainen/Granlund (Granlund [one goal] replaced Kuivalainen [4 goals] to start 2nd)

January 2   Czechoslovakia 6   Canada 5

First Period

1. Czechoslovakia, Hamrlik (Palffy) 7:31
2. Czechoslovakia, Janos (Rucinsky) .... 12:36(pp)
3. Canada, Falloon (Lindros, Marshall) 19:45

PENALTIES: Kuntos (Cze) 8:20, Rice (Can) 11:28, Rice (Can) 15:25

Second Period

4. Czechoslovakia, Stumpel (Palffy, Meluzin) 5:36
5. Canada, Johnson (Brisebois) 8:52
6. Czechoslovakia, Madovy (Kuntos).. 14:02
7. Canada, Craig (Lindros, Sevigny)... 18:49(pp)

8. Canada, Lindros (Craig) 19:11

    PENALTIES: Kuntos (Cze) 3:25, Madovy (Cze) 17:15, Droppa (Cze) 20:00

Third Period

9. Canada, Craig (Lindros, Slaney) 7:45
10. Czechoslovakia, Uharchek (Rucinsky, Slegr)............................. 15:55(pp)
11. Czechoslovakia, Rucinsky (Slegr, Janos) 17:25

    PENALTIES: Sillinger (Can) 9:26, Rice (Can) 14:02

Shots on Goal:

Canada	9	15	9	**33**
Czechoslovakia	13	10	15	**38**

In Goal:

    Canada — Kidd
    Czechoslovakia — Hnilicka

January 4   *Canada 3*   *Soviet Union 2*

First Period

1. Canada, Sevigny (Lindros)..5:12(pp)
2. Canada, Rice (Sillinger, Dykhuis)...15:15

    PENALTIES: Ozolinsh (Sov) 4:18, Slaney (Can) 5:54

Second Period

3. Soviet Union, Zholtok (unassisted) 11:20

    PENALTIES: none

Third Period

4. Soviet Union, Ozolinsh (unassisted) 3:50
5. Canada, Slaney (Marshall)...14:47

    PENALTIES: Bure (Sov) & Craig (Can) 7:42

Shots on Goal:

Canada	11	6	3	**20**
Soviet Union	8	5	17	**30**

In Goal:

    Canada — Kidd
    Soviet Union — Sviagin

TEAM CANADA FINAL STATISTICS
1991 WORLD JUNIOR CHAMPIONSHIPS

			GP	G	A	P	PIM
88	F	Eric Lindros	7	6	11	17	6
15	F	Mike Craig	7	6	5	11	8

234

24	D	Patrice Brisebois	7	1	6	7	2
21	F	Kent Manderville	7	1	6	7	0
22	F	Pierre Sevigny	7	4	2	6	8
16	F	Mike Sillinger	7	4	2	6	2
8	F	Greg Johnson	7	4	2	6	0
9	F	Pat Falloon	7	3	3	6	2
12	F	Steve Rice(C)	7	4	1	5	8
11	F	Scott Thornton	7	3	1	4	0
19	F	Kris Draper	7	1	3	4	0
2	D	Jason Marshall	7	0	4	4	6
6	D	Chris Snell	7	0	4	4	0
27	D	John Slaney	7	1	2	3	6
18	F	Dale Craigwell	7	1	2	3	0
4	D	Karl Dykhuis	7	0	3	3	2
26	F	Martin Lapointe	7	0	3	3	2
7	D	David Harlock	7	0	2	2	2
10	F	Brad May	7	1	0	1	2
28	D	Scott Niedermayer	7	0	0	0	0
1	G	Trevor Kidd	6	0	0	0	0
29	G	Felix Potvin	2	0	0	0	0

In Goal

	GP	W-L-T	MINS	GA	SO	AVG
Trevor Kidd	6	4–1–0	340	13	1	2.25
Felix Potvin	2	1–0–0	80	5	0	3.75

Goalie Notes:

1. Kidd [no goals] replaced Potvin [4 goals] to start 2nd, December 30 vs. Sweden

Coach   Dick Todd
Assistants   Perry Pearn / Alain Vigneault

CANADIAN OFFICIALS AT THE 1991 WORLD JUNIOR CHAMPIONSHIPS

Blaine Angus (referee)   5 games
Jeff Gardiner (linesman)   6 games
Mike Hasenfrantz (linesman)   5 games

TEAM CANADA ROSTER SUMMARY

Team Canada players   22
Drafted Into NHL   22
Played In NHL   22
Returning Players   6   (Brisebois, Craig, Draper, Lindros, Manderville, Rice)

PLAYER REPRESENTATION BY LEAGUE

OHL	7	(Craigwell, Draper, Lindros, May, Rice, Slaney, Snell)
WHL	5	(Falloon, Kidd, Marshall, Niedermayer, Sillinger)
QMJHL	4	(Brisebois, Lapointe, Potvin, Sevigny)
NHL	2	(Craig, Thornton)
U.S. COLLEGE	3	(Harlock, Johnson, Manderville)
OTHER*	1	(Dykhuis)

Canadian Olympic Team

PLAYER REPRESENTATION BY AGE

19-year-olds	15	(Brisebois, Craig, Craigwell, Draper, Harlock, Johnson, Manderville, Marshall, May, Potvin, Rice, Sevigny, Sillinger, Snell, Thornton)
18-year-olds	4	(Dykhuis, Falloon, Kidd, Slaney)
17-year-olds	3	(Lapointe, Lindros, Niedermayer)

PLAYERS' CAREER PROFILES

Patrice Brisebois
Drummondville Voltigeurs (QMJHL)
Selected 30th overall by Montreal at 1989 Draft
Played in the NHL 1990 to present

Mike Craig
Minnesota North Stars (NHL)
Last Junior team: Oshawa Generals (OHL)
Selected 28th overall by Minnesota at 1989 Draft
Played in the NHL 1990–97

Dale Craigwell
Oshawa Generals (OHL)
Selected 199th overall by San Jose at 1991 Draft
Played in the NHL 1991–94

Kris Draper
Ottawa 67's (OHL)
Selected 62nd overall by Winnipeg at 1989 Draft
Played in the NHL 1990 to present

Karl Dykhuis
Canadian Olympic Team
Selected 16th overall by Chicago at 1990 Draft
Played in the NHL 1991 to present

Pat Falloon
Spokane Chiefs (WHL)
Selected 2nd overall by San Jose at 1991 Draft
Played in the NHL 1991 to present

David Harlock
University of Michigan Wolverines (CCHA)
Selected 24th overall by New Jersey at 1990 Draft
Played in the NHL 1993–96

Greg Johnson
University of North Dakota Fighting Sioux (WCHA)
Selected 33rd overall by Philadelphia at 1989 Draft
Played in the NHL 1993 to present

Trevor Kidd — Brandon Wheat Kings (WHL)
Selected 11th overall by Calgary at 1990 Draft
Played in the NHL 1991 to present

Martin Lapointe — Laval Titans (QMJHL)
Selected 10th overall by Detroit at 1991 Draft
Played in the NHL 1991 to present

Eric Lindros — Oshawa Generals (OHL)
Selected 1st overall by Quebec at 1991 Draft
Played in the NHL 1992 to present

Kent Manderville — Cornell University Big Red (ECAC)
Selected 24th overall by Calgary at 1989 Draft
Played in the NHL 1991 to present

Jason Marshall — Tri-City Americans (WHL)
Selected 9th overall by St. Louis at 1989 Draft
Played in the NHL 1991 to present

Brad May — Niagara Falls Thunder (OHL)
Selected 14th overall by Buffalo at 1990 Draft
Played in the NHL 1991 to present

Scott Niedermayer — Kamloops Blazers (WHL)
Selected 3rd overall by New Jersey at 1991 Draft
Played in the NHL 1991 to present

Felix Potvin — Chicoutimi Sagueneens (QMJHL)
Selected 31st overall by Toronto at 1990 Draft
Played in the NHL 1991 to present

Steve Rice — Kitchener Rangers (OHL)
Selected 20th overall by Rangers at 1989 Draft
Played in the NHL 1990 to present

Pierre Sevigny — St. Hyacinthe Lasers (QMJHL)
Selected 51st overall by Montreal at 1989 Draft
Played in the NHL 1993 to present

Mike Sillinger — Regina Pats (WHL)
Selected 11th overall by Detroit at 1989 Draft
Played in the NHL 1990 to present

John Slaney — Cornwall Royals (OHL)
Selected 9th overall by Washington at 1990 Draft
Played in the NHL 1993 to present

Chris Snell — Ottawa 67's (OHL)
Selected 145th overall by Buffalo at 1991 Draft
Played in the NHL 1993–95

Scott Thornton — Toronto Maple Leafs (NHL)
Last Junior team: Belleville Bulls (OHL)
Selected 3rd overall by Toronto at 1989 Draft
Played in the NHL 1990 to present

1992 WORLD JUNIOR CHAMPIONSHIPS GERMANY, DECEMBER 26, 1991-- JANUARY 4, 1992

FINAL PLACINGS

GOLD MEDAL	CIS
SILVER MEDAL	Sweden
BRONZE MEDAL	United States
Fourth Place	Finland
Fifth Place	Czechoslovakia
Sixth Place	**CANADA**
Seventh Place	Germany*
Eighth Place	Switzerland**

* promoted from "B" pool in 1991
** relegated to "B" pool for 1993

ALL-STAR TEAM

GOAL	Mike Dunham (United States)
DEFENCE	Scott Niedermayer (Canada)
	Janne Gronvall (Finland)
FORWARD	Alexei Kovalev (CIS)
	Michael Nylander (Sweden)
	Peter Ferraro (United States)

DIRECTORATE AWARDS

BEST GOALIE	Mike Dunham (United States)
BEST DEFENCEMAN	Darius Kasparaitis (CIS)
BEST FORWARD	Michael Nylander (Sweden)

COACH RICK CORNACCHIA

While the CAHA was trying to establish continuity in its coaching ranks, 1992's World Junior entry suffered a blip in the hiring of a head coach. Dick Todd had been first an assistant and then head coach for the juniors, but pulled himself from further committments as he felt his duties with the Peterborough Petes were suffering. One of the two assistants under Todd the previous year was naturally first in line as a replacement, but both declined. Alain Vigneault expressed a concern for his Hull Olympiques team, and the second assistant, Perry Pearn, did not want to commit to the juniors so long as Dave King was considering adding him to the Olympic team staff. A new man had to be brought in.

Ten candidates were interviewed: Rick Cornacchia, Joe Canale (Chicoutimi, QMJHL), Danny Flynn (Sault Ste. Marie, OHL), Gary Agnew (London, OHL), Alain Chaney (Beauport, QMJHL), Bob Loucks (Lethbridge, WHL), Tom Renney (Kamloops, WHL), Brad Tippet (Regina, WHL), Don McKee (University of Waterloo, CIAU), and Dave Siciliano (Thunder Bay, Tier II). The committee making the decision was a cross-section of junior hockey: CAHA president Murray Costello, vice-president Bob Nicholson, and the three CHL commissioners, Dave Branch (OHL), Ed Chynoweth (WHL), and Gilles Courteau (QMJHL).

In early June the hiring of Cornacchia was announced. Renney and Agnew were named as assistants.

THE CAMPS

An evaluation camp was held in Calgary in August 1991 to determine who would be invited to the tryouts in December. The final camp was held December 13–18 in Kitchener. Two exhibition games were also scheduled, the first against the Kitchener Selects on December 16 (a 6–5 loss), the second against the Guelph Selects two nights later (a 3–1 win). The team travelled to the Canadian Forces Base in Germany for five days of training, then played two preparatory games, December 21 against the German juniors (a 2–0 win), and two nights later against an outfit called Eishockey Bad Tolz, a Division II team playing out of Bad Tolz, Germany (an easy 12–2 walkover).

Cornacchia made three series of cuts to the roster. After the first exhibition game, four players were released: Grant Marshall and Brett Seguin of Ottawa (OHL), Michael Stewart of Michigan State, and Yves Sarault of the St.-Jean Lynx. After the win over the Guelph all-star team, five more players were sent back to junior: Chris Pronger to Peterborough, Francois Groleau to Shawinigan, Aaron Ward to the University of Michigan, Terry Chitaroni to Sudbury, and Yanic Dupre to Drummondville. That reduced the roster to twenty-seven. Five more players were let go the day before the team flew to Europe: Chris Osgood of Brandon and Martin Brodeur of St. Hyacinthe, two goalies who are now among the best in the world, Glen Murray of Sudbury, Dean McAmmond of Prince Albert, and Martin d'Orsonnens of Clarkson University.

NEW YEAR, NEW POLITICS

The World Juniors, always held at the end of one year and the start of the next, was not a time for New Year's parties. Curfews were generally ten or eleven o'clock, to prevent champagne drinking and late-night carousing. But in 1992, a new era in Russian history began with the dissolution of the Soviet Union. At Bundesleistungszentrum Arena (usually referred to usually as BLZ arena) in Fussen, the hammer and sickle flag was secretly lowered and it was announced that for the rest of the tournament the team would be called the Commonwealth of Independent States (CIS). No new flag was provided, and the CCCP jerseys remained in use. A new era of political freedom in the Soviet Union created a fractured hockey program, since many of the Soviet Union's best players were from Latvia, Belarus, Lithuania, Kazahkstan, the Ukraine, and other new states within the empire. The IIHF defused any potential controversy surrounding the name change by stating that if the CIS won a medal the players would be able to keep it. (A long-standing IIHF edict stipulates that a player cannot represent two countries at a single event.)

ERIC LINDROS

This was Lindros's third World Juniors, and "l'affaire Lindros" was in full swing in Quebec. Lindros had been drafted first overall by the Nordiques in the summer, but refused to play under Marcel Aubut. He was instead skating anywhere and everywhere but where he should have been — the NHL. He began the 1991–92 season playing for Canada at the Canada Cup and flourished under the sharp tutelage of coach Mike Keenan, who used the teenage behemoth to minimalist perfection in Canada's win.

Lindros rejoined his junior team in the OHL, the Oshawa Generals, before attending the WJC camp in Kitchener. He was a guest attendee, leaving December 16 to join the Canadian Olympic team in Ottawa for an exhibition against the U.S.A. He re-joined the juniors in Fussen, Germany on December 23, and after the WJC played in the Olympics under Dave King before returning to Oshawa for the end of the OHL season.

By the time he reached Fussen, Lindros was the centre of attention in hockey. He was well-travelled, tired, and by no means ready to make his

*Eric Lindros of the Oshawa Generals was one of only three
players to compete in three World Juniors for Canada.*

contribution commensurate with the two gold medals he had won with the
juniors previously. Under the circumstances, he wasn't likely to excel, and
his losing battle with a viral infection weakened his play. No matter how sick
he became, team doctor Duncan Colby could not prescribe anything that
wouldn't cause Lindros to fail the doping test, so his recuperation, while
natural, was greatly slowed.

DOPING

One player from each team is randomly selected after a game to provide a
sample of urine. This is then divided into two specimens. The first is analysed,
and if the result is negative, all is well. If it is positive, the governing body is
notified and the player is ineligible to compete until the second sample is
analysed, at which the player (or his representative), an IIHF representative,
and the analyst must be present. If this is positive, a suspension is automatic.
There are six kinds of banned substances: stimulants (for example, caffeine),
narcotic analgesics (codeine), anabolic steroids, Beta blockers, diuretics, and
peptide hormones and analogues.

MEDALS

Between 1977, when the first World Juniors were held, and the games in 1992, the Amercians had won just one medal (a bronze in 1986) and had placed higher than Canada only once (sixth to Canada's seventh in 1981). Yet after Canada's disappointing sixth place in Germany and the Americans' surprise bronze medal performance, the Americans began waving their medals at the Canadians and taunting, "You guys got nothing and we got something." Class, as they say, will out. Wait until next year.

TOURNAMENT FORMAT

A simple round-robin formula was used. All nations were grouped into one division. Ties would be decided first by head-to-head meetings, then goal differential, then goal ratio (goals-for divided by goals-allowed).

THE OPPOSITION

CIS (COMMONWEALTH OF INDEPENDENT STATES)

Alexandre Cherbayev, Ravile Gousmanov, Darius Kasparaitis, Artem Kopot, Konstantin Korotkov, Alexandre Kouzminski, Alexei Kovalev, Sergei Krivo-krasov, Denis Metliouk, Boris Mironov, Andrei Nikolishin, Sandis Ozolinsh, Alexandre Sverjov, Alexei Trochtchinski, Denis Vinokourov, Mikhail Volkov, Alexei Yashin, Alexei Zhitnik, Sergei Zholtok, Vladislav Bouline, Nikolai Khabibulin, Ildar Moukhomet

CZECHOSLOVAKIA

Jan Alinc, Jan Caloun, Tomas Chlubna, Michal Chromco, Ivan Droppa, Roman Hamrlik, Milan Hnilicka, Frantisek Kaberle, Patrik Luza, Roman Meluzin, Igor Murin, Milan Nedoma, Zigmund Palffy, Robert Petrovicky, Martin Prochazka, Patrik Rimmel, Miroslav Skovira, Martin Straka, Viktor Ujcik, Jan Vopat, Marek Zadina, Jiri Zelenka

FINLAND

Tuomas Gronman, Janne Gronvall, Petri Gunther, Sami Kapanen, Ilpo Kauhanen, Marko Kiprusov, Jussi Kiuru, Pasi Kuivalainen, Tero Lehtera, Jere Lehtinen, Mikko Luovi, Pasi Maattanen, Jarno Miikkulainen, Janne Niinimaa, Jani Nikko, Petteri Nummelin, Jukka Ollila, Sakari Palsola, Marko Tuomainen, Jarkko Varvio, Tony Virta, Juha Ylonen

GERMANY

Christian Althoff, Till Feser, Timo Gschwill, Peter Hartung, Robert Hock, Frank Hohenadl, Henrik Holscher, Markus Kehle, Josef Lehner, Andreas Loth, Mirko Ludemann, Ronny Martin, Hans-Jorg Mayer, Oliver Mayer, Andreas Naumann, Thomas Schubert, Jens Schwabe, Marc Seliger, Michael Smazal, Stefan Ustorf, Thomas Wilhelm, Steffen Ziesche

SWEDEN

Greger Artursson, Calle Carlsson, Patrik Ekholm, Peter Forsberg, Kristian Gahn, Jens Hemstrom, Jonas Hoglund, Fredrik Jax, Andreas Johansson, Jacob Karlsson, Stefan Ketola, Stefan Klockare, Roger Kyro, Magnus Lindqvist, Markus Naslund, Bjorn Nord, Johan Norgren, Mattias Norstrom, Michael Nylander, Mikael Renberg, Niklas Sundblad, Rolf Wanhainen

SWITZERLAND

Marco Bayer, Michael Blaha, Laurent Bucher, Nicola Celio, Michael Diener, Ivan Gazzaroli, Tiziano Gianini, Gilles Guyaz, Noel Guyaz, Christian Hofstetter, Mathias Holzer, Pauli Jaks, Claude Luthi, Daniel Meier, Sasha Ochsner, Bjorn Schneider, Bernhard Schumperli, Martin Steinegger, Gaetan Voisard, Marc Weber, Lars Weibe, Gerd Zenhausern

UNITED STATES

Brent Bilodeau, Rich Brennan, Jim Campbell, Mike Dunham, Chris Ferraro, Peter Ferraro, Todd Hall, Brian Holzinger, Chris Imes, Steve Konowalchuk, Scott Lachance, John Lilley, Brian Mueller, Pat Peake, Mike Prendergast, Brian Rafalski, Brian Rolston, Corwin Saurdiff, Marty Schriner, Ryan Sittler, Keith Tkachuk, Chris Tucker

FINAL STANDINGS

	GP	W	L	T	GF	GA	P	GAA	SO	PIM
CIS	7	6	1	0	39	13	12	1.86	2	129
Sweden	7	5	1	1	41	24	11	3.43	0	116
United States	7	5	2	0	30	22	10	3.14	0	88
Finland	7	3	3	1	22	21	7	3.00	1	86*
Czechoslovakia	7	3	4	0	28	25	6	3.57	0	100
CANADA	7	2	3	2	21	30	6	4.29	0	122
Germany	7	1	6	0	15	40	2	5.71	0	88
Switzerland	7	1	6	0	19	40	2	5.71	0	96

* won Fair Play Cup

RESULTS

December 26	Fussen	Canada 5	Germany 4
	Fussen	Sweden 8	Czechoslovakia 4
	Kaufbeuren	CIS 10	Switzerland 2
	Fussen	United States 5	Finland 1
December 27	Fussen	Canada 6	Switzerland 4
	Kaufbeuren	Finland 5	Czechoslovakia 1
	Fussen	CIS 4	Sweden 3
	Fussen	United States 6	Germany 2
December 29	Kaufbeuren	Canada 2	Sweden 2
	Fussen	CIS 4	Finland 1
	Fussen	Czechoslovakia 8	Germany 2
	Fussen	United States 5	Switzerland 1
December 30	Fussen	Canada 2	Finland 2
	Fussen	Switzerland 4	Czechosloavkia 2
	Fussen	CIS 7	Germany 0
	Kaufbeuren	Sweden 8	United States 6
January 1	Fussen	United States 5	Canada 3
	Fussen	Sweden 4	Switzerland 3
	Kaufbeuren	Finland 2	Germany 0
	Fussen	Czechoslovakia 5	CIS 2
January 2	Fussen	Czechoslovakia 6	Canada 1
	Fussen	Finland 7	Switzerland 3
	Fussen	Sweden 10	Germany 1
	Kaufbeuren	CIS 5	United States 0
January 4	Fussen	CIS 7	Canada 2
	Fussen	Sweden 6	Finland 4
	Kaufbeuren	Germany 6	Switzerland 2
	Fussen	United States 3	Czechoslovakia 2

TEAM CANADA GAME SUMMARIES

December 26   *Canada 5*   *Germany 4*

First Period

1. Canada, Poulin (Daniels) .... 10:15(pp)
2. Canada, Sydor (Lindros) .... 13:48(pp)

   PENALTIES: Bombardir (Can) 0:25, Slaney (Can) 4:14, Lindros (Can) 5:52, Gschwill (Ger) 9:35, Schneider (Can) 11:40, O. Mayer (Ger) 12:30

Second Period

3. Germany, Martin (Schwabe, Schubert)...................................... 8:17(pp)

4. Germany, Smazal (Ustorf) 8:52
5. Germany, Ziesche (Loth) 12:46
6. Canada, Wright (unassisted) 15:01

> PENALTIES: Gschwill (Ger) 3:18, Wright (Can) & Smazal (Ger) 6:45, Sydor (Can) 7:29, Hohenadl (Ger) 9:10, Holscher (Ger) 10:23, Dykhuis (Can) 17:47

Third Period

7. Germany, Naumann (H. Mayer) .... 5:16(pp)
8. Canada, Sydor (Nelson, Slaney)...13:14
9. Canada, Poulin (Daniels) 19:40

> PENALTIES: O. Mayer (Ger) 1:07, Kariya (Can) 3:24, Niedermayer (Can) 4:50, Feser (Ger) 9:08

Shots on Goal:

Canada	9	15	10	**34**
Germany	7	9	9	**25**

In Goal:

> Canada — Kidd
> Germany — Seliger

December 27   *Canada 6*   *Switzerland 4*

First Period

1. Canada, Junker (Lindros, Kariya)... 2:21
2. Switzerland, Luthi (Zenhausern) 8:07
3. Canada, Lapointe (Poulin, Daniels) 16:38

> PENALTIES: Stevenson (Can) 2:53, A. Schneider (Can) 8:52, Lapointe (Can) 10:42, Guyaz (Swi) 13:59

Second Period

4. Canada, Cullimore (Lindros) 15:22
5. Canada, Lindros (Slaney, Daniels) 18:03

> PENALTIES: Luthi (Swi) 4:20, Poulin (Can) 8:55, Dykhuis (Can) 10:39

Third Period

6.   Switzerland, Blaha (B. Schneider) 0:25
7.   Switzerland, Schumperli (Celio, Gianini).............................. 5:35(pp)
8.   Canada, Sydor (Bombardir, Lindros).. 11:20
9.   Canada, Daniels (Lindros, Slaney)..12:56
10. Switzerland, Celio (unassisted) 15:08

> PENALTIES: Lapointe (Can) & Steinegger (Swi) 1:10, A. Schneider (Can) 1:20, Stevenson (Can) 4:25, Stevenson (Can) 7:00, Stevenson (Can) 12:01, B. Schneider (Swi) 12:28, Voisard (Swi) 15:08

Shots on Goal:

Canada	17	31	18	**66**
Switzerland	12	14	12	**38**

In Goal:

Canada — Kidd

Switzerland — Jaks

December 29   *Canada 2*   *Sweden 2*

First Period

1. Sweden, Naslund (Renberg, Forsberg) 3:43
2. Canada, Junker (Lapointe, Hughes) 19:06

PENALTIES: Wright (Can) & Carlsson (Swe) 4:51, Sundblad (Swe) 5:44, Bombardir (Can) 11:25, Niedermayer (Can) 14:03, Daniels (Can — misconduct) 17:10

Second Period

3. Canada, Lapointe (Sydor, Junker) .... 2:04(pp)

PENALTIES: Norstrom (Swe) 1:33, Lindros (Can — double minor) 7:25

Third Period

4. Sweden, Renberg (Nylander).. 19:53

PENALTIES: Lindros (Can) 13:41, Wright (Can) & Gahn (Swe) 17:52, Hemstrom (Swe) 19:53

Shots on Goal:

Canada	8	9	5	**22**
Sweden	25	14	24	**63**

In Goal:

Canada — Kidd

Sweden — Lindqvist

December 30   *Canada 2*   *Finland 2*

First Period

1. Finland, Varvio (Ylonen).. 4:07
2. Canada, Lindros (Bombardir).. 9:38

PENALTIES: Wright (Can) 14:08

Second Period

No Scoring

PENALTIES: Niedermayer (Can) 6:55, Niedermayer (Can) 13:09, Daniels (Can) 15:40

Third Period

3. Canada, Slaney (Stevenson) 6:50
4. Finland, Lehtera (Lehtinen, Virta).. 8:29

PENALTIES: Lapointe (Can) 4:16, Virta (Fin) 8:49, Gronman (Fin) 12:04, Lindros (Can) 20:00

Shots on Goal:

Canada	19	14	16	**49**
Finland	19	24	23	**66**

In Goal:

Canada — Kidd

Finland — Kauhanen

January 1   *United States 5*   *Canada 3*

First Period

1. United States, Konowalchuk (C. Ferraro) 11:15
2. Canada, Daniels (Junker) 12:26
3. Canada, Daniels (Lindros) .... 15:14(pp)

PENALTIES: Lilley (U.S.) 0:25, Penney (Can) 3:02, Brennan (U.S.) 3:17, Schriner (U.S.) 14:45

Second Period

4. United States, C. Ferraro (Lachance, P. Ferraro) 17:56

PENALTIES: Konowalchuk (U.S.) 6:07, Sydor (Can) 7:29, P. Ferraro (U.S.) 12:28, Wright (Can) 19:21

Third Period

5. United States, C. Ferraro (P. Ferraro) 6:03
6. United States, Rolston (unassisted) .... 14:19(pp)
7. Canada, Nelson (Stevenson) 14:48
8. United States, Konowalchuk (Peake) .... 19:40(en)

PENALTIES: Junker (Can) 0:50, Schriner (U.S.) 10:55, Cullimore (Can) 14:00

Shots on Goal:

Canada	22	12	20	**54**
United States	10	14	13	**37**

In Goal:

Canada — Kidd

United States — Dunham

January 2   *Czechoslovakia 6*   *Canada 1*

First Period

1. Canada, Lapointe (Poulin) 1:10
2. Czechoslovakia, Petrovicky (unassisted) 1:37
3. Czechoslovakia, Ujcik (Rimmel, Petrovicky) .... 15:50(pp)

PENALTIES: Palffy (Cze) 3:09, Lapointe (Can) 12:05, Wright (Can) 14:06, Stevenson (Can) & Caloun (Cze) 16:14

Second Period

4. Czechoslovakia, Caloun (Rimmel, Ujcik)......................................4:47(pp)
5. Czecholosvakia, Caloun (Straka, Vopat) 7:16
6. Czechoslovakia, Petrovicky (Rimmel) ....15:55(sh)

PENALTIES: Ujcik (Cze) 1:35, Wright (Can — double minor) 4:03, Chlubna (Cze) 9:40, Chlubna (Cze) 14:41

Third Period

7. Czechoslovakia, Zelenka (Rimmel, Petrovicky)............................9:28(pp)

PENALTIES: Nedoma (Cze) & Nelson (Can) 0:55, Daniels (Can) 2:34, Junker (Can) 7:57, Hamrlik (Cze) 12:01, Slaney (Can) 12:15, Rimmel (Cze) 14:18, Dykhuis (Can) 16:24, Luza (Cze) 18:21, Caloun (Cze) 19:13

Shots on Goal:

Canada	7	10	14	31
Czechoslovakia	16	12	13	41

In Goal:

Canada — Kidd
Czechoslovakia — Hnilicka

January 4   *CIS 7*   *Canada 2*

First Period

1. CIS, Korotkov (Volkov) 0:15
2. Canada, Lapointe (Lindros) ....11:42(sh)
3. CIS, Cherbayev (Zholtok) ....17:03(sh)

PENALTIES: Lindros (Can) 5:36, Ozolinsh (CIS) 8:21, Stevenson (Can) 10:39, Mironov (CIS) 16:11, Stevenson (Can) 18:29

Second Period

4. Canada, Kariya (Bombardir, Lindros)..13:37
5. CIS, Metliouk (Krivokrasov)..16:05
6. CIS, Kouzminski (Kovalev)..18:36

PENALTIES: Matvichuk (Can) 5:20, Korotkov (CIS — misconduct) 6:52, Dykhuis (Can) 14:03, Niedermayer (Can) & Sverjov (CIS) 17:01

Third Period

7. CIS, Kouzminski (Kovalev, Ozolinsh)..6:07(pp)
8. CIS, Cherbayev (unassisted) 11:30
9. CIS, Korotkov (Zholtok, Cherbayev) 14:07

PENALTIES: Slaney (Can) 5:56, Daniels (Can) 18:06, Lapointe (Can) 20:00

Shots on Goal:

Canada	8	8	6	22
CIS	16	19	8	43

In Goal:

Canada — Kidd
CIS — Khabibulin

TEAM CANADA FINAL STATISTICS
1992 WORLD JUNIOR CHAMPIONSHIPS

			GP	G	A	P	PIM
88	F	Eric Lindros(C)	7	2	8	10	12
14	F	Kimbi Daniels	7	3	4	7	16
22	F	Martin Lapointe(A)	7	4	1	5	10
5	D	Darryl Sydor(A)	7	3	1	4	4
11	F	Steve Junker	7	2	2	4	4
19	F	Patrick Poulin	7	2	2	4	2
77	D	John Slaney	7	1	3	4	6
55	D	Brad Bombardir	7	0	3	3	4
7	F	Jeff Nelson	7	1	1	2	2
18	F	Paul Kariya	6	1	1	2	2
23	F	Turner Stevenson	7	0	2	2	14
12	F	Tyler Wright	7	1	0	1	16
2	D	Jassen Cullimore	7	1	0	1	2
9	F	Ryan Hughes	7	0	1	1	0
44	D	Scott Niedermayer	7	0	0	0	10
24	D	Karl Dykhuis	7	0	0	0	8
17	F	Andy Schneider	7	0	0	0	6
8	F	Chad Penney	7	0	0	0	2
13	D	Richard Matvichuk	4	0	0	0	2
1	G	Trevor Kidd	7	0	0	0	0
16	F	David St. Pierre	7	0	0	0	0

In Goal

	GP	W-L-T	MINS	GA	SO	AVG
Trevor Kidd	7	2–3–2	420	29	0	4.29
Mike Fountain		did not play				

Coach   Rick Cornacchia
Assistants Tom Renney/Gary Agnew

CANADIAN OFFICIALS AT THE 1992
WORLD JUNIOR CHAMPIONSHIPS

Daryl Borden (referee)   3 games
Mike Burton (linesman)   7 games

TEAM CANADA ROSTER SUMMARY

Team Canada players   21
Drafted Into NHL   20 (all but Schneider)
Played In NHL   20 (all but St. Pierre)
Returning Players   6 (Dykhuis, Kidd, Lapointe, Lindros, Niedermayer, Slaney)

PLAYER REPRESENTATION BY LEAGUE

OHL   4 (Cullimore, Lindros, Penney, Slaney)
WHL   8 (Junker, Matvichuk, Nelson, Niedermayer, Schneider,
      Stevenson, Sydor, Wright)
QMJHL   3 (Lapointe, Poulin, St. Pierre)
NHL   1 (Daniels)
U.S. COLLEGE   3 (Bombardir, Hughes, Kariya)
OTHER*   2 (Dykhuis, Kidd)
* Canadian Olympic Team

PLAYER REPRESENTATION BY AGE

19-year-olds   13 (Bombardir, Cullimore, Daniels, Dykhuis, Hughes,
      Junker, Nelson, St. Pierre, Schneider, Slaney, Stevenson,
      Sydor)
18-year-olds   7 (Lapointe, Lindors, Matvichuk, Niedermayer, Penney,
      Poulin, Wright)
17-year-olds   1 (Kariya)

PLAYERS' CAREER PROFILES

Brad Bombardir   University of North Dakota Fighting Sioux (WCHA)
      Selected 56th overall by New Jersey at 1990 Draft
      Played in the NHL 1997 to present
Jassen Cullimore   Peterborough Petes (OHL)
      Selected 29th overall by Vancouver at 1991 Draft
      Played in the NHL 1994 to present
Kimbi Daniels   Philadelphia Flyers (NHL)
      last junior team: Swift Current Broncos (WHL)
      Selected 44th overall by Philadelphia at 1990 Draft
      Played in the NHL 1990–92
Karl Dykhuis   Canadian National Team
      Selected 16th overall by Chicago at 1990 Draft
      Played in the NHL 1991–97
Ryan Hughes   Cornell University Big Red (ECAC)
      Selected 22nd overall by Quebec at 1990 Draft
      Played in the NHL 1995–96

Steve Junker	Spokane Chiefs (WHL)
	Selected 92nd overall by Islanders at 1991 Draft
	Played in the NHL 1992–94
Paul Kariya	University of Maine Black Bears (HE)
	Selected 4th overall by Anaheim at 1993 Draft
	Played in the NHL 1994 to present
Trevor Kidd	Canadian National Team
	Selected 11th overall by Calgary at 1990 Draft
	Played in the NHL 1991 to present
Martin Lapointe	Laval Titans (QMJHL)
	Selected 10th overall by Detroit at 1991 Draft
	Played in the NHL 1991 to present
Eric Lindros	Oshawa Generals (OHL)
	Selected 1st overall by Quebec at 1991 Draft
	Played in the NHL 1992 to present
Rick Matvichuk	Saskatoon Blades (WHL)
	Selected 8th overall by Minnesota at 1991 Draft
	Played in the NHL 1992 to present
Jeff Nelson	Prince Albert Raiders (WHL)
	Selected 36th overall by Washington at 1991 Draft
	Played in the NHL 1994–96
Scott Niedermayer	Kamloops Blazers (WHL)
	Selected 3rd overall by New Jersey at 1991 Draft
	Played in the NHL 1991 to present
Chad Penney	North Bay Centennials (OHL)
	Selected 25th overall by Ottawa at 1992 Draft
	Played in the NHL 1993–94
Patrick Poulin	St. Hyacinthe Laser (QMJHL)
	Selected 9th overall by Hartford at 1991 Draft
	Played in the NHL 1991 to present
David St. Pierre	Verdun College Francais (QMJHL)
	Selected 173rd overall by Calgary at 1991 Draft
	Did not play in the NHL
Andy Schneider	Swift Current Broncos (WHL)
	Not drafted
	Played in the NHL 1993–94
John Slaney	Cornwall Royals (OHL)
	Selected 9th overall by Washington at 1990 Draft
	Played in the NHL 1993 to present
Turner Stevenson	Seattle Thunderbirds (WHL)
	Selected 12th overall by Montreal at 1990 Draft
	Played in the NHL 1992 to present
Darryl Sydor	Kamloops Blazers (WHL)
	Selected 7th overall by Los Angeles at 1990 Draft
	Played in the NHL 1991 to present

Tyler Wright   Swift Current Broncos (WHL)
                      Selected 12th overall by Edmonton at 1991 Draft
                      Played in the NHL 1992 to present

1993 WORLD JUNIOR CHAMPIONSHIPS SWEDEN, DECEMBER 26, 1992-- JANUARY 4, 1993

FINAL PLACINGS

GOLD MEDAL	**CANADA**
SILVER MEDAL	Sweden
BRONZE MEDAL	Czech & Slovak Republics
Fourth Place	United States
Fifth Place	Finland
Sixth Place	Russia
Seventh Place	Germany
Eighth place	Japan*

promoted from "B" pool in 1992; relegated to "B" pool for 1994

ALL-STAR TEAM

GOAL	Manny Legace (Canada)
DEFENCE	Brent Tully (Canada)
	Kenny Jonsson (Sweden)
FORWARD	Paul Kariya (Canada)
	Markus Naslund (Sweden)
	Peter Forsberg (Sweden)

DIRECTORATE AWARDS

BEST GOALIE	Manny Legace (Canada)
BEST DEFENCEMAN	Janne Gronvall (Finland)
BEST FORWARD	Peter Forsberg (Sweden)

COACH PERRY PEARN

Befitting the mandate of the Program of Excellence, Pearn graduated from the ranks of assistant coach of two gold-medal winning teams in 1990 and 1991 to head coach for this 1993 entry at the World Juniors. His appointment was due largely to his international experience after a sixth-place showing the previous year under a coaching staff that was without any. New assistant Siciliano, who had been an assistant and head coach with Canada's under-18 team, and Canale was assistant for Canada's under-18 entry at the Phoenix Cup in Japan in 1991 in which Canada won a silver medal.

Pearn began as a spare-part member of the University of Alberta team, coached by Clare Drake. Drake became his mentor, and after Pearn graduated from U of A he became an assistant for the Northern Alberta Institute of Technology Ookpiks and became head coach in 1978. In the ensuing years, NAIT won five CCHA titles, and Pearn's successes led to an assistant coaching job with the national under-18 team in 1986. He acted as assistant to Dave King's national team for the 1990–91 season.

Pearn had to prepare for the summer evaluation camp in Kitchener from August 15 to 22. Then he went on a scouting mission to Europe for September. He spent October and November travelling Canada scouting talent, and in December and January he led the team to the final camp and tournament.

THE UNKINDEST CUTS

Of the thirty-three players invited to the camp in Kitchener from December 13 to 18, eleven were cut: Norm Maracle (Saskatoon, WHL), Jocelyn Thibault (Sherbrooke, QMJHL), Nick Stajduhar (London, OHL), Brendan Witt (Seattle, WHL), Dean Melanson (St. Hyacinthe, QMJHL), Shane Peacock (Lethbridge, WHL), Curtis Bowen (Ottawa, OHL), Todd Warriner (Windsor, OHL), Jason Arnott (Oshawa, OHL), Kevin Brown (Niagara Falls, OHL), and Grant Marshall (Ottawa, OHL).

The final spot was taken by Mike Rathje, whose availability was almost scuppered by a trading card contract. Rathje was playing junior with the Medicine Hat Tigers, who had an exclusive deal with Classic Cards for player images. However, all players on the Junior Nationals had to sign a waiver for Upper Deck cards, exclusive producers of a WJC card set. A deal was eventually reached so Rathje could be on both sets.

The final team had youth but was not lacking in experience. Most players were seventeen- and eighteen-year-olds, and only three were returnees from 1992. But fourteen members of the team had played on the under-seventeen

Manny Legace had a perfect 6-0-0 record and
was the key to Canada's gold medal victory in 1993.

or under-eighteen team. This gave the juniors speed and size, and it meant the system of development in Canada was working.

THE EXHIBITIONS

The camp team played two friendly games, one against the Kitchener Selects on December 16 (a 6–1 win), one the next night against Team Guelph (a 5–2 win). The final team played Division 1 team Lekslands 1F in Lekslands, Sweden, on December 21 (a 1–1 tie). The next night they played the Swedish Juniors in Hofors, Sweden (an 8–5 loss).

GAVLE, SWEDEN

Located about two hundred kilometres north of Stockholm, Gavle was infamous for being the most radioactive area in Europe in 1986 because of the Chernobyl nuclear disaster in the Ukraine. The city had been cleaned up, however, and hosted the tournament admirably.

THE INSPIRATION

Prior to every game, the Canadians watched an inspirational video shot to the music of Bon Jovi's song "Keep the Faith," in which some of Canada's greatest goals were shown: Paul Henderson's goal in 1972, Darryl Sittler's Canada Cup game winner in 1976, Mario Lemieux converting Wayne Gretzky's pass in 1987, and John Slaney's dramatic goal late in the third period of Canada's 1991 World Junior gold. Said Tyler Wright, "It's very moving. It focuses on hard work, character, and determination. Those are the things we need here in order to succeed." Coach Pearn agreed: "The video gives the boys a sense of focus," he said.

During the second intermission of the game against Finland, Canada was leading 2–1 but being outplayed. Canada could put a clinch on gold with a strong third period. Pearn came into the dressing room, cleared off the trainer's table, and placed his championship ring from 1991 on the bare table. Before the team went back onto the ice, he reminded the players that this is what they were playing for. They won 3–2.

MISCELLANY

Sweden was certain to be Canada's biggest threat with Peter Forsberg (who set a record for most points, thirty-one, and most assists, twenty-four), Kenny Jonsson, Mats Lindgren, Markus Naslund (record for most goals, thirteen), and Niklas Sundblad. Forsberg incited the Canadians' wrath by predicting a win prior to their game, and the resultant 5–4 loss to the Canadians forced Peter the Great to *manger his mots*, as it were.

The most interesting entry in the tournament was Japan, competing in the "A" pool for the first time and led by Hiroyuki Miura, who was drafted by Montreal in round eleven of the entry draft in 1992.

The Americans were having troubles icing a respectable team. The year before, they had flaunted their medals at the closing ceremonies. This year, Canada whitewashed them 3–0 in the round robin and then deprived the Americans of a medal. In the final game, a Canadian win would have given the States a bronze medal. Canada's loss pushed the Czech-Slovak team into the medals and the Americans out.

Paul Kariya, arguably the greatest player in the world today, was one of so many Canadian stars who honed his skills at the World Juniors.

POLITICS

At the previous year's WJC, the Soviet Union became the Commonwealth of Independent States on New Year's Day. This year, the breakup of Czechoslovakia welcomed the new year. The team remained intact for the rest of the tournament, but the Czechoslovakian flag and anthem were replaced by the IIHF flag and anthem, and the team was referred to as the Czech and Slovak Republics.

TOURNAMENT FORMAT

No change in the structure was made from last year. Eight teams, one round-robin of play. Ties in the standings were broken by head-to-head results. Thus, Canada's win over Sweden gave it the gold medal.

THE OPPOSITION

CZECH/SLOVAK REPUBLICS

Radim Bicanek, Vaclav Burda, Michal Cerny, Pavol Demitra, Frantisek Kaberle, Roman Kadera, Richard Kapus, Tomas Klimt, Kamil Kolacek, Pavel Kowalczyk, Patrik Krisak, Pavel Malac, Igor Murin, Stanislav Neckar, Tomas Nemcicky, Pavel Rajnoha, Miroslav Skovira, Ondrej Steiner, Petr Ton, Zdenek Touzimsky, Jan Vopat, David Vyborny

FINLAND

Jarkko Glad, Tuomas Gronman, Janne Gronvall, Markus Hatinen, Sami Helenius, Timo Hirvonen, Sami Kapanen, Ilpo Kauhanen, Jussi Kiuru, Tom Koivisto, Saku Koivu, Antti Laaksonen, Jere Lehtinen, Mikko Luovi, Janne Nikko, Jukka Ollila, Ville Peltonen, Kimmo Rintanen, Pasi Saarela, Kalle Sahlstedt, Kimmo Timonen, Jonni Vauhkonen

GERMANY

Fabian Brannstrom, Ralf Dobrzynski, James Dresler, Sven Felski, Andre Grein, Robert Hock, Rafael Jedamzik, Markus Kempf, Thomas Knobloch, Mike Losch, Mirko Ludemann, Michael Maass, Stefan Mann, Jochen Molling, Matthias Mosebach, Marc Pethke, Michael Schmi, Moritz Schmidt, Marc Seliger, Alexander Serikow, Heiko-Michael Smazal, Norbert Zabel

JAPAN

Tomohiro Baba, Yutaka Ebata, Ken'ichi Hiraiwa, Akira Ihara, Yuji Iizuka, Shiro Ishiguro, Gen Ishioka, Akihito Isojima, Shin'ichi Itabashi, Yutaka Kawaguchi, Hironori Kawashima, Hiroyuki Miura, Ohno Naoto, Mitsuaki Nitta, Tsutsumi Otomo, Junji Sakata, Hideyuki Sano, Yuichi Sasaki, Daisuke Sasoya, Taiji Susumago, Hideji Tshuchida, Shinjiro Tsuji

RUSSIA

Igor Alexandrov, Oleg Belov, Sergei Brylin, Alexander Cherbayev, Maxim Galanov, Sergei Gonchar, Alexander Guliavtsev, Igor Ivanov, Nikolai Khabibulin, Sergei Klimovich, Victor Kozlov, Sergei Marchkov, Artur Oktjabrev, Alexei Poliakov, Nikolai Semin, Stanislav Shalnov, Vadim Sharifianov, Vitali Tomilin, Nikolai Tsulygin, Andrei Yakhanov, Alexei Yashin, Pavel Yevstegneyev

SWEDEN

Clas Eriksson, Peter Forsberg, Edvin Frylen, Mikael Hakansson, Niclas Havelid, Andreas Johansson, Daniel Johansson, Hans Jonsson, Kenny Jonsson, Mats Lindgren, Fredrik Lindqvist, Mikael Magnusson, Johan Manss, Markus Naslund, Reine Rauhala, Petter Ronnqvist, Roger Rosen, Andreas Salomonsson, Niklas Sundblad, Niklas Sundstrom, Johan Tornberg, Magnus Wernblom

UNITED STATES

Adam Bartell, Brent Bilodeau, Dan Brierley, Jeff Callinan, Jim Campbell, Jim Carey, Adam Deadmarsh, John Emmons, Chris Ferraro, Peter Ferraro, Liam Garvey, Todd Hall, Brady Kramer, Todd Marchant, Pat Mikesch, Pat Peake, Mike Pomichter, Brian Rafalski, Brian Rolston, Ryan Sittler, Mark Strobel, David Wilkie

FINAL STANDINGS

	GP	W	L	T	GF	GA	P	GAA	SO	PIM
CANADA	7	6	1	0	37	17	12	2.43	1	147
Sweden	7	6	1	0	53	15	12	2.14	0	175
Czech/Slovak	7	4	2	1	38	27	9	3.86	0	98
United States	7	4	3	0	32	23	8	3.29	0	106
Finland	7	3	3	1	31	20	7	2.86	2	153
Russia	7	2	3	2	26	20	6	2.86	2	96
Germany	7	1	6	0	16	37	2	5.29	0	128
Japan	7	0	7	0	9	83	0	11.87	0	88*

* won Fair Play Cup

RESULTS

December 26	Gavle	Canada 3	United States 0
	Falun	Russia 16	Japan 0
	Bollnas	Finland 5	Czech/Slovak 2
	Gavle	Sweden 4	Germany 2
December 27	Gavle	Canada 5	Sweden 4
	Falun	Russia 4	Germany 0
	Gavle	Finland 7	Japan 0
	Uppsala	Czech/Slovak 6	United States 5
December 29	Gavle	Canada 9	Russia 1
	Hofors	Finland 11	Germany 0
	Gavle	Sweden 7	Czech/Slovak 2
	Falun	United States 12	Japan 2

December 30	Uppsala	Canada 3	Finland 2
	Gavle	Czech/Slovak 1	Russia 1
	Gavle	Sweden 20	Japan 1
	Bollnas	United States 4	Germany 3
Janaury 1	Gavle	Canada 5	Germany 2
	Skutskar	Czech/Slovak 14	Japan 2
	Gavle	Finland 1	Russia 1
	Uppsala	Sweden 4	United States 2
January 2	Hudkisvall	Canada 8	Japan 1
	Gavle	Sweden 9	Finland 2
	Uppsala	Czech/Slovak 6	Germany 3
	Gavle	United States 4	Russia 2
January 4	Gavle	Czech/Slovak 7	Canada 4
	Hofors	Germany 6	Japan 3
	Gavle	Sweden 5	Russia 1
	Gavle	United States 5	Finland 3

TEAM CANADA GAME SUMMARIES

December 26 *Canada 3* *United States 0*

First Period

1. Canada, Lafayette (McAmmond) .... 12:15(pp)

   PENALTIES: Lapointe (Can) 2:16, Garvey (U.S.) 5:23, Sittler (U.S.) 11:00, Smith (Can) 12:24, Hall (U.S.) 19:35

Second Period

2. Canada, Shantz (Smith, Pronger) .... 1:18(pp)
3. Canada, Gendron (Daigle, Dawe) 16:47

   PENALTIES: Werenka (Can) 2:45, Rathje (Can) 4:43, Rathje (Can) 7:20, Garvey (U.S.) 10:13, Marchant (U.S.) 14:22

Third Period

No Scoring

   PENALTIES: Aucoin (Can) 7:32, Pronger (Can) 8:07

Shots on Goal:

Canada	11	12	4	**27**
United States	9	9	13	**31**

In Goal:

Canada — Legace
United States — Carey

December 27   *Canada 5*   *Sweden 4*

First Period

1. Sweden, Sundstrom (Forsberg, Naslund) ....6:43(pp)

    PENALTIES: Sundblad (Swe) 1:24, Wernblom (Swe) 2:07, Tornberg (Swe) 3:43, Tully (Can) 6:26, Sundblad (Swe) 7:24, McAmmond (Can) 8:49, Frylen (Swe) 10:51, Wright (Can) 15:25

Second Period

2. Canada, Lapointe (Tully, Kariya)...5:04
3. Sweden, Sundstrom (Johansson, Forsberg) ....8:22(pp)
4. Canada, Intranuovo (Wright, Niedermayer) 13:19
5. Canada, Bes (Aucoin)...17:12

    PENALTIES: Intranuovo (Can) & Dawe (Can) & Johansson (Swe) & Tornberg (Swe) 7:13, Aucoin (Can) 7:44, Lindgren (Swe) 9:01, Pronger (Can) 9:32, Jonsson (Swe) 13:37, Daigle (Can — major, game misconduct) 15:18, Lindgren (Swe) 19:44, Werenka (Can — minor, misconduct) 19:56

Third Period

6. Canada, Kariya (Lapointe, Rathje) 3:42
7. Sweden, Naslund (Forsberg, Sundstrom) 4:27
8. Canada, Wright (Niedermayer, Intranuovo).....................................5:05
9. Sweden, Forsberg (unassisted) ....8:49(pp)

    PENALTIES: Kariya (Can) 6:27, Rathje (Can) 8:18, McAmmond (Can) 9:57, Jonsson (Swe — minor, misconduct) 13:06, Naslund (Swe — major) 13:39

Shots on Goal:

Canada	10	12	17	**39**
Sweden	9	15	9	**33**

In Goal:

Canada — Legace
Sweden — Ronnqvist

December 29   *Canada 9*   *Russia 1*

First Period

1. Canada, Pronger (Shantz) 8:00
2. Canada, Intranuovo (unassisted) ....13:53(sh)
3. Canada, Gratton (Kariya, Lapointe) ....15:57(pp)

    PENALTIES: Tomilin (Rus) 2:09, Aucoin (Can) 3:24, Intranuovo (Can) 11:38, Bes (Can) 12:13, Sharifianov (Rus) 14:48, Werenka (Can) 16:42, Belov (Rus) 19:08

Second Period

4. Canada, Rathje (unassisted) ....10:02(pp)
5. Russia, Brylin (Belov) 15:35

    PENALTIES: Gratton (Can) 0:59, Smith (Can) 6:14, Oktjabrev (Rus) 8:29, Semin (Rus) 9:01, Shalnov (Rus) 12:06, Pronger (Can) 14:47, Marchkov (Rus) 16:29

Third Period

6. Canada, Dawe (Daigle) 3:27
7. Canada, Gendron (Daigle, Dawe) 11:28
8. Canada, Lapointe (Kariya, Gratton) 14:18
9. Canada, Intranuovo (Wright, Smith) .... 16:57(pp)
10. Canada, Gendron (Dawe) 18:23

PENALTIES: Klimovich (Rus) 8:35, Werenka (Can) 11:56, Oktjabrev (Rus) 14:52, Gonchar (Rus) 15:31

Shots on Goal:

Canada	10	10	16	**36**
Russia	19	12	13	**44**

In Goal:

Canada — Legace
Russia — Khabibulin

December 30   *Canada 3*   *Finland 2*

First Period

1. Canada, Gendron (Daigle) 6:55
2. Canada, Smith (Kariya, Lapointe) .... 19:44(pp)

PENALTIES: Smith (Can) 7:59, Gronman (Fin) 15:39, Saarela (Fin) 18:49

Second Period

3. Finland, Rintanen (Lehtinen, Koivu) 15:24

PENALTIES: Can bench (served by Niedermayer) 0:00, Hirvonen (Fin) 2:34, Sahlstedt (Fin) 4:43, Rathje (Can) 7:13, Dawe (Can) 11:18, Bes (Can) 16:58, Rintanen (Fin) 18:52

Third Period

4. Canada, Wright (Intranuovo, Tully) 4:04
5. Finland, Lehtinen (Peltonen, Koivu) 7:01

PENALTIES: Shantz (Can) 9:10, McAmmond (Can) 17:14

Shots on Goal:

Canada	16	10	10	**36**
Finland	26	12	22	**60**

In Goal:

Canada — Legace
Finland — Kauhanen

January 1   *Canada 5*   *Germany 2*

First Period

1. Germany, Zabel (Brannstrom, Serikow) 6:04
2. Canada, Rathje (Lafayette) 8:17
3. Canada, Tully (Pronger) .... 8:54(pp)

     PENALTIES: Zabel (Ger) 8:48, Aucoin (Can) 9:20, Rathje (Can) 9:44

Second Period

4. Canada, Lafayette (Shantz) .... 7:11(sh)
5. Canada, Kariya (Gratton) 9:55
6. Germany, Hock (Brannstrom, Mosebach) 13:43

     PENALTIES: Tully (Can) 6:57, Niedermayer (Can) 11:05, Wright (Can) 16:01, Hock (Ger) 17:12

Third Period

7. Canada, Werenka (Shantz, Wright) 10:01

     PENALTIES: Rathje (Can) 1:29, Ger bench 3:07, Dawe (Can) & Ger bench 5:42, Lapointe (Can) 11:22, Wright (Can) 13:05, Ger bench 14:03, Tully (Can) 17:57

Shots on Goal:

Canada	16	17	5	**38**
Germany	9	12	4	**25**

In Goal:

     Canada — Legace
     Germany — Seliger

January 2   *Canada 8*   *Japan 1*

First Period

1. Canada, Lapointe (Bes) 1:38
2. Japan, Sasoya (Tsuchida, Kawaguchi) 11:41
3. Canada, Dawe (Gendron, Daigle) 12:17
4. Canada, Lapointe (Bes, Smith) 14:48
5. Canada, Lafayette (Shantz) .... 16:35(pp)
6. Canada, Bes (Kariya) 18:10

     PENALTIES: Tully (Can) 3:13, Miura (Jap) 15:35, Sano (Jap) 18:23

Second Period

7. Canada, Bes (Lapointe, Kariya) 16:01

     PENALTIES: Itabashi (Jap) 3:00, Tsuji (Jap) 4:30, Kawashima (Jap) 7:57, McAmmond (Can) 10:20, Ihara (Jap) 17:53

Third Period

8. Canada, Wright (Intranuovo, Niedermayer) 8:06

9. Canada, Dawe (Gendron) 8:37

PENALTIES: Dawe (Can) 3:09, Shantz (Can) 4:22, Ebata (Jap) 8:44, Miura (Jap) 13:02, Kawashima (Jap) 16:07, Gendron (Can) 18:38

Shots on Goal:

Canada	24	23	20	**67**
Japan	10	5	5	**20**

In Goal:

Canada — Legace
Japan — Baba

January 4   *Czech/Slovak Republics 7 Canada 4*

First Period

1. Canada, Gendron (Daigle) 12:45
2. Czech/Slovak, Cerny (Ton) 13:16
3. Czech/Slovak, Krisak (unassisted) 15:51

PENALTIES: Cerny (CzSl) 1:34, Daigle (Can) 7:15, Smith (Can) 8:27, McAmmond (Can) 17:19

Second Period

4. Canada, Shantz (unassisted) 0:47
5. Czech/Slovak, Vyborny (penalty shot) 11:58
6. Canada, Gratton (Pronger) .... 17:25(pp)

PENALTIES: Tully (Can) 1:23, McAmmond (Can) 7:22, Smith (Can) 8:43, Vyborny (CzSl) 16:50, Nemcicky (CzSl) 18:44

Third Period

7. Czech/Slovak, Steiner (unassisted) 3:20
8. Czech/Slovak, Cerny (Ton, Rajnoha) 5:39
9. Canada, Lapointe (Rathje) .... 13:08(pp)
10. Czech/Slovak, Nemcicky (unassisted) 18:29
11. Czech/Slovak, Vopat (Vyborny, Demitra) .... 19:40(pp)

PENALTIES: Lapointe (Can) 6:31, Demitra (CzSl) 12:36, Tully (Can) 19:15

Shots on Goal:

Canada	10	13	11	**34**
Czech/Slovak	12	11	10	**33**

In Goal:

Canada — DeRouville
Czech/Slovak — Murin

TEAM CANADA FINAL STATISTICS
1993 WORLD JUNIOR CHAMPIONSHIPS

			GP	G	A	P	PIM
22	F	Martin Lapointe(C)	7	5	4	9	6
18	F	Paul Kariya	7	2	6	8	2
32	F	Martin Gendron	7	5	2	7	2
10	F	Jason Dawe	7	3	3	6	8
12	F	Tyler Wright(A)	7	3	3	6	6
9	F	Ralph Intranuovo	7	3	3	6	4
29	F	Jeff Shantz	7	2	4	6	4
19	F	Alexandre Daigle	7	0	6	6	27
11	F	Jeff Bes	7	3	2	5	4
21	F	Nathan Lafayette	7	3	1	4	0
33	D	Mike Rathje	7	2	2	4	12
7	F	Chris Gratton	7	2	2	4	2
15	D	Jason Smith	7	1	3	4	10
6	D	Chris Pronger	7	1	3	4	6
2	D	Brent Tully	7	1	2	3	12
23	F	Rob Niedermayer	7	0	3	3	4
4	D	Darcy Werenka	7	1	0	1	18
16	D	Dean McAmmond	7	0	1	1	12
3	D	Adrian Aucoin(A)	7	0	1	1	8
14	D	Joel Bouchard	7	0	0	0	0
30	G	Manny Legace	6	0	0	0	0
31	G	Philippe DeRouville	1	0	0	0	0

In Goal

	GP	W–L–T	MINS	GA	SO	AVG
Manny Legace	6	6–0–0	360	10	1	1.67
Philippe DeRouville	1	0–1–0	60	7	0	7.00

Coach   Perry Pearn
Assistants Dave Siciliano/Joe Canale

CANADIAN OFFICIALS AT THE 1993
WORLD JUNIOR CHAMPIONSHIPS

Benoit Lapointe (referee)   3 games
Dave Taveroff (linesman)   6 games

TEAM CANADA ROSTER SUMMARY

Team Canada players   22
Drafted Into NHL   22
Played In NHL   20 (all but Bes, Tully)
Returning Players   3 (Kariya, Lapointe, Wright)

PLAYER REPRESENTATION BY LEAGUE

OHL   8   (Bes, Dawe, Gratton, Intranuovo, Lafayette, Legace, Pronger, Tully)
WHL   7   (McAmmond, Niedermayer, Rathje, Shantz, Smith, Werenka, Wright)
QMJHL   5   (Bouchard, Daigle, DeRouville, Gendron, Lapointe)
U.S. COLLEGE   1   (Kariya)
OTHER*   1   (Aucoin)

* *Canadian National Team*

PLAYER REPRESENTATION BY AGE

19-year-olds   12 (Aucoin, Bes, Dawe, Intranuovo, Lafayette, Lapointe, Legace, McAmmond, Shantz, Smith, Werenka, Wright)
18-year-olds   8 (Bouchard, Daigle, DeRouville, Gendron, Kariya, Pronger, Rathje, Tully)
17-year-olds   2 (Gratton, Niedermayer)

PLAYERS' CAREER PROFILES

Adrian Aucoin   Canadian National Team
Selected 117th overall by Vancouver at 1992 Draft
Played in the NHL 1994 to present

Jeff Bes   Guelph Storm (OHL)
Selected 58th overall by Minnesota at 1992 Draft
Did not play in the NHL

Joel Bouchard   Verdun College Francais (QMJHL)
Selected 129th overall by Calgary at 1992 Draft
Played in the NHL 1994 to present

Alexandre Daigle   Victoriaville Tigers (QMJHL)
Selected 1st overall by Ottawa at 1993 Draft
Played the NHL 1993 to present

Jason Dawe   Peterborough Petes (OHL)
Selected 35th overall by Buffalo at 1991 Draft
Played in the NHL 1993 to present

Philippe DeRouville   Verdun College Francais (QMJHL)
Selected 115th overall by Pittsburgh at 1992 Draft
Played in the NHL 1994 to present

Martin Gendron   St.-Hyacinthe Laser (QMJHL)
Selected 71st overall by Washington at 1992 Draft
Played in the NHL 1994–98

Chris Gratton   Kingston Frontenacs (OHL)
Selected 3rd overall by Tampa Bay at 1993 Draft
Played in the NHL 1993–98

Ralph Intranuovo   Sault Ste. Marie Greyhounds (OHL)
Selected 96th overall by Edmonton at 1992 Draft
Played in the NHL 1994–98

Paul Kariya   University of Maine Black Bears (HE)
Selected 4th overall by Anaheim at 1993 Draft
Played in the NHL 1994 to present

Nathan Lafayette   Newmarket Royals (OHL)
Selected 65th overall by St. Louis at 1991 Draft
Played in the NHL 1993 to present

Martin Lapointe   Laval Titans (QMJHL)
Selected 10th overall by Detroit at 1991 Draft
Played in the NHL 1991 to present

Manny Legace   Niagara Falls Thunder (OHL)
Selected 188th overall by Hartford at 1993 Draft
Played in the NHL 1998 to present

Dean McAmmond   Prince Albert Raiders (WHL)
Selected 22nd overall by Chicago at 1991 Draft
Played in the NHL 1991 to present

Rob Niedermayer   Medicine Hat Tigers (WHL)
Selected 5th overall by Florida at 1993 Draft
Played in the NHL 1993 to present

Chris Pronger   Peterborough Petes (OHL)
Selected 2nd overall by Hartford at 1993 Draft
Played in the NHL 1993 to present

Mike Rathje   Medicine Hat Tigers (WHL)
Selected 3rd overall by San Jose at 1992 Draft
Played in the NHL 1993 to present

Jeff Shantz   Regina Pats (WHL)
Selected 36th overall by Chicago at 1992 Draft
Played in the NHL 1993 to present

Jason Smith   Regina Pats (WHL)
Selected 18th overall by New Jersey at 1992 Draft
Played in the NHL 1993 to present

Brent Tully   Peterborough Petes (OHL)
Selected 93rd overall by Vancouver at 1992 Draft
Did not play in the NHL

Darcy Werenka	Brandon Wheat Kings (WHL)
	Selected 37th overall by Rangers at 1991 Draft
	Played in the NHL 1992–96
Tyler Wright	Swift Current Broncos (WHL)
	Selected 12th overall by Edmonton at 1991 Draft
	Played in the NHL 1992 to present

1994 WORLD JUNIOR CHAMPIONSHIPS CZECH REPUBLIC, DECEMBER 26, 1993-- JANUARY 4, 1994

FINAL PLACINGS

GOLD MEDAL	**CANADA**
SILVER MEDAL	Sweden
BRONZE MEDAL	Russia
Fourth Place	Finland
Fifth Place	Czech Republic
Sixth Place	United States
Seventh Place	Germany
Eighth Place	Switzerland*

promoted from "B" pool in 1993; relegated to "B" pool for 1995

ALL-STAR TEAM

GOAL	Evgeny Riabchikov (Russia)
DEFENCE	Kenny Jonsson (Sweden)
	Kimmo Timonen (Finland)
FORWARD	Niklas Sundstrom (Sweden)
	Valeri Bure (Russia)
	David Vyborny (Czech Republic)

DIRECTORATE AWARDS

BEST GOALIE	Jamie Storr (Canada)
BEST DEFENCEMAN	Kenny Jonsson (Sweden)
BEST FORWARD	Niklas Sundstrom (Sweden)

COACH JOE CANALE

In 1970, Canale began coaching at the lower levels of hockey — midget AA and AAA, juvenile AA, junior C, and junior AA. He was coach of the Shawinigan Cataracts until the early morning of February 20, 1978, when the RCMP knocked on his door with a warrant for his arrest. He was charged with trafficking narcotics (mescaline) at a Montreal bar of which he was part owner. He was convicted, sentenced to four years in prison, and that seemed to be the end of the line for him. However, after eighteen months, he was paroled, then pardoned, but getting back into hockey proved difficult.

He coached the Sud-Ouest AA team to two championships in Montreal, then Montreal-Bourassa AAA with Pierre Turgeon on it, and took Quebec to a gold medal at the Esso Cup midget tournament. In 1990 he made it back to junior hockey, as coach of the Chicoutimi Sagueneens. He was voted coach of the year his first season with the Sags. Like his predecessor for the national team, Perry Pearn, he was an assistant coach before being hired to lead the team at the WJC in the Czech Republic, taking time off from his coaching duties with the Beauport Harfangs.

THE FINAL CAMP

Thirty-two players were invited to camp in Kitchener beginning December 13. Coach Canale's prime interests were skating ability and speed, realising once again that the larger European ice surface would be a factor in team strategy.

The team played two exhibition games, the first a 3–3 tie against an OHL select team at the Kinsmen Arena in Kitchener, the second a 4–3 loss to a university select team backed by junior goalie Jamie Storr. The coaching staff wanted to make all its cuts by December 17, but players were close in skill, and only two were cut on schedule, Jason Gladney of Kitchener and Daniel Guerard of Verdun.

Among the final cuts made by Coach Canale were Ed Jovanovski and Jeff O'Neill, both of whom have gone on to careers in the NHL and once again proving the depth of the Canadian team. Canale can't be condemned for cutting the two future stars (he won gold) but being cut from this one team did not doom the pro careers of either Jovanowski or O'Neill. On the 19th, after the final roster had been selected, the team flew from Toronto to Ambri in Switzerland, where they held a five-day mini-camp intended to help them come together as a team. On Christmas Eve they headed for Ostrava in the Czech Republic and played their first tournament game two days later.

*Canada beat Sweden 6-4 in this game to win gold, thanks in part to
hits such as Nick Stajduhar's on Tre Kronor's Peter Gerhardsson.*

TOURNAMENT FORMAT

Eight teams were grouped in one division to play a single round robin.
Head-to-head results and then goal differential were used to determine
placings in the standings in case of a tie.

THE OPPOSITION

CZECH REPUBLIC

Tomas Blazek, Pavel Kowalczyk, Marek Malik, Josef Marha, Jaroslav Miklen,
Milan Navratil, Zdenek Nedved, Libor Prochazka, Ladislav Prokupek, Vaclav
Prospal, Pavel Rajnoha, Zdenek Sedlak, Viacheslav Skuta, Robert Slavik,
Lukas Smital, Jaroslav Spacek, Ondrej Steiner, Petr Sykora, Radim Tesarik,
Tomas Vlasak, David Vyborny, Pavel Zubicek

FINLAND

Antti Aalto, Petri Engman, Tuomas Gronman, Tommi Hamalainen, Jani
Hassinen, Jere Karalahti, Jari Kauppila, Teemu Kohvakka, Tom Koivisto, Saku

Koivu, Juha Lind, Jussi Markkanen, Tommi Miettinen, Niko Mikkola, Janne Niinimaa, Jani Nikko, Veli-Pekka Nutikka, Jussi Tarvainen, Jukka Tiilikainen, Kimmo Timonen, Mikko Turunen, Jonni Vauhkonen

GERMANY

Fabian Brannstrom, Marco Eltner, Sven Felski, Christian Gegenfurtner, Erich Goldmann, Rudolf Gorgenlander, Carsten Gossmann, Jochen Hecht, Rafael Jedamzik, Thomas Knobloch, Daniel Korber, Markus Krawinkel, Mike Losch, Stefan Mann, Stephan Retzer, Andreas Schneider, Marc Seliger, Alexander Serikow, Patrick Solf, Stefan Ustorf, Sven Valenti, Markus Wieland

RUSSIA

Evgeni Babariko, Maxim Bets, Sergei Brylin, Valeri Bure, Alexei Chikalin, Pavel Desiatkov, Alexander Kharlamov, Sergei Kondrashkin, Denis Kuzmenko, Konstantin Kuzmichev, Alexander Osadchi, Dmitri Podlegayev, Evgeny Riabchikov, Vadim Sharifianov, Maxim Smelnitsky, Ilya Stashenkov, Maxim Sushinski, Nikolai Tsulygin, Maxim Tsvetkov, Vasily Turkovsky, Oleg Tverdovsky, Nikolai Zavarukhin

SWEDEN

Johan Davidsson, Anders Eriksson, Jonas Forsberg, Edvin Frylen, Peter Gerhardsson, Johan Hagman, Mikael Hakansson, Mathias Johansson, Daniel Johansson, Kenny Jonsson, Mats Lindgren, Joakim Lundberg, Fredrik Modin, Mattias Ohlund, Peter Olsson, Roger Rosen, Anders Soderberg, Peter Strom, Niklas Sundstrom, Per Svartvadet, Dick Tarnstrom, Mattias Timander

SWITZERLAND

Robin Bauer, Claudio Bayer, Patric Della Rossa, Sven Dick, Patrick Fischer, Reto Germann, Daniel Giger, Brund Habisreutinger, Jacub Horak, Vjeran Ivankovic, Marcel Jenni, Matthias Keller, Marco Kloti, Patrick Looser, Thierry Paterlini, Jorg Reber, Marco Schellenberg, Pascal Sommer, Stefano Togni, Lars Weibel, Michel Zeiter, Jerry Zuurmond

UNITED STATES

Kevyn Adams, Jason Bonsignore, Andy Brink, Jon Coleman, Adam Deadmarsh, Aaron Ellis, John Emmons, Ashlin Halfnight, Kevin Hilton, Jason Karmanos, Toby Kvalevog, Bob Lachance, Jamie Langenbrunner, Jason McBain, Chris O'Sullivan, Jay Pandolfo, Richard Park, Deron Quint, Ryan Sittler, Blake Sloan, John Varga, David Wilkie

FINAL STANDINGS

	GP	W	L	T	GF	GA	P	GAA	SO	PIM
CANADA	7	6	0	1	39	20	13	2.86	0	142
Sweden	7	6	1	0	35	16	12	2.29	1	82*
Russia	7	5	1	1	23	17	11	2.43	1	98
Finland	7	4	3	0	27	24	8	3.43	1	124
Czech Republic	7	3	4	0	31	29	6	4.14	1	114
United States	7	1	5	1	20	33	3	4.71	0	119
Germany	7	1	6	0	10	26	2	3.71	0	113
Switzerland	7	0	6	1	10	30	1	4.29	0	98

* won Fair Play Cup

RESULTS

December 26	Frydek-Mistek	Canada 5	Switzerland 1
	Ostrava	Sweden 4	Germany 1
	Ostrava	Russia 5	Czech Republic 1
	Frydek-Mistek	Finland 5	United States 2
December 27	Ostrava	Canada 5	Germany 2
	Ostrava	Sweden 3	Russia 0
	Frydek-Mistek	Finland 7	Czech Republic 3
	Frydek-Mistek	Switzerland 1	United States 1
December 29	Frydek-Mistek	Canada 3	Russia 3
	Frydek-Mistek	Czech Republic 6	Switzerland 0
	Ostrava	Sweden 6	Finland 2
	Ostrava	United States 7	Germany 2
December 30	Ostrava	Canada 6	Finland 3
	Ostrava	Czech Republic 6	Germany 2
	Frydek-Mistek	Sweden 6	Switzerland 2
	Frydek-Mistek	Russia 4	United States 3
January 1	Frydek-Mistek	Canada 8	United States 3
	Ostrava	Finland 4	Switzerland 2
	Frydek-Mistek	Sweden 6	Czech Republic 4
	Ostrava	Russia 1	Germany 0
January 2	Ostrava	Canada 6	Czech Republic 4
	Frydek-Mistek	Finland 2	Germany 0
	Frydek-Mistek	Russia 5	Switzerland 3
	Ostrava	Sweden 6	United States 1
January 4	Ostrava	Canada 6	Sweden 4
	Ostrava	Germany 3	Switzerland 1
	Frydek-Mistek	Russia 5	Finland 4
	Frydek-Mistek	Czech Republic 7	United States 3

TEAM CANADA GAME SUMMARIES

December 26   Canada 5   Switzerland 1

First Period

1. Switzerland, Fischer (Paterlini) 1:59
2. Canada, Harvey (unassisted) 9:13
3. Canada, Stajduhar (Peca) .... 15:55(pp)

    PENALTIES: Bannister (Can) 2:51, Peca (Can) 6:26, Germann (Swi) 10:38, Zeiter (Swi) 11:08, McCabe (Can) 12:46, Looser (Swi — double minor) 15:35, Bannister (Can) 18:17

Second Period

4. Canada, Gendron (Dube)... 2:37(pp)

    PENALTIES: Jenni (Swi) 0:59, Harvey (Can) 3:20, Dube (Can) 6:48, Togni (Swi) 7:19, Peca (Can) 8:12, Tully (Can) 8:30, McCabe (Can) 9:52, Della Rossa (Swi) 10:08, Bannister (Can) 10:37, Dick (Swi) 10:47, Gendron (Can) 15:15, Della Rossa (Swi) 17:32

Third Period

5. Canada, Peca (Gendron, Stajduhar) .... 4:33(pp)
6. Canada, Carter (Bannister, Harvey).. 6:16

    PENALTIES: Paterlini (Swi) 3:13, Reber (Swi) 4:10, Peca (Can) 8:07, Bowen (Can) 11:13, Bouchard (Can) 11:39, Gavey (Can) 11:50, Sommer (Swi) 15:14

Shots on Goal:

Canada	14	15	16	**45**
Switzerland	12	15	13	**40**

In Goal:

    Canada — Storr
    Switzerland — Weibel

December 27   Canada 5   Germany 2

First Period

1. Germany, Eltner (Knobloch) .... 4:10(pp)
2. Canada, Harvey (Murray) .... 10:14(pp)
3. Germany, Mann (Losch, Schneider).. 18:15

    PENALTIES: Stajduhar (Can) 2:26, Harvey (Can) & Gavey (Can — misconduct) 5:13, Felski (Ger) 9:59, Stajduhar (Can) 18:55, Tully (Can) & Schneider (Ger) 19:23

Second Period

4. Canada, Gavey (Peca)... 13:11(pp)
5. Canada, Girard (unassisted) 15:29

    PENALTIES: Jedamzik (Ger) 11:32, Jedamzik (Ger) 16:30, Gavey (Can) & Ustorf (Ger) 19:53

Third Period

6. Canada, Girard (Harvey) .... 13:05(pp)
7. Canada, Gendron (Allison).. 18:31(pp)

PENALTIES: Bouchard (Can) 5:43, Eltner (Ger) 12:17, Felski (Ger) & Bannister (Can) 14:13, Gavey (Can) 15:07, Losch (Ger) 16:57, Felski (Ger — minor, game misconduct) 17:34

Shots on Goal:

Canada	10	9	19	38
Germany	15	13	11	39

In Goal:

Canada — Storr
Germany — Seliger

December 29   Canada 3   Russia 3

First Period

1. Canada, Harvey (Stajduhar, Gavey) .... 4:53(pp)

PENALTIES: Sharifianov (Rus) 1:22, Tsulygin (Rus) 2:59, Sushinski (Rus) 4:19, Botterill (Can) 8:06, Turkovsky (Rus) 12:16, Can bench 14:41, Harvey (Can) 16:30

Second Period

2. Canada, Carter (Bannister)... 14:28

PENALTIES: McCabe (Can) 2:56, Tsvetkov (Rus) 14:56, Gendron (Can) 17:52

Third Period

3. Canada, Allison (Dube) .... 5:14(pp)
4. Russia, Brylin (Tverdovsky)... 12:20
5. Russia, Kharlamov (Tverdovsky, Brylin) .... 17:47(pp)
6. Russia, Sushinkski (Brylin, Bure) 19:05

PENALTIES: Sharifianov (Rus) 3:18, Dube (Can) 13:43, Tully (Can) 17:35

Shots on Goal:

Canada	14	13	13	40
Russia	11	12	17	40

In Goal:

Canada — Storr
Russia — Riabchikov

December 30   Canada 6   Finland 3

First Period

1. Canada, Botterill (Gendron, Bannister) 1:24

2. Finland, Lind (unassisted) .... 18:26(sh)

PENALTIES: Stajduhar (Can) 2:18, Karalahti (Fin) 3:34, Aalto (Fin) 5:39, Lind (Fin) 8:59, Gavey (Can) 14:07, Tiilikainen (Fin) 17:24

Second Period

3. Canada, Murray (Carter) .... 6:44(pp)
4. Finland, Koivu (unassisted) 11:15
5. Canada, Dube (Girard) 15:03

PENALTIES: Tiilikainen (Fin) 0:17, Botterill (Can) 4:07, Witt (Can) & Tully (Can — misconduct) 5:07, Gavey (Can) 9:52, Peca (Can) & Mikkola (Fin) 12:02, Dube (Can) & Hassinen (Fin) 18:28

Third Period

6. Finland, Karalahti (Miettinen) 2:12
7. Canada, Carter (Friesen, Stajduhar) 3:39
8. Canada, Girard (Murray, Bannister) 15:21
9. Canada, Girard (unassisted) .... 19:10(en)

PENALTIES: Aalto (Fin) & Murray (Can) 1:06, Bowen (Can) 6:47, Murray (Can) 7:40, Gavey (Can) 8:37, Kohvakka (Fin) 11:34

Shots on Goal:

Canada	12	12	12	36
Finland	13	15	15	43

In Goal:

Canada — Fernandez

Finland — Engman

January 1   *Canada 8*   *United States 3*

First Period

1. Canada, Peca (unassisted) 2:50
2. United States, Varga (Karmanos, Quint) 9:46
3. United States, Wilkie (O'Sullivan, Adams) 12:03
4. Canada, Bowen (unassisted) 13:00
5. Canada, Harvey (Gavey, Armstrong) 13:31
6. Canada, Dube (Tully) 13:52

PENALTIES: none

Second Period

7. Canada, Allison (Bouchard, Dube) .... 7:55(pp)
8. Canada, Dube (Girard) 18:30

PENALTIES: Karmanos (U.S.) 6:17, Witt (Can) 11:04

Third Period

9. Canada, Gavey (Carter, Friesen) 2:52
10. United States, Langenbrunner (Brink, Wilkie) 7:08
11. Canada, Gendron (unassisted) 19:14

PENALTIES: Witt (Can) 8:19, Bowen (Can) 12:01

Shots on Goal:

Canada	13	12	8	**33**
United States	16	9	16	**41**

In Goal:

Canada — Fernandez
United States — Ellis/Kvalevog (Kvalevog [4 goals] replaced Ellis [4 goals] at 13:52 of 1st)

January 2   Canada 6   Czech Republic 4

First Period

1. Czech Republic, Marha (unassisted) 2:30
2. Canada, Convery (unassisted) 5:18
3. Canada, Gendron (Allison)... 9:45(pp)

   PENALTIES: Bowen (Can) 2:39, Bowen (Can) 5:52, Vyborny (CzR) & Skuta (CzR) 9:19, Gavey (Can) 13:12, Bouchard (Can) 18:23, Malik (CzR) 18:45

Second Period

4. Czech Republic, Sedlak (Smital) 6:57
5. Czech Republic, Sykora (Zubicek, Rajnoha) 8:27
6. Canada, Dube (Allison, Stajduhar) .... 13:23(pp)
7. Canada, Girard (Allison)... 15:37

   PENALTIES: Allison (Can) 1:32, Gavey (Can) 9:18, Spacek (CzR) 11:31, Kowalczyk (CzR) 18:13

Third Period

8. Czech Republic, Vlasak (Malik) 6:54
9. Canada, Gavey (Harvey) 7:49
10. Canada, Bowen (Murray, Gendron) 16:34

   PENALTIES: Prokupek (CzR) 3:13

Shots on Goal:

Canada	6	15	9	**30**
Czech Republic	17	10	15	**42**

In Goal:

Canada — Fernandez
Czech Republic — Slavik

January 4   Canada 6   Sweden 4

First Period

1. Canada, Dube (Allison, Gendron)... 13:42(pp)
2. Canada, Allison (Dube) 17:05
3. Sweden, Lindgren (unassisted) 17:23

4. Sweden, Modin (Johansson, Ohlund) .... 19:33(pp)

   PENALTIES: Botterill (Can) 5:59, Tarnstrom (Swe) 11:43, Botterill (Can) & Eriksson (Swe) 17:50, Bannister (Can) 19:02

Second Period

5. Canada, Gendron (unassisted) 4:14
6. Canada, Gavey (Girard) 12:25
7. Canada, Gendron (Allison, Dube) .... 19:47(pp)

   PENALTIES: Dube (Can) 6:13, Girard (Can) & Jonsson (Swe) 7:10, Sundstrom (Swe) 10:11, Gendron (Can) & Hakansson (Swe) 11:28, Dube (Can) 13:33, Lundberg (Swe) 18:52, Jonsson (Swe) 19:32

Third Period

8. Sweden, Lindgren (Sundstrom) .... 8:53(pp)
9. Sweden, Tarnstrom (Johansson) 9:47
10. Canada, Girard (unassisted) .... 19:54(sh-en)

    PENALTIES: Stajduhar (Can) 7:11, Bouchard (Can) 7:32, Lindgren (Swe) 10:18, Bouchard (Can) 19:08, Convery (Can) 19:54

Shots on Goal:

Canada	13	13	5	31
Sweden	16	14	19	49

In Goal:

Canada — Storr
Sweden — Olsson

TEAM CANADA FINAL STATISTICS
1994 WORLD JUNIOR CHAMPIONSHIPS

			GP	G	A	P	PIM
32	F	Martin Gendron	7	6	4	10	6
9	F	Yanick Dube	7	5	5	10	10
18	F	Rick Girard	7	6	3	9	2
8	F	Jason Allison	7	3	6	9	2
10	F	Todd Harvey(A)	7	4	3	7	6
22	F	Aaron Gavey	7	4	2	6	26
19	F	Anson Carter	7	3	2	5	0
14	D	Nick Stajduhar	7	1	4	5	8
27	F	Mike Peca	7	2	2	4	8
28	F	Marty Murray	7	1	3	4	4
5	D	Drew Bannister	7	0	4	4	10
20	F	Curtis Bowen	7	2	0	2	10
25	D	Jeff Friesen	5	0	2	2	0
23	F	Jason Botterill	6	1	0	1	8
12	F	Brandon Convery	7	1	0	1	2
2	D	Brent Tully(C)	7	0	1	1	16
24	D	Joel Bouchard	7	0	1	1	10

34	D	Chris Armstrong	6	0	1	1	0
4	D	Bryan McCabe	7	0	0	0	6
6	D	Brendan Witt(A)	7	0	0	0	6
1	G	Jamie Storr	4	0	0	0	0
30	G	Emmanuel Fernandez	3	0	0	0	0

In Goal

	GP	W–L–T	MINS	GA	SO	AVG
Jamie Storr	4	3–0–1	240	10	0	2.50
Emmanuel Fernandez	3	3–0–0	180	10	0	3.33

Coach　　　Joe Canale
Assistants　Mike Johnston/Dan Flynn

CANADIAN OFFICIALS AT THE 1994 WORLD JUNIOR CHAMPIONSHIPS

Sylvain Bibeau (referee)	4 games
Jean-Yves Malliet (linesman)	6 games

TEAM CANADA ROSTER SUMMARY

Team Canada players　22
Drafted Into NHL　22
Played In NHL (to date) 17　(all but Armstrong, Bowen, Dube, Girard, Tully)
Returning Players　3　(Bouchard, Gendron, Tully)

PLAYER REPRESENTATION BY LEAGUE

OHL　　　　　10　(Allison, Bannister, Bowen, Convery, Gavey, Harvey, Peca, Stajduhar, Storr, Tully)
WHL　　　　　6　(Armstrong, Friesen, Girard, McCabe Murray, Witt)
QMJHL　　　　4　(Bouchard, Dube, Fernandez, Gendron)
U.S. COLLEGE　2　(Botterill, Carter)

PLAYER REPRESENTATION BY AGE

19-year-olds　　13　(Bannister, Bouchard, Bowen, Carter, Convery, Dube, Fernandez, Gavey, Gendron, Girard, Peca, Stajduhar, Tully)
18-year-olds　　6　(Allison, Armstrong, Harvey, McCabe, Murray, Witt)
17-year-olds　　3　(Botterill, Friesen, Storr)

PLAYERS' CAREER PROFILES

Jason Allison   London Knights (OHL)
Selected 17th overall by Washington at 1993 Draft
Played in the NHL 1993 to present

Chris Armstrong   Moose Jaw Warriors (WHL)
Selected 57th overall by Florida at 1993 Draft
Has not yet played in the NHL

Drew Bannister   Sault Ste. Marie Greyhounds (OHL)
Selected 26th overall by Tampa Bay at 1992 Draft
Played the NHL 1995 to present

Jason Botterill   University of Michigan Wolverines (CCHA)
Selected 20th overall by Dallas at 1994 Draft
Played in the NHL 1997 to present

Joel Bouchard   Verdun College Francais (QMJHL)
Selected 129th overall by Calgary at 1992 Draft
Played in the NHL 1994 to present

Curtis Bowen   Ottawa 67's (OHL)
Selected 22nd overall by Detroit at 1992 Draft
Has not yet played in the NHL

Anson Carter   Michigan State University Spartans (CCHA)
Selected 220th overall by Quebec at 1992 Draft
Played in the NHL 1996 to present

Brandon Convery   Niagara Falls Thunder (OHL)
Selected 8th overall by Toronto at 1992 Draft
Played in the NHL 1995 to present

Yannick Dube   Laval Titans (QMJHL)
Selected 117th overall by Vancouver at 1994 Draft
Has not yet played in the NHL

Emmanuel Fernandez   Laval Titans (QMJHL)
Selected 52nd overall by Quebec at 1992 Draft
Played in the NHL 1994 to present

Jeff Friesen   Regina Pats (WHL)
Selected 11th overall by San Jose at 1994 Draft
Played in the NHL 1994 to present

Aaron Gavey   Sault Ste. Marie Greyhounds (OHL)
Selected 74th overall by Tampa Bay at 1992 Draft
Played the NHL 1995 to present

Martin Gendron   Hull Olympiques (QMJHL)
Selected 71st overall by Washington at 1992 Draft
Played in the NHL 1994 to present

Rick Girard   Swift Current Broncos (WHL)
Selected 46th overall by Vancouver at 1993 Draft
Has not yet played in the NHL

Todd Harvey   Detroit Jr. Red Wings (OHL)
                     Selected 9th overall by Dallas at 1993 Draft
                     Played in the NHL 1994 to present
Bryan McCabe   Spokane Chiefs (WHL)
                     Selected 40th overall by Islanders at 1993 Draft
                     Played in the NHL 1995 to present
Marty Murray   Brandon Wheat Kings (WHL)
                     Selected 96th overall by Calgary at 1993 Draft
                     Played in the NHL 1995 to present
Mike Peca   Ottawa 67's (OHL)
                     Selected 40th overall by Vancouver at 1992 Draft
                     Played in the NHL 1993 to present
Nick Stajduhar   London Knights (OHL)
                     Selected 16th overall by Edmonton at 1993 Draft
                     Played in the NHL 1995–96
Jamie Storr   Owen Sound Platers (OHL)
                     Selected 7th overall by Los Angeles at 1994 Draft
                     Played in the NHL 1994 to present
Brent Tully   Peterborough Petes (OHL)
                     Selected 93rd overall by Vancouver at 1992 Draft
                     Has not yet played in the NHL
Brendan Witt   Seattle Thunderbirds (WHL)
                     Selected 11th overall by Washington at 1993 Draft
                     Played in the NHL 1995 to present

1995 WORLD JUNIOR CHAMPIONSHIPS CANADA, DECEMBER 26, 1994-- JANUARY 4, 1995

FINAL PLACINGS

GOLD MEDAL   **CANADA**
SILVER MEDAL   Russia
BRONZE MEDAL   Sweden
Fourth Place   Finland
Fifth Place   United States
Sixth Place   Czech Republic
Seventh Place   Germany
Eighth Place   Ukraine*

* promoted from "B" pool in 1994
note: no team was relegated to "B" pool from this year's tournament because
in 1996 the "A" pool expanded to ten teams and a new round-robin format

ALL-STAR TEAM

GOAL   Igor Karpenko (Ukraine)
DEFENCE   Bryan McCabe (Canada)
           Anders Eriksson (Sweden)
FORWARD   Jason Allison (Canada)
           Eric Daze (Canada)
           Marty Murray (Canada)

DIRECTORATE AWARDS

BEST GOALIE   Evgeny Tarasov (Russia)
BEST DEFENCEMAN   Bryan McCabe (Canada)
BEST FORWARD   Marty Murray (Canada)

COACH DON HAY

Hay was coach of the Memorial Cup champion Kamloops Blazers. He was an assistant coach with the team for seven years (1985–92) and became head coach in 1992. After three successful years in the WHL, he coached the Phoenix Coyotes for 1996–97.

Just as junior coaches use the junior leagues to gain experience for the World Juniors, so too does the tournament provide excellent apprenticeship for the NHL. Of the nineteen coaches from 1977 to 1998, eight have gone on to the NHL.

THE HOCKEY ATMOSPHERE, DECEMBER 1994

The 1994–95 season was the darkest hour in the NHL's history. An owners' lockout and an impasse between owners and players forced the cancellation of half the season and threw the year into disarray. To watch kids skate in the name of country was therefore particularly enjoyable. It also showed the pro game in an even poorer light. When Edmonton Oiler goalie Curtis Joseph helped raise a WJC banner at the Coliseum, one fan yelled, "Get back to work, ya bum."

SHAPING THE TEAM

Because of the lockout, all under-20 NHLers were available to play at the World Juniors, most notably Ryan Smyth, Alexandre Daigle, Jason Allison, Todd Harvey, and Jeff Friesen, all of whom had made their NHL teams but had no games to play because of the lockout (though technically they were in junior at the time they were selected to the team).

Coach Hay's most controversial cut at the December camp was the release of Brett Lindros, behemoth brother of Eric and a 1st-round draft choice by the Islanders. When he arrived at camp, a beaming Brett exclaimed, "Look around. This is the next wave of players in the NHL." But Hay was confident in his decision: "There were four guys — Jason Allison, Shean Donovan, Todd Harvey, and Eric Daze — who outplayed him. The bottom line is he didn't show the speed for the international game." Lindros seemed like a great NHL prospect, but his career ended due to concussions. Today, Allison and Daze are among the best young players in the NHL.

Lindros was a name and seemed to be a sure future NHL superstar, and when he was cut, a number of important facts about the junior team became clear. One, a future NHL star does not necessarily make a great international junior. Two, names don't make teams, contributors do. Three, the team might

Shean Donovan bears down on German goaler Oliver Hausler
who surrendered all eight goals in Canada's 8-1 win.

just as well have won with him in the lineup as without. The decision by Hay
was bold. Had Brett made the team, no one would have criticised Hay.
Without Lindros, Hay would have faced a great deal of scrutiny had the team
lost gold.

EXHIBITIONS

Playing as host nation always provided advantages for Team Canada. For one,
there was no extensive travel. For another, the Europeans had to adjust to
the smaller ice surface. Hay's troops played two exhibition games just before
Christmas, beating Finland 4–1 and the Swedes 5–2 two nights later, both at
the Canada Games Arena in Grand Prairie, Alberta.

STICKING TOGETHER

Hay brought to the team superb motivational skills. For example, on Christmas Night, when the team met to celebrate their holiday together, they took
an ordinary stick and covered it in white tape and wrote "respect" on it. It
was passed around and everyone wrote the name of someone he would

dedicate the tournament to. The stick went everywhere with the team, a constant reminder of commitment and family spirit.

The idea was first used by Hay with Kamloops, and it showed his coaching approach. "Hockey has changed so much in the last ten years," he said. "It's changed from the Xs and Os to the motivational part of the game. Players are so smart nowadays, they can adjust very quickly to what coaches explain to them. It's the mental part that's really big in the games."

ANOTHER CARD DILEMMA

Just as in 1993 when the team almost lost Mike Rathje because of playing card contracts, this year's team faced a similar problem. Pinnacle produced a special set of cards to commemorate the WJC, but could not include Jason Botterill, a U.S. Collegian, because NCAA rules prohibit players from being used in card sets. Rather than print twenty-one players, Pinnacle decided to cut Chad Allan, as well, to ensure an even twenty in the set.

Alexandre Daigle was a Canadian rarity at the World Juniors, the only player to participate in two tournaments, not consecutively, in 1993 and then 1995.

CANADA'S ACCOMPLISHMENTS

This was one of the most talented and successful teams ever to represent Canada internationally. The team scored forty-nine goals, second only to fifty-four goals in 1986. The only period they didn't score a goal was the second period of the last game of the tournament against Sweden. Their twenty-three power-play goals were a tournament record, as was the perfect 7–0 won-loss record. Five players finished with ten points or more — another record — and four of the six first-team all-star spots were taken by Canadians.

TOURNAMENT FORMAT

No change from the norm. Eight teams played a round-robin within one large grouping. In the case of a tie, the head-to-head match was the first deciding factor, then goal differential, then goals quotient (goals-for divided by goals-against).

THE OPPOSITION

CZECH REPUBLIC

Tomas Blazek, Petr Buzek, Petr Cajanek, Miloslav Guren, Milan Hejduk, Jan Hlavac, Jan Hrdina, Ladislav Kohn, Vlastimil Kroupa, Jaroslav Kudrna, Marek Malik, Josef Marha, Michal Marik, Zdenek Nedved, Pavel Nestak, Angel Nikolov, Vaclav Prospal, Frantisek Ptacek, Petr Sykora, Pavel Trnka, Vaclav Varada, Marek Zidlicky

FINLAND

Antti Aalto, Miika Elomo, Niko Halttunen, Tommi Hamalainen, Jani Hassinen, Mikko Helisten, Martti Jarventie, Miska Kangasniemi, Jere Karalahti, Miikka Kiprusoff, Petri Kokko, Toni Makiaho, Jussi Markkanen, Tommi Miettinen, Janne Niinimaa, Veli-Pekka Nutikka, Tommi Rajamaki, Timo Salonen, Tommi Sova, Jussi Tarvainen, Kimmo Timonen, Juha Vuorivirta

GERMANY

Tino Boos, Lars Bruggemann, Hubert Buchwieser, Eric Dylla, Marco Eltner, Thorsten Fendt, Kai Fischer, Erich Goldmann, Oliver Hausler, Jochen Hecht, Florian Keller, Stephan Lahn, Stefan Mann, Andreas Renz, Stephan Retzer, Matthias Sanger, Florian Schneider, Alexander Serikow, Marco Sturm, Stefan Tillert, Sven Valenta, Markus Wieland, Martin Williams

SWEDEN

Jonas Andersson-Junkka, Per-Johan Axelsson, Daniel Back, Anders Burstrom, Johan Davidsson, Anders Eriksson, Johan Finnstrom, Jonas Forsberg, Fredrik Johansson, Andreas Karlsson, Jesper Mattsson, Peter Nylander, Mattias Ohlund, Kristoffer Ottosson, Mathias Pihlstrom, Henrik Smangs, Anders Soderberg, Peter Strom, Niklas Sundstrom, Per Svartvadet, Dick Tarnstrom, Daniel Tjarnquist

RUSSIA

Artem Anisimov, Ruslan Batyrchine, Pavel Boichenko, Alexander Boikov, Vadim Charifianov, Vladimir Chebaturkin, Vadim Epanshintsev, Anvar Gatiatoulline, Sergei Goussev, Alexander Kharlamov, Dmitri Klevakin, Alexandre Koroliouk, Denis Kouzmenko, Igor Melyakov, Valentin Morozov, Mikhail Okhotnikov, Ramil Saioulline, Evgeny Tarasov, Ilja Vorobiev, Sergei Vychedkevitch, Vitali Yachmenev, Nikolai Zavaroukhin

UKRAINE

Alexei Bernatsky, Sergei Chubenko, Boris Chursin, Danil Didkovsky, Igor Drifan, Alexander Fyodorov, Alexandre Govorun, Sergei Karnaukh, Igor Karpenko, Sergei Kharchenko, Andrei Kurilko, Andrei Kuzminsky, Alexei Lazarenko, Yuri Ljaskovsky, Denis Lobanovsky, Dmitri Mozheiko, Alexandre Mukhanov, Roman Salnikov, Vladislav Shevtchenko, Vitaly Tretiakov, Oleg Tsirkunov, Igor Yankovitch

UNITED STATES

Shawn Bates, Jon Battaglia, Bryan Berard, Reg Berg, Doug Bonner, Jason Bonsignore, Mike Crowley, Adam Deadmarsh, Rory Fitzpatrick, John Grahame, Mike Grier, Sean Haggerty, Ashlin Halfnight, Kevin Hilton, Chris Kelleher, Brian LaFleur, Jamie Langenbrunner, Jeff Mitchell, Richard Park, Deron Quint, Dan Tompkins, Landon Wilson

FINAL STANDINGS

	GP	W	L	T	GF	GA	P	GAA	SO	PIM
CANADA	7	7	0	0	49	22	14	3.14	0	68*
Russia	7	5	2	0	36	24	10	3.43	0	123
Sweden	7	4	2	1	35	21	9	3.00	0	82
Finland	7	3	3	1	29	26	7	3.71	0	155
United States	7	3	4	0	28	33	6	4.71	0	165
Czech Republic	7	3	4	0	43	26	6	3.71	1	219
Germany	7	1	6	0	17	55	2	7.86	0	148
Ukraine	7	1	6	0	12	42	2	6.00	0	139

* won Fair Play Cup

RESULTS

December 26	Red Deer	Canada 7	Ukraine 1
	Leduc	Sweden 10	Germany 2
	Spruce Grove	Czech Republic 3	Finland 0
	Innisfail	United States 4	Russia 3
December 27	Red Deer	Canada 9	Germany 1
	Stettler	Russia 4	Czech Republic 3
	Rocky Mtn House	Finland 6	Ukraine 2
	Red Deer	Sweden 4	United States 2
December 29	Red Deer	Canada 8	United States 3
	Red Deer	Sweden 4	Czech Republic 3
	Edmonton	Russia 4	Ukraine 2
	Wetaskiwin	Finland 7	Germany 1
December 30	Calgary	Canada 7	Czech Republic 5
	Sherwood Park	Sweden 7	Ukraine 1
	Lacombe	Russia 8	Germany 1
	Red Deer	Finland 7	United States 5
January 1	Edmonton	Canada 6	Finland 4
	Calgary	Russia 6	Sweden 4
	Red Deer	Czech Republic 10	Ukraine 1
	Edmonton	United States 5	Germany 3
January 2	Red Deer	Canada 8	Russia 5
	Calgary	Sweden 3	Finland 3
	Red Deer	Czech Republic 14	Germany 3
	Camrose	Ukraine 3	United States 2
January 4	Red Deer	Canada 4	Sweden 3
	Red Deer	Russia 6	Finland 2
	Stettler	Germany 6	Ukraine 2
	Ponoka	United States 7	Czech Republic 5

TEAM CANADA GAME SUMMARIES

December 26   *Canada 7*   *Ukraine 1*

First Period

1. Canada, Friesen (Allison, McCabe) ....4:02(pp)

    PENALTIES: Jovanovski (Can) 1:56, Karpenko (Ukr) 3:08, Mukhanov (Ukr) 3:38

Second Period

2. Canada, Rivers (Murray, Courville)..2:45(pp)
3. Canada, Courville (O'Neill) 3:25
4. Canada, Murray (Allison)...5:35(pp)

5. Canada, Murray (Allison, O'Neill) ....7:36(pp)
6. Ukraine, Chubenko (Chursin, Kuzminsky) .... 17:47(pp)

   PENALTIES: Mukhanov (Ukr) 2:39, Bernatsky (Ukr) 5:01, Drifan (Ukr) 6:30, Lazarenko (Ukr) 12:49, Botterill (Can) 16:38, Friesen (Can) 18:53

Third Period

7. Canada, Smyth (unassisted) 15:14
8. Canada, Daze (Smyth, O'Neill) .... 19:17(pp)

   PENALTIES: Daigle (Can) 13:02, Yankovitch (Ukr) 17:39

Shots on Goal:

Canada	16	25	19	60
Ukraine	4	9	2	15

In Goal:

Canada — Storr
Ukraine — Karpenko

December 27   *Canada 9*   *Germany 1*

First Period

1. Canada, Smyth (Tucker) 2:10
2. Canada, Daigle (unassisted) 4:05

   PENALTIES: Boos (Ger) 6:05, Bruggemann (Ger) 10:38, Courville (Can) 10:55, Boos (Ger) 15:58, Renz (Ger) 18:09, Jovanovski (Can) 19:20

Second Period

3. Canada, Jovanovski (Murray) 3:25
4. Canada, Jovanovski (unassisted)... 3:59
5. Canada, Murray (McCabe) ....7:12(pp)
6. Germany, Retzer (Hecht) 8:36
7. Canada, Daze (unassisted) 8:55
8. Canada, Redden (Smyth, Tucker) .... 12:07(pp)
9. Canada, Harvey (Redden) .... 16:53(pp)

   PENALTIES: Courville (Can) 2:03, Bruggemann (Ger) 3:18, Tillert (Ger) 6:13, Williams (Ger) 11:43, Goldmann (Ger — minor, misconduct) 12:53, Eltner (Ger) 15:23, Schneider (Ger) 16:34, Ger bench 20:00

Third Period

10. Canada, Friesen (Daigle) ....0:55(pp)

   PENALTIES: Smyth (Can) 2:59, Rivers (Can) 8:23, Donovan (Can) 9:43

Shots on Goal:

Canada	26	20	13	59
Germany	4	8	8	20

In Goal:

Canada — Cloutier
Germany — Hausler

December 29 · *Canada 8* · *United States 3*

First Period

1. Canada, McCabe (Murray, Allison) 1:17
2. Canada, Friesen (Daigle, McCabe) 5:10
3. Canada, Harvey (Daigle, Friesen) 16:38
4. Canada, Pederson (Botterill, Baumgartner) 17:23

    PENALTIES: Wilson (U.S.) 5:25, Harvey (Can) 7:54, Baumgartner (Can) 12:45, Halfnight (U.S.) 18:12, O'Neill (Can) 19:56

Second Period

5. United States, Wilson (Deadmarsh, Park) .... 0:35(pp)
6. Canada, Redden (McCabe, Daigle) .... 2:37(pp)
7. Canada, Daze (Rivers, O'Neill) .... 13:12(pp)
8. Canada, O'Neill (Tucker, Smyth) .... 19:43(pp)

    PENALTIES: Bonsignore (U.S.) 2:00, Haggerty (U.S.) 11:26, Crowley (U.S.) 17:06, Fitzpatrick (U.S.) 19:12

Third Period

9. United States, Langenbrunner (Crowley) 7:35
10. Canada, Friesen (Daigle, Rivers) .... 13:02(pp)
11. United States, Bates (unassisted) .... 16:40(sh)

    PENALTIES: Grier (U.S.) 1:06, Grahame (U.S.) 2:30, Donovan (Can) 6:04, Botterill (Can) 7:03, Park (U.S. — major, game misconduct) 12:00, Baumgartner (Can) 17:26

Shots on Goal:

Canada	17	11	6	**34**
United States	4	4	5	**13**

In Goal:

Canada — Storr
United States — Bonner/Grahame (Grahame [4 goals] replaced Bonner [4 goals] to start 2nd)

December 30 · *Canada 7* · *Czech Republic 5*

First Period

1. Canada, Allison (McCabe, Daze) .... 9:14(pp)
2. Czech Republic, Marha (unassisted) 19:37

    PENALTIES: Malik (CzR) 7:22, Trnka (CzR) 8:52, Harvey (Can) 11:17, Buzek (CzR) 15:21

Second Period

3. Czech Republic, Nedved (Malik) 0:16
4. Czech Republic, Cajanek (unassisted) 3:50
5. Canada, McCabe (Rivers) .... 9:10(pp)

6. Canada, Murray (Allison, Smyth) 9:52
7. Czech Republic, Marha (Prospal).. 11:21
8. Canada, Harvey (Tucker) 12:35
9. Czech Republic, Kudrna (Marha, Prospal) 18:04

   PENALTIES: Kohn (CzR) 8:25, Kajanek (CzR — misconduct) 9:52, Allison (Can) 13:25, Storr (Can) 14:34, Malik (CzR) 15:57

Third Period

10. Canada, Redden (Daigle, Sorochan) 15:51
11. Canada, Rivers (unassisted) 17:36
12. Canada, Friesen (unassisted) ....19:29(en-sh)

   PENALTIES: Buzek (CzR) 2:45, Kohn (CzR) 5:27, Cajanek (CzR) 13:51, Donovan (Can) 18:04, Cajanek (CzR — game misconduct) 20:00

Shots on Goal:

Canada	11	8	12	**31**
Czech Republic	9	14	11	**34**

In Goal:

Canada — Storr
Czech Republic — Marik

January 1   *Canada 6*   *Finland 4*

First Period

1. Canada, Courville (Allison, Murray) 0:44

   PENALTIES: Sova (Fin) 9:32, Smyth (Can) 12:02, Karalahti (Fin) 15:34

Second Period

2. Canada, McCabe (Murray, Allison).. 3:18
3. Canada, Harvey (Friesen, McCabe) ....4:26(pp)
4. Finland, Kokko (Niinimaa, Sova) ....5:32(pp)
5. Canada, Daze (Murray, Allison) .... 13:50(pp)
6. Finland, Niinimaa (Aalto) 19:35
7. Finland, Tarvainen (Timonen) 19:47

   PENALTIES: Hamalainen (Fin) 3:56, Courville (Can) 5:10, Allan (Can) 10:44, Rajamaki (Fin) 13:11, Salonen (Fin) 16:41

Third Period

8. Canada, Murray (McCabe, Allison) 2:36
9. Canada, Daigle (Courville).. 4:58
10. Finland, Nutikka (penalty shot) ....12:52(sh)

   PENALTIES: Sorochan (Can) 7:21, Makiaho (Fin) 11:40, Aalto (Fin — minor, misconduct) 13:07

Shots on Goal:

Canada	10	15	12	**37**
Finland	7	18	18	**43**

In Goal:

Canada — Cloutier
Finland — Markkanen

January 2   Canada 8   Russia 5

First Period

1. Russia, Klevakin (Kharlamov) 6:01
2. Canada, Allison (Courville) 6:42
3. Canada, Daze (Murray, McCabe) .... 19:06(pp)

   PENALTIES: McCabe (Can) 3:47, Botterill (Can) & Rus bench 11:11, Daigle (Can) 16:10, Okhotnikov (Rus) 18:50

Second Period

4. Canada, Daze (Botterill, Pederson) 0:32
5. Russia, Koroliouk (Morozov, Chebaturkin) .... 7:46(pp)
6. Russia, Koroliouk (Saioulline, Morozov) 8:32
7. Canada, Rivers (Murray, Allison) 16:09
8. Canada, Daze (Botterill, Pederson) 18:08

   PENALTIES: Anisimov (Rus) 5:17, Allison (Can) 6:48, Sorochan (Can) 13:41, Koroliouk (Rus) 13:41, Koroliouk (Rus — major, misconduct, game misconduct) 18:59

Third Period

9. Canada, Harvey (Daigle).. 2:29(pp)
10. Canada, O'Neill (Smyth) .... 2:48(pp)
11. Canada, Murray (Daze, Allison).. 3:07(pp)
12. Russia, Charifianov (Vychedkevitch, Batyrchine) .... 9:44(pp)
13. Russia, Yachmenev (Epanshintsev) 18:09

   PENALTIES: Batyrchine (Rus) 4:14, Friesen (Can) 9:17, Rus bench 11:53, Allison (Can) 18:18

Shots on Goal:

Canada	7	14	15	36
Russia	4	12	4	20

In Goal:

Canada — Storr
Russia — Kouzmenko/Tarasov (Tarasov [one goal] replaced Kouzmenko [7 goals] at 2:48 of 3rd)

January 4   Canada 4   Sweden 3

First Period

1. Canada, Harvey (Daigle, Redden) 9:25
2. Canada, Allison (Murray, McCabe) .... 10:34(pp)

3. Canada, Pederson (Botterill) 13:12
4. Sweden, Soderberg (Tarnstrom, Karlsson) 17:00

> PENALTIES: Sundstrom (Swe) 10:07, Allan (Can) 18:50

Second Period

No Scoring

> PENALTIES: Sorochan (Can) 10:59, Johansson (Swe) 19:32

Third Period

5. Canada, Daze (Allison) .... 0:08(pp)
6. Sweden, Sundstrom (Svartvadet, Andersson-Junkka) 17:48
7. Sweden, Strom (Andersson-Junkka, Mattsson) 18:24

> PENALTIES: Eriksson (Swe — double minor) 14:38, McCabe (Can) 17:25

Shots on Goal:

Canada	10	7	8	25
Sweden	8	6	7	21

In Goal

Canada — Cloutier
Sweden — Soderberg

TEAM CANADA FINAL STATISTICS
1995 WORLD JUNIOR CHAMPIONSHIPS

			GP	G	A	P	PIM
28	F	Marty Murray	7	6	9	15	0
9	F	Jason Allison(A)	7	3	12	15	6
4	D	Bryan McCabe(A)	7	3	9	12	4
24	F	Eric Daze	7	8	2	10	0
19	F	Alexandre Daigle	7	2	8	10	4
25	F	Jeff Friesen	7	5	2	7	4
20	F	Ryan Smyth	7	2	5	7	4
10	F	Todd Harvey(C)	7	6	0	6	4
12	D	Jamie Rivers	7	3	3	6	2
17	F	Jeff O'Neill	7	2	4	6	2
6	D	Wade Redden	7	3	2	5	0
8	F	Larry Courville	7	2	3	5	6
23	F	Denis Pederson	7	2	2	4	0
21	F	Jason Botterill	7	0	4	4	6
16	F	Darcy Tucker	7	0	4	4	0
14	D	Ed Jovanovski	7	2	0	2	4
7	D	Lee Sorochan	7	0	1	1	6
5	D	Nolan Baumgartner	7	0	1	1	4
22	F	Shean Donovan	7	0	0	0	6
3	D	Chad Allan	7	0	0	0	4

1	G	Jamie Storr	4	o	o	o	2
30	G	Dan Cloutier	3	o	o	o	o

In Goal

	GP	W-L-T	MINS	GA	SO	AVG
Dan Cloutier	3	3—0—0	180	8	o	2.67
Jamie Storr	4	4—0—0	240	14	o	3.50

Coach Don Hay
Assistants Mike Johnston / Alain Rajotte

CANADIAN OFFICIALS AT THE 1995 WORLD JUNIOR CHAMPIONSHIPS

Brad Meier (referee)
Sylvain Cloutier (linesman)
Darren Gibbs (linesman)

TEAM CANADA ROSTER SUMMARY

Team Canada players   22
Drafted Into NHL   22
Played In NHL (to date)   20   (all but Allan, Sorochan)
Returning Players   8   (Allison, Botterill, Daigle, Friesen, Harvey, McCabe, Murray, Storr)

PLAYER REPRESENTATION BY LEAGUE

OHL	9	(Allison, Cloutier, Courville, Donovan, Harvey, Jovanovski, O'Neill, Rivers, Storr)
WHL	10	(Allan, Baumgartner, Friesen, McCabe, Murray, Pederson, Redden, Smyth, Sorochan, Tucker)
QMJHL	2	(Daigle, Daze)
U.S. COLLEGE	1	(Botterill)

PLAYER REPRESENTATION BY AGE

19-year-olds	12	(Allison, Courville, Daigle, Daze, Donovan, Harvey, McCabe, Murray, Pederson, Rivers, Sorochan, Tucker)
18-year-olds	9	(Allan, Baumgartner, Botterill, Cloutier, Friesen, Jovanovski, O'Neill, Smith, Storr)
17-year-olds	1	(Redden)

PLAYERS' CAREER PROFILES

Chad Allan
Saskatoon Blades (WHL)
Selected 65th overall by Vancouver at 1994 Draft
Played in the NHL 1998 to present

Jason Allison
London Knights (OHL)
Selected 17th overall by Washington at 1993 Draft
Played in the NHL 1993 to present

Nolan Baumgartner
Kamloops Blazers (WHL)
Selected 10th overall by Washington at 1994 Draft
Played in the NHL 1995 to present

Jason Botterill
University of Michigan Wolverines (CCHA)
Selected 20th overall by Dallas at 1994 Draft
Played in the NHL 1997 to present

Dan Cloutier
Sault Ste. Marie Greyhounds (OHL)
Selected 26th overall by Rangers at 1994 Draft
Played in the NHL 1998 to present

Larry Courville
Oshawa Generals (OHL)
Selected 119th overall by Winnipeg at 1993 Draft
Played in the NHL 1995 to present

Alexandre Daigle
Victoriaville Tigers (QMJHL)
Selected 1st overall by Ottawa at 1993 Draft
Played in the NHL 1993 to present

Eric Daze
Beauport Harfangs (QMJHL)
Selected 90th overall by Chicago at 1993 Draft
Played in the NHL 1994 to present

Shean Donovan
Ottawa 67's (OHL)
Selected 28th overall by San Jose at 1993 Draft
Played in the NHL 1994 to present

Jeff Friesen
Regina Pats (WHL)
Selected 11th overall by San Jose at 1994 Draft
Played in the NHL 1994 to present

Todd Harvey
Detroit Whalers (OHL)
Selected 9th overall by Dallas at 1993 Draft
Played in the NHL 1994 to present

Ed Jovanovski
Windsor Spitfires (OHL)
Selected 1st overall by Florida at 1994 Draft
Played in the NHL 1994 to present

Bryan McCabe
Spokane Chiefs (WHL)
Selected 40th overall by Islanders at 1993 Draft
Played in the NHL 1995 to present

Marty Murray
Brandon Wheat Kings (WHL)
Selected 96th overall by Calgary at 1993 Draft
Played in the NHL 1995 to present

Jeff O'Neill	Guelph Storm (OHL) Selected 5th overall by Hartford at 1994 Draft Played in the NHL 1995 to present
Denis Pederson	Prince Albert Raiders (WHL) Selected 13th overall by New Jersey at 1993 Draft Played in the NHL 1995 to present
Wade Redden	Brandon Wheat Kings (WHL) Selected 2nd overall by Islanders at 1995 Draft Played in the NHL 1996 to present
Jamie Rivers	Sudbury Wolves (OHL) Selected 63rd overall by St. Louis at 1993 Draft Played in the NHL 1995 to present
Ryan Smyth	Moose Jaw Warriors (WHL) Selected 6th overall by Edmonton at 1994 Draft Played in the NHL 1994 to present
Lee Sorochan	Lethbridge Broncos (WHL) Selected 34th overall by Rangers at 1993 Draft Has not yet played in the NHL
Jamie Storr	Owen Sound Platers (OHL) Selected 7th overall by Los Angeles at 1994 Draft Played in the NHL 1994 to present
Darcy Tucker	Kamloops Blazers (WHL) Selected 151st overall by Montreal at 1993 Draft Played in the NHL 1995 to present

1996 WORLD JUNIOR CHAMPIONSHIPS UNITED STATES, DECEMBER 26, 1995-- JANUARY 4, 1996

FINAL PLACINGS

GOLD MEDAL	**CANADA**
SILVER MEDAL	Sweden
BRONZE MEDAL	Russia
Fourth Place	Czech Republic
Fifth Place	United States
Sixth Place	Finland
Seventh Place	Slovakia*
Eighth Place	Germany
Ninth Place	Switzerland*
Tenth Place	Ukraine**

promoted from "B" pool in 1995
**relegated to "B" pool for 1997*

ALL-STAR TEAM

GOAL	Jose Theodore (Canada)
DEFENCE	Nolan Baumgartner (Canada)
	Mattias Ohlund (Sweden)
FORWARD	Jarome Iginla (Canada)
	Johan Davidsson (Sweden)
	Alexei Morozov (Russia)

DIRECTORATE AWARDS

BEST GOALIE	Jose Theodore (Canada)
BEST DEFENCEMAN	Mattias Ohlund (Sweden)
BEST FORWARD	Jarome Iginla (Canada)

COACH MARCEL COMEAU

Comeau was a coach everyone could admire, for, as they say, he paid his dues. Comeau's dues were paid over eleven years as a player with the Saginaw Gears in the IHL — "the I." He first coached in 1983, with the Saskatoon Blades, won a Memorial Cup six years later, and moved to the New Haven Nighthawks of the AHL. He was fired midway through his second season, and at the start of the 1991–92 season joined the Kelowna Rockets of the WHL as coach until 1996. He was hired partly because of his participation in the under-18 Mexico Cup, where he led Canada to a gold in 1994 with two assistants, Terry Bangen and Blair MacKasey. Ironically, McKasey, who grew up in Montreal, is bilingual; Comeau grew up in the West and speaks only English.

TEAM MOTTO: *Find a way.*

THE PROGRAM: SCOUTING AND INVITING

The development system begins in the provinces, where five regional under-17 teams are put together and given international competition. From this comes one elite under-18 team that will travel abroad to tournaments. Profiles, assessments, and development charts are used to determine who will be invited to the evaluation camp in the summer for the world juniors. This list is augmented by scouts who travel year-round.

As chief scout Ray Payne pointed out, the difference between the work of an NHL scout and a CHA scout is great: "The pros look at who might develop into a player four or five years down the road, and they look at anybody who might be a late-round draft pick. With the junior team here I was scouting in September for December and I'm just looking at the cream of the crop."

Comeau coached the under-18 team to a gold medal. It is not surprising that seven members from the 1993 bronze-medal team were with his world juniors for 1996: Daymond Langkow, Jose Theodore, Chad Allan, Rhett Warrener, Curtis Brown, Mike Watt, and Jason Podollan.

THE CUTS

The team's pre-tournament, six-day camp opened December 13 in Campbellton, New Brunswick. Four days later, the team beat an Atlantic universities all-star aggregation 6–1. Then came the cuts: Brad Lukowich (Kamloops, WHL), Jason Doig (Winnipeg Jets, NHL), Jay McKee (Niagara Falls, OHL), Justin Kurtz (Brandon, WHL), Craig Hillier (Ottawa, OHL), Martin Biron

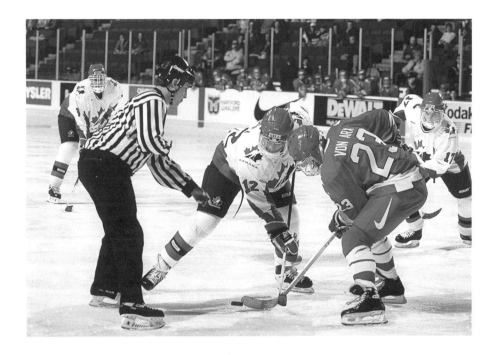

Jarome Iginla faces off with Switzerland's Reto von Arx during Canada's surprisingly slim 2-1 win.

(Beauport, QMJHL), Daniel Briere (Beauport, QMJHL), and Dan Cleary (Drummondville, QMJHL).

THE WORLD JUNIOR CHALLENGE TOURNAMENT

Canada, the Czech Republic, and Germany played in the World Junior Challenge, a warm-up for the WJC. The three-nation, round-robin tournament was held before Christmas, and Canada won the event by beating the Czechs 4–2 at Harbour Station in Saint John, the Germans 11–0 in Fredericton, and the Czechs again 7–4 in the finals at Moncton.

TOURNAMENT FORMAT

The World Junior championships changed radically for these 1996 games, as ten nations were now competing instead of eight. Two divisions of five teams each were created, and a dynamic playoff showdown replaced the more staid round-robin format. The preliminary round consisted of four round-robin games, with the top team in each division earning spots in the semi-finals.

The second- and third-place team from each division had a one-game playoff to earn the other two spots, the second in one division playing the third in the other and vice versa. The semi-finals winners played for the gold medal, and the semis losers played for the bronze. Ties in the preliminary round would be broken, as always, first by head-to-head results and then goal differential.

There was a full round-robin in the relegation round between the four teams that did not advance to the playoffs. Previous results between those nations counted, and the team that finished fourth was demoted to the "B" pool for next year's tournament.

Team Canada's captain, Nolan Baumgartner, watches the slot while goalie Jose Theodore recovers during Canada's 4-1 win over Sweden.

THE OPPOSITION

CZECH REPUBLIC

Michal Bros, Miroslav Guren, Milan Hejduk, Jan Hlavac, Robert Jindrich, Martin Koudelka, Ondrej Kratena, Pavel Kubina, Ladislav Kudrna, Marek Melenovsky, Jan Nemecek, Ales Pisa, Jiri Polak, Marek Posmyk, Pavel Rosa, Zdenek Skorepa, Jan Tomajko, Vaclav Varada, Tomas Vokoun, Marek Vorel, Jan Zurek

FINLAND

Miika Elomo, Tommi Hirvonen, Martti Jarventie, Juho Jokinen, Tommi Kallio, Miikka Kiprusoff, Arto Kuki, Jukka Laamanen, Kimmo Lotvonen, Toni Lydman, Marko Makinen, Antti-Jussi Niemi, Pasi Petrilainen, Mika Puhakka, Lauri Puolanne, Tommi Rajamaki, Teemu Riihijarvi, Timo Salonen, Janne Salpa, Jussi Tarvainen, Vesa Toskala, Juha Vuorivirta

GERMANY

Frank Appel, David Berge, Oliver Bernhardt, Lars Bruggemann, Markus Draxler, Thorsten Fendt, Kai Fischer, Stephen Gerike, Erich Goldmann, Jochen Hecht, Klaus Kathan, Florian Keller, Sebastian Klenner, Martin Kropf, Boris Lingemann, Niki Mondt, Andreas Morczinietz, Markus Pottinger, Andreas Renz, Stephan Retzer, Daniel Schury, Marco Sturm, Thomas Vogel

RUSSIA

Alexei Egorov, Vadim Epanshintsev, Ilya Gorokhov, Dmitri Klevakin, Alexei Kolkunov, Alexander Koroliouk, Sergei Luchinkin, Igor Meliakov, Alexei Morozov, Dmitri Nabokov, Mikhail Okhotnikov, Andrei Petrakov, Evgeny Petroshinin, Andrei Petrunin, Dmitri Riabykin, Sergei Samsonov, Ruslan Shafikov, Sergei Shalamai, Alexei Vasiliev, Anton Zelenov, Sergei Zimakov, Andrei Zuzin

SLOVAKIA

Jiri Bicek, Ivan Ciernik, Miroslav Droppa, Josef Drzik, Juraj Durco, Michal Handzus, Robert Jurcak, Mario Kazda, Marcel Kuris, Richard Lintner, Vladimir Orsagh, Stanislav Petrik, Andrei Podkonicky, Daniel Socha, Radovan Somik, Juraj Stefanka, Radoslav Suchy, Robert Tomik, Lubomir Vaic, Rudolf Vercik, Lubomir Visnovsky, Richard Zednik

SWEDEN

Niklas Anger, Anders Burstrom, Johan Davidsson, Nils Ekman, Johan Finnstrom, David Halvardsson, Peter Hogardh, Kim Johnsson, Fredrik Loven, Per-Anton Lundstrom, Johan Molin, Fredrik Moller, Magnus Nilsson, Markus Nilsson, Peter Nylander, Mattias Ohlund, Kristoffer Ottosson, Samuel Pahlsson, David Petrasek, Per Ragnar Bergkvist, Daniel Tjarnkvist, Patrik Wallenberg

SWITZERLAND

Daniel Aegertner, Mattia Baldi, Andre Baumann, Paolo Della Bella, Fabian Guignard, Sandy Jeannin, Michael Kress, Philippe Marquis, Dominic Meier, Laurent Muller, Martin Pluss, Arne Ramholt, Michel Riesen, Sandro Rizzi, Stephane Rosset, Frederic Rothen, Ivo Ruthemann, Mathias Seger, Nicolas Steiger, Mark Streit, Reto von Arx, Christian Wohlwend

UKRAINE

Andrei Bakunenko, Vladislav Chevchenko, Sergei Chubenko, Sergei Dechevyi, Danil Didkovski, Ruslan Fedotenko, Juri Gorulko, Alexander Iakovenko, Igor Karpenko, Oleg Krikunenko, Alexei Lazarenko, Dmitri Mozheiko, Alexander Mukhanov, Vasil Polonitsky, Sergei Revenko, Sergei Sadii, Roman Salnikov, Valeri Seredenko, Dmitri Tolkunov, Andre Voouch, Nikolai Yaprintsev, Alexander Zinevitch

UNITED STATES

Bryan Berard, Reg Berg, Chris Bogas, Brian Boucher, Ben Clymer, Matt Cullen, Chris Drury, Jeff Farkas, Casey Hankinson, Matt Herr, Jeff Kealty, Marc Magliarditi, Michael McBain, Jeremiah McCarthy, Mark Parrish, Tom Poti, Erik Rasmussen, Marty Reasoner, Wyatt Smith, Brian Swanson, Mike Sylvia, Mike York

FINAL STANDINGS PRELIMINARY ROUND

Group A

	GP	W	L	T	GF	GA	P
CANADA	4	4	0	0	19	4	8
United States	4	2	2	0	13	17	4
Finland	4	2	2	0	14	10	4
Switzerland	4	1	3	0	10	14	2
Ukraine	4	1	3	0	9	20	2

Results

December 26	Worcester	Canada 6	United States 1
	Marlborough	Finland 5	Switzerland 1
December 27	Amherst	Canada 2	Switzerland 1
	Boston	Ukraine 4	United States 3
December 28	Boston	Finland 4	Ukraine 1
December 29	Boston	Canada 3	Finland 1
	Springfield	United States 4	Switzerland 3
December 30	Marlborough	Switzerland 5	Ukraine 3
December 31	Boston	Canada 8	Ukraine 1
	Amherst	United States 5	Finland 4

Group B

	GP	W	L	T	GF	GA	P
Czech Republic	4	2	0	2	15	10	6
Russia	4	2	1	1	19	12	5

Sweden	4	2	1	1	14	7	5
Slovakia	4	0	1	3	11	17	3
Germany	4	0	3	1	11	24	1

Results

December 26	Amherst	Czech Republic 5	Russia 3
	Worcester	Sweden 6	Slovakia 0
December 27	Boston	Slovakia 3	Russia 3
	Amherst	Czech Republic 6	Germany 3
December 28	Boston	Sweden 6	Germany 2
December 29	Boston	Czech Republic 4	Slovakia 4
	Springfield	Russia 5	Sweden 2
December 30	Marlborough	Germany 4	Slovakia 4
December 31	Boston	Czech Republic 0	Sweden 0
	Amherst	Russia 8	Germany 2

FINAL STANDINGS RELEGATION ROUND

	GP	W	L	T	GF	GA	P
Slovakia	3	2	0	1	17	10	5
Germany	3	1	0	2	12	7	4
Switzerland	3	1	1	1	11	13	3
Ukraine	3	0	3	0	6	16	0

Carry-Over Results

Germany 4	Slovakia 4
Switzerland 5	Ukraine 3

Results

January 2	Marlborough	Germany 3	Switzerland 3
	Marlborough	Slovakia 6	Ukraine 3
January 3	Marlborough	Slovakia 7	Switzerland 3
	Marlborough	Germany 5	Ukraine 0

MEDAL ROUND

Quarter-finals

January 1	Amherst	Sweden 3	United States 0
	Amherst	Russia 6	Finland 2

Semi-finals

| January 3 | Boston | Canada 4 | Russia 3 |
| | Boston | Sweden 8 | Czech Republic 2 |

Fifth Place Game

| January 4 | Marlboro | United States 8 | Finland 7 (OT) |

Bronze Medal Game

| January 4 | Chestnut Hill | Russia 4 | Czech Republic 1 |

Gold Medal Game

| January 4 | Chestnut Hill | Canada 4 | Sweden 1 |

AGGREGATE STANDINGS

(ordered according to final placings)

	GP	W	L	T	GF	GA	GAA	SO	PIM
CANADA	6	6	0	0	27	8	1.33	0	80
Sweden	7	4	2	1	26	13	1.86	3	96
Russia	7	4	2	1	32	19	2.71	0	52
Czech Republic	6	2	2	2	18	22	3.67	1	85
United States	6	3	3	0	21	27	4.50	0	233
Finland	6	2	4	0	23	24	4.00	0	247
Slovakia	6	2	1	3	24	23	3.83	0	143
Germany	6	1	3	2	19	27	4.50	1	155
Switzerland	6	1	4	1	16	24	4.00	0	258
Ukraine	6	1	5	0	12	31	5.17	0	196

TEAM CANADA GAME SUMMARIES

December 26 *Canada 6* *United States 1*

First Period

1. Canada, Holland (Gordon, Langkow) 1:24
2. Canada, Botterill (McCauley, Wright)... 4:47
3. Canada, Gauthier (Redden, Podollan)... 13:30(pp)

PENALTIES: Berard (U.S.) 2:32, Larsen (Can) 5:10, Gauthier (Can) 9:20, Clymer (U.S.) 12:07, Baumgartner (Can) & Sylvia (U.S.) 14:33, Domenichelli (Can) & Kealty (U.S.) 15:33

Second Period

4. Canada, Langkow (Iginla) 1:10
5. Canada, Domenichelli (Langkow, Iginla)...................................... 5:04(pp)

PENALTIES: Holland (Can) 2:41, Clymer (U.S.) 4:37, Baumgartner (Can) 9:15, Botterill (Can) 19:11, Baumgartner (Can — minor, misconduct) 19:57

Third Period

6. United States, Reasoner (Berard, Clymer) .... 0:35(pp)
7. Canada, Larsen (unassisted) 7:56

>   PENALTIES: Berard (U.S.) 8:13, Mills (Can) 14:54, Gauthier (Can) 18:56

Shots on Goal:

Canada	15	12	9	36
United States	6	12	14	32

In Goal:

>   Canada — Theodore
>   United States — Boucher

December 27   *Canada 2*   *Switzerland 1*

First Period

No Scoring

>   PENALTIES: Muller (Swi) 2:18, McCauley (Can) 5:13, Muller (Swi) 8:49, Iginla (Can — double minor) & Domenichelli (Can) 13:06, Gauthier (Can) 16:54

Second Period

1. Canada, Wright (McCauley, Botterill) 10:53

>   PENALTIES: Steiger (Swi) 3:29, Baumann (Swi) 7:16, Allan (Can) 13:16

Third Period

2. Switzerland, Muller (Baldi) 9:11
3. Canada, Dube (Podollan) 11:33

>   PENALTIES: Seger (Swi) 9:26, Domenichelli (Can) & von Arx (Swi) 9:45, Guignard (Swi) 16:59

Shots on Goal:

Canada	5	13	11	29
Switzerland	11	9	16	36

In Goal:

>   Canada — Denis
>   Switzerland — Della Bella

December 29   *Canada 3*   *Finland 1*

First Period

1. Canada, Baumgartner (Iginla) .... 17:23(pp)

>   PENALTIES: Baumgartner (Can) 3:05, Elomo (Fin) 7:05, Riihijarvi (Fin) 16:45

Second Period

2. Canada, Dube (Brown) 13:53

>   PENALTIES: Rajamaki (Fin) 15:05, Salonen (Fin) & Redden (Can) 18:33, Baumgartner (Can) 19:48

Third Period

3. Finland, Elomo (Riihijarvi)..14:59
4. Canada, Iginla (Dube) ....19:28(pp-en)

   PENALTIES: Riihijarvi (Fin) 2:53, Salonen (Fin) 4:34, Podollan (Can) 6:13, Rajamaki (Fin) & Langkow (Can) 8:40, Larsen (Can) 12:45, Hirvonen (Fin) 18:48, Mills (Can) 19:46

Shots on Goal:

Canada	14	23	9	46
Finland	15	8	7	30

In Goal:

Canada — Theodore
Finland — Kiprusoff

December 31   *Canada 8*   *Ukraine 1*

First Period

1. Canada, McCauley (Domenichelli, Gordon)..........................8:44

   PENALTIES: Warrener (Can) 9:06, Bakunenko (Ukr) 10:35, Revenko (Ukr) 13:07

Second Period

2. Canada, Iginla (Gordon, Domenichelli)..........................5:48(pp)
3. Canada, Dube (Podollan, Watt) 8:23
4. Canada, Dube (unassisted) 14:12
5. Canada, Holland (Iginla, Gordon)..........................19:51(pp)

   PENALTIES: Gorulko (Ukr) 1:51, Didkovski (Ukr) 4:07, Baumgartner (Can) 16:34, Tolkunov (Ukr) 19:39

Third Period

6. Canada, Iginla (Larsen) 4:23
7. Canada, Iginla (McCauley, Domenichelli) 7:04
8. Canada, Allan (Baumgartner, Watt) 8:51
9. Ukraine, Yaprintsev (Salnikov, Fedotenko) ....12:10(pp)

   PENALTIES: Didkovski (Ukr) 4:23, Holland (Can) 10:33, Salnikov (Ukr) 15:48

Shots on Goal:

Canada	24	24	15	63
Ukraine	3	9	4	16

In Goal:

Canada — Denis
Ukraine — Karpenko

January 3   Canada 4   Russia 3

First Period

1. Canada, Podollan (Gauthier).. 8:41(pp)
2. Russia, Morozov (Shafikov, Nabokov) .... 11:24(pp)

    PENALTIES: Korolyuk (Rus) 7:04, Allan (Can) 10:35, Allan (Can) 14:07

Second Period

3. Canada, Watt (Redden, Dube).. 11:11(pp)
4. Canada, Podollan (Botterill, Holland) 12:43
5. Russia, Petroshinin (Nabokov) 15:39

    PENALTIES: Epanshintsev (Rus) 9:07, Meliakov (Rus) 9:52, Wright (Can) 13:12

Third Period

6. Canada, Iginla (unassisted) .... 6:40(sh)
7. Russia, Morozov (Nabokov, Shafikov) .... 10:34(pp)

    PENALTIES: Watt (Can) 5:13, Watt (Can) 9:35, Epanshintsev (Rus — misconduct) 20:00

Shots on Goal:

Canada	10	10	8	28
Russia	19	16	14	49

In Goal:

    Canada — Thoedore
    Russia — Egorov

January 4   Canada 4   Sweden 1

First Period

1. Canada, Langkow (Iginla) 1:36
2. Sweden, Nilsson (unassisted) 8:41

    PENALTIES: Ohlund (Swe) 9:46, Watt (Can) 14:10, Petrasek (Swe) 19:28

Second Period

3. Canada, Langkow (Iginla) .... 13:00(pp)
4. Canada, Domenichelli (Langkow, Iginla)... 14:12

    PENALTIES: Burstrom (Swe) 8:44, Johnsson (Swe) 11:05, Brown (Can) 14:51

Third Period

5. Canada, McCauley (Wright, Botterill) 8:12

    PENALTIES: Nilsson (Swe — minor, misconduct) 10:12, Warrener (Can) 18:47

Shots on Goal:

Canada	6	12	17	35
Sweden	13	8	12	33

In Goal:

    Canada — Theodore

    Sweden — Bergkvist

TEAM CANADA FINAL STATISTICS
1996 WORLD JUNIOR CHAMPIONSHIPS

			GP	G	A	P	PIM
12	F	Jarome Iginla	6	5	7	12	4
9	F	Christian Dube	6	4	2	6	0
14	F	Daymond Langkow	5	3	3	6	2
17	F	Hnat Domenichelli	6	2	3	5	6
8	F	Alyn McCauley	6	2	3	5	2
22	F	Jason Podollan	6	2	3	5	2
19	F	Jason Botterill(A)	6	1	3	4	2
16	F	Robb Gordon	6	0	4	4	0
3	D	Jason Holland	6	2	1	3	4
18	F	Mike Watt	6	1	2	3	6
10	F	Jamie Wright	6	1	2	3	2
5	D	Nolan Baumgartner(C)	6	1	1	2	22
21	D	Denis Gauthier	6	1	1	2	6
23	F	Brad Larsen	6	1	1	2	4
6	D	Wade Redden	6	0	2	2	2
7	D	Chad Allan(A)	6	1	0	1	6
11	F	Curtis Brown	5	0	1	1	2
24	F	Craig Mills	6	0	0	0	4
30	D	Rhett Warrener	6	0	0	0	4
4	D	Chris Phillips	6	0	0	0	0
1	G	Jose Theodore	4	0	0	0	0
31	G	Marc Denis	2	0	0	0	0

In Goal

	GP	W-L-T	MINS	GA	SO	AVG
Marc Denis	2	2-0-0	120	2	0	1.00
Jose Theodore	4	4-0-0	240	6	0	1.50

Coach   Marcel Comeau

Assistants   Terry Bangen/Blair MacKasey

CANADIAN OFFICIALS AT THE 1996
WORLD JUNIOR CHAMPIONSHIPS

Mark Joannette (referee)	3 games
Serge Carpentier (linesman)	5 games
Todd Thomander (linesman)	3 games

TEAM CANADA ROSTER SUMMARY

Team Canada players   22
Drafted Into NHL   22
Played In NHL (to date) 20 (all but Allan, Gordon)
Returning Players   4   (Allan, Baumgartner, Botterill, Redden)

PLAYER REPRESENTATION BY LEAGUE

OHL   3 (McCauley, Mills, Wright)
WHL   13 (Allan, Baumgartner, Brown, Domenichelli, Gordon, Holland, Iginla, Langkow, Larsen, Phillips, Podollan, Redden, Warrener)
QMJHL   4 (Denis, Dube, Gautheir, Theodore)
U.S. COLLEGE   2 (Botterill, Watt)

PLAYER REPRESENTATION BY AGE

19-year-olds   15 (Allan, Baumgartner, Botterill, Brown, Domenichelli, Gauthier, Gordon, Holland, Langkow, Mills, Podollan, Theodore, Warrener, Watt, Wright)
18-year-olds   6 (Denis, Dube, Iginla, Larsen, McCauley, Redden)
17-year-olds   1 (Phillips)

PLAYERS' CAREER PROFILES

Chad Allan   Saskatoon Blades (WHL)
Selected 65th overall by Vancouver at 1994 Draft
Has not yet played in the NHL

Nolan Baumgartner   Kamloops Blazers (WHL)
Selected 10th overall by Washington at 1994 Draft
Played in the NHL 1995 to present

Jason Botterill   University of Michigan Wolverines (CCHA)
Selected 20th overall by Dallas at 1994 Draft
Played in the NHL 1997 to present

Curtis Brown   Prince Albert Raiders (WHL)
Selected 43rd overall by Buffalo at 1994 Draft
Played in the NHL 1994 to present

Marc Denis   Chicoutimi Sagueneens (QMJHL)
Selected 25th overall by Avalanche at 1995 Draft
Played in the NHL 1996 to present

Hnat Domenichelli   Kamloops Blazers (WHL)
Selected 83rd overall by Hartford at 1994 Draft
Played in the NHL 1996 to present

Christian Dube   Sherbrooke Faucons (QMJHL)
                      Selected 39th overall by Rangers at 1995 Draft
                      Played in the NHL 1996 to present
Denis Gauthier   Drummondville Voltigeurs (QMJHL)
                      Selected 20th overall by Calgary at 1995 Draft
                      Played in the NHL 1997 to present
Robb Gordon   Kelowna Rockets (WHL)
                      Selected 39th overall by Vancouver at 1994 Draft
                      Has not yet played in the NHL
Jason Holland   Kamloops Blazers (WHL)
                      Selected 38th overall by Islanders at 1994 Draft
                      Played in the NHL 1996 to present
Jarome Iginla   Kamloops Blazers (WHL)
                      Selected 11th overall by Dallas at 1995 Draft
                      Played in the NHL 1995 to present
Daymond Langkow   Tri-City Americans (WHL)
                      Selected 5th overall by Tampa Bay at 1995 Draft
                      Played in the NHL 1995 to present
Brad Larsen   Swift Current Broncos (WHL)
                      Selected 53rd overall by Ottawa at 1995 Draft
                      Played in the NHL 1997 to present
Alyn McCauley   Ottawa 67's (OHL)
                      Selected 79th overall by New Jersey at 1995 Draft
                      Played in the NHL 1997 to present
Craig Mills   Belleville Bulls (OHL)
                      Selected 108th overall by Winnipeg at 1994 Draft
                      Played in the NHL 1995 to present
Chris Phillips   Prince Albert Raiders (WHL)
                      Selected 1st overall by Ottawa at 1996 Draft
                      Played in the NHL 1997 to present
Jason Podollan   Spokane Chiefs (WHL)
                      Selected 31st overall by Florida at 1994 Draft
                      Played in the NHL 1996 to present
Wade Redden   Brandon Wheat Kings (WHL)
                      Selected 2nd overall by Islanders at 1995 Draft
                      Played in the NHL 1996 to present
Jose Theodore   Hull Olympiques (QMJHL)
                      Selected 44th overall by Montreal at 1994 Draft
                      Played in the NHL 1995 to present
Rhett Warrener   Saskatoon Blades (WHL)
                      Selected 27th overall by Florida at 1994 Draft
                      Played in the NHL 1995 to present
Mike Watt   Michigan State University Spartans (CCHA)
                      Selected 32nd overall by Edmonton at 1994 Draft
                      Played in the NHL 1997 to present

Jamie Wright   Guelph Storm (OHL)
Selected 98th overall by Dallas at 1996 Draft
Played in the NHL 1997 to present

1997 WORLD JUNIOR CHAMPIONSHIPS SWITZERLAND, DECEMBER 26, 1996-- JANUARY 4, 1997

FINAL PLACINGS

GOLD MEDAL	**CANADA**
SILVER MEDAL	United States
BRONZE MEDAL	Russia
Fourth Place	Czech Republic
Fifth Place	Finland
Sixth Place	Slovakia
Seventh Place	Switzerland
Eighth Place	Sweden
Ninth Place	Germany
Tenth Place	Poland*

promoted from "B" pool in 1996; relegated to "B" pool for 1998

ALL-STAR TEAM

GOAL	Brian Boucher (United States)
DEFENCE	Chris Phillips (Canada)
	Mark Streit (Switzerland)
FORWARD	Christian Dube (Canada)
	Sergei Samsonov (Russia)
	Michael York (United States)

DIRECTORATE AWARDS

BEST GOALIE	Marc Denis (Canada)
BEST DEFENCEMAN	Joseph Corvo (United States)
BEST FORWARD	Alexei Morozov (Russia)

COACH MIKE BABCOCK

Babcock's first coaching gig came when he taught a group of profs at McGill University the finer arts of the game while he was an undergrad. He taught in England for a year and coached Red Deer College for three years. In 1991, he was appointed head coach of the Moose Jaw Warriors (WHL), but was fired after two seasons. In 1993, he molded the hapless University of Lethbridge team into CIAU champions. The next year he was back in the WHL, with the Spokane Chiefs. Now in his third year at Lethbridge, he was appointed head coach of Canada's national junior team for the '97 tournament.

Boyd Devereaux was key to Canada's gold medal in Switzerland, scoring four goals including the game winner against the U.S. in the finals.

RED, WHITE, AND GOLD

SELECTION CAMP

At the summer camp in August in Calgary, coach Babcock knew exactly what kind of team he wanted to assemble: "We are looking for our players to play the way Canadians have played forever — a tenacious team who will crash the net, play with a lot of pride and with a controlled aggression."

The team was abetted by the presence of two NHLers, Christian Dube from the Rangers and Jeff Ware of the Leafs. Dube, though born in Quebec, grew up in Switzerland while his father, a former NHLer, coached and scouted there.

Not all players at camp were cut at one time. Rather, they left in dribs and drabs. On December 15, Eric Belanger of Beauport left the team after suffering an abdominal strain. The next day, Babcock cut three players — Craig Hillier, Dan Cleary, and J.P. Dumont. That night, the Nats were soundly beaten by an OUAA all-star team 5–2 in an exhibition game in Kitchener, and the next day the pattern was repeated: in the morning, Byron Ritchie of Lethbridge was let go, and in the evening the team fought back for a 3–2 win over another University Selects team. The juniors left for Switzerland the morning of December 18, but not before the final painful five players were cut to pare the roster down to tournament size. Gone were Zenith Komarniski (Tri-City), Darryl Laplante (Moose Jaw), Stephane Robidas (Shawinigan), Philippe Audet (Granby), and Sebastien Charpentier (Shawinigan).

In Europe, the team played three exhibition games in Wichtracht, Switzerland. They beat the Finns 3–2 on December 20, rallied to tie the ever-improving Swiss 3–3 two nights later, and were shut out by the Czech Republic 3–0 on December 23.

THE INSPIRATION

The players were shown the now famous video featuring Canada's greatest moments in international hockey. Babcock interpreted the video this way: "The message to the players was, 'You are not alone. All the players before you are with you.'"

Just before the players left for Europe, they were given a red-and-white session with NHL goaler Mike Liut, who told them of his international experiences and what putting on the national sweater should mean.

MEMORIES

Before the game against Switzerland, Canadian captain and Swift Current Bronco Brad Larsen spoke to the team about the tragic bus crash in Swift

Current a decade earlier, on December 30, 1986, in which four players were killed. Trent Kresse, Scotty Kruger, Chris Mantyka, and Brent Ruff died in a crash survived by twenty-three others, including Joe Sakic, and no event could make more poignant the connection between team and individual, family and team, and hockey and life.

TEAM STRATEGY

Discipline. Controlled emotion. Relentless puck pursuit. Crash the net.

THE TURNING POINT

Because Canada's teams are almost always put together at the last minute and never stay together long, team cohesion and chemistry are essential. Nothing bonds a family or a team more quickly, more emotionally, and more completely than adversity. Going overseas to compete is always a positive, and poor refereeing can bring out the best in the boys.

The Canadian team started out slowly and steadily improved as the tournament went on. The turning point came late in the second period in the

Canada tied the Czech Republic 3-3 in the final game of the preliminary round to advance to the medal round where they won three in a row to take gold.

game against the Russians. Jason Doig received a five-minute major for slashing and an automatic game misconduct, and Canada was already trailing 2–1. They played with guts and glory and didn't allow a single shot during the five minutes they were short-handed. Early in the third period, thirty-six seconds after the penalty ended, Boyd Devereaux tied the game. Alyn McCauley did not lose a single faceoff in the third period, and Devereaux scored again midway through the period to give Canada the lead.

TOURNAMENT FORMAT

Two divisions of five teams were created, and each country played four games in a round-robin series. The top team from each division advanced to the semi-finals, and the second and third place teams played for the other two spots. The second place team from one division played the third place team from the other, and vice versa. The two semi-finals winners went on to play for the gold medal, and the semi-finals losers played for the bronze.

THE OPPOSITION

CZECH REPUBLIC

Jiri Burger, Michal Horak, David Hruska, Petr Kadlec, Ondrej Kratena, Pavel Kriz, Ladislav Kudrna, Radek Matejovsky, Marek Melenovsky, Petr Mudroch, Jiri Novotny, Libor Pavlis, Kamil Piros, Ales Pisa, Marek Posmyk, Radek Prochazka, Martin Richter, Martin Spanhel, Martin Streit, Adam Svoboda, Petr Tenkrat, Marek Zidlicky

FINLAND

Aki-Peterri Berg, Santeri Heiskanen, Tomi Hirvonen, Petri Isotalus, Olli Jokinen, Tommi Kallio, Pekka Kangasalusta, Niko Kapanen, Toni Lydman, Illka Mikkola, Antti-Jussi Niemi, Ville Nieminen, Mika Noronen, Esa Pirnes, Teemu Riihijaervi, Sami-Ville Salomaa, Sami Salonen, Eero Somervuori, Vesa Toskala, Jarkko Vaeaenaenen, Timo Vertala, Juha Viinikainen

GERMANY

Nils Antons, Michael Bakos, David Berge, Thomas Dolak, Alexander Erdmann, Thorsten Fendt, Kai Fischer, Sven Gerike, Sascha Goc, Jochen Hecht, Benjamin Hinterstocker, Klaus Kathan, Daniel Kreutzer, Boris Lingemann, Dennis Meyer, Niki Mondt, Markus Poettinger, Nico Pyka, Andreas Renz, Christian Schoenmoser, Patrick Senger, Thorsten Walz

POLAND

Maciej Baran, Adam Borzecki, Rafal Cychowski, Lukasz Gil, Lukasz Kiedewicz, Jaroslaw Klys, Jaroslaw Kuc, Sebastian Labus, Leszek Laszkiewicz, Krzysztof Lipkowski, Sebastian Pajerski, Rafal Piekarski, Maciej Radwanski, Piotr Sarnik, Rafal Selega, Damian Slabon, Robert Suchomski, Mariusz Trzopek, Rafal Twardy, Tomasz Wawrzkiewicz, Bartolomiej Wrobel, Pawel Zwolinski

RUSSIA

Vladimir Antipov, Yuri Boutsayev, Mikhail Donika, Radmir Faizov, Sergei Fedotov, Roustem Gabdoulline, Ilya Gorokhov, Denis Khlopotnov, Alexei Kolkunov, Oleg Kvacha, Roman Liachenko, Andrei Markov, Alexei Morozov, Oleg Orekhovsky, Andrei Petrunine, Sergei Samsonov, Konstantin Sidulov, Alexander Trofimov, Alexei Vasiliev, Dmitri Vlasenkov, Alexander Volchkov, Andrei Zuzin

SLOVAKIA

Peter Barinka, Peter Bartek, Jiri Bicek, Ivan Ciernik, Miroslav Droppa, Jurai Durco, Michal Handzus, Marian Hossa, Richard Lintner, Erik Marinov, Ratislav Pavlikovsky, Pavol Pekarik, Stanislav Petrik, Jozef Potac, Richard Richnak, Pavol Rieciciar, Jan Simco, Peter Slamiar, Radovan Somik, Martin Spillar, Martin Tomas, Lubomir Vaic

SWEDEN

Henrik Andersson, Niklas Anger, Per Anton Lundstrom, Robert Borgqvist, Josef Boumedienne, Mikael Burakovsky, Daniel Carlsson, Jonas Elofsson, David Engblom, Linus Fagemo, Johan Forsander, Emanuel Fredriksson, Per Gustafsson, Per Hallberg, Kristian Huselius, Ragnar Karlsson, Fredrik Loven, Marcus Nilsson, Timmy Pettersson, Henrik Rehnberg, Patrik Wallenberg, Peter Wallin

SWITZERLAND

David Aebischer, Rolf Badertscher, Mattia Baldi, Andre Baumann, Bjorn Christen, Paolo Della Bella, Michel Faeh, Patrik Fischer, Stefan Grauwiler, Michel Mouther, Laurent Mueller, Martin Pluess, Philipp Portner, Michel Riesen, Sandro Rizzi, Sascha Schneider, Mario Schocher, Matthias Seger, Mark Streit, Rene Stuessi, Jan Von Arx, Benjamin Winkler

UNITED STATES

Blake Bellefeuille, Brian Boucher, Jesse Boulerice, Ben Clymer, Joseph Corvo, Robert Esche, Jeff Farkas, Chris Hajt, Daniel Lacouture, Paul Mara, Michael McBain, Mark Parrish, Daniel Peters, Tobias Petersen, Thomas Poti, Erik Rasmussen, Marty Reasoner, Jason Sessa, Benjamin Simon, Wyatt Smith, Michael York, Jerry Young

FINAL STANDINGS

Group A

	GP	W	L	T	GF	GA	P
United States	4	3	0	1	18	5	7
CANADA	4	2	0	2	15	9	6
Czech Republic	4	1	1	2	13	8	4
Switzerland	4	1	2	1	8	11	3
Germany	4	0	4	0	5	26	0

Results

December 26	Geneva	United States 4	Switzerland 0
	Morges	Czech Republic 8	Germany 2
December 27	Geneva	Canada 4	Germany 1
	Morges	Czech Republic 1	Switzerland 1
December 28	Geneva	Canada 4	United States 4
December 29	Geneva	Switzerland 6	Germany 2
	Geneva	United States 2	Czech Republic 1
December 30	Geneva	Canada 4	Switzerland 1
December 31	Geneva	Canada 3	Czech Republic 3
	Geneva	United States 8	Germany 0

Group B

	GP	W	L	T	GF	GA	P
Russia	4	3	0	1	20	5	7
Finland	4	3	1	0	17	9	6
Slovakia	4	2	2	0	17	13	4
Sweden	4	1	2	1	10	10	3
Poland	4	0	4	0	6	33	0

Results

December 26	Geneva	Russia 4	Slovakia 3
	Morges	Finland 7	Poland 0
December 27	Geneva	Slovakia 4	Sweden 1
	Morges	Russia 12	Poland 0
December 28	Morges	Finland 4	Sweden 2
December 29	Morges	Slovakia 7	Poland 4
	Morges	Russia 4	Finland 2
December 30	Morges	Sweden 7	Poland 2
December 31	Morges	Finland 4	Slovakia 3
	Morges	Sweden 0	Russia 0

RELEGATION ROUND FINAL STANDINGS

	GP	W	L	T	GF	GA	P
Switzerland	3	3	0	0	18	5	6
Sweden	3	2	1	0	17	10	4
Germany	3	1	2	0	11	14	2
Poland	3	0	3	0	3	20	0

Carry-over Results

Sweden 7	Poland 2
Switzerland 6	Germany 2

Results

January 2	Morges	Switzerland 6	Poland 1
	Morges	Sweden 8	Germany 2
January 3	Morgues	Germany 7	Poland 0
	Morgues	Switzerland 6	Sweden 2

Playoffs (second and third place teams)

January 1	Geneva	Canada 7	Slovakia 2
	Geneva	Czech Republic 3	Finland 2 (so)

Semi-finals

January 3	Geneva	Canada 3	Russia 2
	Geneva	United States 5	Czech Republic 2

Fifth Place Game

January 3	Morges	Finland 6	Slovakia 4

Bronze Medal Game

January 4	Geneva	Russia 4	Czech Republic 1

Gold Medal Game

January 4	Geneva	Canada 2	United States 0

AGGREGATE STANDINGS

(ordered according to final placings)

	GP	W	L	T	GF	GA	GAA	SO	PIM
CANADA	7	5	0	2	27	13	1.86	1	109
United States	6	4	1	1	23	9	1.50	2	62
Russia	6	4	1	1	26	9	1.50	2	56*
Czech Republic	7	2	3	2	19	19	2.71	0	84
Finland	6	4	2	0	25	16	2.67	1	66
Slovakia	6	2	4	0	23	26	4.33	0	118

Switzerland	6	3	2	1	20	14	2.33	0	163
Sweden	6	2	3	1	20	18	3.00	1	111
Germany	6	1	5	0	14	34	5.67	1	92
Poland	6	0	6	0	7	46	7.67	0	64

* won Fair Play Cup

TEAM CANADA GAME SUMMARIES

December 27   Canada 4   Germany 1

First Period

1. Germany, Fendt (Kreutzer) .... 3:18(pp)
2. Canada, Isbister (unassisted) .... 17:23(pp)

   PENALTIES: Hamilton (Can) 1:18, Wallin (Can) 2:15, Senger (Ger) 4:54, Hinterstocker (Ger) 10:31, Senger (Ger) 16:32

Second Period

3. Canada, Mann (unassisted) 12:21

   PENALTIES: Kathan (Ger) 8:07, Ware (Can) 12:36, Lingemann (Ger) 17:50

Third Period

4. Canada, Jackman (Dube) 3:50
5. Canada, Thornton (Briere, Mann) .... 11:26(pp)

   PENALTIES: Larsen (Can) 5:31, Hecht (Ger) 10:02, Hay (Can) 14:36, Hecht (Ger) 18:53

Shots on Goal:

Canada	9	10	15	34
Germany	9	7	6	22

In Goal:

Canada — Denis
Germany — Fischer

December 28   Canada 4   United States 4

First Period

1. Canada, Dube (Doig) 1:18
2. United States, Parrish (Young) 1:48
3. United States, Farkas (Smith) .... 4:43(sh)
4. Canada, Dube (unassisted) .... 8:52(pp)

   PENALTIES: Farkas (U.S.) 3:34, Parrish (U.S.) 7:00, Rasmussen (U.S.) 8:17, Mann (Can) 9:10, McBain (U.S.) 10:07, Isbister (Can) 17:43

Second Period

5. Canada, Briere (Isbister) 6:24

   PENALTIES: York (U.S.) 8:17, Doig (Can) 17:00

Third Period

6. United States, Lacouture (Boulerice) 0:28

7. United States, Young (Poti) 15:46

8. Canada, Schaefer (Mann) 16:54

    PENALTIES: Sarich (Can) 2:43

Shots on Goal:

Canada	9	10	13	**32**
United States	8	8	10	**26**

In Goal:

    Canada — Denis

    United States — Boucher

December 30   *Canada 4*   *Switzerland 1*

First Period

1. Switzerland, Riesen (unassisted) 16:35

    PENALTIES: Seger (Swi) 3:19, Isbister (Can) 4:17, Ware (Can) 7:52, Isbister (Can) 12:54, Baldi (Swi) 17:48

Second Period

2. Canada, Isbister (Briere) 1:32

3. Canada, Dube (Isbister) .... 11:22(pp)

    PENALTIES: Phillips (Can) 5:38, Faeh (Swi) 10:24, Grauwiler (Swi) 13:59

Third Period

4. Canada, Thornton (McCauley, Briere) 3:34

5. Canada, Mann (Doig) 15:30

    PENALTIES: Grauwiler (Swi) 1:21, Hamilton (Can) 9:17, Doig (Can) 16:20, Sarich (Can) & Schneider (Swi) 18:00

Shots on Goal:

Canada	9	14	12	**35**
Switzerland	11	5	5	**21**

In Goal:

    Canada — Denis

    Switzerland — Aebischer

December 31   *Canada 3*   *Czech Republic 3*

First Period

1. Canada, Letowski (Thornton) 9:42

2. Czech Republic, Matejovsky (Zidlicky) 10:17

    PENALTIES: Mudroch (CzR) 2:00, Doig (Can) 5:30, Wallin (Can) 10:43, Hamilton (Can) 15:28

Second Period

3. Czech Republic, Melenovsky (unassisted) 6:33
4. Canada, Jackman (Mann) .... 8:22(pp)

PENALTIES: Zidlicky (CzR) 1:28, Larsen (Can) 4:02, Kriz (CzR — minor, misconduct) 7:48, Mann (Can) 11:56, Kadlec (CzR) 15:30

Third Period

5. Canada, Mann (Dube) 15:30
6. Czech Republic, Burger (Kratena) .... 19:50(sh)

PENALTIES: Phillips (Can) 1:09, Schaefer (Can) 5:04, Wallin (Can) 12:35, Richter (CzR) 17:55

Shots on Goal:

Canada	4	17	8	29
Czech Republic	8	7	7	22

In Goal:

Canada — Denis
Czech Republic — Svoboda

January 1　　　*Canada 7*　　　*Slovakia 2*

First Period

No Scoring

PENALTIES: Lintner (Slo) 1:06, Lintner (Slo) 3:41, Whitfield (Can) 7:59, Mann (Can) 10:57, Ciernik (Slo) 15:23

Second Period

1. Canada, Briere (Isbister) 5:07
2. Canada, Whitfield (Thornton, Mann) .... 7:35(pp)
3. Slovakia, Hossa (Vaic, Pavlikovsky) .... 12:25(pp)
4. Canada, Schaefer (Dube, McCauley) .... 18:49(pp)

PENALTIES: Slamiar (Slo) 7:13, Isbister (Can) 11:27, Doig (Can) 14:52, Durco (Slo — minor) & Letowski (Can — double minor) 17:40, Lintner (Slo — minor, misconduct) 18:32

Third Period

5. Slovakia, Rieciciar (Handzus, Somik) 1:15
6. Canada, Isbister (unassisted) 4:51
7. Canada, Devereaux (McCauley) 5:59
8. Canada, Letowski (unassisted) 11:50
9. Canada, Dube (Schaefer) .... 16:28(pp)

PENALTIES: Barinka (Slo) 1:42, Potac (Slo — minor) & Mann (Can — double minor) 9:40, Doig (Can) 12:25, Pavlikovsky (Slo) 16:12, Ware (Can) 17:41

Shots on Goal:

Canada	9	4	8	21
Slovakia	8	13	18	39

In Goal:

Canada — Denis
Slovakia — Petrik

January 3   *Canada 3*   *Russia 2*

First Period

1. Russia, Morozov (Sidulov) .... 11:53(pp)
2. Canada, Schaefer (McCauley) .... 18:10(pp)

PENALTIES: Doig (Can) 10:02, Briere (Can) 12:44, Kvacha (Rus) 16:28

Second Period

3. Russia, Gabdoulline (Volchkov) 9:56

PENALTIES: Markov (Rus) 2:49, Sarich (Can) 5:51, Zuzin (Rus) 10:15, Whitfield (Can) 12:56, Doig (Can — spearing major, game misconduct) 15:13

Third Period

4. Canada, Devereaux (McCauley) 0:49
5. Canada, Devereaux (Larsen, Phillips) 9:44

PENALTIES: Vasiliev (Rus) 4:07, Larsen (Can) 14:40

Shots on Goal:

Canada	13	6	8	27
Russia	13	4	11	28

In Goal:

Canada — Denis
Russia — Faizov

January 4   *Canada 2*   *United States 0*

First Period

No Scoring

PENALTIES: McCauley (Can) 12:20, Young (U.S.) 15:25

Second Period

1. Canada, Devereaux (Letowski) 8:38

PENALTIES: Briere (Can) 0:34, Peters (U.S.) 10:18, Schaefer (Can) 14:15

Third Period

2. Canada, Isbister (Briere) 3:09

PENALTIES: Bellefeuille (U.S.) 7:56

Shots on Goal:

Canada	10	12	13	35
United States	7	9	7	23

In Goal:

Canada — Denis

United States — Boucher

TEAM CANADA FINAL STATISTICS
1997 WORLD JUNIOR CHAMPIONSHIPS

			GP	G	A	P	PIM
12	F	Brad Isbister	7	4	3	7	8
9	F	Christian Dube(A)	7	4	3	7	0
10	F	Cameron Mann	7	3	4	7	10
14	F	Daniel Briere	7	2	4	6	4
18	F	Alyn McCauley(A)	7	0	5	5	2
19	F	Boyd Devereaux	7	4	0	4	0
27	F	Peter Schaefer	7	3	1	4	4
25	F	Joe Thornton	7	2	2	4	0
17	F	Trevor Letowski	7	2	1	3	4
24	D	Richard Jackman	7	2	0	2	0
4	D	Jason Doig	7	0	2	2	37
35	F	Trent Whitfield	7	1	0	1	4
23	F	Brad Larsen(C)	7	0	1	1	6
7	D	Chris Phillips(A)	7	0	1	1	4
3	D	Hugh Hamilton	7	0	0	0	6
22	D	Cory Sarich	7	0	0	0	6
34	D	Jesse Wallin	7	0	0	0	6
33	D	Jeff Ware	7	0	0	0	6
28	F	Dwayne Hay	7	0	0	0	2
31	G	Marc Denis	7	0	0	0	0
20	F	Shane Willis	7	0	0	0	0

In Goal

	GP	W-L-T	MINS	GA	SO	AVG
Marc Denis	7	5—0—2	420	13	1	1.86
Martin Biron	did not play					

Coach   Mike Babcock

Assistants   Mike Pelino/Real Paiement

CANADIAN OFFICIALS AT THE 1997
WORLD JUNIOR CHAMPIONSHIPS

Tom Kowal (referee)	4 games
Ryan Galloway (linesman)	7 games

TEAM CANADA ROSTER SUMMARY

Team Canada Players   21
Drafted In to NHL   21
Played In NHL (to date) 14 (all but Hamilton, Jackman, Letowski, Sarich,
       Schaefer, Wallin, Whitfield, Willis)
Returning Players   5   (Denis, Dube, Larsen, McCauley, Phillips)

PLAYER REPRESENTATION BY LEAGUE

OHL   7   (Devereaux, Hay, Jackman, Letowski, Mann, McCauley,
       Thornton)
WHL   9   (Hamilton, Isbister, Larsen, Phillips, Sarich, Schaefer,
       Wallin, Whitfield, Willis)
QMJHL   3   (Briere, Denis, Doig)
NHL   2   (Dube, Ware)

PLAYER REPRESENTATION BY AGE

19-year-olds   15 (Briere, Denis, Doig, Dube, Hamilton, Hay,
       Isbister, Larsen, Letowski, Mann, McCauley, Schaefer,
       Ware, Whitfield, Willis)
18-year-olds   5   (Devereaux, Jackman, Phillips, Sarich, Wallin)
17-year-olds   1   (Thornton)

PLAYERS' CAREER PROFILES

Daniel Briere   Drummondville Voltigeurs (QMJHL)
       Selected 24th overall by Phoenix at 1996 Draft
       Played in the NHL 1997 to present
Marc Denis   Chicoutimi Sagueneens (QMJHL)
       Selected 25th overall by Avalanche at 1995 Draft
       Played in the NHL 1996 to present
Boyd Devereaux   Kitchener Rangers (OHL)
       Selected 6th overall by Edmonton at 1996 Draft
       Played in the NHL 1997 to present
Jason Doig   Granby Predateurs (QMJHL)
       Selected 34th overall by Winnipeg at 1995 Draft
       Played in the NHL 1995 to present
Christian Dube   New York Rangers (NHL)
       Last Junior team: Sherbrooke Faucon (QMJHL)
       Selected 39th overall by Rangers at 1995 Draft
       Played in the NHL 1996 to present
Hugh Hamilton   Spokane Chiefs (WHL)
       Selected 113th overall by Hartford at 1995 Draft
       Has not yet played in the NHL

Dwayne Hay	Guelph Storm (OHL) Selected 43rd overall by Washington at 1995 Draft Played in the NHL 1997 to present
Brad Isbister	Portland Winter Hawks (WHL) Selected 67th overall by Winnipeg at 1995 Draft Played in the NHL 1997 to present
Richard Jackman	Sault Ste. Marie Greyhounds (OHL) Selected 5th overall by Dallas at 1996 Draft Has no yet played in the NHL
Brad Larsen	Swift Current Broncos (WHL) Selected 53rd overall by Ottawa at 1995 Draft Played in the NHL 1997 to present
Trevor Letowski	Sarnia Sting (OHL) Selected 174th overall by Phoenix at 1996 Draft Has not yet played in the NHL
Cameron Mann	Peterborough Petes (OHL) Selected 99th overall by Boston at 1995 Draft Played in the NHL 1997 to present
Alyn McCauley	Ottawa 67's (OHL) Selected 79th overall by New Jersey at 1995 Draft Played in the NHL 1997 to present
Chris Phillips	Prince Albert Raiders (WHL) Selected 1st overll by Ottawa at 1996 Draft Played in the NHL 1997 to present
Corey Sarich	Saskatoon Blades (WHL) Selected 27th overall by Buffalo at 1996 Draft Has not yet played in the NHL
Peter Schaefer	Brandon Wheat Kings (WHL) Selected 66th overall by Vancouver at 1995 Draft Has not yet played in the NHL
Joe Thornton	Sault Ste. Marie Greyhounds (OHL) Selected 1st overall by Boston at 1997 Draft Played in the NHL 1997 to present
Jesse Wallin	Red Deer Rebels (WHL) Selected 26th overall by Detroit at 1996 Draft Has not yet played in the NHL
Jeff Ware	Toronto Maple Leafs (NHL) Last Junior team: Oshawa Generals (OHL) Selected 15th overall by Toronto at 1995 Draft Played in the NHL 1996 to present
Trent Whitfield	Spokane Chiefs (WHL) Selected 100th overall by Boston at 1996 Draft Has not yet played in the NHL

Shane Willis Prince Albert Raiders (WHL)
Selected 56th overall by Tampa Bay at 1995 Draft
Has not yet played in the NHL

1998 WORLD JUNIOR CHAMPIONSHIPS FINLAND, DECEMBER 25, 1997-- JANUARY 3, 1998

FINAL PLACINGS

GOLD MEDAL	Finland
SILVER MEDAL	Russia
BRONZE MEDAL	Switzerland
Fourth Place	Czech Republic
Fifth Place	United States
Sixth Place	Sweden
Seventh Place	Kazakhstan*
Eighth Place	CANADA
Ninth Place	Slovakia
Tenth Place	Germany**

promoted from "B" pool in 1997
**relegated to "B" pool for 1999*

ALL-STAR TEAM

GOAL	David Aebischer (Switzerland)
DEFENCE	Pierre Hedin (Sweden)
	Andrei Markov (Russia)
FORWARD	Olli Jokinen (Finland)
	Eero Somervuori (Finland)
	Maxim Balmochnykh (Russia)

DIRECTORATE AWARDS

BEST GOALIE	David Aebischer (Switzerland)
BEST DEFENCEMAN	Pavel Skrbek (Czech Republic)
BEST FORWARD	Olli Jokinen (Finland)

COACH REAL PAIEMENT

Real Paiement was one of two assistants from 1996, and was selected to head this 1998 team when the other assistant, Mike Pelino, declined. Paiement won a Memorial Cup in his second season with the Chicoutimi Sagueneens and then coached the Moncton Wildcats of the QMJHL. Paiement got involved in coaching as a player-coach for a club team in Dunkirk, France. He returned to Canada in 1985, and for five years coached the Granby Bisons in the Quebec junior league. He returned to Europe for a year, coaching Senfter SG Brunico in the Italian Elite League. It was the combination of Canadian and international experience that made him a qualified candidate for junior coach.

THE CAMPS AND CUTS

The summer camp began August 8 in Toronto and ran for one intense week. Many talented players from the previous year accepting invitations. Joe Thornton, Patrick Marleau, Daniel Tkaczuk, Daniel Cleary, and Jean-Pierre Dumont led the way. Richard Jackman had won gold in '97, but because of discipline problems with the Soo he was not invited to try out for the '98 team. After the camp, two qualified players (17-year-olds Vincent Lecavalier and Manny Malhotra) headed for the Czech Republic to play in an under-18 tournament.

Final selections took place December 12 to 17 in Kitchener. The cuts came only hours before the team packed its bags and headed overseas. Not available to the team were five players in the NHL: Patrick Marleau (San Jose), Boyd Devereaux (Edmonton), Joe Thornton (Boston), Chris Phillips (Ottawa), and Derek Morris (Calgary). Only two players from last year's team went to Finland: Cory Sarich and Jesse Wallin. And, for the first time in years, Canada was sending two new goalies overseas. As with the coaches, preference had always been to see a backup one year go on to be a starter the next.

The last players told to stay behind were Patrick Desrochers (Sarnia, OHL), Nick Boynton (Ottawa, OHL), Colin Pepperall (Erie, OHL), and Dan Cleary (Belleville, OHL). Also cut were Evan Lindsay (Prince Albert, WHL), Brad Stuart (Regina, WHL), Remi Royer (Rouyn, QMJHL), Stefan Cherneski (Brandon, WHL), Jay Legault (London, OHL), and Darren Van Oene (Brandon, WHL).

The team arrived in Stockholm on December 17 for a five-day training session that included two exhibition games, one a 4–3 loss to Sweden, the other a 4–2 win over the Swiss. Against the Swedes, they took a 3–1 lead into the third period, only to lose. Against the Swiss they were behind 1–0 and 2–1, and didn't take the lead until the third.

*Manny Malhotra is one of a few players to step into the NHL his draft
year. After the World Juniors, he was selected 7th overall by the
Rangers in 1998 and made the team in the fall as an 18-year old rookie.*

DANIEL CLEARY

Cleary was by far the most high-profile name to be cut from a team since Brett Lindros in 1995. It was the third successive year Cleary was cut, but the circumstances this time were more complex than the previous two. Cleary had played six games with the Chicago Blackhawks and four with their farm club in Indianapolis, and was sent to his OHL team in Belleville by Chicago expressly to make him free for the World Juniors. Then he was cut. He played the rest of the year in junior rather than with Chicago in the NHL.

TEAM MOTTO: *Pay the price*

EIGHTH

The team faced Finland and Sweden in its first two games. What became immediately clear was that there were problems in every area of team talent and chemistry. Team officials had always done their homework to minimize those chances for failure, but this year things went awry.

Irresponsibility was certainly part of the problem, as team captain Jesse Wallin admitted: "There was a discipline problem off the ice with this team right from the start. What happens off the ice carries over onto the ice."

Paiement dismissed Canada's last two losses, to the U.S. and Kazakhstan, by saying the team folded after their heart-breaking loss to the Russians. More embarrassing was the first period of the game against Russia. Played in Hameenlinaa, the Russians were designated the home team. This meant they could choose whether to wear red or white jerseys. They chose red, but Canada had left their whites behind in Helsinki. For the first period, while a bus went for Canada's white sweaters, the players had to endure the humiliation of having to wear the home whites of the local Hameenlinaa Knights team. That's how the tournament went.

In their loss to Kazakhstan, Canada showed its worst face in international competition. The Kazak players were using antiquated equipment, and as a team had exactly seven spare sticks for the game. Yet this collection of ancient amateurs embarrassed the Canadians, flying to a 4–0 lead and winning 6–3. Canada's last goal came with just three seconds left.

EL NINO AT THE WORLD JUNIORS

The whole tournament was a study in change, displacement, and unpredictability. The team's eighth place finish was thirty-nine seconds away from a potential berth in the semi-finals. Canada lost by one goal to both finalists,

Vincent Lecavalier played in the Prospects Game at
Maple Leaf Gardens shortly after being part of a disappointing
eighth place finish by Canada just a few weeks earlier in Finland.

yet lost 6–3 to a Kazakhstan team that had been destroyed 14–1 by the Finns. The Swiss, remarkably, were gold medal contenders through and through. The Swedes lost to the Czech Republic 2–1; Canada whipped the Czechs 5–0. Yet the Swedes completely dominated Canada. The Finns had won gold only once, yet they went undefeated.

TOURNAMENT FORMAT

A shorter round robin allowed for quick elimination of the weakest two teams while the top eight went to the playoffs. The two teams that didn't qualify played a two-game total-goals series to determine which would be relegated to the "B" pool the following year. A ten-minute overtime was used for ties only in the playoffs, after which a shootout would settle a winner.

THE OPPOSITION

CZECH REPUBLIC

Pavel Bacho, Radek Duda, Lukas Galvas, Jan Hejda, Tomas Kaberle, Pavel Kabrt, Ales Kotalik, Vlastimil Lakosil, Petr Mudroch, Ivo Novotny, Kamil Piros, Marek Posmyk, Radek Prochazka, Karel Rachunek, Robert Schnabel, Pavel Selinger, Pavel Skrbek, Patrik Stefan, Josef Straka, Adam Svoboda, Petr Sykora, Martin Tomasek

FINLAND

Timo Ahmaoja, Olli Ahonen, Johannes Alanen, Niklas Backstrom, Toni Dahlman, Teemu Elomo, Niklas Hagman, Olli Jokinen, Tomi Kallarsson, Kari Kalto, Niko Kapanen, Marko Kauppinen, Jyrki Louhi, Ilkka Mikkola, Mika Noronen, Pasi Petrilainen, Pasi Puistola, Timo Seikkula, Eero Somervuori, Ari Vallin, Tomek Valtonen, Timo Vertala

GERMANY

Nils Antons, Michael Bakos, Bjorn Barta, Boris Blank, Gordon Borberg, Leonardo Conti, Thomas Dolak, Robert Francz, Sacha Goc, Benjamin Hinterstocker, Christoph Jahns, Markus Jocher, Daniel Kreutzer, Torsten Kunz, Bjorn Leonhardt, Niki Mondt, Andreas Morczinietz, Andreas Paderhuber, Markus Pottinger, Martin Schweiger, Patrick Senger, David Sulkovski, Nicolai Tittus

KAZAKHSTAN

Sergei Aksyutenko, Sergei Alexandrov, Nikolai Antropov, Maxim Belyayev, Andrei Gavrillin, Anton Komissarov, Roman Krivomazov, Vitali Litvinov,

Vladimir Logvin, Evgeny Lyapunov, Mikhail Medvedev, Vitali Novopashin, Anton Petrov, Alexander Pokladov, Vadim Riffel, Denis Shemelin, Andrei Sidorenko, Viacheslav Tregubov, Andrei Troschinsky, Dmitri Upper, Georgi Xandopulo, Pavel Yakovlev

RUSSIA

Maxim Afinogenov, Vladimir Antipov, Denis Arkhipov, Maxim Balmochnykh, Mikhail Chernov, Artem Chubarov, Mikhail Donika, Denis Khlopotnov, Alexei Krovopuskov, Andrei Kruchinin, Oleg Kvasha, Roman Lyashenko, Andrei Markov, Igor Mikhailov, Dimitri Mylnikov, Valeri Pokrovski, Sergei Shikhanov, Denis Shvidky, Andrei Sidyakin, Alexei Tezikov, Vitali Vishnevsky, Dimitri Vlassenkov

SLOVAKIA

Karol Bartanus, Peter Bartek, Marian Cisar, Adrian Daniel, Stanislav Fatyka, Peter Gallo, Stanislav Gron, Ladislav Harabin, Marian Hossa, Miroslav Kovacik, Martin Kucera, Boris Majesky, Ladislav Nagy, Martin Nemcek, Vladimir Nemec, Andrei Podkonicky, Pavol Rieciciar, Jan Simko, Martin Spillar, Andrei Szoke, Martin Tomas, Marek Topoli

SWEDEN

Andreas Andersson, Josef Boumedienne, Kim Cannerholm, Jonas Elofsson, Johan Eriksson, Johan Forsander, Per Hallberg, Pierre Hedin, Johan Holmqvist, Mikael Holmqvist, Kristian Huselius, Mattias Karlin, Magnus Nilsson, Marcus Nilsson, Niklas Persson, Henrik Petre, Jan Sandstrom, Henrik Sedin, Daniel Sedin, Mikael Simons, Henrik Tallinder, Andreas Westlund

SWITZERLAND

David Aebischer, Marco Buhrer, Ralph Bundi, Alex Chatelain, Bjorn Christen, Flavien Conne, Patrick Fischer, Sven Lindemann, Michel Mouther, Laurent Muller, Marc Reichert, Alain Reist, Michel Riesen, Sandro Rizzi, Mario Schocher, Rene Stussi, Julien Vauclair, Jan von Arx, Marc Werlen, Adrian Wichser, Markus Wuthrich, Thomas Ziegler

UNITED STATES

Jesse Boulerice, Kevin Colley, Joe Dusbabek, Robert Esche, Jeff Farkas, Brian Gionta, Scott Gomez, Chris Hajt, Ty Jones, Kevin Kellett, Dustin Kuk, Jay Leach, David Legwand, Paul Mara, Aaron Miskovich, Mike Mottau, Jean-Marc Pelletier, Toby Peterson, Ben Simon, Chris St. Croix, Nikos Tselios, Mike York

FINAL STANDINGS PRELIMINARY ROUND

POOL A

	GP	W	L	T	GF	GA	P
Finland	4	3	0	1	17	10	7
Czech Republic	4	2	1	1	16	12	5
Sweden	4	2	2	0	16	6	4
CANADA	4	2	2	0	9	7	4
Germany	4	0	4	0	1	24	0

Results

December 25	Helsinki	Finland 3	Canada 2
	Hemeenlinaa	Czech Republic 2	Sweden 1
December 26	Helsinki	Sweden 4	Canada 0
	Hameenlinaa	Finland 5	Germany 0
December 27	Helsinki	Czech Republic 9	Germany 1
December 28	Helsinki	Canada 5	Czech Republic 0
	Helsinki	Finland 4	Sweden 3
December 29	Helsinki	Sweden 8	Germany 0
December 30	Helsinki	Canada 2	Germany 0
	Helsinki	Finland 5	Czech Republic 5

POOL B

	GP	W	L	T	GF	GA	P
Russia	4	3	0	1	22	6	7
Switzerland	4	2	1	1	14	8	5
United States	4	2	2	0	17	12	4
Kazakhstan	4	1	3	0	8	29	2
Slovakia	4	1	3	0	9	15	2

Results

December 25	Hemeenlinaa	Russia 12	Kazakhstan 1
	Helsinki	Slovakia 6	United States 3
December 26	Helsinki	United States 8	Kazakhstan 2
	Hameenlinaa	Switzerland 3	Slovakia 1
December 27	Helsinki	Switzerland 3	Russia 3
December 28	Hameenlinaa	Kazakhstan 5	Slovakia 2
	Hameenlinaa	Russia 3	United States 2
December 29	Hameenlinaa	Switzerland 7	Kazakhstan 0
December 30	Hameenlinaa	Russia 4	Slovakia 0
	Hameenlinaa	United States 4	Switzerland 1

RELEGATION ROUND FINAL RESULTS

| January 1 | Helsinki | Slovakia 9 | Germany 0 |
| January 3 | Helsinki | Slovakia 8 | Germany 3 |

Slovakia wins total goals series 17–3; Germany relegated to "B" pool for 1999

PLACEMENT ROUND RESULTS
(losers of quarter-finals)

| January 2 | Hameenlinaa | United States 3 | Canada 0 |
| | Hameenlinaa | Sweden 5 | Kazakhstan 1 |

Fifth Place Game

| January 3 | Hameenlinaa | United States 4 | Sweden 3 |

Seventh Place Game

| January 3 | Hameenlinaa | Kazakhstan 6 | Canada 3 |

PLAYOFFS

Quarter-finals

December 31	Hameenlinaa	Russia 2	Canada 1 (OT)
	Helsinki	Finland 14	Kazakhstan 1
	Helsinki	Switzerland 2	Sweden 1 (OT)
	Hameenlinaa	Czech Republic 4	United States 1

Semi-finals

| January 1 | Helsinki | Russia 5 | Czech Republic 1 |
| | Helsinki | Finland 2 | Switzerland 1 |

Bronze Medal Game

| January 3 | Helsinki | Switzerland 4 | Czech Republic 3 (OT) |

Gold Medal Game

| January 3 | Helsinki | Finland 2 | Russia 1 |

AGGREGATE STANDINGS
(ordered according to final placings)

	GP	W	L	T	GF	GA	GAA	SO	PIM
Finland	7	6	0	1	35	13	1.86	1	64*
Russia	7	5	1	1	30	10	1.43	1	84
Switzerland	7	4	2	1	21	14	2.00	1	78
Czech Republic	7	3	3	1	24	22	3.14	0	88

United States	7	4	3	0	25	19	2.71	1	138
Sweden	7	3	4	0	25	13	1.86	2	114
Kazakhstan	7	2	5	0	16	51	7.29	0	82
CANADA	7	2	5	0	13	18	2.57	2	124
Slovakia	6	3	3	0	26	18	2.83	1	183
Germany	6	0	6	0	4	41	6.83	0	194

* won Fair Play Cup

TEAM CANADA GAME SUMMARIES

December 26   Finland 3   Canada 2

First Period

No Scoring

PENALTIES: Brewer (Can) 1:06, Ahmaoja (Fin) 7:34, Komarniski (Can) 12:05, Vallin (Fin) 17:39, Lecavalier (Can) 18:55

Second Period

1. Canada, Ward (unassisted) 10:02
2. Finland, Kauppinen (Vallin, Kalto) 13:01

PENALTIES: Van Ryn (Can) 5:31, Tkaczuk (Can) 10:24, Kallarsson (Fin) 13:33, Willsie (Can) 16:19

Third Period

3. Finland, Somervuori (Jokinen) .... 7:27(pp)
4. Canada, Tanguay (Tkaczuk) 11:39
5. Finland, Hagman (Somervuori, Jokinen) 16:20

PENALTIES: Ference (Can) 6:30, Vertala (Fin) 7:55, Puistola (Fin) 14:01, Begin (Can) 16:45, Komarniski (Can — minor, misconduct) 19:40

Shots on Goal:

Canada	6	4	8	**18**
Finland	12	11	15	**38**

In Goal:

Canada — Garon
Finland — Noronen

December 26   Sweden 4   Canada 0

First Period

1. Sweden, Nilsson (Forsander) .... 6:56(pp)
2. Sweden, Hedin (unassisted) 17:32

PENALTIES: Van Ryn (Can) 5:22, Holden (Can) 8:23, Persson (Swe) 11:54, Petre (Swe) 13:03, Begin (Can) 19:03, Nilsson (Swe) 19:54

Second Period

3. Sweden, D. Sedin (Petre) 2:55

    PENALTIES: Brewer (Can) 5:46, Komarniski (Can) 8:05, Persson (Swe) 10:40, Corso (Can) & Petre (Swe) 13:24, Corso (Can) 17:15, Ference (Can) 19:58

Third Period

4. Sweden, Cannerholm (Nilsson) 6:45

    PENALTIES: Tallinder (Swe) 3:38, M. Holmqvist (Swe) 14:39, Blanchard (Can) 15:34, Willsie (Can) & Sandstrom (Swe) 19:59

Shots on Goal:

Canada	7	10	5	22
Sweden	15	11	9	35

In Goal:

Canada — Luongo
Sweden — J. Holmqvist

December 28   *Canada 5*   *Czech Republic 0*

First Period

1. Canada, Holden (Corso) 10:10
2. Canada, Cooke (Sarich) .... 11:10(pp)

    PENALTIES: Galvas (CzR) 5:29, McLean (Can) 6:59, Rachunek (CzR) 10:58, Straka (CzR) 16:33

Second Period

3. Canada, Tanguay (McLean) 6:45
4. Canada, McLean (Tanguay, Brewer) .... 10:40(sh)
5. Canada, Holden (Corso) 18:05

    PENALTIES: Brewer (Can) 0:18, Skrbek (CzR) 4:44, Begin (Can) 7:07, Blanchard (Can) 9:23, Wallin (Can) 18:34

Third Period

No Scoring

    PENALTIES: Tomasek (CzR) 2:11, Duda (CzR) 6:33, Novotny (CzR) 9:05, Begin (Can) 9:47

Shots on Goal:

Canada	9	7	6	22
Czech Republic	7	10	5	22

In Goal:

Canada — Garon
Czech Republic — Svoboda/Lakosil (Lakosil [one goal] replaced Svoboda [4 goals] at 15:46 of 2nd)

December 30   Canada 2   Germany 0

First Period

No Scoring

> PENALTIES: Wallin (Can) 5:37, Goc (Ger) 12:01, Ger bench 13:47, Cooke (Can) 14:53

Second Period

1. Canada, Bradley (Cooke, Lecavalier) 8:05

> PENALTIES: Tanguay (Can) 1:51, McLean (Can) 14:37, Bakos (Ger) 19:40

Third Period

2. Canada, Lecavalier (Bradley) 14:59

> PENALTIES: Tkaczuk (Can) 3:42, Komarniski (Can) 3:48, Sarich (Can) 11:42, Sulkovski (Ger) 16:03

Shots on Goal:

Canada	2	16	10	**28**
Germany	6	4	7	**17**

In Goal:

> Canada — Garon
> Germany — Leonhardt

December 31   Russia 2   Canada 1

First Period

1. Russia, Vlassenkov (Lyashenko) 18:01

> PENALTIES: Rus bench 2:37, Brewer (Can) & Arkhipov (Rus) 6:37, Can bench (served by Ference) 11:25, Cooke (Can) 19:36

Second Period

No Scoring

> PENALTIES: Kruchinin (Rus) 4:43, Chernov (Rus) 5:11, Ward (Can) 12:51

Third Period

2. Canada, Tkaczuk (Willsie, Blanchard) 2:31

> PENALTIES: Vlassenkov (Rus) 6:43, Lyashenko (Rus) 16:48

Overtime

3. Russia, Afinogenov (Balmochnykh) 9:21

> PENALTIES: none

Shots on Goal:

Canada	4	6	9	4	**23**
Russia	10	5	7	6	**28**

In Goal:

> Canada — Garon
> Russia — Khlopotnov

January 2   *United States 3*   *Canada 0*

First Period

1. United States, York (Mottau) .... 5:59(pp)

    PENALTIES: Blanchard (Can) & Gionta (U.S.) 5:24, Luongo (Can) 5:36, St. Croix (U.S.) 12:46, Sarich (Can) 13:35, Pelletier (U.S.) 17:18, Komarniski (Can) 18:57

Second Period

2. United States, Dusbabek (Mara) 19:31

    PENALTIES: Cooke (Can) 3:26, Bradley (Can) 7:47, Komarniski (Can) 13:40

Third Period

3. United States, Farkas (unassisted) .... 19:25(en)

    PENALTIES: Mara (U.S.) 10:42, Hajt (U.S.) 11:08

Shots on Goal:

Canada	5	3	7	15
United States	19	16	5	40

In Goal:

    Canada — Luongo
    United States — Pelletier

January 3   *Kazakhstan 6*   *Canada 3*

First Period

1. Kazakhstan, Troschinsky (Antropov) 3:45
2. Kazakhstan, Alexandrov (Troschinsky, Antropov) .... 13:14(pp)

    PENALTIES: Pokladov (Kaz) 4:13, Ference (Can) 8:09, Sarich (Can) 11:54, Shemelin (Kaz) 16:54, Lecavalier (Can) & Sidorenko (Kaz) 19:00

Second Period

3. Kazakhstan, Troschinsky (Alexandrov, Novopashin) .... 11:47(sh)
4. Kazakhstan, Troschinsky (Antropov) 14:00

    PENALTIES: Begin (Can) 1:26, Blanchard (Can) 6:41, Alexandrov (Kaz) 6:46, Antropov (Kaz) 7:18, Petrov (Kaz) 10:28, Holden (Can) 12:32, Komarniski (Can) 14:00, Logvin (Kaz) 17:23, Komarniski (Can) 19:24

Third Period

5. Canada, Holden (Blanchard) .... 7:25(pp)
6. Canada, Holden (Ference, Corso) .... 10:10(pp)
7. Kazakhstan, Komissarov (Xandopulo) 18:21
8. Kazakhstan, Riffel (unassisted) .... 19:20(en)
9. Canada, Tkaczuk (Willsie, Brewer) 19:57

    PENALTIES: Litvinov (Kaz) 6:36, Litvinov (Kaz) 9:47, Holden (Can — minor, misconduct) 10:37, Petrov (Kaz) 12:41

Shots on Goal:

Canada	10	20	13	**43**
Kazakhstan	5	6	6	**17**

In Goal:

Canada — Garon/Luongo (Luongo [2 goals] replaced Garon [4 goals at 14:00 of 2nd)
Kazakhstan — Krivomazov

TEAM CANADA FINAL STATISTICS
1998 WORLD JUNIOR CHAMPIONSHIPS

			GP	G	A	P	PIM
21	F	Josh Holden	7	4	0	4	16
10	F	Daniel Tkaczuk	7	2	1	3	4
19	F	Alex Tanguay	7	2	1	3	2
15	F	Daniel Corso	7	0	3	3	4
12	F	Matt Cooke	6	1	1	2	6
14	F	Vincent Lecavalier	7	1	1	2	4
16	F	Brett McLean	7	1	1	2	4
28	F	Matt Bradley	7	1	1	2	2
7	D	Sean Blanchard	7	0	2	2	8
3	D	Eric Brewer	7	0	2	2	8
24	F	Brian Willsie	7	0	2	2	4
20	F	Jason Ward	7	1	0	1	2
2	D	Brad Ference	7	0	1	1	6
22	D	Cory Sarich(A/C)	7	0	1	1	6
5	D	Zenith Komarniski	7	0	0	0	26
11	F	Steve Begin(A)	7	0	0	0	10
26	D	Mike Van Ryn	7	0	0	0	4
4	D	Jesse Wallin(C)	4	0	0	0	4
1	G	Roberto Luongo	3	0	0	0	2
18	F	Jean-Pierre Dumont	7	0	0	0	0
6	F	Manny Malhotra	7	0	0	0	0
32	G	Mathieu Garon	5	0	0	0	0

Captain Notes:

Wallin captain vs. Finland, Sweden, Czech Republic, Germany
Sarich captain vs. Russia, United States, Kazakhstan

In Goal

	GP	W-L-T	MINS	GA	SO	AVG
Mathieu Garon	5	2–3–0	284	14	2	2.96
Roberto Luongo	3	0–2–0	146	9	0	3.70

Goalie Notes:

1. Luongo [2 goals] replaced Garon [4 goals] at 14:00 of 2nd, January 3 vs. Kazakhstan

Coach   Real Paiement
Assistant   Terry Bangen/Peter DeBoer

CANADIAN OFFICIALS AT THE 1998 WORLD JUNIOR CHAMPIONSHIPS

Stephane Auger (referee)	6 games
Jeff Bradley (linesman)	5 games

TEAM CANADA SUMMARY

Team Canada players	22	
Drafted Into NHL	22	
Played In NHL (to date)	6	(Begin, Brewer, Cooke, Dumont, Lecavalier, Malhotra)
Returning Players	2	(Sarich, Wallin)

PLAYER REPRESENTATION BY LEAGUE

OHL	7	(Blanchard, Bradley, Cooke, Malhotra, Tkaczuk, Ward, Willsie)
WHL	7	(Brewer, Ference, Holden, Komarniski, McLean, Sarich, Wallin)
QMJHL	7	(Begin, Corso, Dumont, Garon, Lecavalier, Luongo, Tanguay)
U.S. COLLEGE	1	(Van Ryn)

PLAYER REPRESENTATION BY AGE

19-year-olds	12	(Garon, Wallin, Blanchard, Sarich, Begin, Cooke, Corso, McLean, Dumont, Holden, Willsie, Bradley)
18-year-olds	8	(Luongo, Ference, Brewer, Komarniski, Van Ryn, Tkaczuk, Tanguay, Ward)
17-year-olds	2	(Lecavalier, Malhotra)

PLAYERS' CAREER PROFILES

Steve Begin	Val d'Or Foreurs (QMJHL)
	Selected 40th overall by Calgary at 1996 Draft
	Played in the NHL 1997 to present
Sean Blanchard	Ottawa 67's (OHL)
	Selected 99th overall by Los Angeles at 1997 Draft
	Has not yet played in the NHL

Matt Bradley   Kingston Frontenacs (OHL)
Selected 102nd overall by San Jose at 1996 Draft
Has not yet played in the NHL

Eric Brewer   Prince George Cougars (WHL)
Selected 5th overall by Islanders at 1997 Draft
Played in the NHL 1998 to present

Matt Cooke   Windsor Spitfires (OHL)
Selected 144th overall by Vancouver at 1997 Draft
Played in the NHL 1998 to present

Daniel Corso   Victoriaville Tigers (QMJHL)
Selected 169th overall by St. Louis at 1996 Draft
Has not yet played in the NHL

Jean-Pierre Dumont   Val d'Or Foreurs (QMJHL)
Selected 3rd overall by Islanders at 1996 Draft
Played in the NHL 1998 to present

Brad Ference   Spokane Chiefs (WHL)
Selected 10th overall by Vancouver at 1997 Draft
Has not yet played in the NHL

Mathieu Garon   Victoriaville Tigers (QMJHL)
Selected 44th overall by Montreal at 1996 Draft
Has not yet played in the NHL

Josh Holden   Regina Pats (WHL)
Selected 12th overall by Vancouver at 1996 Draft
Has not yet played in the NHL

Zenith Komarniski   Spokane Chiefs (WHL)
Selected 75th overall by Vancouver at 1996 Draft
Has not yet played in the NHL

Vincent Lecavalier   Rimouski Oceanic (QMJHL)
Selected 1st overall by Tampa Bay at 1998 Draft
Played in the NHL 1998 to present

Roberto Luongo   Val d'Or Foreurs (QMJHL)
Selected 4th overall by Islanders at 1997 Draft
Has not yet played in the NHL

Manny Malhotra   Guelph Storm (OHL)
Selected 7th overall by Rangers at 1998 Draft
Played in the NHL 1998 to present

Brett McLean   Kelowna Rockets (WHL)
Selected 242nd overall by Dallas at 1997 Draft
Has not yet played in the NHL

Cory Sarich   Saskatoon Blades (WHL)
Selected 27th overall by Buffalo at 1996 Draft
Has not yet played in the NHL

Alex Tanguay   Halifax Mooseheads (QMJHL)
Selected 12th overall by Avalanche at 1998 Draft
Has not yet played in the NHL

Daniel Tkaczuk   Barrie Colts (OHL)
                        Selected 6th overall by Calgary at 1997 Draft
                        Has not yet played in the NHL
Mike Van Ryn   University of Michigan Wolverines (CCHA)
                        Selected 26th overall by New Jersey at 1998 Draft
                        Has not yet played in the NHL
Jesse Wallin   Red Deer Rebels (WHL)
                        Selected 26th overall by Detroit at 1996 Draft
                        Has not yet played in the NHL
Jason Ward   Erie Otters (OHL)
                        Selected 11th overall by Montreal at 1997 Draft
                        Has not yet played in the NHL
Brian Willsie   Guelph Storm (OHL)
                        Selected 146th overall by Avalanche at 1996 Draft
                        Has not yet played in the NHL

1999 WORLD JUNIOR CHAMPIONSHIPS CANADA, DECEMBER 26, 1998-- JANUARY 5, 1999

COACH TOM RENNEY

George Burnett won the Memorial Cup with the Guelph Storm in spring '98 and was hired by the CHA just weeks later to lead Canada to recovery from 1998's disastrous eighth place finish. No sooner had he accepted the appointment than he was offered an assistant coach's job with the Mighty Ducks of Anaheim in the NHL. He resigned on August 18, 1998 to take on the pro challenge and two weeks later Tom Renney was named as his replacement. Renney had been coach of the Vancouver Canucks for 1996–97 but was replaced after the team failed to make the playoffs that season.

The committee that made the hiring decision included CHA president Bob Nicholson, WHL commissioner Dev Dley, OHL president David Branch, QMJHL preisdent Gilles Courteau, and CHA vice-president Sheldon Landsbury. The group passed over Burnett's assistants, Claude Julien and Stan Butler, who remained in that secondary capacity for Renney. Renney's international track record includes a gold medal as head coach at the World Championships in 1994 and followed an awful sixth place finish at the world juniors in 1992 when he acted as Rick Cornacchia's assistant. He also won the Memorial Cup as bench boss with the Kamloops Blazers in '92.

RECOVERING FROM THE DEBACLE

Canada's eighth-place finish in 1998 was its worst performance at the World Juniors. On the upside, after the previous worst showing, sixth place in 1992, Canada went on to win gold the next fiive years, the first team to accomplish such a feat. While pessimists point to the showing as a sign of deteriorating skills and eroding international success, history has long proven Canada to be a resilient, ever-consistent winner with but the occasional blip of poor performance.

WORLD-WIDE DEFENCE

Scoring has not necessarily disappeared in the NHL, but defence has certainly been able to overwhelm scorers with increasing success in the past five years, partly because expansion has weakened talent, partly because desperate coaches with thin talent have opted for defence over offence, partly because goalies are becoming better each year. But the defensive tendencies are not limited to the NHL. At the World Championships in the spring of 1998, talent-laden teams from Sweden and Finland played a best-of-two finals that resulted in scores of 1–0 and 0–0. (In the event of a tie, a ten-minute overtime decided the winner.)

So, too, with the World Juniors, as this chart shows. Either the next generation of NHLers will be even more defensive or the next generation of coaches already is, but scoring is down and shutouts are up.

TGP = total games played in the tournament
SO = shutouts, all teams
GPG = average number of goals per game, both teams

YEAR	TGP	SO	GPG
1977	28	4	8.96
1978	25	2	9.92
1979	22	3	7.77
1980	20	1	8.90
1981	20	0	10.35
1982	28	4	10.07
1983	28	3	9.18
1984	28	2	9.68
1985	28	5	8.21
1986	28	4	8.79
1987	27	5	10.07
1988	28	2	8.82
1989	28	3	9.07
1990	28	3	9.32
1991	28	5	9.04
1992	28	3	7.68
1993	28	5	8.64
1994	28	4	6.96
1995	28	1	8.89
1996	31	5	7.03
1997	31	8	6.58
1998	34	9	6.44

Traditionally, the more teams in the tournament, the weaker the competition, which should increase goals scored because of blow-outs. Not so at the World Juniors, where shutouts have increased and scoring decreased in the last four years, despite the increase from eight teams to ten in 1996.

TUNEUP

To prepare for the Worlds, Canada's juniors will be part of a four-team mini-tournament to be held in Kenora and Dryden, Ontario from December 19 to 24. Other competing nations will include Finland, Russia, and Switzerland, and should give coach Renney an excellent opportunity to prepare his team for Winnipeg and to evaluate the abilities of his players as a cohesive unit.

PRE-WJC TOURNAMENT SCHEDULE

December 19	Dryden	Finland vs. Russia
December 20	Kenora	Canada vs. Switzerland
December 21	Kenora	Switzerland vs. Finland
December 22	Kenora	Canada vs. Russia
December 23	Kenora	Canada vs. Finland
	Dryden	Switzerland vs. Russia

SUMMER CAMP ROSTER

From August 11–16, the Canadian team held their annual summer evaluation camp in Winnipeg, attended by 41 players. The final camp, to be held at the start of December, would see 32 players invited, some not necessarily from this group if they had performed well during the junior or college season to that date.

GOALIES

MATHIEU CHOUINARD (6′1″ 200 lbs.)
   b. Laval, Quebec, April 11, 1980
   Shawinigan Cataracts (QMJHL)/Drafted 15th overall by Ottawa in 1998
PAT DESROCHERS (6′4″ 195 lbs.)
   b. Penetang, Ontario, October 27, 1979
   Sarnia Sting (OHL)/Drafted 14th overall by Phoenix in 1998
ROBERTO LUONGO (6′2″ 185 lbs.)
   b. St.-Leonard, Quebec, April 4, 1979
   Val d'Or Foreurs (QMJHL)/Drafted 4th overall by Islanders in 1997
SCOTT MEYERS (5′11″ 172 lbs.)
   b. Winnipeg, Manitoba, June 11, 1979
   Prince George Cougars (WHL)/Drafted 110th overall by Pittsburgh in 1998

DEFENCEMEN

BRYAN ALLEN (6'5" 208 lbs.)
  b. Kingston, Ontario, August 21, 1980
  Shawinigan Cataracts (QMJHL)/Drafted 4th overall by Vancouver in 1998

MATHIEU BIRON (6'7" 212 lbs.)
  b. Lac St. Charles, Quebec, April 29, 1980
  Shawinigan Cataracts (QMJHL)/Drafted 21st overall by Los Angeles in 1998

NICK BOYNTON (6'2" 210 lbs.)
  b. Nobleton, Ontario, January 14, 1979
  Ottawa 67's (OHL)/Drafted 9th overall by Washington in 1997

ERIC BREWER (6'3" 195 lbs.)
  b. Vernon, British Columbia, April 17, 1979
  Prince George Cougars (WHL)/Drafted 5th overall by Islanders in 1997

JOEY DIPENTA (6'2" 205 lbs.)
  b. Barrie, Ontario, February 25, 1979
  Boston University (HE)/Drafted 61st overall by Florida in 1998

ANDREW FERENCE (5'10" 180 lbs.)
  b. Edmonton, Alberta, March 17, 1979
  Portland Winter Hawks (WHL)/Drafted 208th overall by Pittsburgh in 1997

BRAD FERENCE (6'3" 196 lbs.)
  b. Calgary, Alberta, April 2, 1979
  Spokane Chiefs (WHL)/Drafted 10th overall by Vancouver in 1997

SCOTT HANNAN (6'2" 210 lbs.)
  b. Richmond, British Columbia, January 23, 1979
  Kelowna Rockets (WHL)/Drafted 23rd overall by San Jose in 1997

BURKE HENRY (6'2" 190 lbs.)
  b. Ste. Rose du Lac, Manitoba, January 21, 1979
  Brandon Wheat Kings (WHL)/Drafted 73rd overall by Rangers in 1997

ROBYN REGEHR (6'2" 210 lbs.)
  b. Recife, Brazil, April 19, 1980
  Kamloops Blazers (WHL)/Drafted 19th overall by Colorado in 1998

BRAD STUART (6'3" 215 lbs.)
  b. Rocky Mountain House, Alberta, November 6, 1979
  Regina Pats (WHL)/Drafted 3rd overall by San Jose in 1998

LUC THEORET (6'2" 203 lbs.)
  b. Winnipeg, Manitoba, July 30, 1979
  Lethbridge Broncos (WHL)/Drafted 101st overall by Buffalo in 1997

MIKE VAN RYN (6'1" 190 lbs.)
  b. London, Ontario, May 16, 1979
  University of Michigan (CCHA)/Drafted 26th overall by New Jersey in 1998

FORWARDS

RAMZI ABID (6'2" 195 lbs.)
>   b. Montreal, Quebec, March 24, 1980
>   Chicoutimi Sagueneens (QMJHL)/Drafted 28th overall by Colorado in 1998

SCOTT BARNEY (6'4" 197 lbs.)
>   b. Oshawa, Ontario, March 27, 1979
>   Peterborough Petes (OHL)/Drafted 29th overall by Los Angeles in 1997

MARK BELL (6'3" 185 lbs.)
>   b. St. Paul's, Ontario, August 5, 1980
>   Ottawa 67's (OHL)/Drafted 8th overall by Chicago in 1998

BLAIR BETTS (6'2" 183 lbs.)
>   b. Edmonton, Alberta, February 16, 1980
>   Prince George Cougars (WHL)/Drafted 33rd overall by Calgary in 1998

JOHNATHAN CHEECHOO (6' 205 lbs.)
>   b. Moose Factory, Ontario, July 15, 1980
>   Belleville Bulls (OHL)/Drafted 29th overall by San Jose in 1998

JASON CHIMERA (6' 160 lbs.)
>   b. Edmonton, Alberta, May 2, 1979
>   Medicine Hat Tigers (WHL)/Drafted 121st overall by Edmonton in 1997

ERIC CHOUINARD (6'2" 195 lbs.)
>   b. Atlanta, Georgia, July 8, 1980
>   Quebec Remparts (QMJHL)/Drafted 16th overall by Montreal in 1998

MIKE COMRIE (5'9" 170 lbs.)
>   b. Edmonton, Alberta, September 11, 1980
>   St. Albert Saints (AJHL)/Draft eligible in 1999

HAROLD DRUKEN (6' 205 lbs.)
>   b. St. John's, Newfoundland, January 26, 1979
>   Plymouth Whalers (OHL)/Drafted 36th overall by Vancouver in 1997

RICO FATA (6' 202 lbs.)
>   b. Sault Ste. Marie, Ontario, February 12, 1980
>   London Knights (OHL)/Drafted 6th overall by Calgary in 1998
>   (currently in the NHL)

RANDY FITZGERALD (5'11" 175 lbs.)
>   b. Toronto, Ontario, September 5, 1979
>   Plymouth Whalers (OHL)/Drafted 199th overall by Carolina in 1997

SIMON GAGNE (6' 165 lbs.)
>   b. Ste. Foy, Quebec, February 29, 1980
>   Quebec Remparts (QMJHL)/Drafted 22nd overall by Philadelphia in 1998

JEFF HEEREMA (6'1" 171 lbs.)
>   b. Thunder Bay, Ontario, January 17, 1980
>   Sarnia Sting (OHL)/Drafted 11th overall by Carolina in 1998

VINCENT LECAVALIER (6'4" 180 lbs.)
   b. Ile Bizard, Quebec, April 21, 1980
   Rimouski Oceanic (QMJHL)/Drafted 1st overall by Tampa Bay in 1998
   Invited to camp but did not attend
   (currently in the NHL)

JAY LEGAULT (6'5" 205 lbs.)
   b. Peterborough, Ontario, May 15, 1979
   London Knights (OHL)/Drafted 72nd overall by Anaheim in 1997

ADAM MAIR (6'1" 195 lbs.)
   b. Hamilton, Ontario, February 15, 1979
   Owen Sound Platers (OHL)/Drafted 84th overall by Toronto in 1997

MANNY MALHOTRA (6'2" 210 lbs.)
   b. Mississauga, Ontario, May 18, 1980
   Guelph Storm (OHL)/Drafted 7th overall by Rangers in 1998

BRENDEN MORROW (5'11" 195 lbs.)
   b. Carlisle, Saskatchewan, January 16, 1979
   Portland Winter Hawks (WHL)/Drafted 25th overall by Dallas in 1997

JUSTIN PAPINEAU (5'11" 160 lbs.)
   b. Ottawa, Ontario, January 15, 1980
   Belleville Bulls (OHL)/Drafted 46th overall by Los Angeles in 1998

JEREMY REICH (6'1" 190 lbs.)
   b. Craik, Saskatchewan, February 11, 1979
   Swift Current Broncos (WHL)/Drafted 39th overall by Chicago in 1997

TYLER RENNETTE (6'1" 184 lbs.)
   b. North Bay, Ontario, April 16, 1979
   Erie Otters (OHL)/Drafted 40th overall by St. Louis in 1997
   Suffered a concussion during camp and sent home

ALEX TANGUAY (6' 180 lbs.)
   b. Ste.-Justine, Quebec, November 21, 1979
   Halifax Mooseheads (QMJHL)/Drafted 12th overall by Colorado in 1998

DANIEL TKACZUK (6'1" 190 lbs.)
   b. Toronto, Ontario, June 10, 1979
   Barrie Colts (OHL)/Drafted 6th overall by Calgary in 1997

JASON WARD (6'2" 190 lbs.)
   b. Chapleau, Ontario, January 16, 1979
   Windsor Spitfires (OHL)/Drafted 11th overall by Montreal in 1997

MATT ZUTEK (6'4" 218 lbs.)
   b. Oakville, Ontario, March 12, 1979
   Ottawa 67's (OHL)/Drafted 15th overall by Los Angeles in 1997

TOURNAMENT FORMAT

The ten participating nations are divided into two pools of five teams each, the top four advancing to the medal round, the bottom team from each playing a two-game total goals series to determine which team is relegated to the "B" pool for the 2000 tournament. The fourth team from one division plays the first team from the other, and vice versa, and the second from one plays the third from the other in a one-game elimination format.

SCHEDULE

Group A	Group B
CANADA	Belarus*
Czech Republic	Kazakhstan
Finland	Russia
Slovakia	Sweden
United States	Switzerland
* promoted from B pool in 1998	

December 26	Brandon	Czech Republic vs. Slovakia
	Winnipeg	Finland vs. United States
	Winnipeg	Sweden vs. Russia
	Selkirk	Belarus vs. Switzerland
December 27	Brandon	Canada vs. Slovakia
	Portage	Kazakhstan vs. Belarus
December 28	Winnipeg	Canada vs. Finland
	Brandon	Czech Republic vs. United States
	Winnipeg	Switzerland vs. Sweden
	Portage	Russia vs. Kazakhstan
December 29	Winnipeg	Slovakia vs. Finland
	Brandon	Belarus vs. Russia
December 30	Winnipeg	Canada vs. Czech Republic
	Selkirk	Slovakia vs. United States
	Brandon	Switzerland vs. Kazakhstan
	Morden	Sweden vs. Belarus
December 31	Winnipeg	Canada vs. United States
	Selkirk	Finland vs. Czech Republic
	Brandon	Russia vs. Switzerland
	Teulon	Kazakhstan vs. Sweden

January 2	Winnipeg	Quarter-final	B2 vs. A3
	Winnipeg	Quarter-final	A2 vs. B3
January 3	Winnipeg	Relegation	A4 vs. B5
	Portage	Relegation	B4 vs. A5
January 4	Winnipeg	B1 vs. winner of A2/B3	
	Brandon	Loser B2/A3 vs. Loser A2/B3	
	Winnipeg	A1 vs. Winner of B2/A3	
	Selkirk	Relegation	A5 vs. B5
	Morden	Relegation	A4 vs. B4
January 5	Winnipeg	Bronze Medal	Semi-final losers
	Winnipeg	Gold Medal	Semi-final winners

TEAM CANADA GUIDE AND RECORD BOOK FOR THE WORLD JUNIOR CHAMPIONSHIPS

ALL-TIME PLAYER AND COACHING REGISTER

For player register, statistics are for games played, goals, assists, points, final placing of team; for goalies, statistics are for games played, won-lost-tied record, minutes played, goals against, shutouts, goals against average, assists, penalty minutes, final placing of team

PLAYER REGISTER

CHAD ALLAN Defence 6'1" 192 lbs.
b. Saskatoon, Saskatchewan, July 12, 1976

1995	7	0	0	0	4	G
1996	6	1	0	1	6	G
2 years	13	1	0	1	10	G/G

JASON ALLISON Forward 6'3" 205 lbs.
b. North York, Ontario, May 29, 1975

1994	7	3	6	9	2	G
1995	7	3	12	15	6	G
2 years	14	6	18	24	8	G/G

RAY ALLISON Forward 6' 199 lbs.
b. Cranbrook, British Columbia, March 4, 1959

| 1979 | 5 | 0 | 5 | 5 | 4 | 5th |

JOHN ANDERSON Forward 5'11" 189 lbs.
b. Toronto, Ontario, March 28, 1957

| 1977 | 7 | 10 | 5 | 15 | 4 | S |

DAVE ANDREYCHUK Forward 6'3" 195 lbs.
b. Hamilton, Ontario, September 29, 1963

| 1983 | 7 | 6 | 5 | 11 | 14 | B |

CHRIS ARMSTRONG Defence 6'1" 184 lbs.
b. Regina, Saskatchewan, June 26, 1975

| 1994 | 6 | 0 | 1 | 1 | 0 | G |

SCOTT ARNIEL Forward 6'1" 170 lbs.
b. Kingston, Ontario, September 17, 1962

1981	5	3	1	4	4	7th
1982	7	5	6	11	4	G
2 years	12	8	7	15	8	G

FRED ARTHUR Defence 6'5" 210 lbs.
b. Toronto, Onario, March 6, 1961

| 1981 | 5 | 0 | 2 | 2 | 10 | 7th |

ADRIAN AUCOIN Defence 6'1" 194 lbs.
b. Ottawa, Ontario, July 3, 1973

| 1993 | 7 | 0 | 1 | 1 | 8 | G |

WARREN BABE Forward 6'3" 192 lbs.
b. Bow Island, Alberta, September 7, 1968

| 1988 | 7 | 0 | 2 | 2 | 10 | G |

WAYNE BABYCH Forward 5'11" 191 lbs.
b. Edmonton, Alberta, June 6, 1958

| 1978 | 6 | 5 | 5 | 10 | 4 | B |

DREW BANNISTER Defence 6'1" 195 lbs.
b. Belleville, Ontario, September 4, 1974

| 1994 | 7 | 0 | 4 | 4 | 10 | G |

STU BARNES Centre 5'11" 175 lbs.
b. Spruce Grove, Alberta, December 25, 1970

| 1990 | 7 | 2 | 4 | 6 | 6 | G |

BOB BASSEN Forward 5'10" 180 lbs.
b. Calgary, Alberta, May 6, 1965

| 1985 | 7 | 2 | 0 | 2 | 8 | G |

NOLAN BAUMGARTNER Defence 6'1" 187 lbs. *b.* Calgary, Alberta, March 23, 1976

1995	7	0	1	1	4	G
1996	6	1	1	2	22	G
2 years	13	1	2	3	26	G/G

YVES BEAUDOIN Defence 5'11" 180 lbs.
b. Pointe-aux-Trembles, Quebec, January 7, 1965

| 1985 | 7 | 0 | 3 | 3 | 4 | G |

DAVE BECKON Forward 5'9" 173 lbs.
b. Burlington, Ontario, March 19, 1961

| 1980 | 5 | 2 | 2 | 4 | 2 | 5th |

STEVE BEGIN Forward 6' 188 lbs.
b. Trois-Rivieres, Quebec, June 14, 1978

| 1998 | 7 | 0 | 0 | 0 | 10 | 8th |

TIM BERNHARDT Goalie 5'9" 162 lbs.
b. Sarnia, Ontario, January 17, 1958

| 1978 | 3 | 3--0--0 | 180 | 6 | 1 | 2.000 | 0 | 3rd |

BRAD BERRY Defence 6'2" 190 lbs.
b. Bashaw, Alberta, April 1, 1965

| 1985 | 7 | 0 | 1 | 1 | 2 | G |

JEFF BES Forward 6' 186 lbs.
b. Tillsonburg, Ontario, July 31, 1973

| 1993 | 7 | 3 | 2 | 5 | 4 | G |

ALLAN BESTER Goalie 5'7" 150 lbs.
b. Hamilton, Ontario, March 26, 1964

| 1984 | 2 | 2--0--0 | 120 | 2 | 1 | 1.00 | 0 | 0 | 4th |

JEFF BEUKEBOOM Defence 6'4" 210 lbs.
b. Ajax, Ontario, March 28, 1965

| 1985 | 3 | 1 | 0 | 1 | 4 | G |

CRAIG BILLINGTON Goalie 5'10" 160 lbs.
b. London, Ontario, September 11, 1966

1985	5	3--0--2	300	12	1	2.60	0	0	G
1986	5	3--2--0	300	14	0	2.80	0	0	S
2 yrs	10	6--2--2	600	26	1	2.60	0	0	G/S

SEAN BLANCHARD Defence 6' 201 lbs.
b. Garson, Ontario, March 29, 1978

| 1998 | 7 | 0 | 2 | 2 | 8 | 8th |

FRED BOIMISTRUCK Defence 5'11" 191 lbs. *b.* Sudbury, Ontario, November 4, 1962

| 1981 | 5 | 3 | 0 | 3 | 8 | 7th |

BRAD BOMBARDIR Defence 6'2" 190 lbs.
b. Powell River, British Columbia, May 5, 1972

| 1992 | 7 | 0 | 3 | 3 | 4 | 6th |

JASON BOTTERILL Forward 6'3" 205 lbs.
b. Edmonton, Alberta, May 19, 1976

1994	6	1	0	1	8	G
1995	7	0	4	4	6	G
1996	6	1	3	4	2	G
3 years	19	2	7	9	16	G/G/G

JOEL BOUCHARD Defence 6' 190 lbs.
b. Montreal, Quebec, January 23, 1974

1993	7	0	0	0	0	G
1994	7	0	1	1	10	G
2 years	14	0	1	1	10	G/G

PAUL BOUTILIER Defence 6' 190 lbs.
b. Halifax, Nova Scotia, May 3, 1963

1982	7	2	4	6	4	G
1983	7	2	3	5	2	B
2 years	14	4	7	11	6	G/B

TERRY BOVAIR Forward 6' 198 lbs.
b. Burlington, Ontario, January 15, 1960

| 1980 | 5 | 2 | 2 | 4 | 10 | 5th |

CURTIS BOWEN Forward 6'1" 189 lbs.
b. Kenora, Ontario, March 24, 1974

1994	7	2	0	2	10	G

BRIAN BRADLEY Forward 5'10" 170 lbs.
b. Kitchener, Ontario, January 21, 1965

1985	7	7	5	12	2	G

MATT BRADLEY Forward 6'1" 188 lbs.
b. Stittsville, Ontario, June 13, 1978

1998	7	1	1	2	2	8th

ERIC BREWER Defence 6'3" 196 lbs.
b. Kamloops, British Columbia,
April 17, 1979

1998	7	0	2	2	8	8th

DANIEL BRIERE Forward 5'9" 160 lbs.
b. Gatineau, Quebec, October 6, 1977

1997	7	2	4	6	4	G

ROB BRIND'AMOUR Forward 6' 190 lbs.
b. Ottawa, Ontario, August 9, 1970

1989	7	2	3	5	4	4th

PATRICE BRISEBOIS Defence 6'1" 170 lbs.
b. Montreal, Quebec, January 27, 1971

1990	7	2	2	4	6	G
1991	7	1	6	7	2	G
2 years	14	3	8	11	8	G/G

CURTIS BROWN Forward 6' 182 lbs.
b. Seniac, Saskatchewan,
February 12, 1976

1996	5	0	1	1	2	G

KEITH BROWN Defence 6'1" 192 lbs.
b. Corner Brook, Newfoundland,
May 6, 1960

1979	5	0	2	2	0	5th

ROB BROWN Forward 5'11" 188 lbs.
b. Kingston, Ontario, April 10, 1968

1988	7	6	2	8	2	G

SEAN BURKE Goalie 6'3" 195 lbs.
b. Windsor, Ontario, January 29, 1967

1986	2	2--0--0	120	7	0	3.50	0	0	S

GARTH BUTCHER Defence 6' 196 lbs.
b. Regina, Saskatchewan, January 8, 1963

1982	7	1	3	4	0	G

LYNDON BYERS Forward 6'1" 185 lbs.
b. Nipawin, Saskatchewan,
February 29, 1964

1984	6	1	1	2	4	4th

ERIC CALDER Defence 6'1" 184 lbs.
b. Kitchener, Ontario, July 26, 1963

1981	5	1	0	1	4	7th

BILL CAMPBELL Defence 6' 170 lbs.
b. Montreal, Quebec, March 20, 1964

1981	5	0	1	1	2	7th

FRANK CAPRICE Goalie 5'9" 149 lbs.
b. Hamilton, Ontario, May 12, 1962

1982	3	3--0--0	180	7	0	2.33	0	0	G

TERRY CARKNER Defence 6'4" 202 lbs.
b. Smiths Falls, Ontario, March 7, 1966

1986	7	0	4	4	0	S

ANSON CARTER Forward 6'1" 175 lbs.
b. Toronto, Ontario, June 6, 1974

1994	7	3	2	5	0	G

ANDREW CASSELS Forward 5'11" 187 lbs.
b. Bramalea, Ontario, July 23, 1969

1989	7	2	5	7	2	4th

BRUCE CASSIDY Defence 6'1" 180 lbs.
b. Ottawa, Ontario, May 20, 1965

1984	7	0	1	1	4	4th

ANDRE CHARTRAIN Forward 5'8" 175 lbs.
b. Beaconsfield, Quebec, March 24, 1962

1981	5	2	1	3	2	7th

STEVE CHIASSON Defence 6′ 200 lbs.
b. Barrie, Ontario, April 14, 1967

| 1987 | 6 | 2 | 2 | 4 | 16 | DQ |

DAVE CHYZOWSKI Forward 6′1″ 192 lbs.
b. Edmonton, Alberta, July 11, 1971

| 1990 | 7 | 9 | 4 | 13 | 2 | G |

DINO CICCARELLI Forward 5′11″ 185 lbs.
b. Sarnia, Ontario, February 8, 1960

| 1980 | 5 | 5 | 1 | 6 | 2 | 5th |

ROB CIMETTA Forward 6′1″ 191 lbs.
b. Toronto, Ontario, February 15, 1970

| 1989 | 7 | 7 | 4 | 11 | 4 | 4th |

CARMINE CIRELLA Forward 6′4″ 215 lbs.
b. Hamilton, Ontario, January 16, 1960

| 1980 | 5 | 2 | 3 | 5 | 14 | 5th |

JOE CIRELLA Defence 6′2″ 190 lbs.
b. Stoney Creek, Ontario, May 9, 1963

| 1983 | 7 | 0 | 0 | 0 | 6 | B |

WENDEL CLARK Forward 5′11″ 190 lbs.
b. Kelvington, Saskatchewan,
October 25, 1966

| 1985 | 7 | 4 | 2 | 6 | 10 | G |

DAN CLOUTIER Goalie 6′1″ 187 lbs
b. Mont-Laurier, Quebec, April 22, 1976

| 1995 | 3 | 3--0--0 | 180 | 8 | 0 | 2.67 | 0 | 0 | G |

AL CONROY Forward 5′7″ 165 lbs.
b. Calgary, Alberta, January 17, 1966

| 1986 | 7 | 4 | 4 | 8 | 6 | S |

JOE CONTINI Forward 5′10″ 178 lbs.
b. Galt, Ontario, January 29, 1957

| 1977 | 7 | 4 | 6 | 10 | 38 | S |

BRANDON CONVERY Forward 6′1″ 180 lbs.
b. Kingston, Ontario, February 4, 1974

| 1994 | 7 | 1 | 0 | 1 | 2 | G |

MATT COOKE Forward 6′1″ 195 lbs.
b. Stirling, Ontario, September 7, 1978

| 1998 | 6 | 1 | 1 | 2 | 6 | 8th |

YVON CORRIVEAU Forward 6′1″ 200 lbs.
b. Welland, Ontario, February 8, 1967

| 1987 | 6 | 2 | 1 | 3 | 4 | DQ |

DANIEL CORSO Forward 5′10″ 161 lbs.
b. St. Hubert, Quebec, April 3, 1978

| 1998 | 7 | 0 | 3 | 3 | 4 | 8th |

SHAYNE CORSON Forward 6′1″ 187 lbs.
b. Midland, Ontario, August 13, 1966

1985	7	3	3	6	2	G
1986	7	7	7	14	6	S
2 years	14	10	10	20	8	G/S

ALAIN COTE Defence 5′11″ 200 lbs.
b. Montmagny, Quebec, April 14, 1967

| 1986 | 7 | 1 | 4 | 5 | 6 | S |

SYLVAIN COTE Defence 6′ 175 lbs.
b. Quebec City, Quebec, January 19, 1966

1984	7	0	1	1	13	4th
1986	7	1	4	5	4	S
2 years	14	1	5	6	17	S

YVES COURTEAU Forward 6′1″ 185 lbs.
b. Montreal, Quebec, April 25, 1964

| 1984 | 7 | 0 | 1 | 1 | 0 | 4th |

RUSS COURTNALL Forward 5′10″ 175 lbs.
b. Duncan, British Columbia, June 2, 1965

| 1984 | 7 | 7 | 6 | 13 | 0 | 4th |

LARRY COURVILLE Forward 6′2″ 184 lbs.
b. Timmins, Ontario, April 2, 1975

| 1995 | 7 | 2 | 3 | 5 | 6 | G |

MIKE CRAIG Forward 6′1″ 167 lbs.
b. St. Mary's, Ontario, June 6, 1971

1990	7	3	0	3	8	G
1991	7	6	5	11	8	G
2 years	14	9	5	14	16	G/G

DALE CRAIGWELL Forward 5'10" 178 lbs.
b. Toronto, Ontario, April 24, 1971

| 1991 | 7 | 1 | 2 | 3 | 0 | G |

MARC CRAWFORD Forward 5'11" 183 lbs.
b. Belleville, Ontario, February 13, 1961

| 1981 | 5 | 1 | 3 | 4 | 4 | 7th |

ADAM CREIGHTON Forward 6'5" 200 lbs.
b. Burlington, Ontario, June 2, 1965

| 1985 | 7 | 8 | 4 | 12 | 4 | G |

DOUG CROSSMAN Defence 6'2" 190 lbs.
b. Peterborough, Ontario, May 30, 1960

| 1980 | 5 | 0 | 2 | 2 | 2 | 5th |

JASSEN CULLIMORE Defence 6'5" 220 lbs.
b. Simcoe, Ontario, December 4, 1972

| 1992 | 7 | 1 | 0 | 1 | 2 | 6th |

DAN CURRIE Forward 6' 178 lbs.
b. Burlington, Ontario, March 15, 1968

| 1988 | 7 | 4 | 3 | 7 | 2 | G |

DENIS CYR Forward 5'10" 180 lbs.
b. Verdun, Quebec, February 4, 1961

| 1981 | 5 | 2 | 1 | 3 | 0 | 7th |

PAUL CYR Forward 5'11" 185 lbs.
b. Port Alberti, British Columbia,
October 31, 1963

1982	7	4	6	10	12	G
1983	7	1	3	4	19	B
2 years	14	5	9	14	31	G/B

ALEXANDRE DAIGLE Forward 6' 165 lbs.
b. Montreal, Quebec, February 7, 1975

1993	7	0	6	6	27	G
1995	7	2	8	10	4	G
2 years	14	2	14	16	31	G/G

J.J. DAIGNEAULT Defence 5'11" 180 lbs.
b. Montreal, Quebec, October 12, 1965

| 1984 | 7 | 0 | 2 | 2 | 2 | 4th |

PAT DALEY Forward 6'1" 176 lbs.
b. Marieville, France, March 27, 1959

| 1978 | 6 | 3 | 2 | 5 | 2 | B |

KIMBI DANIELS Forward 5'10" 175 lbs.
b. Brandon, Manitoba, January 19, 1972

| 1992 | 7 | 3 | 4 | 7 | 16 | 6th |

JASON DAWE Forward 5'10" 193 lbs.
b. North York, Ontario, May 29, 1973

| 1993 | 7 | 3 | 3 | 6 | 8 | G |

ERIC DAZE Forward 6'5" 204 lbs.
b. Montreal, Quebec, July 2, 1975

| 1995 | 7 | 8 | 2 | 10 | 0 | G |

GILBERT DELORME Defence 5'11"
202 lbs. b. Boucherville, Quebec,
November 25, 1962

| 1981 | 5 | 1 | 0 | 1 | 0 | 7th |

MARC DENIS Goalie 6'1" 193 lbs.
b. Montreal, Quebec, August 1, 1977

1996	2	2--0--0	120	2	0	1.00	0	0	G
1997	7	5--0--2	420	13	1	1.86	0	0	G
2 yrs	9	7--0--2	540	15	1	1.67	0	0G/G

DALE DERKATCH Forward 5'6" 140 lbs.
b. Preeceville, Saskatchewan,
October 17, 1964

1983	7	3	4	7	2	B
1984	7	5	0	5	4	4th
2 years	14	8	4	12	6	B

PHILIPPE DEROUVILLE Goalie 6'2"
180 lbs. b. Victoriaville, Quebec,
August 7, 1974

| 1993 | 1 | 0--1--0 | 60 | 7 | 0 | 7.00 | 0 | 0 | G |

ERIC DESJARDINS Defence 6' 182 lbs.
b. Rouyn, Quebec, June 14, 1969

1988	7	0	0	0	6	G
1989	7	1	4	5	6	4th
2 years	14	1	4	5	12	G

BOYD DEVEREAUX Forward 6'2" 190 lbs.
b. Seaforth, Ontario, April 16, 1978

| 1997 | 7 | 4 | 0 | 4 | 0 | G |

GERALD DIDUCK Defence 6'2" 202 lbs.
b. Edmonton, Alberta, April 6, 1965

| 1984 | 7 | 0 | 0 | 0 | 4 | 4th |

ROB DIMAIO Forward 5'10" 187 lbs.
b. Calgary, Alberta, February 19, 1968

| 1988 | 7 | 1 | 0 | 1 | 10 | G |

JASON DOIG Defence 6'3" 218 lbs.
b. Montreal, Quebec, January 29, 1977

| 1997 | 7 | 0 | 2 | 2 | 37 | G |

BOBBY DOLLAS Defence 6'2" 210 lbs.
b. Montreal, Quebec, January 31, 1965

| 1985 | 7 | 0 | 2 | 2 | 12 | G |

HNAT DOMENICHELLI
Forward 5'11" 179 lbs.
b. Edmonton, Alberta, February 17, 1976

| 1996 | 6 | 2 | 3 | 5 | 6 | G |

SHEAN DONOVAN Forward 6'1" 172 lbs.
b. Timmins, Ontario, January 22, 1975

| 1995 | 7 | 0 | 0 | 0 | 6 | G |

PETER DOURIS Forward 6' 195 lbs.
b. Toronto, Ontario, February 19, 1966

| 1986 | 7 | 4 | 2 | 6 | 6 | S |

KRIS DRAPER Forward 5'10" 189 lbs.
b. Toronto, Ontario, May 24, 1971

1990	7	0	2	2	4	G
1991	7	1	3	4	0	G
2 years	14	1	5	6	4	G/G

CHRISTIAN DUBE Forward 5'11" 186 lbs.
b. Sherbrooke, Quebec, April 25, 1977

1996	6	4	2	6	0	G
1997	6	4	2	6	0	G
2 years	12	8	4	12	0	G/G

YANICK DUBE Forward 5'9" 170 lbs.
b. Gaspe, Quebec, June 14, 1974

| 1994 | 7 | 5 | 5 | 10 | 10 | G |

RON DUGUAY Forward 6'2" 210 lbs.
b. Sudbury, Ontario, July 6, 1957

| 1977 | 7 | 1 | 4 | 5 | 11 | S |

JEAN-PIERRE DUMONT Forward 6' 195 lbs.
b. Montreal, Quebec, April 1, 1978

| 1998 | 7 | 0 | 0 | 0 | 0 | 8th |

KARL DYKHUIS Defence 6'2" 184 lbs.
b. Sept-Iles, Quebec, July 8, 1972

1991	7	0	3	3	2	G
1992	0	0	0	8	6th	
2 years	14	0	3	3	10	G

MIKE EAGLES Forward 5'11" 185 lbs.
b. Sussex, New Brunswick, March 7, 1963

| 1983 | 7 | 2 | 4 | 6 | 2 | B |

BRUCE EAKIN Forward 5'10" 185 lbs.
b. Winnipeg, Manitoba,
September 28, 1962

| 1982 | 7 | 4 | 7 | 11 | 4 | G |

JEFF EATOUGH Forward 5'9" 168 lbs.
b. Toronto, Ontario, June 2, 1963

| 1981 | 5 | 1 | 2 | 3 | 4 | 7th |

PAT ELYNUIK Forward 6' 181 lbs.
b. Foam Lake, Saskatchewan,
October 30, 1967

| 1987 | 6 | 6 | 5 | 11 | 2 | DQ |

DEAN EVASON Forward 5'10" 175 lbs.
b. Flin Flon, Manitoba, August 22, 1964

| 1984 | 7 | 6 | 1 | 7 | 0 | 4th |

PAT FALLOON Forward 5'10" 192 lbs.
b. Foxwarren, Manitoba,
September 22, 1972

| 1991 | 7 | 3 | 3 | 6 | 2 | G |

DAVE FENYVES Defence 5'11" 188 lbs.
b. Dunnville, Ontario, April 29, 1960

| 1980 | 5 | 0 | 0 | 0 | 8 | 5th |

BRAD FERENCE Defence 6'3" 190 lbs.
b. Calgary, Alberta, April 2, 1979

| 1998 | 7 | 0 | 1 | 1 | 6 | 8th |

EMMANUEL FERNANDEZ Goalie 6' 170 lbs.
b. Etobicoke, Ontario, August 27, 1974

| 1994 | 3 | 3--0--0 | 180 | 10 | 0 | 3.33 | 0 | 0 | G |

STEPHANE FISET Goalie 6' 175 lbs.
b. Montreal, Quebec, June 17, 1970

1989	6	3--2--1	329	18	0	3.27	0	0	4th
1990	7	5--1--1	420	18	1	2.57	0	0	G
2 yrs	13	8--3--2	749	36	1	2.88	0	0	G

BORIS FISTRIC Defence 6'3" 220 lbs.
b. Edmonton, Alberta, September 15, 1960

| 1979 | 5 | 0 | 0 | 0 | 22 | 5th |

PAT FLATLEY Forward 6'2 195 lbs.
b. Toronto, Ontario, October 3, 1963

| 1983 | 7 | 4 | 0 | 4 | 6 | B |

THEOREN FLEURY Forward 5'8" 160 lbs.
b. Oxbow, Saskatchewan, June 29, 1968

1987	6	2	3	5	2	DQ
1988	7	6	2	8	4	G
2 years	13	8	5	13	6	G

MIKE FORBES Defence 6'2" 200 lbs.
b. Brampton, Ontario, September 20, 1957

| 1977 | 7 | 0 | 1 | 1 | 22 | S |

COREY FOSTER Defence 6'3" 202 lbs.
b. Ottawa, Ontario, October 27, 1969

| 1989 | 7 | 1 | 3 | 4 | 4 | 4th |

DWIGHT FOSTER Forward 5'10" 190 lbs.
b. Toronto, Ontario, April 2, 1957

| 1977 | 7 | 2 | 4 | 6 | 4 | S |

NORM FOSTER Goalie 5'9" 175 lbs.
b. Vancouver, British Columbia, February 10, 1965

| 1985 | 2 | 2--0--0 | 120 | 1 | 1 | 0.50 | 0 | 0 | G |

GUY FOURNIER Forward 5'11" 176 lbs.
b. Portneuf, Quebec, January 30, 1962

| 1981 | 5 | 1 | 2 | 3 | 0 | 7th |

JIM FOX Forward 5'8" 170 lbs.
b. Coniston, Ontario, May 18, 1960

| 1980 | 5 | 3 | 2 | 5 | 0 | 5th |

CURT FRASER Forward 6' 190 lbs.
b. Cincinnati, Ohio, January 12, 1958

| 1978 | 5 | 0 | 2 | 2 | 0 | B |

JEFF FRIESEN Forward 5'11" 185 lbs.
b. Meadow Lake, Saskatchewan, August 5, 1976

1994	5	0	2	2	0	G
1995	7	5	2	7	4	G
2 years	12	5	4	9	4	G/G

DAVE GAGNER Forward 5'10" 185 lbs.
b. Chatham, Ontario, December 11, 1964

| 1984 | 7 | 4 | 2 | 6 | 4 | 4th |

BILL GARDNER Forward 5'10" 170 lbs.
b. Toronto, Ontario, May 19, 1960

| 1980 | 5 | 0 | 4 | 4 | 14 | 5th |

MATHIEU GARON Goalie 6'1" 193 lbs.
b. Chandler, Quebec, January 9, 1978

| 1998 | 5 | 2--3--0 | 284 | 14 | 2 | 2.96 | 0 | 0 | 8th |

MIKE GARTNER Forward 6' 180 lbs.
b. Ottawa, Ontario, October 29, 1959

| 1978 | 6 | 3 | 3 | 6 | 4 | B |

JEAN-MARC GAULIN Forward 5'10" 180 lbs.
b. Balve, Germany, March 3, 1962

| 1981 | 5 | 2 | 0 | 2 | 4 | 7th |

DENIS GAUTHIER Defence 6'1" 195 lbs.
b. Montreal, Quebec, October 1, 1976

| 1996 | 6 | 1 | 1 | 2 | 6 | G |

AARON GAVEY Forward 6' 170 lbs.
b. Sudbury, Ontario, February 22, 1974

1994	7	4	2	6	26	G

MARTIN GELINAS Forward 5'11" 195 lbs.
b. Shawinigan, Quebec, June 5, 1970

1989	7	0	2	2	8	4th

MARTIN GENDRON Forward 5'8" 180 lbs.
b. Valleyfield, Quebec, February 15, 1974

1993	7	5	2	7	2	G
1994	7	6	4	10	6	G
2 years	14	11	6	17	8	G/G

DOUG GILMOUR Forward 5'11" 157 lbs.
b. Kingston, Ontario, June 25, 1963

1981	5	0	0	0	0	7th

RICK GIRARD Forward 5'11" 176 lbs.
b. Edmonton, Alberta, May 1, 1974

1994	7	6	3	9	2	G

ROBB GORDON Forward 6' 195 lbs.
b. Surrey, British Columbia,
January 13, 1976

1996	6	0	4	4	0	G

TOM GRAOVAC Goalie 6'3" 184 lbs.
b. January 26, 1961

1981	3	1--0--0	87	5	0	3.45	0	0	7th

CHRIS GRATTON Forward 6'3" 198 lbs.
b. Brantford, Ontario, July 5, 1975

1993	7	2	2	4	6	G

DAN GRATTON Forward 6'1" 200 lbs.
b. Brantford, Ontario, December 17, 1966

1985	7	2	3	5	16	G

ADAM GRAVES Forward 6'1" 191 lbs.
b. Toronto, Ontario, April 12, 1968

1988	7	5	0	5	4	G

JEFF GREENLAW Forward 6'2" 195 lbs.
b. Toronto, Ontario, February 28, 1968

1986	7	3	1	4	4	S

WAYNE GRETZKY Forward 5'11" 165 lbs.
b. Brantford, Ontario, January 26, 1961

1978	6	8	9	17	2	B

MARC HABSCHIED Forward 6' 180 lbs.
b. Wymark, Saskatchewan, March 1, 1963

1982	7	6	6	12	2	G

KEVIN HALLER Defence 6'2" 180 lbs.
b. Trochu, Alberta, December 5, 1970

1990	7	2	2	4	8	G

CRAIG HALLIDAY Forward 5'10" 191 lbs.
b. May 2, 1962

1981	5	0	0	0	2	7th

HUGH HAMILTON Defence 6'1" 175 lbs.
b. Saskatoon, Saskatchewan,
February 11, 1977

1997	7	0	0	0	6	G

DAVID HARLOCK Defence 6'2" 195 lbs.
b. Toronto, Ontario, March 16, 1971

1991	7	0	2	2	2	G

CRAIG HARTSBURG Defence 6'1" 190 lbs.
b. Stratford, Ontario, June 29, 1959

1978	6	1	4	5	8	B

TODD HARVEY Forward 6' 190 lbs.
b. Hamilton, Ontario, February 17, 1975

1994	7	4	3	7	6	G
1995	7	6	0	6	4	G
2 years	14	10	3	13	10	G/G

DALE HAWERCHUK Forward 5'11" 170 lbs.
b. Toronto, Ontario, April 4, 1963

1981	5	5	4	9	2	7th

GREG HAWGOOD Defence 5'9" 185 lbs.
b. Edmonton, Alberta, August 10, 1968

1987	6	2	2	4	6	DQ
1988	7	1	8	9	6	G
2 years	13	3	10	13	12	G

DWAYNE HAY Forward 6'1" 205 lbs.
b. London, Ontario, February 11, 1977

1997	7	0	0	0	2	G

STEVE HAZLETT Forward 5'9" 170 lbs.
b. Sarnia, Ontario, December 12, 1957

1977	7	6	1	7	2	S

RANDY HEATH Forward 5'8" 165 lbs.
b. Vancouver, British Columbia,
November 11, 1964

1984	7	3	6	9	12	4th

JASON HERTER Defence 6'1" 196 lbs.
b. Hafford, Saskatchewan, October 2, 1970

1990	7	0	1	1	2	G

ANDRE HIDI Forward 6'1" 198 lbs.
b. Toronto, Ontario, June 5, 1960

1980	5	2	0	2	2	5th

BILL HOBBINS Forward 5'10" 195 lbs.
b. Edmonton, Alberta, April 13, 1960

1979	5	0	1	1	4	5th

DAN HODGSON Forward 5'11" 170 lbs.
b. Pt. Vermillion, Alberta, August 29, 1965

1984	7	1	4	5	4	4th
1985	7	5	2	7	0	G
2 years	14	6	6	12	4	G

JOSH HOLDEN Forward 6' 170 lbs.
b. Calgary, Alberta, January 18, 1978

1998	7	4	0	4	16	8th

JASON HOLLAND Defence 6'2" 200 lbs.
b. Morinville, Alberta, April 30, 1976

1996	6	2	1	3	4	G

DENIS HOULE Forward 5'11" 175 lbs.
b. Sudbury, Ontario, August 19, 1958

1977	7	0	1	1	0	S

BRUCE HOWES Defence 6'2" 201 lbs.
b. New Westminster, British Columbia,
July 4, 1960

1979	5	0	1	1	2	5th

WILLIE HUBER Defence 6'5" 228 lbs.
b. Strasskirchen, Germany,
January 15, 1958

1977	7	1	2	3	11	S
1978	6	0	2	2	2	B
2 years	13	1	4	5	13	S/B

KERRY HUFFMAN Defence 6'2" 185 lbs.
b. Peterborough, Ontario, January 3, 1968

1987	6	0	1	1	4	DQ

RYAN HUGHES Forward 6'1" 180 lbs.
b. Montreal, Quebec, January 17, 1972

1992	7	0	1	1	0	6th

JODY HULL Forward 6'2" 200 lbs.
b. Cambridge, Ontario, February 2, 1969

1988	7	2	1	3	2	G

DAVE HUNTER Forward 5'11" 195 lbs.
b. Petrolia, Ontario, January 1, 1958

1977	7	6	0	6	4	S

JAROME IGINLA Forward 6'1" 193 lbs.
b. St. Albert, Alberta, July 1, 1977

1996	6	5	7	12	4	G

RALPH INTRANUOVO Forward 5'8" 170 lbs.
b. East York, Ontario, December 11, 1973

1993	7	3	2	5	4	G

RANDY IRVING Forward 6'1" 199 lbs.
b. Victoria, British Columbia,
August 12, 1959

1979	5	4	2	6	8	5th

BRAD ISBISTER Forward 6'2" 225 lbs.
b. Edmonton, Alberta, May 7, 1977

1997	7	4	3	7	8	G

RICHARD JACKMAN Defence 6'2" 171 lbs.
b. Toronto, Ontario, June 28, 1978

1997	7	2	0	2	0	G

JEFF JACKSON Forward 6' 195 lbs.
b. Chatham, Ontario, April 24, 1965

1985	7	1	7	8	10	G

AL JENSEN Goalie 5'10" 180 lbs.
  b. Hamilton, Ontario, November 27, 1958

1977	7	5--1--1	420	20	1	2.86	0	0	S
1978	3	1--2--0	180	12	0	4.00	0	0	B
2 yrs	10	6--3--1	600	32	1	3.16	0	0	S/B

TREVOR JOHANSEN Defence 5'9" 200 lbs.
  b. Thunder Bay, Ontario, March 30, 1957

| 1977 | 7 | 0 | 3 | 3 | 10 | S |

GREG JOHNSON Forward 5'10" 173 lbs.
  b. Thunder Bay, Ontario, March 16, 1971

| 1991 | 7 | 4 | 2 | 6 | 0 | G |

GREG JOHNSTON Forward 6'1" 190 lbs.
  b. Barrie, Ontario, January 14, 1965

| 1985 | 7 | 2 | 0 | 2 | 2 | G |

YVAN JOLY Forward 5'8" 170 lbs.
  b. Hawkesbury, Ontario, February 6, 1960

1979	5	2	0	2	2	5th
1980	5	3	0	3	8	5th
2 years	10	5	0	5	10	—

CHRIS JOSEPH Defence 6'2" 194 lbs.
  b. Burnaby, British Columbia,
  September 10, 1969

1987	6	1	1	2	14	DQ
1988	7	1	2	3	8	G
2 years	13	2	3	5	22	G

ED JOVANOVSKI Defence 6'2" 210 lbs.
  b. Windsor, Ontario, June 26, 1976

| 1995 | 7 | 2 | 0 | 2 | 4 | G |

STEVE JUNKER Forward 6' 182 lbs.
  b. Castlegar, British Columbia,
  June 25, 1972

| 1992 | 7 | 2 | 2 | 4 | 4 | 6th |

PAUL KARIYA Forward 5'10" 157 lbs.
  b. Vancouver, British Columbia,
  October 16, 1974

1992	6	1	1	2	2	6th
1993	7	2	6	8	2	G
2 years	13	3	7	10	4	G

MIKE KEANE Forward 5'10" 179 lbs.
  b. Winnipeg, Manitoba, May 29, 1967

| 1987 | 6 | 0 | 0 | 0 | 4 | DQ |

MIKE KEATING Forward 6' 185 lbs.
  b. Toronto, Ontario, January 21, 1957

| 1977 | 7 | 0 | 2 | 2 | 0 | S |

JOHN PAUL KELLY Forward 6' 212 lbs.
  b. Edmonton, Alberta, November 15, 1959

| 1979 | 5 | 0 | 0 | 0 | 10 | 5th |

SHELDON KENNEDY
  Forward 5'10" 170 lbs.
  b. Elkhorn, Manitoba, June 15, 1969

1988	7	4	2	6	6	G
1989	7	3	4	7	14	4th
2 years	14	7	6	13	20	G

TREVOR KIDD Goalie 6'1" 168 lbs.
  b. Dugald, Manitoba, March 29, 1972

1991	6	4--1--0	340	13	1	2.25	0	0	G
1992	7	2--3--2	420	29	0	4.14	0	0	6th
2 yrs	13	6--4--2	760	42	1	3.32	0	0	G

JOHN KIRK Forward 6' 190 lbs.
  b. September 19, 1961

| 1981 | 5 | 4 | 3 | 7 | 24 | 7th |

TERRY KIRKHAM Forward 5'9" 162 lbs.
  b. Vancouver, British Columbia,
  February 4, 1959

| 1979 | 5 | 2 | 1 | 3 | 2 | 5th |

BILL KITCHEN Defence 6'1" 200 lbs.
  b. Schomberg, Ontario, October 2, 1960

| 1980 | 5 | 0 | 1 | 1 | 10 | 5th |

GORD KLUZAK Defence 6'4" 215 lbs.
  b. Climax, Saskatchewan, March 4, 1964

| 1982 | 7 | 0 | 1 | 1 | 4 | G |

ZENITH KOMARNISKI Defence 6'2" 190 lbs.
  b. Edmonto, Alberta, August 13, 1978

| 1998 | 7 | 0 | 0 | 0 | 26 | 8th |

GARY LACEY Forward 6'3" 202 lbs.
b. Sudbury, Ontario, May 24, 1964

| 1984 | 5 | 0 | 0 | 4 | 4th |

NATHAN LAFAYETTE Forward 6' 190 lbs.
b. New Westminster, British Columbia,
February 17, 1993

| 1993 | 7 | 3 | 1 | 4 | 0 | G |

RICK LAFERRIERE Goalie 5'9" 170 lbs.
b. Hawkesbury, Ontario, January 3, 1961

| 1980 | 4 | 2--2--0 | 240 | 13 | 0 | 3.25 | 0 | 2 | 5th |

DAN LAMBERT Defence 5'7" 173 lbs.
b. St. Boniface, Manitoba,
January 12, 1970

| 1989 | 7 | 1 | 2 | 3 | 4 | 4th |

DAYMOND LANGKOW
Forward 5'10" 170 lbs.
b. Sherwood Park, Alberta,
September 27, 1976

| 1996 | 5 | 3 | 3 | 6 | 2 | G |

MARC LANIEL Defence 6'1" 185 lbs.
b. Scarborough, Ontario, January 16, 1968

| 1988 | 7 | 1 | 2 | 3 | 6 | G |

RICK LANZ Defence 6'1" 195 lbs.
b. Karlouy Vary, Czechoslovakia,
September 16, 1961

| 1980 | 5 | 0 | 1 | 1 | 6 | 5th |

MARTIN LAPOINTE Forward 5'11" 194 lbs.
b. Ville Ste. Pierre, Quebec,
September 12, 1973

1991	7	0	3	3	2	G
1992	7	4	1	5	10	6th
1993	7	5	4	9	6	G
3 years	21	9	8	17	18	G/G

BRAD LARSEN Forward 6' 200 lbs.
b. Nakusp, British Columbia,
January 28, 1977

1996	6	1	1	2	4	G
1997	7	0	1	1	6	G
2 years	13	1	2	3	10	G/G

DAVID LATTA Forward 6' 187 lbs.
b. Thunder Bay, Ontario, January 3, 1967

| 1987 | 6 | 4 | 6 | 10 | 12 | DQ |

DEREK LAXDAL Forward 6'2" 196 lbs.
b. St. Boniface, Manitoba,
February 21, 1966

| 1986 | 7 | 1 | 4 | 5 | 6 | S |

JAMIE LEACH Forward 6'1" 195 lbs.
b. Winnipeg, Maitoba, August 25, 1969

| 1989 | 7 | 1 | 4 | 5 | 2 | 4th |

VINCENT LECAVALIER
Forward 6'4" 180 lbs.
b. Ile Bizard, Quebec, April 21, 1980

| 1998 | 7 | 1 | 1 | 2 | 4 | 8th |

GARY LEEMAN Defence 5'11" 168 lbs.
b. Toronto, Ontario, February 19, 1964

1983	7	1	2	3	2	B
1984	7	3	8	11	10	4th
2 years	14	4	10	14	12	B

MANNY LEGACE Goalie 5'9" 162 lbs.
b. Toronto, Ontario, February 4, 1973

| 1993 | 6 | 6--0--0 | 360 | 10 | 1 | 1.67 | 0 | 0 | G |

MOE LEMAY Forward 5'11" 185 lbs.
b. Saskatoon, Saskatchewan,
February 18, 1962

| 1982 | 7 | 2 | 0 | 2 | 4 | G |

CLAUDE LEMIEUX Forward 6' 220 lbs.
b. Buckingham, Quebec, July 16, 1965

| 1985 | 6 | 3 | 2 | 5 | 6 | G |

MARIO LEMIEUX Forward 6'2" 190 lbs.
b. Montreal, Quebec, October 5, 1965

| 1983 | 7 | 5 | 5 | 10 | 10 | B |

TREVOR LETOWSKI Forward 5'10" 175 lbs.
b. Thunder Bay, Ontario, April 5, 1977

| 1997 | 7 | 2 | 1 | 3 | 4 | G |

TREVOR LINDEN Forward 6′2″ 177 lbs.
b. Medicine Hat, Alberta, April 11, 1970

1988	7	1	0	1	0	G

ERIC LINDROS Forward 6′5″ 220 lbs.
b. Toronto, Ontario, February 28, 1973

1990	7	4	0	4	14	G
1991	7	6	11	17	6	G
1992	7	2	8	10	12	6th
3 years	21	12	19	31	32	G/G

DARCY LOEWEN Forward 5′10″ 185 lbs.
b. Calgary, Alberta, February 26, 1969

1989	7	1	1	2	12	4th

ROBERTO LUONGO Goalie 6′2″ 185 lbs.
b. Montreal, Quebec, April 4, 1979

1998	3	0--2--0	146	9	0	3.70	0	2	8th

GARY LUPUL Forward 5′9″ 172 lbs.
b. Powell River, British Columbia, April 4, 1959

1979	5	2	1	3	0	5th

JOHN MACLEAN Forward 6′ 195 lbs.
b. Oshawa, Ontario, November 20, 1964

1984	7	7	2	9	6	4th

SCOTT MACLEOD Forward 5′10″ 170 lbs.
b. Vancouver, British Columbia, May 17, 1959

1979	5	1	2	3	4	5th

STEWART MALGUNAS Defence 5′11″ 184 lbs.
b. Prince George, British Columbia, April 21, 1970

1990	7	0	1	1	0	G

MANNY MALHOTRA Forward 6′1″ 210 lbs.
b. Mississauga, Ontario, April 18, 1980

1998	7	0	0	0	0	8th

KENT MANDERVILLE Forward 6′3″ 193 lbs.
b. Edmonton, Alberta, April 12, 1971

1990	7	1	2	3	0	G
1991	7	1	6	7	0	G
2 years	14	2	8	10	0	G/G

CAMERON MANN Forward 6′ 190 lbs.
b. Thompson, Manitoba, April 20, 1977

1997	7	3	4	7	10	G

BRAD MARSH Defence 6′3″ 210 lbs.
b. London, Ontario, March 31, 1958

1977	7	1	3	4	16	S
1978	6	0	4	4	2	B
2 years	13	1	7	8	18	S/B

JASON MARSHALL Defence 6′2″ 188 lbs.
b. Cranbrook, British Columbia, February 22, 1971

1991	7	0	4	4	6	G

RICHARD MATVICHUK
Defence 6′2″ 190 lbs.
b. Edmonton, Alberta, February 5, 1973

1992	4	0	0	0	2	6th

BRAD MAY Forward 6′ 200 lbs.
b. Toronto, Ontario, November 29, 1971

1991	7	1	0	1	2	G

DEAN McAMMOND Defence 6′ 180 lbs.
b. Grand Cache, Alberta, June 15, 1973

1993	7	0	1	1	12	G

WAYNE McBEAN Defence 6′2″ 200 lbs.
b. Calgary, Alberta, February 21, 1969

1988	7	1	0	1	2	G

BRYAN McCABE Defence 6′2″ 185 lbs.
b. St. Catharines, Ontario, June 8, 1975

1994	7	0	0	0	6	G
1995	7	3	9	12	4	G
2 years	14	3	9	12	10	G/G

ALYN McCAULEY Forward 5′11″ 185 lbs.
b. Brockville, Ontario, May 29, 1977

1996	6	2	3	5	2	G
1997	7	0	5	5	2	G
2 years	13	2	8	10	4	G/G

DALE McCOURT Forward 5′10″ 180 lbs.
b. Falconbridge, Ontario, January 26, 1957

1977	7	10	8	18	14	S

SCOTT McCRADY Defence 6'2" 190 lbs.
b. Calgary, Alberta, October 30, 1968

1988	7	0	1	1	8	G

BRAD McCRIMMON Defence 5'11" 193 lbs.
b. Dodsland, Saskatchewan,
March 29, 1959

1978	6	0	2	2	4	B
1979	5	1	2	3	2	5th
2 years	11	1	4	5	6	B

JOHN McINTYRE Forward 6'1" 182 lbs.
b. Ravenswood, Ontario, April 29, 1969

1989	7	1	0	1	4	4th

TONY McKEGNEY Forward 6'1" 198 lbs.
b. Montreal, Quebec, February 15, 1958

1978	6	2	6	8	0	B

BRETT McLEAN Forward 5'10" 187 lbs.
b. Comox, British Columbia,
August 14, 1978

1998	7	1	1	2	4	8th

DAVE McLLWAIN Forward 6' 176 lbs.
b. Seaforth, Ontario, January 9, 1967

1987	6	4	3	7	2	DQ

ROLLIE MELANSON Goalie 5'10" 178 lbs.
b. Moncton, New Brunswick,
June 28, 1960

1979	2	0--0--0	120	3	0	1.50	0	0	5th

SCOTT MELLANBY Forward 6'1" 200 lbs.
b. Montreal, Quebec, June 11, 1966

1986	7	5	4	9	6	S

LARRY MELNYK Defence 6' 180 lbs.
b. New Westminster, British Columbia,
February 21, 1960

1979	5	1	1	2	2	5th

SCOTT METCALFE Forward 6' 192 lbs.
b. Mississauga, Ontario, January 6, 1967

1987	6	2	5	7	12	DQ

CORRADO MICALEF Goalie 5'8" 172 lbs.
b. Montreal, Quebec, April 20, 1961

1981	4	0--3--1	213	20	0	5.63	0	0	7th

CRAIG MILLS Forward 5'11" 190 lbs.
b. Toronto, Ontario, August 27, 1976

1996	6	0	0	0	4	G

JOHN MINER Defence 5'10" 180 lbs.
b. Moose Jaw, Saskatchewan,
August 28, 1965

1985	7	0	2	2	12	G

MIKE MOFFAT Goalie 5'11" 169 lbs.
b. Galt, Ontario, February 4, 1962

1982	4	3--0--1	240	7	1	1.75	0	0	G

MIKE MOLLER Forward 6'1" 190 lbs.
b. Calgary, Alberta, June 16, 1962

1982	7	5	9	14	6	G

RANDY MOLLER Defence 6'2" 205 lbs.
b. Red Deer, Alberta, August 23, 1963

1982	7	0	3	3	2	G

DAVE MORRISON Forward 6'1" 190 lbs.
b. Toronto, Ontario, June 12, 1962

1982	7	1	2	3	0	G

MARK MORRISON Forward 5'9" 160 lbs.
b. Delta, British Columbia,
March 11, 1963

1982	7	3	7	10	0	G
1983	7	3	2	5	0	B
2 years	14	6	9	15	0	G/B

GUS MORSCHAUSER Goalie 5'9" 163 lbs.
b. Kitchener, Ontario, March 26, 1969

1989	2	0--0--0	91	5	0	3.30	0	0	4th

DAVE MOYLAN Defence 6'2" 194 lbs.
b. Tillsonburg, Ontario, August 13, 1967

1986	7	1	2	3	0	S

KIRK MULLER Forward 6' 185 lbs.
b. Kingston, Ontario, February 8, 1966

1984	7	2	3	5	16	4th

JOE MURPHY Forward 6'1" 170 lbs.
b. London, Ontario, October 16, 1967

| 1986 | | 7 | 4 | 10 | 14 | 2 | S |

LARRY MURPHY Defence 6'1" 210 lbs.
b. Scarborough, Ontario, March 8, 1961

| 1980 | | 5 | 1 | 0 | 1 | 4 | 5th |

ROB MURPHY Forward 6'3" 203 lbs.
b. Hull, Quebec, April 7, 1969

| 1989 | | 7 | 1 | 0 | 1 | 8 | 4th |

MARTY MURRAY Forward 5'9" 160 lbs.
b. Deloraine, Manitoba, February 16, 1975

1994		7	1	3	4	4	G
1995		7	6	9	15	0	G
2 years		14	7	12	19	4	G/G

TROY MURRAY Forward 5'11" 190 lbs.
b. Calgary, Alberta, July 31, 1962

| 1982 | | 7 | 4 | 4 | 8 | 4 | G |

MIKE NEEDHAM Forward 5'10" 196 lbs.
b. Fort Saskatchewan, Alberta,
March 25, 1970

| 1990 | | 7 | 3 | 4 | 7 | 2 | G |

JEFF NELSON Forward 6'1" 180 lbs.
b. Prince Albert, Saskatchewan,
December 18, 1972

| 1992 | | 7 | 1 | 1 | 2 | 2 | 6th |

STEVE NEMETH Forward 5'9" 175 lbs.
b. Calgary, Alberta, February 11, 1967

| 1987 | | 6 | 4 | 4 | 8 | 4 | DQ |

ROB NIEDERMAYER Forward 6'1" 178 lbs.
b. Cassiar, British Columbia,
December 28, 1974

| 1993 | | 7 | 0 | 2 | 2 | 2 | G |

SCOTT NIEDERMAYER Defence 6' 200 lbs.
b. Edmonton, Alberta, August 31, 1973

1991		7	0	0	0	0	G
1992		7	0	0	0	10	6th
2 years		14	0	0	0	10	G

JOE NIEUWENDYK Forward 6'2" 187 lbs.
b. Oshawa, Ontario, September 10, 1966

| 1986 | | 7 | 5 | 7 | 12 | 6 | S |

DWAYNE NORRIS Forward 5'10" 178 lbs.
b. St. John's, Newfoundland,
January 8, 1970

| 1990 | | 7 | 2 | 4 | 6 | 2 | G |

GARY NYLUND Defence 6'4" 207 lbs.
b. Surrey, British Columbia,
October 28, 1963

| 1982 | | 7 | 1 | 3 | 4 | 0 | G |

SELMAR ODELEIN Defence 6'1" 190 lbs.
b. Quill Lake, Saskatchewan,
April 11, 1966

1985		7	1	5	6	8	G
1986		7	0	1	1	6	S
2 years		14	1	6	7	14	G/s

JOHN OGRODNICK Forward 6' 190 lbs.
b. Ottawa, Ontario, June 20, 1959

| 1979 | | 5 | 3 | 0 | 3 | 4 | 5th |

JEFF O'NEILL Forward 6' 186 lbs.
b. Richmond Hill, Ontario,
February 23, 1976

| 1995 | | 7 | 2 | 4 | 6 | 2 | G |

DAVE ORLESKI Forward 6'3" 210 lbs.
b. Edmonton, Alberta, December 26, 1959

| 1979 | | 5 | 2 | 0 | 2 | 0 | 5th |

MARK PATERSON Defence 5'11" 180 lbs.
b. Ottawa, Ontario, February 22, 1964

| 1984 | | 7 | 0 | 1 | 1 | 10 | 4th |

RICK PATERSON Forward 5'9" 187 lbs.
b. Kingston, Ontario, February 10, 1958

| 1978 | | 6 | 1 | 2 | 3 | 0 | B |

JAMES PATRICK Defence 6'2" 180 lbs.
b. Winnipeg, Manitoba, June 14, 1963

1982		7	0	2	2	6	G
1983		7	0	2	2	4	B
2 years		14	0	4	4	10	G/B

MIKE PECA   Forward 5'11" 175 lbs.
b. Toronto, Ontario, March 26, 1974

| 1994 | 7 | 2 | 2 | 4 | 8 | G |

DENIS PEDERSON   Forward 6'2" 195 lbs.
b. Prince Albert, Saskatchewan,
September 10, 1975

| 1995 | 7 | 2 | 2 | 4 | 0 | G |

MARK PEDERSON   Forward 6'1" 192 lbs.
b. Medicine Hat, Alberta, January 14, 1968

| 1988 | 7 | 1 | 2 | 3 | 4 | G |

SCOTT PELLERIN   Forward 5'11" 195 lbs.
b. Shediac, New Brunswick,
January 9, 1970

| 1990 | 7 | 2 | 0 | 2 | 2 | G |

CHAD PENNEY   Forward 6' 195 lbs.
b. St. John's, Newfoundland,
September 18, 1973

| 1992 | 7 | 0 | 0 | 0 | 2 | 6th |

CHRIS PHILLIPS   Defence 6'2" 200 lbs.
b. Fort McMurray, Alberta, March 9, 1978

1996	6	0	0	0	0	G
1997	7	0	1	1	4	G
2 years	13	0	1	1	4	G/G

MARK PLANTERY   Defence 6'1" 185 lbs.
b. St. Catharines, Ontario,
August 14, 1959

| 1977 | 7 | 0 | 1 | 1 | 2 | S |

ADRIEN PLAVSIC   Defence 6'1" 195 lbs.
b. Montreal, Quebec, January 13, 1970

| 1990 | 7 | 0 | 1 | 1 | 8 | G |

JASON PODOLLAN   Forward 6'1" 181 lbs.
b. Vernon, British Columbia,
February 18, 1976

| 1996 | 6 | 2 | 3 | 5 | 2 | G |

FELIX POTVIN   Goalie 6'1" 183 lbs.
b. Montreal, Quebec, June 23, 1971

| 1991 | 2 | 0--0--0 | 80 | 3 | 0 | 2.25 | 0 | 0 | G |

PATRICK POULIN   Forward 6'1" 212 lbs.
b. Vanier, Quebec, April 23, 1973

| 1992 | 7 | 2 | 2 | 4 | 2 | 6th |

CHRIS PRONGER   Defence 6'5" 173 lbs.
b. Dryden, Ontario, October 10, 1974

| 1993 | 7 | 1 | 3 | 4 | 6 | G |

BRIAN PROPP   Forward 5'9" 185 lbs.
b. Lanigan, Saskatchewan,
February 15, 1959

| 1979 | 5 | 2 | 1 | 3 | 2 | 5th |

YVES RACINE   Defence 6' 194 lbs.
b. Matane, Quebec, February 7, 1969

| 1989 | 7 | 0 | 0 | 0 | 6 | 4th |

ROB RAMAGE   Defence 6'2" 195 lbs.
b. Byron, Ontario, January 11, 1959

1977	7	0	2	2	2	S
1978	6	1	3	4	6	B
2 years	13	1	5	6	8	S/B

MIKE RATHJE   Defence 6'5" 205 lbs.
b. Mannville, Alberta, May 11, 1974

| 1993 | 7 | 2 | 2 | 4 | 12 | G |

DAN RATUSHNY   Defence 6'1" 202 lbs.
b. Nepean, Ontario, September 29, 1970

| 1990 | 7 | 2 | 2 | 4 | 4 | G |

ERROL RAUSSE   Forward 5'10" 181 lbs.
b. Quesnel, British Columbia,
May 18, 1959

| 1979 | 5 | 1 | 1 | 2 | 2 | 5th |

KENT REARDON   Forward 6'1" 175 lbs.
b. Calgary, Alberta, May 14, 1959

| 1979 | 5 | 2 | 2 | 4 | 6 | 5th |

MARK RECCHI   Forward 5'10" 188 lbs.
b. Kamloops, British Columbia,
February 1, 1968

| 1988 | 7 | 0 | 5 | 5 | 4 | G |

WADE REDDEN   Defence 6′1″ 193 lbs.
b. Lloydminster, Saskatchewan,
June 12, 1977

1995	7	3	2	5	0	G
1996	6	0	2	2	2	G
2 years	13	3	4	7	2	G/G

MARK REEDS   Forward 5′10″ 188 lbs.
b. Burlington, Ontario, January 24, 1960

| 1980 | 5 | 1 | 0 | 1 | 2 | 5th |

MIKE RICCI   Forward 6′1″ 191 lbs.
b. Scarborough, Ontario,
October 27, 1971

1989	7	5	2	7	6	4th
1990	5	0	4	4	0	G
2 years	12	5	6	11	6	G

STEVE RICE   Forward 6′1″ 209 lbs.
b. Kitchener, Ontario, May 26, 1971

1990	7	2	0	2	16	G
1991	7	4	1	5	8	G
2 years	14	6	1	7	24	G/G

LUKE RICHARDSON   Defence 6′3″ 197 lbs.
b. Ottawa, Ontario, March 26, 1969

| 1987 | 6 | 0 | 0 | 0 | 0 | DQ |

STEPHANE RICHER   Forward 6′2″ 200 lbs.
b. Ripon, Quebec, June 7, 1966

| 1985 | 7 | 4 | 3 | 7 | 2 | G |

PIERRE RIOUX   Forward 5′9″ 165 lbs.
b. Quebec City, Quebec, February 1, 1962

| 1982 | 7 | 3 | 3 | 6 | 4 | G |

JAMIE RIVERS   Defence 6′1″ 185 lbs.
b. Ottawa, Ontario, March 16, 1975

| 1995 | 7 | 3 | 3 | 6 | 2 | G |

GARY ROBERTS   Forward 6′1″ 187 lbs.
b. North York, Ontario, May 23, 1966

| 1986 | 7 | 6 | 3 | 9 | 6 | S |

LUC ROBITAILLE   Forward 6′1″ 185 lbs.
b. Montreal, Quebec, February 17, 1966

| 1986 | 7 | 3 | 5 | 8 | 2 | S |

STEPHANE ROY   Forward 6′ 182 lbs.
b. Cap Rouge, Quebec, June 29, 1967

| 1987 | 6 | 0 | 1 | 1 | 6 | DQ |

ROY RUSSELL   Forward 5′8″ 155 lbs.
b. Manchester, England, April 7, 1963

| 1981 | 5 | 0 | 0 | 0 | 0 | 7th |

BRAD RYDER   Forward 6′ 189 lbs.
b. Toronto, Ontario, October 16, 1961

| 1980 | 4 | 1 | 1 | 2 | 14 | 5th |

DAVID ST. PIERRE   Forward 6′ 180 lbs.
b. Montreal, Quebec, March 22, 1972

| 1992 | 7 | 0 | 0 | 0 | 0 | 6th |

JOE SAKIC   Forward 5′11″ 185 lbs.
b. Burnaby, British Columbia, July 7, 1969

| 1988 | 7 | 3 | 1 | 4 | 2 | G |

JIM SANDLAK   Forward 6′3″ 207 lbs.
b. Kitchener, Ontario, December 12, 1966

1985	5	1	0	1	6	G
1986	7	5	7	12	16	S
2 years	12	6	7	13	22	G/s

EVERETT SANIPASS   Forward 6′2″ 198 lbs.
b. Moncton, New Brunswick,
February 13, 1968

| 1987 | 6 | 3 | 2 | 5 | 8 | DQ |

MIKE SANDS   Goalie 5′8″ 155 lbs.
b. Mississauga, Ontario, April 6, 1963

| 1983 | 5 | 2--2--1 | 240 | 14 | 1 | 3.50 | 0 | 0 | B |

CORY SARICH   Defence 6′3″ 175 lbs.
b. Saskatoon, Saskatchewan,
August 16, 1978

1997	7	0	0	0	6	G
1998	7	0	1	1	6	8th
2 years	14	0	1	1	12	G

REGINALD SAVAGE   Forward 5′10″ 185 lbs.
b. Montreal, Quebec, May 1, 1970

| 1989 | 7 | 4 | 5 | 9 | 4 | 4th |

ROBERT SAVARD Defence 5'11" 189 lbs.
b. Sudbury, Ontario, March 16, 1961

1981	5	0	2	2	2	7th

PETER SCHAEFER Forward 6' 187 lbs.
b. Yellow Grass, Saskatchewan,
July 12, 1977

1997	7	3	1	4	4	G

ANDY SCHNEIDER Forward 5'9" 165 lbs.
b. Edmonton, Alberta, March 29, 1972

1992	7	0	0	0	6	6th

AL SECORD Forward 6'1" 205 lbs.
b. Sudbury, Ontario, March 3, 1958

1977	7	2	2	4	10	S

RIC SEILING Forward 6'1" 178 lbs.
b. Elmira, Ontario, December 15, 1957

1977	7	3	3	6	8	S

TOM SEMENCHUK Goalie 5'7" 160 lbs.
b. Winnipeg, Manitoba, September 13, 1959

1979	3	0--0--0	180	7	0	2.33	0	0	5th

PIERRE SEVIGNY Forward 6' 189 lbs.
b. Trois-Rivieres, Quebec,
September 8, 1971

1991	7	4	2	6	8	G

BRENDAN SHANAHAN Forward 6'3" 206 lbs.
b. Mimico, Ontario, January 23, 1969

1987	6	4	3	7	4	DQ

DARRIN SHANNON Forward 6'2" 190 lbs.
b. Barrie, Ontario, December 8, 1969

1989	7	1	3	4	10	4th

JEFF SHANTZ Forward 6' 175 lbs.
b. Duchess, Alberta, October 10, 1973

1993	7	2	4	6	2	G

BRAD SHAW Defence 5'11" 160 lbs.
b. Cambridge, Ontario, April 28, 1964

1983	7	1	1	2	2	B
1984	7	0	2	2	0	4th
2 years	14	1	3	4	2	B

GEOFF SHAW Forward 6' 185 lbs.
b. November 26, 1958

1977	7	3	1	4	21	S

GORD SHERVEN Forward 6' 184 lbs.
b. Mankota, Saskatchewan,
August 21, 1963

1983	7	1	3	4	0	B

MIKE SILLINGER Forward 5'11" 190 lbs.
b. Regina, Saskatchewan, June 29, 1971

1991	7	4	2	6	2	G

SEAN SIMPSON Goalie 5'11" 157 lbs.
b. Gloucester, Ontario, August 10, 1968

1980	5	0	2	2	0	5th

SHAWN SIMPSON Goalie 5'11" 180 lbs.
b. Gloucester, Ontario, August 10, 1968

1987	4	2--1--1	200	13	0	3.90	0	0	DQ

JOHN SLANEY Defence 6' 187 lbs.
b. St. John's, Newfoundland,
February 7, 1972

1991	7	1	2	3	6	G
1992	7	1	3	4	6	6th
2 years	14	2	5	7	12	G

BOBBY SMITH Forward 6'4" 210 lbs.
b. North Sydney, Nova Scotia,
February 12, 1958

1978	3	1	4	5	0	B

GEOFF SMITH Defence 6'3" 191 lbs.
b. Edmonton, Alberta, March 7, 1969

1989	7	0	1	1	4	4th

JASON SMITH Defence 6'3" 185 lbs.
b. Calgary, Alberta, November 2, 1973

1993	7	1	3	4	10	G

STUART SMITH Defence 6'1" 185 lbs.
b. Toronto, Ontario, March 17, 1960

1980	5	0	1	1	10	5th

STAN SMYL Forward 5′8″ 200 lbs.
b. Glendon, Alberta, January 28, 1958

| 1978 | 6 | 1 | 1 | 2 | 6 | B |

RYAN SMYTH Forward 6′1″ 183 lbs.
b. Banff, Alberta, February 21, 1976

| 1995 | 7 | 2 | 5 | 7 | 4 | G |

CHRIS SNELL Defence 5′10″ 198 lbs.
b. Regina, Saskatchewan, May 12, 1971

| 1991 | 7 | 0 | 4 | 4 | 0 | G |

LEE SOROCHAN Defence 6′2″ 205 lbs.
b. Edmonton, Alberta, September 9, 1975

| 1995 | 7 | 0 | 1 | 1 | 6 | G |

NICK STAJDUHAR Defence 6′2″ 190 lbs.
b. Kitchener, Ontario, December 6, 1974

| 1994 | 7 | 1 | 4 | 5 | 8 | G |

MIKE STAPLETON Forward 5′10″ 175 lbs.
b. Sarnia, Ontario, May 5, 1966

| 1986 | 7 | 3 | 3 | 6 | 6 | S |

TURNER STEVENSON Forward 6′3″ 206 lbs.
b. Prince George, British Columbia,
May 18, 1972

| 1992 | 7 | 0 | 2 | 2 | 14 | 6th |

JAMIE STORR Goalie 6′1″ 168 lbs.
b. Brampton, Ontario, December 28, 1975

1994	4	3--0--1	240	10	0	2.50	0	0	G
1995	4	4--0--0	240	14	0	3.50	0	2	G
2 yrs	8	7--0--1	480	24	0	3.00	0	2	G/G

TODD STRUEBY Forward 6′1″ 191 lbs.
b. Lanningan, Saskatchewan, June 15, 1963

| 1982 | 7 | 0 | 5 | 5 | 4 | G |

DARRYL SYDOR Defence 6′ 190 lbs.
b. Edmonton, Alberta, May 13, 1972

| 1992 | 7 | 3 | 1 | 4 | 4 | 5th |

STEVE TAMBELLINI Forward 6′ 190 lbs.
b. Trail, British Columbia, May 14, 1958

| 1978 | 6 | 2 | 2 | 4 | 0 | B |

ALEX TANGUAY Forward 6′ 180 lbs.
b. Ste. Justine, Quebec,
November 21, 1979

| 1998 | 7 | 2 | 1 | 3 | 2 | 8th |

TONY TANTI Forward 5′10″ 190 lbs.
b. Mississauga, Ontario,
September 7, 1963

| 1983 | 7 | 0 | 4 | 4 | 6 | B |

JOSE THEODORE Goalie 5′11″ 175 lbs.
b. Laval, Quebec, September 13, 1976

| 1996 | 4 | 4--0--0 | 240 | 6 | 0 | 1.50 | 0 | 0 | G |

JOE THORNTON Forward 6′4″ 186 lbs.
b. London, Ontario, July 2, 1979

| 1997 | 7 | 2 | 2 | 4 | 0 | G |

SCOTT THORNTON Forward 6′2″ 200 lbs.
b. London, Ontario, January 9, 1971

| 1991 | 7 | 3 | 1 | 4 | 0 | G |

DANIEL TKACZUK Forward 6′ 195 lbs.
b. Mississauga, Ontario, June 10, 1979

| 1998 | 7 | 2 | 1 | 3 | 4 | 8th |

LARRY TRADER Defence 6′2″ 195 lbs.
b. Barry's Bay, Ontario, July 7, 1963

| 1983 | 7 | 2 | 3 | 5 | 8 | B |

DARCY TUCKER Forward 5′10″ 163 lbs.
b. Castor, Alberta, March 15, 1975

| 1995 | 7 | 0 | 4 | 4 | | G |

BRENT TULLY Defence 6′3″ 185 lbs.
b. Peterborough, Ontario, March 26, 1974

1993	7	1	2	3	12	G
1994	7	0	1	1	16	G
2 years	14	1	3	4	28	G/G

PIERRE TURGEON Forward 6′1″ 204 lbs.
b. Rouyn, Quebec, August 28, 1969

| 1987 | 6 | 3 | 0 | 3 | 2 | DQ |

SYLVAIN TURGEON Forward 6′ 185 lbs.
b. Noranda, Quebec, January 17, 1965

| 1983 | 7 | 4 | 2 | 6 | 8 | B |

RICK VAIVE Forward 6' 180 lbs.
b. Ottawa, Ontario, May 14, 1959

1978		6	3	0	3	4	B

MIKE VAN RYN Defence 6'1" 186 lbs.
b. London, Ontario, May 14, 1979

1998		7	0	0	0	4	8th

STEVE VEILLEUX Defence 6' 194 lbs.
b. Lachenaie, Quebec, March 9, 1969

1989		7	0	0	0	8	4th

PAT VERBEEK Forward 5'8" 176 lbs.
b. Sarnia, Ontario, May 24, 1964

1983		7	2	2	4	6	B

MIKE VERNON Goalie 5'9" 150 lbs.
b. Calgary, Alberta, February 24, 1963

1983	4	2--0--0	180	10	1	3.33	1	0	B

EMANUEL VIVEIROS
Defence 5'11" 170 lbs.
b. St. Albert, Alberta, January 8, 1966

1986		7	1	1	2	2	S

JIMMY WAITE Goalie 5'11" 162 lbs.
b. Sherbooke, Quebec, April 15, 1969

1987	3	2--0--0	160	10	0	3.75	0	0	DQ
1988	7	6--0--1	419	16	0	2.29	0	2	G
2 yrs	10	8--0--1	579	26	0	2.69	0	2	G

JESSE WALLIN Defence 6'2" 186 lbs.
b. Saskatoon, Saskatchewan,
March 10, 1978

1997		7	0	0	0	6	G
1998		4	0	0	0	4	8th
2 years		11	0	0	0	10	G

RYAN WALTER Forward 6' 195 lbs.
b. New Westminster, British Columbia,
April 23, 1958

1978		6	5	3	8	4	B

WES WALZ Forward 5'11" 181 lbs.
b. Calgary, Alberta, May 15, 1970

1990		7	2	3	5	0	G

JASON WARD Forward 6'2" 193 lbs.
b. Oshawa, Ontario, January 16, 1979

1998		7	1	0	1	2	8th

JEFF WARE Defence 6'4" 225 lbs.
b. Toronto, Ontario, May 19, 1977

1997		7	0	0	0	6	G

RHETT WARRENER Defence 6'1" 209 lbs.
b. Saskatoon, Saskatchewan,
January 27, 1976

1996		6	0	0	0	4	G

MIKE WATT Forward 6'1" 212 lbs.
b. Egmondville, Ontario, March 31, 1976

1996		6	1	2	3	6	G

DARCY WERENKA Defence 6'2" 210 lbs.
b. Edmonton, Alberta, May 13, 1973

1993		7	1	0	1	18	G

GLEN WESLEY Defence 6'1" 192 lbs.
b. Red Deer, Alberta, October 2, 1968

1987		6	2	1	3	4	DQ

TRENT WHITFIELD Forward 5'11" 180 lbs.
b. Estevan, Saskatchewan, June 17, 1977

1997		7	1	0	1	4	G

JIM WIEMER Defence 6'4" 200 lbs.
b. Sudbury, Ontario, January 9, 1961

1980		5	2	2	4	2	5th

SHANE WILLIS Forward 6'1" 185 lbs.
b. Edmonton, Alberta, June 13, 1977

1997		7	0	0	0	0	G

BRIAN WILLSIE Forward 6' 179 lbs.
b. London, Ontario, March 16, 1978

1998		7	0	2	2	4	8th

CAREY WILSON Forward 6'1" 192 lbs.
b. Winnipeg, Manitoba, May 11, 1962

1982		7	4	1	5	6	G

BRENDAN WITT Defence 6′1″ 210 lbs.
 b. Humbolt, Saskatchewan,
 February 20, 1975

| 1994 | | 7 | 0 | 0 | 0 | 6 | G |

KEN WREGGET Goalie 6′1″ 182 lbs.
 b. Brandon, Manitoba, March 25, 1964

| 1984 | 5 | 2--2--1 | 300 | 14 | 1 | 2.80 | 0 | 0 | 4th |

JAMIE WRIGHT Forward 5′11″ 172 lbs.
 b. Elmira, Ontario, May 13, 1976

| 1996 | | 6 | 1 | 2 | 3 | 2 | G |

TERRY WRIGHT Goalie 5′7″ 160 lbs.
 b. Sault Ste. Marie, Ontario, June 19, 1960

| 1980 | 1 | 0--0--0 | 60 | 5 | 0 | 5.00 | 0 | 0 | 5th |

TYLER WRIGHT Forward 5′11″ 170 lbs.
 b. Canora, Saskatchewan, April 6, 1973

1992	7	1	0	1	16	6th
1993	7	3	3	6	6	G
2 years	14	4	3	7	22	G

BRIAN YOUNG Defence 6′1″ 183 lbs.
 b. Jasper, Alberta, October 2, 1958

| 1978 | | 6 | 0 | 2 | 2 | 2 | B |

STEVE YZERMAN Forward 5′10″ 173 lbs.
 b. Cranbrook, British Columbia,
 May 9, 1965

| 1983 | | 7 | 2 | 3 | 5 | 2 | B |

COACHES' REGISTER

MIKE BABCOCK
b. Saskatoon, Saskatchewan,
March 29, 1963

1997	6	4	0	2	G

JOE CANALE
b. Montreal, Quebec, September 21, 1949

1994	7	6	1	0	G

DAVE CHAMBERS
b. Toronto, Ontario, May 7, 1940

1988	7	6	1	0	G

GUY CHARRON
b. Verdun, Quebec, January 14, 1949

1990	7	5	1	1	G

MARCEL COMEAU
b. Edmonton, Alberta, March 1, 1953

1996	6	6	0	0	G

RICK CORNACCHIA
b. Monteleone, Italy, February 6, 1951

1992	7	2	2	3	6th

DON HAY
b. Kamloops, British Columbia,
February 13, 1954

1995	7	7	0	0	G

MIKE KEENAN
b. Toronto, Ontario, October 21, 1949

1980	6	4	2	0	5th

BOB KILGER
b. Cornwall, Ontario, June 29, 1944

1981	6	2	3	1	7th

BRIAN KILREA
b. Ottawa, Ontario, October 21, 1934

1984	7	4	1	2	4th

DAVE KING
b. Saskatoon, Saskatchewan,
December 22, 1947

1982	7	6	1	0	G
1983	7	4	1	2	B
Totals	14	10	2	2	G/B

ERNIE MCLEAN
b. Estevan, Saskatchewan, November 3, 1932

1979	6	4	2	0	5th

REAL PAIEMENT
b. Dollard-des-Ormeaux,
September 30, 1959

1988	7	2	5	0	8th

PERRY PEARN
b. St. Albert, Alberta, June 6, 1951

1993	7	6	0	1	G

TERRY SIMPSON
b. Prince Albert, Saskatchewan,
August 30, 1943

1985	7	5	2	0	G
1986	7	5	2	0	S
Totals	14	10	4	0	G/S

BERT TEMPLETON
b. Irvine, Scotland, May 11, 1940

1977	7	5	1	1	S
1987	6	4	1	1	DQ
Totals	13	9	2	2	S

ORVAL TESSIER
b. Cornwall, Ontario, June 30, 1933

1978	6	4	2	0	B

DICK TODD
b. Toronto, Ontario, June 3, 1945

1991	7	5	1	1	G

TOM WEBSTER
b. Kirkland Lake, Ontario, October 4, 1948

1989	7	4	1	2	4th

ALL-TIME TEAM
AND
INDIVIDUAL RECORDS

ALL-TIME TEAM RECORDS

LONGEST WINNING STREAK

18 games	December 30, 1994--December 27, 1997
7 games	December 31, 1987--December 29, 1988

LONGEST UNDEFEATED STREAK

27 games	December 26, 1993--January 4, 1997
13 games	December 30, 1986--December 29, 1988
12 games	December 23, 1984--January 1, 1986

LONGEST LOSING STREAK

3 games	January 1--4, 1992
	December 31, 1997--January 3, 1998

LONGEST WINLESS STREAK

5 games	December 29, 1991--January 4, 1992
3 games	December 30, 1982--January 2, 1983

GOAL SCORING RECORDS, TEAM

MOST GOALS FOR, GAME (all games with ten goals or more)

18	December 27, 1985	Canada 18	West Germany 2
	December 30, 1986	Canada 18	Poland 3
14	December 23, 1976	Canada 14	Poland 0
13	January 4, 1983	Canada 13	Norway 0
12	December 28, 1983	Canada 12	Switzerland 0
	December 25, 1984	Canada 12	Poland 1
	December 26, 1985	Canada 12	Switzerland 1
	December 28, 1989	Canada 12	Poland 0
11	December 30, 1980	Canada 11	Austria 1
	December 29, 1981	Canada 11	West Germany 3
	January 1, 1982	Canada 11	Switzerland 1
10	December 31, 1978	Canada 10	Norway 1
	December 29, 1990	Canada 10	Norway 1

MOST GOALS AGAINST, GAME

8	December 28, 1979	Soviet Union 8	Canada 5
7	December 31, 1980	United States 7	Canada 3
	December 30, 1982	Soviet Union 7	Canada 3
	January 4, 1989	Soviet Union 7	Canada 2
	January 4, 1992	CIS 7	Canada 2
	January 4, 1993	Czech/Slovak 7	Canada 4

MOST GOALS BOTH TEAMS, GAME (all games 14+)

21	December 30, 1986	Canada 18	Poland 3
20	December 27, 1985	Canada 18	West Germany 2
14	December 30, 1979	Canada 9	Switzerland 5
	December 29, 1981	Canada 11	West Germany 3
	January 1, 1983	Canada 7	Czechoslovakia 7

SCORELESS GAMES

Canada has never been involved in a scoreless game at the
World Junior Championships

MOST GOALS FOR, PERIOD

7   2nd period, December 28, 1983 vs. Switzerland
     1st period, December 27, 1985 vs. West Germany
     1st period, December 30, 1986 vs. Poland
     1st period, December 28, 1989 vs. Poland

MOST GOALS AGAINST, PERIOD

6   1st period, January 2, 1977 vs. Soviet Union
     2nd period, January 1, 1983 vs. Czechoslovakia

MOST GOALS BOTH TEAMS, PERIOD

11   2nd period, January 1, 1983
     (Czechoslovakia 6 goals, Canada 5 goals)
8   3rd period, December 30, 1986
     (Canada 6 goals, Poland 2 goals)

HIGHEST TIE SCORES

7--7   January 1, 1983 vs. Czechoslovakia
6--6   December 27, 1986 vs. Finland

ALL POWER-PLAY AND SHORT-HANDED GOALS
RECORDS, FOR AND AGAINST

	FOR		AGAINST	
	PP	SH	PP	SH
1977	7	2	10	0
1978	6	0	5	0
1979	5	0	4	0
1980	3	3	6	0

1981	5	0	3	1
1982	4	0	5	1
1983	8	1	4	1
1984	6	0	3	1
1985	9	0	3	0
1986	10	2	5	0
1987	7	1	7	1
1988	9	2	8	0
1989	8	1	8	0
1990	7	1	5	0
1991	7	2	2	1
1992	4	1	8	2
1993	10	2	4	0
1994	14	2	4	1
1995	23	1	5	2
1996	9	1	4	0
1997	9	0	3	2
1998	3	1	4	1

MOST POWER-PLAY GOALS, TEAM, ONE GAME

5	December 26, 1994	Canada 7	Ukraine 1
4	December 23, 1976	Canada 14	Poland 0
	December 25, 1984	Canada 12	Poland 1
	December 27, 1985	Canada 18	West Germany 2
	December 27, 1993	Canada 5	Germany 2
	December 27, 1994	Canada 9	Germany 1
	December 29, 1994	Canada 8	United States 3
	January 2, 1995	Canada 8	Russia 5

MOST POWER-PLAY GOALS TEAM, ONE PERIOD

3	1st period, December 23, 1976	Canada 14	Poland 0
	1st period, December 27, 1985	Canada 18	West Germany 2
	2nd period, January 1, 1986	Canada 6	Finland 5
	2nd period, December 27, 1994	Canada 9	Germany 1
	2nd period, December 29, 1994	Canada 8	United States 3
	3rd period, January 2, 1995	Canada 8	Russia 5

MOST POWER-PLAY GOALS AGAINST, GAME

3	December 25, 1976	Canada 4	Czechoslovakia 4
	December 31, 1987	Canada 5	United States 4
	December 28, 1988	Canada 7	West Germany 4
	January 4, 1989	Soviet Union 7	Canada 2
	January 2, 1992	Czechoslovakia 6	Canada 1
	December 27, 1992	Canada 5	Sweden 4

MOST POWER-PLAY GOALS AGAINST, PERIOD

3	3rd period, December 28, 1988	Canada 7	West Germany 4
2	2nd period, December 26, 1976	Canada 6	Finland 4
	1st period, January 2, 1977	Soviet Union 6	Canada 4
	3rd period, December 31, 1987	Canada 5	United States 4

MOST SHORT-HANDED GOALS FOR, GAME

2	December 30, 1979	Canada 9	Switzerland 5

MOST SHORT-HANDED GOALS AGAINST, GAME & PERIOD

Canada has never allowed more than one short-handed goal in any game or period

ALL-TIME INDIVIDUAL RECORDS

MOST WORLD JUNIOR CHAMPIONSHIPS PARTICIPATED IN

3	Eric Lindros (1990/91/92)
	Martin Lapointe (1991/92/93)
	Jason Botterill (1994/95/96)

MOST MEDALS WON

3	Jason Botterill (all gold)

MOST GAMES PLAYED

21	Eric Lindros (1990/91/92)
	Martin Lapointe (1991/92/93)
19	Jason Botterill (1994/95/96)

MOST POINTS, CAREER

31	Eric Lindros (1990/91/92)
24	Jason Allison (1994/95)
19	Shayne Corson (1985/86)
	Marty Murray (1994/95)

MOST POINTS, ONE WJC

18	Dale McCourt (1977)
17	Eric Lindros (1991)
15	Jason Allison (1995)

MOST GOALS, CAREER

12	Eric Lindros (1990/91/92)
11	John Anderson (1977)
	Martin Gendron (1993/94)
10	Todd Harvey (1994/95)

MOST GOALS, ONE WJC

11	John Anderson (1977)
10	Dale McCourt (1977)
9	Dave Chyzowski (1990)

MOST ASSISTS, CAREER

19	Eric Lindros (1990/91/92)
18	Jason Allison (1994/95)
14	Alexandre Daigle (1993/95)
12	Marty Murray (1994/95)

MOST ASSISTS, ONE WJC

12	Jason Allison (1995)
11	Eric Lindros (1991)
10	Marty Murray (1995)

MOST PENALTY MINUTES, CAREER

38	Joe Contini (1977)
37	Jason Doig (1997)
32	Eric Lindros (1990/91/92)
31	Paul Cyr (1982/83)
	Alexandre Daigle (1993/95)

MOST PENALTY MINUTES, ONE WJC

38	Joe Contini (1977)
37	Jason Doig (1997)
27	Alexandre Daigle (1993)
26	Aaron Gavey (1994)
	Zenith Komarniski (1998)

MOST GOALS, ONE GAME (all hat tricks)

4	Mario Lemieux, January 4, 1983 vs. Norway
3	Dave Hunter, December 23, 1976 vs. Poland
	Dale McCourt, December 23, 1976 vs. Poland
	Dale McCourt, December 25, 1976 vs. Czechoslovakia
	John Anderson, January 1, 1977 vs. United States
	Wayne Gretzky, December 23, 1977 vs. West Germany
	Wayne Gretzky, December 25, 1977 vs. Czechoslovakia
	Wayne Babych, January 1, 1978 vs. Sweden
	Dino Ciccarelli, December 28, 1979 vs. Soviet Union
	Troy Murray, December 29, 1981 vs. West Germany
	Dave Andreychuk, January 4, 1983 vs. Norway
	Russ Courtnall, December 28, 1983 vs. Switzerland
	Dean Evason, December 28, 1983 vs. Switzerland
	Russ Courtnall, December 29, 1983 vs. West Germany
	Adam Creighton, December 28, 1984 vs. United States
	Jim Sandlak, December 26, 1985 vs. Switzerland
	Scott Mellanby, December 27, 1985 vs. West Germany
	Dave McLlwain, December 26, 1986 vs. Switzerland

Adam Graves, January 3, 1988 vs. West Germany
Eric Daze, January 2, 1995 vs. Russia
Jarome Iginla, December 31, 1995 vs. Ukraine

MOST HAT TRICKS, CAREER & ONE WJC

2   Dale McCourt (1977)
Wayne Gretzky (1978)
Russ Courtnall (1984)

MOST POINTS, ONE GAME

7   Dave Andreychuk, January 4, 1983 vs. Norway
               (3 goals, 4 assists)
6   Wayne Gretzky, December 25, 1977 vs. Czechoslovakia
               (3 goals, 3 assists)
Mario Lemieux, January 4, 1983 vs. Norway
               (4 goals, 2 assists)
5   Dale McCourt, December 23, 1976 vs. Poland
               (3 goals, 2 assists)
Wayne Gretzky, December 23, 1977 vs. West Germany
               (3 goals, 2 assists)
Russ Courtnall, December 28, 1983 vs. Switzerland
               (3 goals, 2 assists)
Dave McLlwain, December 26, 1986 vs. Switzerland
               (3 goals, 2 assists)
Steve Nemeth, December 30, 1986 vs. Poland
               (2 goals, 3 assists)
Mike Needham, December 28, 1989 vs. Poland
               (2 goals, 3 assists)
Eric Lindros, December 26, 1990 vs. Switzerland
               (one goal, 4 assists)
Eric Lindros, December 27, 1991 vs. Switzerland
               (one goal, 4 assists)

MOST ASSISTS, ONE GAME

4   Paul Cyr, January 1, 1982 vs. Switzerland
Dave Andreychuk, January 4, 1983 vs. Norway
Joe Murphy, December 27, 1985 vs. West Germany
Eric Lindros, December 26, 1990 vs. Switzerland
Eric Lindros, December 27, 1991 vs. Switzerland
Alexandre Daigle, December 29, 1994 vs. United States
Jason Allison, January 1, 1995 vs. Finland

MOST POINTS, ONE PERIOD

4   Wayne Gretzky, 1st period, December 23, 1977 vs. West Germany
               (2 goals, 2 assists)
Dave McLlwain, 1st period, December 26, 1986 vs. Switzerland
               (2 goals, 2 assists)
3   Dale McCourt, 2nd period, December 23, 1976 vs. Poland
               (2goals, one assist)

Mark Morrison, 1st period, January 1, 1982 vs. Switzerland
(2 goals, one assist)
Paul Cyr, 1st period, January 1, 1982 vs. Switzerland
(3 assists)
Shayne Corson, 3rd period, December 25, 1984 vs. Poland
(2 goals, one assist)
Stephane Richer, 3rd period, December 25, 1984 vs. Poland
(one goal, 2 assists)
Dan Hodgson, 3rd period, December 26, 1984 vs. West Germany
(2 goals, one assist)
Evertett Sanipass, 1st period, December 30, 1986 vs. Poland
(2 goals, one assist)
Mike Needham, 3rd period, December 28, 1989 vs. Poland
(2 goals, one assist)
Jason Dawe, 3rd period, December 29, 1992 vs. Russia
(one goal, 2 assists)

MOST GOALS, ONE PERIOD

3   Jim Sandlak, 2nd period, December 26, 1985 vs. Switzerland
Adam Graves, 1st period, January 3, 1988 vs. West Germany

MOST ASSISTS, ONE PERIOD

3   Paul Cyr, 1st period, January 1, 1982 vs. Switzerland
Joe Nieuwendyk, 1st period, December 26, 1985 vs. Switzerland
Joe Murphy, 1st period, December 27, 1985 vs. West Germany

LONGEST POINT-SCORING STREAK

7 games   Joe Contini, December 23, 1976--January 2, 1977
Dale McCourt, December 23, 1976--January 2, 1977
Theoren Fleury, December 26, 1977--January 4, 1988
Gary Leeman, December 25, 1983--January 3, 1984
Dale Derkatch, December 30, 1983--December 27, 1984
Brian Bradley, December 23, 1984--January 1, 1985
Shayne Corson, December 26, 1985--January 4, 1986
Dave Chyzowski, December 26, 1989--January 4, 1990
Mike Craig, January 4, 1990--January 2, 1991
Bryan McCabe, December 26, 1994--January 4, 1995
Marty Murray, December 26, 1994--January 4, 1995

LONGEST GOAL-SCORING STREAK

6 games   Dale McCourt, December 23, 1976--January 1, 1977
Dave Chyzowski, December 26, 1989--January 3, 1990
Todd Harvey, December 27, 1994--January 4, 1995

LONGEST ASSIST-SCORING STREAK

7 games   Bryan McCabe, December 26, 1994--January 4, 1995
6 games   Greg Hawgood, December 28, 1987--January 4, 1988
5 games   Gary Leeman, December 25--31, 1983
Jim Sandlak, December 26, 1985--January 1, 1986

MOST POWER-PLAY GOALS, CAREER

5	Todd Harvey (1994/95)
	Eric Daze (1995)
4	Jason Allison (1994/95)
	John Anderson (1977)
	Martin Gendron (1993/94)
	Marty Murray (1994/95)
	Theoren Fleury (1987/88)

MOST POWER-PLAY GOALS, ONE WJC

5	Eric Daze (1995)
4	John Anderson (1977)
	Martin Gendron (1994)
	Marty Murray (1995)

MOST POWER-PLAY GOALS, GAME

2	John Anderson, December 23, 1976 vs. Poland
	Shayne Corson, December 25, 1984 vs. Poland
	Peter Douris, December 27, 1985 vs. West Germany
	Mike Needham, December 28, 1989 vs. Poland
	Marty Murray, December 26, 1994 vs. Ukraine
	Josh Holden, January 3, 1998 vs. Kazakhstan

MOST SHORT-HANDED GOALS, CAREER & ONE WJC

2	Dale McCourt (1977)

TWO MEN SHORT-HANDED GOAL

Dale McCourt at 17:26 of 2nd, December 25, 1976 vs. Czechoslovakia

PENALTY SHOTS

FOR

Steve Tambellini (Can) stopped by Jaromir Sindel (Cze), December 25, 1977

AGAINST

Josef Lukac (Cze) stopped by Al Jensen (Can), December 25, 1976
Pius Kuonen (Swi) beat Terry Wright (Can), December 30, 1979
Ladislav Lubina (Cze) stopped by Shawn Simpson (Can), December 29, 1986
Tomas Sandstrom (Swe) stopped by Jimmy Waite (Can), January 2, 1987
David Vyborny (CzR) beat Phillippe DeRouville (Can), January 4, 1993
Veli-Pekka Nutikaa (Fin) beat Dan Cloutier (Can), January 1, 1995

EMPTY NET (EN) GOALS

1. Dale McCourt (Anderson), 19:53 of 3rd, December 26, 1976 vs. Finland
2. Rick Girard (unassisted), 19:10 of 3rd, December 30, 1993 vs. Finland
3. Jeff Friesen (unassisted), 19:29 of 3rd, December 30, 1994 vs. Czech Republic
4. Rick Girard (unassisted), 19:54 of 3rd, January 4, 1994 vs. Sweden
5. Jarome Iginla (Dube), 19:28 of 3rd, December 29, 1995 vs. Finland

EXTRA ATTACKER (EA) GOALS

1. Dale McCourt (unassisted), 19:41 of 3rd, December 25, 1976 vs. Czechoslovakia
2. Larry Trader (Andreychuk), 19:25 of 3rd, January 4, 1983 vs. Norway
3. Rob Cimetta (Ricci, Kennedy), 19:28 of 3rd, January 1, 1989 vs. Czechoslovakia

ALL GOALTENDER RECORDS

YEAR-BY-YEAR SHUTOUTS FOR & AGAINST

YEAR	F	A	YEAR	F	A	YEAR	F	A
1977	1	0	1985	2	0	1993	1	0
1978	1	0	1986	0	0	1994	0	0
1979	0	1	1987	0	0	1995	0	0
1980	0	0	1988	0	0	1996	0	0
1981	0	0	1989	0	0	1997	1	0
1982	1	0	1990	1	0	1998	2	2
1983	2	0	1991	1	0			
1984	2	0	1992	0	0	TOTAL	15	3

MOST SHUTOUTS, CAREER

2	Mathieu Garon (1998)

MOST WJC PARTICIPATED IN, GOALIE

2   Al Jensen (1977/78)
    Craig Billington (1985/86)
    Jimmy Waite (1987/88)
    Stephane Fiset (1989/90)
    Trevor Kidd (1991/92)
    Jamie Storr (1994/95)
    Marc Denis (1996/97)

MOST GAMES PLAYED, GOALIE, CAREER

13   Stephane Fiset (1989/90)
     Trevor Kidd (1991/92)
10   Al Jensen (1977/78)
     Craig Billington (1985/86)
     Jimmy Waite (1987/88)

MOST MINUTES PLAYED, GOALIE, CAREER

760   Trevor Kidd (1991/92)
749   Stephane Fiset (1989/90)
600   Al Jensen (1977/78)
      Craig Billington (1985/86)
579   Jimmy Waite (1987/88)

MOST WINS, GOALIE, CAREER

8	Jimmy Waite (1987/88)
	Stephane Fiset (1989/90)
7	Jamie Storr (1994/95)
	Marc Denis (1996/97)

MOST WINS, GOALIE, ONE WJC

6	Jimmy Waite (1988)
	Manny Legace (1993)
5	Al Jensen (1977)
	Stephane Fiset (1990)
	Marc Denis (1997)

MOST LOSSES, GOALIE, CAREER

4	Trevor Kidd (1991/92)
3	Al Jensen (1977/78)
	Stephane Fiset (1989/90)

MOST LOSSES, GOALIE, ONE WJC

3	Trevor Kidd (1992)
2	Al Jensen (1978)
	Mike Sands (1983)
	Craig Billington (1986)
	Stephane Fiset (1989)
	Roberto Luongo (1998)

MOST SHUTOUTS, ONE WJC

2	Mathieu Garon (1998)

MOST CONSECUTIVE SHUTOUTS

2	Mathieu Garon, December 28–30, 1997

BEST GOALS AGAINST AVERAGE, ONE WJC AND CAREER
(minimum 5 games or 300 minutes)

1.67	Manny Legace (1993)
	Marc Denis (1996/97)
2.60	Craig Billington (1985/86)
2.69	Jimmy Waite (1987/88)

LONGEST SHUTOUT SEQUENCE (IN MINUTES)

151:16	Mathieu Garon, December 26–31, 1997
115:51	Norm Foster, December 25–26, 1984
105:21	Stephane Fiset, December 26–29, 1989

SHUTOUTS IN FIRST WJC GAME PLAYED

Al Jensen	December 23, 1976 vs. Poland
Tim Bernhardt	December 23, 1977 vs. West Germany
Mike Sands	December 26, 1982 vs. West Germany

Allan Bester   December 28, 1983 vs. Switzerland
Trevor Kidd   December 26, 1990 vs. Switzerland
Manny Legace   December 26, 1992 vs. United States

LONGEST WINNING STREAK

6 games   Manny Legace, December 26, 1992--January 2, 1993
4 games   Al Jensen, December 26, 1976--January 1, 1977
                   Jimmy Waite, December 31, 1987--January 4, 1988

LONGEST UNBEATEN STREAK

7 games   Jimmy Waite, December 26, 1987--January 4, 1988
                   Marc Denis, December 27, 1996--January 4, 1997
6 games   Al Jensen, December 23, 1976--January 1, 1977
5 games   Stephane Fiset, December 26, 1989--January 1, 1990

LONGEST LOSING STREAK

3 games   Trevor Kidd, January 1--4, 1992

LONGEST WINLESS STREAK

5 games   Trevor Kidd, December 29, 1991--January 4, 1992

ALL GOALIE ASSISTS

Mike Vernon is the only Canadian goalie to record an assist,
January 4, 1983 vs. Norway

ALL GOALIE PENALTY MINUTES

2   Rick LaFerriere
             Jamie Storr
             Roberto Luongo
             Jimmy Waite

ALL SHOTS ON GOAL RECORDS

MOST SHOTS FOR, GAME

80   December 29, 1976 vs. West Germany
67   December 30, 1980 vs. Austria
              January 2, 1993 vs. Japan
66   January 4, 1983 vs. Norway
              December 27, 1991 vs. Switzerland

MOST SHOTS AGAINST, GAME

66   December 30, 1991 vs. Finland
63   December 29, 1991 vs. Sweden
60   December 30, 1992 vs. Finland
49   January 3, 1996 vs. Russia

MOST SHOTS BOTH TEAMS, GAME

113	December 29, 1976 vs. West Germany
	(Canada 80, West Germany 33)
105	December 30, 1991 vs. Finland
	(Finland 66, Canada 49)
104	December 27, 1991 vs. Switzerland
	(Canada 66, Switzerland 38)
96	December 30, 1992 vs. Finland
	(Finland 60, Canada 36)

MOST SHOTS FOR, PERIOD

31	2nd period, December 27, 1991 vs. Switzerland
28	2nd period, December 29, 1976 vs. West Germany
26	1st period, December 29, 1976 vs. West Germany
	3rd period, December 29, 1976 vs. West Germany
	1st period, December 23, 1977 vs. West Germany
	1st period, December 27, 1994 vs. Germany

MOST SHOTS AGAINST, PERIOD

26	1st period, December 30, 1992 by Finland
25	1st period, December 29, 1991 by Sweden
24	3rd period, December 29, 1991 by Sweden
	2nd period, December 30, 1991 by Finland

MOST SHOTS BOTH TEAMS, PERIOD

45	2nd period, December 27, 1991 vs. Switzerland
	(Canada 31, Switzerland 14)
42	1st period, December 30, 1992 vs. Finland
	(Finland 26, Canada 16)
39	3rd period, December 29, 1976
	3rd period, December 30, 1991 vs. Finland
	(Finland 23, Canada 16)

FEWEST SHOTS FOR, GAME

15	January 2, 1987 vs. Sweden
	January 2, 1998 vs. United States
16	January 1, 1988 vs. Soviet Union
17	December 29, 1987 vs. Finland

FEWEST SHOTS AGAINST, GAME

6	January 4, 1983 by Norway
11	December 29, 1981 by West Germany
12	January 2, 1980 by West Germany
	December 28, 1983 by Switzerland

FEWEST SHOTS BOTH TEAMS, GAME

39	December 29, 1984 vs. Soviet Union
	(Canada 22, Soviet Union 17)
44	December 28, 1997 vs. Czech Republic

(Canada 22, Czech Republic 22)
45   December 30, 1997 vs. Germany
(Canada 28, Germany 17)
46   December 27, 1990 vs. United States
(Canada 25, United States 21)
January 4, 1995 vs. Sweden
(Canada 25, Sweden 21)

FEWEST SHOTS FOR, PERIOD

3   2nd period, December 30, 1978 vs. Sweden
2nd period, January 2, 1998 vs. United States

FEWEST SHOTS AGAINST, PERIOD

0   2nd period, January 4, 1983 vs. Norway
3rd period, December 26, 1985 vs. Switzerland
1   3rd period, January 4, 1983 vs. Norway

FEWEST SHOTS BOTH TEAMS, PERIOD

8   1st period, December 30, 1997 vs. Germany
(Germany 6, Canada 2)
9   1st period, December 29, 1988 vs. United States
(United States 7, Canada 2)
3rd period, January 1, 1993 vs. Germany
(Canada 5, Germany 4)
10   3rd period, January 1, 1989 vs. Czechoslovakia
(Canada 5, Czechoslovakia 5)
2nd period, January 3, 1997 vs. Russia
(Canada 6, Russia 4)

ALL PENALTY RECORDS

FEWEST PENALTY MINUTES GAME, TEAM

4   December 30, 1980 vs. Austria
December 26, 1989 vs. United States
January 4, 1991 vs. Soviet Union
6   December 22, 1981 vs. Finland
January 1, 1994 vs. United States

FEWEST PENALTY MINUTES BOTH TEAMS, GAME

8   December 30, 1979 (Canada 8, Switzerland 0)
January 4, 1991 (Canada 4, Soviet Union 4)
January 1, 1994 (Canada 6, United States 2)
10   December 22, 1981 (Canada 6, Finland 4)
December 26, 1989 (United States 6, Canada 4)

FEWEST PENALTIES GAME, TEAM

2   December 30, 1980 vs. Austria
December 26, 1989 vs. United States

	January 4, 1991 vs. Soviet Union
3	December 22, 1981 vs. Finland
	January 1, 1994 vs. United States

FEWEST PENALTIES BOTH TEAMS, GAME

4	December 30, 1979 (Canada 4, Switzerland 0)
	January 4, 1991 (Canada 2, Soviet Union 2)
	January 1, 1994 (Canada 3, United States 1)
5	December 22, 1981 (Canada 3, Finland 2)
	December 26, 1989 (United States 3, Canada 2)

MOST PENALTY MINUTES, TEAM, GAME

57	December 27, 1992 vs. Sweden
52	December 27, 1979 vs. Finland
47	December 23, 1976 vs. Poland

MOST PENALTY MINUTES, TEAM, PERIOD

45	2nd period, December 27, 1992 vs. Sweden
38	3rd period, December 27, 1979 vs. Finland
26	1st period, December 23, 1976 vs. Poland

MOST PENALTY MINUTES, BOTH TEAMS, GAME

94	December 27, 1992 (Canada 57, Sweden 37)
70	December 27, 1979 (Canada 52, Finland 18)
68	January 2, 1981 (West Germany 36, Canada 32)

MOST PENALTY MINUTES, BOTH TEAMS, PERIOD

55	2nd period, December 27, 1992 (Canada 45, Sweden 10)
52	3rd period, December 27, 1979 (Canada 38, Finland 14)
36	1st period, January 2, 1981 (Canada 18, West Germany 18)

MOST PENALTIES, TEAM, GAME

18	December 27, 1979 vs. Finland
15	December 26, 1993 vs. Switzerland
14	December 27, 1992 vs. Sweden

MOST PENALTIES, TEAM, PERIOD

11	3rd period, December 27, 1979 vs. Finland
8	2nd period, December 27, 1992 vs. Sweden

MOST PENALTIES, BOTH TEAMS, GAME

27	December 27, 1992 (Canada 14, Sweden 13)
	December 26, 1993 (Canada 15, Switzerland 12)
23	December 27, 1979 (Canada 18, Finland 5)
22	January 2, 1981 (Canada 12, West Germany 10)

MOST PENALTIES, BOTH TEAMS, PERIOD

14	3rd period, December 27, 1979 (Canada 11, Finland 3)
13	2nd period, December 27, 1992 (Canada 8, Sweden 5)
12	2nd period, December 26, 1993 (Canada 7, Switzerland 5)

MOST PENALTY MINUTES, INDIVIDUAL, GAME

27   Jason Doig, January 3, 1997
25   Alexandre Daigle, December 27, 1992 vs. Sweden
15   Geoff Shaw, December 23, 1976 vs. Poland
         Paul Cyr, December 30, 1982 vs. Soviet Union

MOST PENALTY MINUTES, INDIVIDUAL, PERIOD

25   Alexandre Daigle, 2nd period, December 27, 1992 vs. Sweden
         Jason Doig, 2nd period, January 3, 1997 vs. Russia
15   Geoff Shaw, 2nd period, December 23, 1976 vs. Poland
         Paul Cyr, 3rd period, December 30, 1982 vs. Soviet Union

MOST PENALTIES, INDIVIDUAL, GAME

4   Turner Stevenson, December 27, 1991 vs. Switzerland
         Nolan Baumgartner, December 26, 1995 vs. United States

MOST PENALTIES, INDIVIDUAL, PERIOD

3   Brad Marsh, 1st period, January 2, 1977 vs. Soviet Union
         Turner Stevenson, 3rd period, December 27, 1991 vs. Switzerland
         Nolan Baumgartner, 2nd period, December 26, 1995 vs. United States

ALL SPEED RECORDS

FASTEST GOAL FROM START OF GAME

11 seconds   Jim Sandlak, December 26, 1985
17 seconds   Scott Arniel, December 29, 1981
18 seconds   Scott Pellerin, December 28, 1989

FASTEST GOAL FROM START OF PERIOD

8 seconds   Eric Daze, 3rd period, January 4, 1995

FASTEST TWO GOALS FROM START OF GAME, TEAM

1:33   December 29, 1981   Scott Arniel scored at 0:17
                                   Troy Murray scored at 1:33

FASTEST TWO GOALS, INDIVIDUAL

9 seconds   Dave Gagner, December 28, 1983
         Scored at 18:29 of 2nd and again at 18:38

FASTEST TWO GOALS, TEAM

8 seconds   January 4, 1983
         Dale Derkatch 19:33 of 1st
         Mario Lemieux 19:41
13 seconds   December 30, 1986
         Everett Sanipass 13:30 of 1st
         Brendan Shanahan 13:43

14 seconds   December 28, 1983
                      Russ Courtnall 18:15 of 2nd
                      Dave Gagner 18:29

15 seconds   December 23, 1977
                      Tony McKegney 8:37 of 1st
                      Wayne Gretzky 8:52

FASTEST TWO GOALS, BOTH TEAMS

9 seconds   January 3, 1984
                      Libor Dolana (Cze) 16:18 of 1st
                      Randy Heath (Can) 16:27

12 seconds   January 1, 1977
                      Jim Penningroth (U.S.) 16:29 of 1st
                      Steve Hazlett (Can) 16:41

FASTEST THREE GOALS, INDIVIDUAL

5:46   Adam Graves, January 3, 1988
              Scored at 4:51/6:54/10:37 of 2nd

FASTEST THREE GOALS, TEAM

23 seconds   2nd period, December 28, 1983
                      Russ Courtnall 18:15
                      Dave Gagner 18:29
                      Dave Gagner 18:38

52 seconds   1st period, January 1, 1994
                      Curtis Bowen 13:00
                      Todd Harvey 13:31
                      Christian Dube 13:52

54 seconds   2nd period, December 28, 1983
                      Dave Gagner 18:29
                      Dave Gagner 18:38
                      Dean Evason 19:23

FASTEST THREE GOALS, BOTH TEAMS

39 seconds   2nd period, January 2, 1979
                      Dave Orleski (Can) 14:15
                      Brad McCrimmon (Can) 14:31
                      Gary DeGrio (U.S.) 14:54

43 seconds   2nd period, January 2, 1981
                      Marc Crawford (Can) 10:22
                      Dieter Hegen (WGer) 10:52
                      John Kirk (Can) 11:05

FASTEST FOUR GOALS, TEAM

1:08   2nd period, December 28, 1983
              Russ Courtnall 18:15
              Dave Gagner 18:29
              Dave Gagner 18:38
              Dean Evason 19:23

FASTEST FOUR GOALS, BOTH TEAMS

1:27	2nd period, January 2, 1981
	Fred Boimistruck (Can) 9:38
	Marc Crawford (Can) 10:22
	Dieter Hegen (WGer) 10:52
	John Kirk (Can) 11:05
	3rd period, January 3, 1984
	Libor Dolana (Cze) 13:43
	Lumir Kotala (Cze) 14:06
	Vladimir Kames (Cze) 14:54
	Dean Evason (Can) 15:10

FASTEST FIVE GOALS, TEAM

3:23	1st period, December 30, 1986
	Everett Sanipass 13:30
	Brendan Shanahan 13:43
	Theoren Fleury 15:22
	Scott Metcalfe 16:17
	Pierre Turgeon 16:53

FASTEST SIX GOALS, TEAM

4:35	1st period, December 30, 1986
	Everett Sanipass 13:30
	Brendan Shanahan 13:43
	Theoren Fleury 15:22
	Scott Metcalfe 16:17
	Pierre Turgeon 16:53
	Everett Sanipass 18:05

FASTEST POWER-PLAY GOAL FROM START OF MAN ADVANTAGE

3 seconds	3rd period, January 1, 1978
	Thomas Jonsson (Swe) penalized at 4:13
	Wayne Babych (Can) scored at 4:16
6 seconds	1st period, January 1, 1993
	Norbert Zabel (Ger) penalized at 8:48
	Brent Tully (Can) scored at 8:54
	2nd period, December 26, 1994
	Alexandre Mukhanov (Ukr) penalized at 2:39
	Jamie Rivers (Can) scored at 2:45

FASTEST SHORT-HANDED GOAL FROM START OF OPPONENT'S MAN ADVANTAGE

14 seconds	2nd period, January 1, 1993
	Brent Tully (Can) penalized at 6:57
	Nathan Lafayette (Can) scored at 7:11
15 seconds	3rd period, December 30, 1990
	David Harlock (Can) penalized at 19:08
	Scott Thornton (Can) scored at 19:23

FASTEST TWO POWER-PLAY GOALS, TEAM

49 seconds	1st period, January 1, 1990
	Patrice Brisebois 16:29 (pp)
	Mike Needham 17:18 (pp)
58 seconds	2nd period, December 27, 1980
	Jeff Eatough 12:54 (pp)
	Dale Hawerchuk 13:52 (pp)

FASTEST TWO POWER-PLAY GOALS, INDIVIDUAL

2:01	Marty Murray, 2nd period, December 26, 1994
	Scored at 5:35 and again at 7:36
2:45	Josh Holden, 3rd period, January 3, 1998
	Scored at 7:25 and again at 10:10

FASTEST THREE POWER-PLAY GOALS, TEAM

38 seconds	3rd period, January 2, 1995
	Todd Harvey 2:29 (pp)
	Jeff O'Neill 2:48 (pp)
	Marty Murray 3:07 (pp)

BROTHERS AT THE WJC

Moller, Mike & Randy
Niedermayer, Rob & Scott
Turgeon, Pierre & Sylvain

YOUNGEST TO PLAY FOR TEAM CANADA AT THE WJC

16	Bill Campbell	16 years, 9 months, 7 days
	Eric Lindros	16 years, 9 months, 28 days
	Wayne Gretzky	16 years, 10 months, 26 days
17	Mike Ricci	17 years, one month, 29 days
	Paul Kariya	17 years, 2 months, 10 days
	Mario Lemieux	17 years, 2 months, 21 days
	Martin Lapointe	17 years, 3 months, 14 days
	Chris Joseph	17 years, 3 months, 16 days
	Pierre Turgeon	17 years, 3 months, 28 days
	Mark Plantery	17 years, 4 months, 9 days
	Jeff Friesen	17 years, 4 months, 21 days
	Eric Calder	17 years, 5 months, one day
	Chris Gratton	17 years, 5 months, 21 days
	Joe Thornton	17 years, 5 months, 24 days
	Doug Gilmour	17 years, 6 months, 2 days
	Wade Redden	17 years, 6 months, 14 days
	Jeff Eatough	17 years, 6 months, 25 days

TEAM CANADA
REGISTER BY
BIRTHPLACE

TOTAL 386

ONTARIO 165
J. Allison, Anderson, Andreychuk, Arniel, Arthur, Aucoin, Bannister, Beckon, Bernhardt, Bes, Bester, Beukeboom, Billington, Blanchard, Boimistruck, Bovair, Bowen, B. Bradley, M. Bradley, Brind'Amour, R. Brown, Burke, Calder, Caprice, Carkner, Carter, Cassels, Cassidy, Chiasson, Ciccarelli, Cimetta, C. Cirella, J. Cirella, Contini, Convery, Cooke, Corriveau, Corson, Courville, Craig, Craigwell, Crawford, Creighton, Crossman, Cullimore, Currie, Dawe, Devereaux, Donovan, Douris, Draper, Duguay, Eatough, Fenyves, Fernandez, Flatley, Forbes, C. Foster, D. Foster, Fox, Gagner, Gardner, Gartner, Gavey, Gilmour, C. Gratton, D. Gratton, Graves, Greenlaw, Gretzky, Harlock, Hartsburg, Harvey, Hawerchuk, Hay, Hazlett, Hidi, Houle, Huffman, Hull, Hunter, Intranuovo, Jackman, Jackson, Jensen, Johansen, Johnson, Johnston, Joly, Jovanovski, Keating, Kitchen, Lacey, Laferriere, Laniel, Latta, Leeman, Legace, Letowski, Lindros, MacLean, Malhotra, Marsh, May, McCabe, McCauley, McCourt, McIntyre, McLlwain, Metcalfe, Mills, Moffat, D. Morrison, Morschauser, Moylan, Muller, J. Murphy, L. Murphy, Nieuwendyk, Ogrodnick, O'Neill, M. Paterson, R. Paterson, Peca, Plantery, Pronger, Ramage, Ratushny, Reeds, Ricci, Rice, Richardson, Rivers, Roberts, Ryder, Sandlak, Sands, Savard, Secord, Seiling, Shanahan, Shannon, B. Shaw, Sean Simpson, Shawn Simpson, S. Smith, Stajduhar, Stapleton, Storr, Tanti, J. Thornton, S. Thornton, Tkaczuk, Trader, Tully, Vaive, Van Ryn, Verbeek, Ward, Ware, Watt, Wiemer, Willsie, J. Wright, Terry Wright

ALBERTA 60
Babe, Babych, Barnes, Bassen, Baumgartner, Berry, Botterill, Chyzowski, Conroy, Diduck, Dimaio, Domenichelli, Ference, Fistric, Girard, Haller, Hawgood, Hobbins, Hodgson, Holden, Holland, Iginla, Isbister, Kelly, Komarniski, Langkow, Linden, Loewen, Manderville, Matvichuk, McAmmond, McBean, McCrady, M. Moller, R. Moller, T. Murray, Needham, Nemeth, S. Niedermayer, Orleski, M. Pederson, Phillips, Rathje, Reardon, Schneider, Shantz, G. Smith, J. Smith, Smyl, Smyth, Sorochan, Sydor, Tucker, Vernon, Viveiros, Walz, Werenka, Wesley, Willis, Young

QUEBEC 59
Beaudoin, Begin, Bouchard, Briere, Brisebois, Campbell, Chartrain, Cloutier, Corso, A. Cote, S. Cote, Courteau, D. Cyr, Daigle, Daigneault, Daze, Delorme, Denis, DeRouville, Desjardins, Doig, Dollas, C. Dube, Y. Dube, Dumont, Dykhuis, Fiset, Fournier, Garon, Gauthier, Gelinas, Gendron, Hughes, Lapointe, Lecavalier, C. Lemieux, M. Lemieux, Luongo, McKegney, Mellanby, Micalef, R. Murphy, Plavsic, Potvin, Poulin, Racine, Richer, Rioux, Robitaille, Roy, St. Pierre, Savage, Sevigny, Tanguay, Theodore, P. Turgeon, S. Turgeon, Veilleux, Waite

BRITISH COLUMBIA 33
R. Allison, Bombardir, Brewer, Courtnall, P. Cyr, N. Foster, Gordon, Heath, Howes, Irving, Joseph, Junker, Kariya, Kirkham, Lafayette, Larsen, Lupul, MacLeod, Malgunas, Marshall, McLean, Melnyk, M. Morrison, R. Niedermayer, Nylund, Podollan, Rausse, Recchi, Sakic, Stevenson, Tambellini, Walter, Yzerman

SASKATCHEWAN 33
Allan, Armstrong, C. Brown, Butcher, Byers, Clark, Derkatch, Elnyuik, Fleury, Friesen, Habscheid, Hamilton, Herter, Kluzak, Lemay, McCrimmon, Miner, Nelson, Odelein, D. Pederson, Propp, Redden, Sarich, Schaefer, Sherven, Sillinger, Snell, Strueby, Wallin, Warrener, Whitfield, Witt, Tyler Wright

MANITOBA 16
Daniels, Eakin, Evason, Falloon, Keane, Kennedy, Kidd, Lambert, Laxdal, Leach, Mann, M. Murray, Patrick, Semenchuk, Wilson, Wregget

NEW BRUNSWICK 4
Eagles, Melanson, Pellerin, Sanipass

NEWFOUNDLAND 4
K. Brown, Norris, Penney, Slaney

NOVA SCOTIA 2
Boutilier, B. Smith

UNKNOWN 4
Graovac, Halliday, Kirk, G. Shaw

PLAYERS WHO WERE BORN
IN ANOTHER COUNTRY

There have been six players who were born outside the country who have represented Canada at the World Junior Championships:

1.	Pat Daley	Marieville, France
2.	Curt Fraser	Cincinnati, Ohio
3.	Jean-Marc Gaulin	Balve, Germany
4.	Willie Huber	Strasskirchen, Germany
5.	Rick Lanz	Karlouy Vary, Czechoslovakia
6.	Roy Russell	Manchester, England

JERSEY NUMBERS

1
Billington, Caprice, Graovac, Jensen, Kidd, LaFerriere, Luongo, Melanson, Morschauser, Sands, Shawn Simpson, Storr, Theodore, Wregget

2
Berry, Carkner, J. Cirella, Cullimore, Ference, Halliday, Hawgood, Marshall, McCrimmon, R. Moller, L. Murphy, Plantery, Ratushny, Tully, Veilleux

3
Allan, Arthur, Aucoin, Brewer, K. Brown, Crossman, Daigneault, Hamilton, Holland, Laniel, Miner, Nylund, Trader, Viveiros, Wesley

4
Chiasson, Delorme, Doig, Dykhuis, C. Foster, Gardner, Hartsburg, Hawgood, Kluzak, Leeman, Malgunas, McCabe, Melnyk, Phillips, B. Shaw, Wallin, Werenka

5
Bannister, Baumgartner, Boutilier, Calder, Dollas, Herter, Howes, Johansen, Joseph, Komarniski, Moylan, M. Paterson, G. Smith, S. Smith, Sydor

6
Cassidy, Clark, Desjardins, Forbes, Haller, Huffman, Kitchen, Malhotra, McCrady, Pronger, Redden, Snell

7
Allan, Blanchard, Gelinas, C. Gratton, Harlock, Huber, MacLeod, McBean, McKegney, Nelson, Odelein, Phillips, Plavsic, Rioux, Savard, B. Shaw, Sorochan

8
J. Allison, Bradley, Chartrain, Courville, Eagles, Johnson, Laxdal, MacLean, McCauley, McIntyre, Ogrodnick, Penney, Recchi, Richardson, Ryder

9
J. Allison, Corriveau, Corson, Courtnall, C. Dube, Y. Dube, Falloon, Fleury, Gilmour, Gretzky, Hughes, Intranuovo, Irving, Joly, Patrick, Ricci

10
Butcher, Dawe, Douris, Fleury, Fox, Harvey, Hawerchuk, Johnston, Linden, Loewen, Mann, May, McCourt, Muller, Norris, Rausse, Tambellini, Tkaczuk, S. Turgeon, J. Wright

11
Begin, Bes, C. Brown, Ciccarelli, Crawford, Creighton, Evason, Hunter, Junker, Keane, Propp, Smyl, Strueby, Tanti, Thornton

12
R. Allison, Convery, Cooke, D. Cyr, Derkatch, Heath, Hidi, Hull, Iginla, Isbister, Jackson, Lemay, Ramage, Rice, Rivers, Roberts, Sanipass, Tyler Wright

13
Matvichuk, Walz

14
Arniel, Bassen, Bouchard, Briere, Contini, Daniels, Hobbins, Jovanovski, Langkow, Lanz, Lecavalier, McLlwain, J. Murphy, R. Murphy, Needham, M. Pederson, Russell, Stajduhar, Walter, Yzerman

15
Andreychuk, Corso, Craig, Elynuik, Graves, Kirkham, M. Moller, Robitaille, G. Shaw, B. Smith, J. Smith

16
Beckon, R. Brown, Chyzowski, Fournier, Gordon, Habscheid, Hodgson, Joly, McAmmond, McLean, Metcalfe, Racine, St. Pierre, Sillinger, Tucker, Young

17
Babe, Domenichelli, Gagner, Hazlett, Huber, Kelly, Letowski, M. Morrison, O'Neill, Reeds, Schneider

18
Craigwell, Dimaio, Dumont, Gaulin, Girard, Kariya, McCauley, Pellerin, Reardon, Savage, Shanahan, Verbeek, Watt

19
Beaudoin, Botterill, Carter, C. Cirella, P. Cyr, Daigle, Devereaux, Draper, Gartner, Houle, Leeman, Nemeth, Nieuwendyk, Orleski, Poulin, Sakic, Tanguay

20
Babych, Boimistruck, Bowen, Brind'Amour, Byers, Flatley, Kennedy, Lupul, Mellanby, Secord, Smyth, P. Turgeon, Ward, Willis, Wilson

21
Botterill, Campbell, S. Cote, Courteau, Desjardins, Fistric, Gauthier, Holden, Keating, Kennedy, Lafayette, C. Lemieux, Manderville, T. Murray, Roy, Sherven, Sean Simpson

22
Arniel, S. Cote, Donovan, Fenyves, Gavey, Greenlaw, Lapointe, Latta, Marsh, Podollan, Sarich, Shannon, Sevigny

23
Botterill, Bovair, Diduck, Larsen, D. Morrison, R. Niedermayer, D. Pederson, Richer, Seiling, Stevenson, Vaive

24
Anderson, Bouchard, Brisebois, A. Cote, Daze, Dykhuis, Eakin, D. Gratton, Jackman, Kirk, Lambert, M. Lemieux, Mills, Wiemer, Willsie

25
Beukeboom, Cassels, Daley, Duguay, Friesen, Stapleton, Thornton

26
Currie, Derkatch, Lapointe, Ricci, Sandlak, Van Ryn

27
Cimetta, Conroy, Eatough, Lacey, Peca, Ramage, Schaefer, Slaney

28
Barnes, Bradley, Hay, Leach, Marsh, M. Murray, S. Niedermayer, R. Paterson

29
Fiset, D. Foster, Fraser, Potvin, Shantz, Waite

30
Bester, Burke, Cloutier, Fernandez, N. Foster, Legace, Micalef, Moffat, Semenchuk, Vernon, Waite, Warrener, Terry Wright

31
Bernhardt, Denis, DeRouville

32
Garon, Gendron

33
Rathje, Ware

34
Armstrong, McCrimmon, Wallin

35
Whitfield

44
S. Niedermayer

55
Bombardir

77
Slaney

88
Lindros

CANADA MEDALS SUMMARY

GOLD	10
SILVER	2
BRONZE	2
4th	2
5th	2
6th	1
7th	1
8th	1
DQ	1
Total	22

MEMORIAL CUP CHAMPIONS
1977 TO PRESENT

1977	New Westminster Bruins (WHL)
1978	New Westminster Bruins (WHL)
1979	Peterborough Petes (OHA)
1980	Cornwall Royals (OHL)
1981	Cornwall Royals (OHL)
1982	Kitchener Rangers (OHL)
1983	Portland Winter Hawks (WHL)
1984	Ottawa 67's (OHL)
1985	Prince Albert Raiders (WHL)
1986	Guelph Platers (OHL)
1987	Medicine Hat Tigers (WHL)
1988	Medicine Hat Tigers (WHL)
1989	Swift Current Broncos (WHL)
1990	Oshawa Generals (OHL)
1991	Spokane Chiefs (WHL)
1992	Kamloops Blazers (WHL)
1993	Sault Ste. Marie Greyhounds (OHL)
1994	Kamloops Blazers (WHL)
1995	Kamloops Blazers (WHL)
1996	Granby Predateurs (QMJHL)
1997	Hull Olympiques (QMJHL)
1998	Portland Winter Hawks (WHL)

YEAR-BY-YEAR RECORD

YEAR	GP	W	L	T	GF	GA	POS
1977	7	5	1	1	50	20	2nd
1978	6	4	2	0	36	18	3rd
1979	5	3	2	0	23	10	5th
1980	5	3	2	0	25	18	5th
1981	5	1	3	1	26	25	7th
1982	7	6	0	1	45	14	1st
1983	7	4	2	1	39	24	3rd
1984	7	4	2	1	39	17	4th
1985	7	5	0	2	44	14	1st
1986	7	5	2	0	54	21	2nd
1987	6	4	1	1	41	23	DQ
1988	7	6	0	1	37	16	1st
1989	7	4	2	1	31	23	4th
1990	7	5	1	1	36	18	1st
1991	7	5	1	1	40	18	1st
1992	7	2	3	2	21	30	6th
1993	7	6	1	0	37	17	1st
1994	7	6	0	1	39	20	1st
1995	7	7	0	0	49	21	1st
1996	6	6	0	0	27	8	1st
1997	7	5	0	2	27	13	1st
1998	7	2	5	0	13	18	8th
Totals	145	98	30	17	779	406	

RECORD BY NATION

(listed alphabetically)

	GP	W	L	T	GF	GA
Austria	1	1	0	0	11	1
CIS	1	0	1	0	2	7
Czechoslovakia	15	4	5	6	56	58
Czech Republic	4	3	0	1	21	12
Czech/Slovak	1	0	1	0	4	7
Finland	19	10	4	5	75	58
Germany	6	6	0	0	30	10
Japan	1	1	0	0	8	1
Kazakhstan	1	0	1	0	3	6
Norway	5	5	0	0	46	6
Poland	5	5	0	0	65	5
Russia	6	4	1	1	28	16
Slovakia	1	1	0	0	7	2
Soviet Union	13	5	7	1	47	53
Sweden	19	12	6	1	82	60
Switzerland	10	10	0	0	73	18
Ukraine	2	2	0	0	15	2
United States	23	18	3	2	110	63
West Germany	12	11	1	0	96	21
Totals	145	98	30	17	779	406

RECORD BY NATION, GAME BY GAME

(from longest rivalry to shortest)

UNITED STATES

YEAR	SCORE	W-L-T	YEAR	SCORE	W-L-T
1977	8--2	W	1988	5--4	W
1978	6--3	W	1989	5--1	W
1979	6--3	W	1990	3--2	W
1980	4--2	W	1991	4--4	T
1981	3--7	L	1992	3--5	L
1982	5--4	W	1993	3--0	W
1983	4--2	W	1994	8--3	W
1984	5--2	W	1995	8--2	W
1985	7--5	W	1996	6--1	W
1986	5--2	W	1997	4--4	T
1987	6--2	W	1997	2--0	W
			1998	0--3	L

Totals vs. United States

GP	W	L	T	GF	GA
23	18	3	2	110	63

FINLAND

YEAR	SCORE	W-L-T			
1977	6--4	W	1988	4--4	T
1979	1--3	L	1989	4--3	W
1980	1--2	L	1990	3--3	T
1982	5--1	W	1991	5--1	W
1983	6--3	W	1992	2--2	T
1984	2--4	L	1993	3--2	W
1985	4--4	T	1994	6--3	W
1986	6--5	W	1995	6--4	W
1987	6--6	T	1996	3--1	W
			1998	2--3	L

Totals vs. Finland

GP	W	L	T	GF	GA
19	10	4	5	75	58

SWEDEN

YEAR	SCORE	W-L-T			
1977	5--3	W	1988	4--2	W
1978	5--6	L	1989	4--5	L
1979	0--1	L	1990	4--5	L
1982	3--2	W	1991	7--4	W
1983	2--5	L	1992	2--2	T
1984	6--2	W	1993	5--4	W
1985	8--2	W	1994	6--4	W
1986	9--2	W	1995	4--3	W
1987	4--3	W	1996	4--1	W
			1998	0--4	L

Totals vs. Sweden

GP	W	L	T	GF	GA
19	12	6	1	82	60

CZECHOSLOVAKIA

YEAR	SCORE	W-L-T			
1977	4--4	T	1985	2--2	T
1978	9--3	W	1986	3--5	L
1978	6--3	W	1987	1--5	L
1981	3--3	T	1988	4--2	W
1982	3--3	T	1989	2--2	T
1983	7--7	T	1990	2--1	W
1984	4--6	L	1991	5--6	L
			1992	1--6	L

Totals vs. Czechoslovakia

GP	W	L	T	GF	GA
15	4	5	6	56	58

SOVIET UNION

YEAR	SCORE	W-L-T	YEAR	SCORE	W-L-T
1977	4--6	L	1985	5--0	W
1978	2--3	L	1986	1--4	L
1980	5--8	L	1987	4--2*	
1981	3--7	L	1988	3--2	W
1982	7--0	W	1989	2--7	L
1983	3--7	L	1990	6--4	W
1984	3--3	T	1991	3--2	W

* suspended (does not count)

Totals vs. Soviet Union

GP	W	L	T	GF	GA
13	5	7	1	47	53

WEST GERMANY

YEAR	SCORE	W-L-T	YEAR	SCORE	W-L-T
1977	9--1	W	1983	4--0	W
1978	8--0	W	1984	7--0	W
1979	6--2	W	1985	6--0	W
1980	6--1	W	1986	18--2	W
1981	6--7	L	1988	8--1	W
1982	11--3	W	1989	7--4	W

Totals vs. West Germany

GP	W	L	T	GF	GA
12	11	1	0	96	21

SWITZERLAND

YEAR	SCORE	W-L-T	YEAR	SCORE	W-L-T
1980	9--5	W	1991	6--0	W
1982	11--1	W	1992	6--4	W
1984	12--0	W	1994	5--1	W
1986	12--1	W	1996	2--1	W
1987	6--4	W	1997	4--1	W

Totals vs. Switzerland

GP	W	L	T	GF	GA
10	10	0	0	73	18

GERMANY

YEAR	SCORE	W-L-T			
1992	5--4	W	1995	9--1	W
1993	5--2	W	1997	4--1	W
1994	5--2	W	1998	2--0	W

Totals vs. Germany

GP	W	L	T	GF	GA
6	6	0	0	30	10

NORWAY

YEAR	SCORE	W-L-T			
1979	10--1	W	1989	7--1	W
1983	13--0	W	1990	6--3	W
			1991	10--1	W

Totals vs. Norway

GP	W	L	T	GF	GA
5	5	0	0	46	6

POLAND

YEAR	SCORE	W-L-T			
1977	14--0	W	1987	18--3	W
1985	12--1	W	1988	9--1	W
			1990	12--0	W

Totals vs. Poland

GP	W	L	T	GF	GA
5	5	0	0	65	5

RUSSIA

YEAR	SCORE	W-L-T			
1993	9--1	W	1996	4--3	W
1994	3--3	T	1997	3--2	W
1995	8--5	W	1998	1--2	L*

Totals vs. Russia

GP	W	L	T	GF	GA
6	4	1	1	28	16

* overtime

CZECH REPUBLIC

YEAR	SCORE	W-L-T			
1994	6--4	W	1997	3--3	T
1995	7--5	W	1998	5--0	W

Totals vs. Czech Republic

GP	W	L	T	GF	GA
4	3	0	1	21	12

UKRAINE

YEAR	SCORE	W-L-T
1995	7--1	W
1996	8--1	W

Totals vs. Ukraine

GP	W	L	T	GF	GA
2	2	0	0	15	2

AUSTRIA

YEAR	SCORE	W-L-T
1981	11--1	W

Totals vs. Austria

GP	W	L	T	GF	GA
1	1	0	0	11	1

COMMONWEALTH OF INDEPENDENT STATES (CIS)

YEAR	SCORE	W-L-T
1992	2--7	L

Totals vs. CIS

GP	W	L	T	GF	GA
1	0	1	0	2	7

CZECH/SLOVAK REPUBLICS

YEAR	SCORE	W-L-T
1993	4--7	L

Totals vs. Czech/Slovak Republics

GP	W	L	T	GF	GA
1	0	1	0	4	7

JAPAN

YEAR	SCORE	W-L-T
1993	8--1	W

Totals vs. Japan

GP	W	L	T	GF	GA
1	1	0	0	8	1

SLOVAKIA

YEAR	SCORE	W-L-T
1997	7--2	W

Totals vs. Slovakia

GP	W	L	T	GF	GA
1	1	0	0	7	2

CHRONOLOGICAL
ORDER OF RESULTS

1977 (Czechoslovakia)

December 23, 1976	Canada 14	Poland 0
December 25, 1976	Canada 4	Czechoslovakia 4
December 26, 1976	Canada 6	Finland 4
December 28, 1976	Canada 5	Sweden 3
December 29, 1976	Canada 9	West Germany 1
January 1, 1977	Canada 8	United States 2
January 2, 1977	Soviet Union 6	Canada 4

1978 (Canada)

December 22, 1977	Canada 6	United States 3
December 23, 1977	Canada 8	West Germany 0
December 25, 1977	Canada 9	Czechoslovakia 3
December 28, 1977	Soviet Union 3	Canada 2
December 31, 1977	Canada 6	Czechoslovakia 3
January 1, 1978	Sweden 6	Canada 5

1979 (Sweden)

December 27, 1978	Finland 3	Canada 1
December 28, 1978	Canada 6	West Germany 2
	(counted twice in standings)	
December 30, 1978	Sweden 1	Canada 0
December 31, 1978	Canada 10	Norway 1
January 2, 1979	Canada 6	United States 3

1980 (Finland)

December 27, 1979	Finland 2	Canada 1
December 28, 1979	Soviet Union 8	Canada 5
December 30, 1979	Canada 9	Switzerland 5
	(counted twice in standings)	
January 1, 1980	Canada 4	United States 2
January 2, 1980	Canada 6	West Germany 1

1981 (West Germany)

December 27, 1980	Canada 3	Czechoslovakia 3
December 28, 1980	Soviet Union 7	Canada 3
December 30, 1980	Canada 11	Austria 1

	(counted twice in standings)	
December 31, 1980	United States 7	Canada 3
January 2, 1981	West Germany 7	Canada 6

1982 (United States)

December 22, 1981	Canada 5	Finland 1
December 23, 1981	Canada 3	Sweden 2
December 26, 1981	Canada 7	Soviet Union 0
December 27, 1981	Canada 5	United States 4
December 29, 1981	Canada 11	West Germany 3
January 1, 1982	Canada 11	Switzerland 1
January 2, 1982	Canada 3	Czechoslovakia 3

1983 (Soviet Union)

December 26, 1982	Canada 4	West Germany 0
December 27, 1982	Canada 4	United States 2
December 29, 1982	Canada 6	Finland 3
December 30, 1982	Soviet Union 7	Canada 3
January 1, 1983	Canada 7	Czechoslovakia 7
January 2, 1983	Sweden 5	Canada 2
January 4, 1983	Canada 13	Norway 0

1984 (Sweden)

December 25, 1983	Finland 4	Canada 2
December 26, 1983	Canada 5	United States 2
December 28, 1983	Canada 12	Switzerland 0
December 29, 1983	Canada 7	West Germany 0
December 31, 1983	Canada 6	Sweden 2
January 2, 1984	Canada 3	Soviet Union 3
January 3, 1984	Czechoslovakia 6	Canada 4

1985 (Finland)

December 23, 1984	Canada 8	Sweden 2
December 25, 1984	Canada 12	Poland 1
December 26, 1984	Canada 6	West Germany 0
December 28, 1984	Canada 7	United States 5
December 29, 1984	Canada 5	Soviet Union 0
December 31, 1985	Canada 4	Finland 4
January 1, 1985	Canada 2	Czechoslovakia 2

1986 (Canada)

December 26, 1985	Canada 12	Switzerland 1
December 27, 1985	Canada 18	West Germany 2
December 29, 1985	Canada 5	United States 2
December 30, 1985	Canada 9	Sweden 2

January 1, 1986	Canada 6	Finland 5
January 2, 1986	Soviet Union 4	Canada 1
January 4, 1986	Czechoslovakia 5	Canada 3

1987 (Czechoslovakia)

December 26, 1986	Canada 6	Switzerland 4
December 27, 1986	Canada 6	Finland 6
December 29, 1986	Czechoslovakia 5	Canada 1
December 30, 1986	Canada 18	Poland 3
January 1, 1987	Canada 6	United States 2
January 2, 1987	Canada 4	Sweden 3
January 4, 1987	Canada 4	Soviet Union 2
	(suspended by brawl in 2nd period)	

1988 (Soviet Union)

December 26, 1987	Canada 4	Sweden 2
December 28, 1987	Canada 4	Czechoslovakia 2
December 29, 1987	Canada 4	Finland 4
December 31, 1987	Canada 5	United States 4
January 1, 1988	Canada 3	Soviet Union 2
January 3, 1988	Canada 8	West Germany 1
January 4, 1988	Canada 9	Poland 1

1989 (United States)

December 26, 1988	Canada 7	Norway 1
December 28, 1988	Canada 7	West Germany 4
December 29, 1988	Canada 5	United States 1
December 31, 1988	Sweden 5	Canada 4
January 1, 1989	Canada 2	Czechoslovakia 2
January 3, 1989	Canada 4	Finland 3
January 4, 1989	Soviet Union 7	Canada 2

1990 (Finland)

December 26, 1989	Canada 3	United States 2
December 28, 1989	Canada 12	Poland 0
December 29, 1989	Canada 6	Norway 3
December 31, 1989	Canada 3	Finland 3
January 1, 1990	Canada 6	Soviet Union 4
January 3, 1990	Sweden 5	Canada 4
January 4, 1990	Canada 2	Czechoslovakia 1

1991 (Canada)

December 26, 1990	Canada 6	Switzerland 0
December 27, 1990	Canada 4	United States 4
December 29, 1990	Canada 10	Norway 1

December 30, 1990	Canada 7	Sweden 4
January 1, 1991	Canada 5	Finland 1
January 2, 1991	Czechoslovakia 6	Canada 5
January 4, 1991	Canada 3	Soviet Union 2

1992 (Germany)

December 26, 1991	Canada 5	Germany 4
December 27, 1991	Canada 6	Switzerland 4
December 29, 1991	Canada 2	Sweden 2
December 30, 1991	Canada 2	Finland 2
January 1, 1992	United States 5	Canada 3
January 2, 1992	Czechoslovakia 6	Canada 1
January 4, 1992	CIS 7	Canada 2

1993 (Sweden)

December 26, 1992	Canada 3	United States 0
December 27, 1992	Canada 5	Sweden 4
December 29, 1992	Canada 9	Russia 1
December 30, 1992	Canada 3	Finland 2
January 1, 1993	Canada 5	Germany 2
January 2, 1993	Canada 8	Japan 1
January 4, 1993	Czech/Slovak 7	Canada 4

1994 (Czech Republic)

December 26, 1993	Canada 5	Switzerland 1
December 27, 1993	Canada 5	Germany 2
December 29, 1993	Canada 3	Russia 3
December 30, 1993	Canada 6	Finland 3
January 1, 1994	Canada 8	United States 3
January 2, 1994	Canada 6	Czech Republic 4
January 4, 1994	Canada 6	Sweden 4

1995 (Canada)

December 26, 1994	Canada 7	Ukraine 1
December 27, 1994	Canada 9	Germany 1
December 29, 1994	Canada 8	United States 3
December 30, 1994	Canada 7	Czech Republic 5
January 1, 1995	Canada 6	Finland 4
January 2, 1995	Canada 8	Russia 5
January 4, 1995	Canada 4	Sweden 3

1996 (United States)

December 26, 1995	Canada 6	United States 1
December 27, 1995	Canada 2	Switzerland 1
December 29, 1995	Canada 3	Finland 1

December 31, 1995	Canada 8	Ukraine 1
January 3, 1996	Canada 4	Russia 3
January 4, 1996	Canada 4	Sweden 1

1997 (Switzerland)

December 27, 1996	Canada 4	Germany 1
December 28, 1996	Canada 4	United States 4
December 30, 1996	Canada 4	Switzerland 1
December 31, 1996	Canada 3	Czech Republic 3
January 1, 1997	Canada 7	Slovakia 2
January 3, 1997	Canada 3	Russia 2
January 4, 1997	Canada 2	United States 0

1998 (Finland)

December 25, 1997	Finland 3	Canada 2
December 26, 1997	Sweden 4	Canada 0
December 28, 1997	Canada 5	Czech Republic 0
December 30, 1997	Canada 2	Germany 0
December 31, 1997	Russia 2	Canada 1 (OT)
January 2, 1998	United States 3	Canada 0
January 3, 1998	Kazakhstan 6	Canada 3

TOURNAMENT ALL-STAR SELECTIONS

1974	Frank Salvie (goal)
	Paul MacIntosh (defence)
	Jim Turkiewicz (defence)
1975	Ed Staniowski (goal)
	Rick Lapointe (defence)
	Dale McMullen (forward)
1976	Peter Marsh (forward)

1977	Dale McCourt (forward)
1978	Wayne Gretzky (forward)
1982	Mike Moffat (goal)
	Gord Kluzak (defence)
	Mike Moller (forward)
1985	Bob Dollas (defence)
1986	Sylvain Cote (defence)
	Shayne Corson (forward)
1988	Jimmy Waite (goal)
	Greg Hawgood (defence)
	Theoren Fleury (forward)
1990	Stephane Fiset (goal)
	Dave Chyzowski (forward)
1991	Mike Craig (forward)
	Eric Lindros (forward)
1992	Scott Niedermayer (defence)
1993	Manny Legace (goal)
	Brent Tully (defence)
	Paul Kariya (forward)
1995	Marty Murray (forward)
	Bryan McCabe (defence)
	Jason Allison (forward)
	Eric Daze (forward)
1996	Nolan Baumgartner (defence)
	Jose Theodore (goal)
	Jarome Iginla (forward)
1997	Chris Phillips (defence)
	Christian Dube (forward)

DIRECTORATE AWARDS

1977	BEST FORWARD	Dale McCourt
1978	BEST FORWARD	Wayne Gretzky
1982	BEST GOALIE	Mike Moffat
	BEST DEFENCEMAN	Gord Kluzak
1985	BEST GOALIE	Craig Billington
1986	BEST FORWARD	Jim Sandlak
1988	BEST GOALIE	Jimmy Waite
1990	BEST GOALIE	Stephane Fiset
1991	BEST FORWARD	Eric Lindros
1993	BEST GOALIE	Manny Legace
1994	BEST GOALIE	Jamie Storr
1995	BEST DEFENCEMAN	Bryan McCabe
	BEST FORWARD	Marty Murray
1996	BEST GOALIE	Jose Theodore
	BEST FORWARD	Jarome Iginla
1997	BEST GOALIE	Marc Denis

CAPTAINS

1977	Dale McCourt
1978	Ryan Walter
1979	John Paul Kelly
1980	Dave Fenyves/Rick Lanz
1981	Marc Crawford
1982	Troy Murray
1983	James Patrick
1984	J. J. Daigneault
1985	Dan Hodgson
1986	Jim Sandlak
1987	Steve Chiasson
1988	Theoren Fleury
1989	Eric Desjardins
1990	Dave Chyzowski/Dan Ratushny/Mike Ricci
1991	Steve Rice
1992	Eric Lindros
1993	Martin Lapointe
1994	Brent Tully
1995	Todd Harvey
1996	Nolan Baumgartner
1997	Brad Larsen
1998	Cory Sarich/Jesse Wallin

CANADIAN OFFICIALS

	REFEREES	LINESMEN
1977	Blair Graham	none
1978	Doug Robb	Maurice Baril
		Louis Therrien
		Nelson Gagnon
		Denis Pierre Perreault
		Serge Girard
		Bob MacMillan
		Michel Stebin
		Jean Maheux
		Jacques Charbonneau
1979	Normand Caisse	
1980	unknown	
1981	Jim Lever	none
1982	Dan Cournoyer	Greg Hilker
	Ron Renneberg	Jim Petschenig
		Ken Skingle
1983	Sandy Proctor	none
1984	none	none
1985	Richard Trottier	none
1986	Dennis Pottage	Ron Rost
	John Willsie	Douglas Brousseau
	Dan Emerson	
	Charles Biehn	
1987	Richard Trottier	none
1988	Dave Lynch	
1989	George McCorry	Jay Sharrers
	Brad Watson	
1990	Kevin Muench	none
1991	Blaine Angus	Jeff Gardiner
	Mike Hasenfratz	
1992	Daryl Borden	Mike Burton
1993	Benoit Lapointe	Dave Taveroff
1994	Sylvain Bibeau	Jean-Yves Malliet
1995	Brad Meier	Sylvain Cloutier
		Darren Gibbs
1996	Mark Joannette	Serge Carpentier
		Todd Thomander
1997	Tom Kowal	Ryan Galloway
1998	Stephane Auger	Jeff Bradley

NHL AFFILIATIONS BY DRAFT OF CANADA'S WORLD JUNIORS

(Of the 386 players to represent Canada at the World Junior Championships, 356 have been drafted into the NHL)

VANCOUVER CANUCKS 29
Allan, Aucoin, Butcher, Caprice, Cooke, Crawford, Cullimore, Y. Dube, Daigneault, Ference, Fraser, Girard, Gordon, Hazlett, Herter, Holden, Komarniski, Lanz, Lemay, Linden, Morschauser, R. Murphy, Peca, Sandlak, Schaefer, Smyl, Tully, Vaive, Veilleux

DETROIT RED WINGS 21
Bowen, Chiasson, C. Cirella, Courteau, Fistric, Graves, Huber, Jensen, Kennedy, Lapointe, Malgunas, McCourt, Micalef, J. Murphy, Ogrodnick, Racine, B. Shaw, Sillinger, Trader, Wallin, Yzerman

BOSTON BRUINS 18
Byers, Cimetta, A. Cote, Forbes, D. Foster, N. Foster, Hawgood, Johnston, Kluzak, Mann, McCrimmon, Melnyk, Moffat, Secord, J. Thornton, Walz, Wesley, Whitfield

BUFFALO SABRES 18
Andreychuk, Beckon, C. Brown, Creighton, P. Cyr, Dawe, Eatough, Haller, Loewen, May, McKegney, M. Moller, Moylan, Sarich, Seiling, Snell, P. Turgeon, Wiemer

TORONTO MAPLE LEAFS 18
Anderson, Bester, Boimistruck, Clark, Convery, Courtnall, Hodgson, Jackson, Johansen, Laxdal, Leeman, McIntyre, Nylund, Potvin, Richardson, S. Thornton, Ware, Wregget

CHICAGO BLACKHAWKS 17
K. Brown, Cassidy, Crossman, Daze, Dykhuis, Gardner, McAmmond, T. Murray, R. Paterson, Sanipass, Shantz, Sean Simpson, Stapleton, Tanti, Waite, Wilson, Young

EDMONTON OILERS 17
Beukeboom, Currie, Derkatch, Devereaux, Habschied, Intranuovo, Metcalfe, Miner, Odelein, Sherven, G. Smith, Smyth, Stajduhar, Strueby, Viveiros, Watt, Tyler Wright

MONTREAL CANADIENS 17
Brisebois, Cassels, Corson, Delorme, Desjardins, Garon, Hunter, Joly, C. Lemieux, Orleski, M. Pederson, Richer, Sevigny, Stevenson, Theodore, Tucker, Ward

WASHINGTON CAPITALS 17
J. Allison, Baumgartner, Beaudoin, Calder, Corriveau, Evason, Gartner, Gendron, Greenlaw, Hay, Nelson, Rausse, Savage, Shawn Simpson, Slaney, Walter, Witt

NEW JERSEY DEVILS 16
Billington, Bombardir, Burke, C. Foster, Harlock, Laniel, MacLean, McCauley, Muller, S. Niedermayer, D. Pederson, Pellerin, Shanahan, J. Smith, Van Ryn, Verbeek

CALGARY FLAMES 15

Begin, Bouchard, B. Bradley, D. Cyr, Eakin, Fleury, Gauthier, Kidd, Manderville, M. Murray, Nieuwendyk, Roberts, St. Pierre, Tkaczuk, Vernon

WINNIPEG JETS 15

Arniel, Barnes, Berry, Courville, Daley, Doig, Dollas, Douris, Draper, Elynuik, Fournier, Hawerchuk, Isbister, Mills, Ratushny

NEW YORK ISLANDERS 14

Boutilier, Brewer, Chyzowski, Diduck, Dimaio, Dumont, Flatley, Holland, Junker, Luongo, McCabe, Melanson, Redden, Tambellini

NEW YORK RANGERS 14

Carkner, Cloutier, C. Dube, Duguay, Gagner, Heath, Keating, Malhotra, M. Morrison, Nemeth, Patrick, Rice, Sorochan, Werenka

HARTFORD WHALERS 13

R. Allison, Arthur, S. Cote, Domenichelli, Hamilton, Hull, Legace, O'Neill, M. Paterson, Poulin, Pronger, S. Smith, S. Turgeon

QUEBEC NORDIQUES 12

Carter, Eagles, Fernandez, Fiset, Gaulin, Hughes, Lambert, Latta, Lindros, R. Moller, Norris, Sakic

LOS ANGELES KINGS 11

Blanchard, Fox, Gelinas, D. Gratton, Kelly, McBean, D. Morrison, L. Murphy, Robitaille, Storr, Sydor

ST. LOUIS BLUES 10

Babych, Brind'Amour, Corso, Gilmour, Houle, Lafayette, Marshall, Plavsic, Reeds, Rivers

MINNESOTA NORTH STARS 9

Babe, Bes, Craig, Hartsburg, Matvichuk, McCrady, Sands, B. Smith, Roy

PITTSBURGH PENGUINS 9

R. Brown, DeRouville, Joseph, Leach, M. Lemieux, McLlwain, Needham, Recchi, Shannon

PHILADELPHIA FLYERS 7

Campbell, Daniels, Huffman, Johnson, Mellanby, Propp, Ricci

DALLAS STARS 6

Botterill, Harvey, Iginla, Jackman, McLean, J. Wright

SAN JOSE SHARKS 6

M. Bradley, Craigwell, Donovan, Falloon, Friesen, Rathje

COLORADO ROCKIES 5

J. Cirella, Contini, Hidi, Laferriere, Ramage

FLORIDA PANTHERS 5

Armstrong, Jovanovski, R. Niedermayer, Podollan, Warrener

OTTAWA SENATORS 4

Daigle, Larsen, Penney, Phillips

TAMPA BAY LIGHTNING 4

Bannister, Gavey, C. Gratton, Willis

COLORADO AVALANCHE 3

Denis, Tanguay, Willsie

ATLANTA FLAMES   2
Bernhardt, Marsh

PHOENIX COYOTES   2
Briere, Letowski

TAMPA BAY LIGHTNING   2
Langkow, Lecavalier

MIGHTY DUCKS OF ANAHEIM   1
Kariya

UNDRAFTED   29
Bassen, Bovair, Chartrain, Ciccarelli, Conroy, Fenyves, Graovac, Gretzky, Halliday, Hobbins, Howes, Irving, Keane, Kirk, Kirkham, Kitchen, Lacey, Lupul, MacLeod, Plantery, Reardon, Rioux, Russell, Ryder, Savard, Schneider, Semenchuk, G. Shaw, Terry Wright

CANADIAN HOCKEY LEAGUE AFFILIATIONS

BY LEAGUE

OHL	143
WHL	122
QMJHL	70
Other	
U.S. College	25
NHL	16
Canadian National/Olympic Team	8
Finnish League	1
IHL	1

ACKNOWLEDGEMENTS

The author would like to thank a number people who have been helpful in putting this book together. To the ever-supportive Kimmo Leinonen at the IIHF. To Bob Nicholson, Scott Smith, Dale Ptycia, Joanne Gray, John MacKinnon, Cindy Nield, and Vernon Doyle at Canadian Hockey. To Jack David, Jennifer Trainor, and Paul Davies at ECW Press for fantastic, pressure-filled skills. To Jefferson Davis and Peggy Mackenzie, hockey-loving oenophiles of the first order. To good luck charms Jon Redfern and Geri Dasgupta. To Birger Nordmark, Igor Kuperman, Tatjana Domke, and Tom Ratschunas for filling in a few salient statistical gaps. To everyone at the Hockey Hall of Fame Resource Centre, particularly Phil Pritchard, Craig Campbell, Jane Rodney, Jacqueline Boughazale, Sophie Harding, Izak Westgate, and the great, golden helmeted Darren Boyko for remarkable persistence and energy. To everyone at the Centre of Excellence in Toronto, notably Marty Savoy, Kevin "Patch" Kloostra, and Chris Hall. To Pierre Sasseville in Sherbrooke, Ghislain and Francis Delage, Rick Cornacchia, Richard Trottier, Ernie McLean, and Dick Todd. To Herb Morrell at the OHA, Jackie at the NHL in T.O., Ed Rowe, former Leaf Gus Bodnar, Dennis Pottage, Bob Nadin, Rick Pereira, Darryl Seibel, Morris Roy, Moira MacElhinney, Edna Barker, and Brent Ladds. And, of course, to my mom (see you in Ottawa once everything is in order!)

PHOTO CREDITS

Canadian Hockey: back cover (bottom), 77, 79, 93, 95, 110, 137, 139, 152, 153, 167, 169, 183, 209, 211, 257, 284, 285

Hockey Hall of Fame: back cover (top), 22, 37, 53, 65, 108, 196
HHOF/Doug MacLellan: front cover, 224, 226, 255
HHOF/David Sandford: author photo, 332
HHOF/Chris Black: 313, 315
HHOF/Oshawa Times: 241
HHOF/Ottawa Citizen: 39

Canapress: 124, 182, 271

Bruce Bennett: 299, 300, 330